BUNCE'S
BIG FAT SHORT HISTORY
OF BRITISH BOXING

www.penguin.co.uk

Also by Steve Bunce

THE FIXER

For more Steve Bunce follow him on @bigdaddybunce

BUNCE'S
BIG FAT SHORT HISTORY
OF BRITISH BOXING

Steve Bunce

BANTAM PRESS

LONDON · TORONTO · SYDNEY · AUCKLAND · JOHANNESBURG

TRANSWORLD PUBLISHERS
61–63 Uxbridge Road, London W5 5SA
www.penguin.co.uk

Transworld is part of the Penguin Random House group of companies
whose addresses can be found at global.penguinrandomhouse.com

First published in Great Britain in 2017 by Bantam Press
an imprint of Transworld Publishers

A CIP catalogue record for this book
is available from the British Library.

ISBN 9780593078709 (cased)
9780593079096 (tpb)

Typeset in 11.5/14.5pt Minion by Falcon Oast Graphic Art Ltd.
Printed and bound by Clays Ltd, Bungay, Suffolk.

Penguin Random House is committed to a sustainable
future for our business, our readers and our planet. This book
is made from Forest Stewardship Council® certified paper.

1 3 5 7 9 10 8 6 4 2

For Jacqueline, my wife.

Dad.

And men we lost along the way:
Mick Carney, Billy Webster, Dean Powell,
Reg Gutteridge, Wally Bartleman, Keith Bunker,
Bradley Stone, Jimmy Murphy, Micky May,
Glyn Leach and Ray Francis.

Contents

Introduction

THIS IS THE FIRST history of modern British boxing since the bare-knuckle heyday of the nineteenth century. It starts at a time when several South American countries were bigger forces in professional boxing and the entire Eastern Bloc was more formidable at amateur boxing than the British. In 1970, make no mistake, it looked like the British were simply not very good at the sport they invented. Not one British boxer held a world title at the start of January that year. What's more, the men in charge of the British boxing business had no idea where their next world champion would come from and often acted like they never cared.

It has all changed. Less than fifty years later, at the very end of 2016, the men in charge of the British boxing business had thirteen world champions to keep busy, boxing in Britain had its own television channel, and fighters could sell 90,000 tickets in just a few hours. British boxers have also won five gold medals at the last three Olympics; in the previous twelve Games British boxers had won just two. This is not a renaissance, it's a revolution.

The fighters, managers, trainers, promoters, fixers, losers, jokers and officials are gathered here, mostly for the first time ever in a book, to have their story told. Every major fight and boxer from 1 January 1970 to 31 December 2016 is here. There is a Bunny Johnson for every Frank Bruno, a Rocky Kelly for every Ricky Hatton, and a Gary Jackymelon for every Ken Buchanan.

It starts with the grizzled veterans of the smoke-filled arenas in the seventies and ends with the glittering new breed of modern boxers. They all fought for the same reasons, thrilled the same fans and left the venues with black eyes, glory, and some with great wealth from pay-per-view revenue. There are others that slipped away under the cover of night, their hats pulled down over their battered faces and their pockets empty. They are all here, crucial to the history with their wins, losses, lunacy, tragedy and triumphs.

There are nights and fights when over 20 million people watched on terrestrial television as men became heroes and household names for ever. There are also trips to foreign fights where terrible judges, hostile crowds and crooked operators ruined British boxers. There are nights that ended at dawn with champagne bottles all over the table and other nights that ended at dawn in lonely vigils under the dim lighting of an intensive care unit.

Not every fighter can be rich, unbeaten and hold a world title, and not every promoter can put on sell-out shows in massive indoor and outdoor arenas. Some of the boxers failed on both sides of the ropes, some walked away without a full explanation, and many have simply vanished. I have collected the names of the lost, neglected and over-looked too, and include hundreds of them here where they belong. And they belong next to British greats like Lloyd Honeyghan, Naseem Hamed, John Conteh, Lennox Lewis and Joe Calzaghe. I realized very early that most of these fighters, even some from only fifteen and twenty years ago, have never appeared in any books, never had their story told and had simply faded away. There are others that shone brightly for such a brief time that a constant reminder of their brilliance never grows old.

The men and women that guided and inspired the fighting men also play their part. The old-fashioned boxing press, too, has an important role that is often ignored in the modern business where the lines have been blurred by online correspondents; the impressive written words of the travelling scribes in the seventies and eighties are often the only remaining history from lost fights. I have gathered together all the proper voices, all the right sources, and used hundreds of my own notepads. I settled an argument on the spelling of a boxer's name from the early seventies by looking in my old autograph book: it was there, and there was no final 'e'.

The dead boxers and fight-game characters speak here, often as they move from amateur to professional to retirement; they get their history alongside the winners and losers they knew, fought, promoted, trained and matched. There are great fighters in these pages that are remembered for the first time, others that seem never to have been out of the news, and yet others that have been saved from general obscurity. They all form a unique story – a big fat short history of British boxing.

1970

*'Our 'Enery has been their best earner for years and this is no way
to treat Britain's greatest boxing hero.'*
Jim Wicks attacks the British Boxing Board of Control

'Can we share this room? My guy's not been given one.'
Angelo Dundee asks Ken Buchanan if there is room for
Muhammad Ali in the dressing room

HENRY COOPER WAS unemployed at the start of the year, his career at a standstill. He looked like one of those south London villains that are forever in the dock at the Old Bailey – the one in the gang that enjoyed removing digits with a rusty saw.

Cooper had quit the sport in 1969 in disgust at the British Boxing Board of Control's refusal to sanction a world heavyweight title fight against Jimmy Ellis. There was an ugly impasse, but Cooper returned to fight for his old British title in March, despite starting to suffer from a series of recurring ailments; his shattered body was shutting down and he had a serious problem with a knee and left elbow aggro. He was an old young man and had first won the British heavyweight title in 1959.

Incidentally, had Ellis and Cooper been made, the plan was for it to be staged in London. There was also the seditious option of moving the fight to Rome or Dublin and snubbing the Board's annoying intransigence. But there was no way Cooper the Brit would ever do that. He was a veteran of the celebrity circuit, the winner of the BBC's

Sports Personality of the Year in 1967, and friends with Princess Anne. Our 'Enery would complain, have a moan, but he would never do anything to harm his image as Mr Britain. However, the window of opportunity slipped away permanently and predictably in February when Joe Frazier, who held the World Boxing Council version of the title, met Ellis and bludgeoned him in four rounds. 'That could have been me, it should have been me,' said the national treasure.

In Cooper's temporary absence Jack Bodell, a man from Swadlincote in Derbyshire, had won his old title. Bodell was variously described as a pig farmer, a chicken farmer and the most awkward British heavyweight in history. There is a touch of truth to all three claims: Bodell kept a few chickens, he had once owned a pig, and he was awkward. They fought at the Empire Pool and Wembley was heaving – Cooper was a massive attraction. At the end of fifteen rounds the verdict and the Lonsdale belt went to Cooper. Bodell had refused to stay down having been dropped three times; he finished the fight covered in blood, cuts and bruises. In the changing room afterwards, as the press boys gathered for nuggets, Cooper was helped out of his boxing boots by Jim Wicks, his manager, who shook his head in disgust at the kicking Bodell's big feet had given Cooper's shins and ankles. Big Jack with his fifties clothes, his dangerous feet and rural occupations was too often laughed at, but he was a decent fighter in many ways and would pull off a massive shock in 1971. He died in 2016 and his obits were warm and funny, and every single one had a picture of the day Muhammad Ali went to Jack's fish and chip shop in Coventry.

Cooper was back at the Empire Pool in November and it was business as usual. The knee and elbow worked and after a few rounds it was clear that José Manuel Urtain was, as Jim Wicks might have said, 'urtin'. It was over in the ninth round with Urtain's right eye closed. Cooper had been in total control, toying at times with the Spaniard. 'Being a strongman doesn't necessarily mean you can fight,' said Cooper when he was reminded of Urtain's history of winning rock-lifting competitions. The newspapers went with 'Curtains for Urtain', which I like. Cooper was still European heavyweight champion and there was just one fight left for him – one that defined the decade and the two men involved.

The real story of the fight was the money that promoter Harry Levene, another devotee of a swollen cigar, was forced to pay Urtain, whose manager was a wealthy industrialist, which could mean all sorts of things in Franco's Spain. The winning purse bid was £68,000, a record for a European title fight, and Levene travelled to the European Boxing Union's office in Rome to personally hand over and watch as the sealed envelopes were opened. Men and women still deliver bids for fights in sealed envelopes. Levene was not convinced Urtain would show and had German heavyweight Jürgen Blin in London as a precaution against the strongman's possible withdrawal. There is little doubt that had Levene lost the bid it would have been a perilous fight and trip for Cooper. Levene knew that the backers of Urtain were not happy losing the bid, not happy with the fight's location. 'They never wanted it in London, not a chance,' said Levene. The fight was the first in Britain to have two judges at ringside and not just the one referee as the ultimate arbiter. Levene, however, refused to pay that cost and the Board had to pick up the tab for the extra officials. Levene was never going to lose a fight for costs.

Ken Buchanan, like Cooper, had also quit in 1969. 'I was not making enough money and I sent my belt back,' said Buchanan. A cancelled world title eliminator had also been a factor, but soothing words from Eddie Thomas, his manager, persuaded the unbeaten fighter to return. At the end of January in Madrid, Ken had a difficult European title fight. 'I took the fight in Madrid knowing that a win would change my life,' he said. The fight was typical of the dozens that took place in the seventies when a British boxer went to Europe and knew that he would encounter both legal and illegal obstacles. At the end of fifteen torrid rounds the local fighter, Miguel Velázquez, was the winner. 'The ref picked the easy way out, he wanted to avoid a riot,' said Buchanan. He had a quick win a few weeks later behind closed doors at one of the private sporting clubs in London's West End. His retirement was over, Buchanan was back.

The main news in the summer of 1970 was the world title fight for

Buchanan. It came from nowhere: he was selected as an easy touch by a man called Dewey Fregatta, a fight fixer from California, who had to find an opponent for the WBA lightweight champion Ismael Laguna. The British promoter Jack Solomons, a man seldom separated from a fine cigar, called Buchanan with the news: 'Hey, you miserable Scotsman, how would you like to fight for the world title?' Buchanan replied instantly without asking the name of the opponent: 'When do I fly?'

He flew in the middle of September to New York for a twelve-day training camp and a short publicity tour. Buchanan and his tiny party were dismissed by Laguna's manager, Cain Young, a man with big ambitions for his elegant Panamanian boxer. It was less than a year since Buchanan had decided to unretire and now he was fighting Laguna, who was impossibly exotic, like most of the fifteen different world champions in 1970. They had names like fictional candy and fought each other in locations so distant they sounded like fantasy.

The Buchanan–Laguna fight was scheduled to take place outdoors at two p.m. in San Juan, Puerto Rico. It started in blinding sun, perhaps as hot as a hundred degrees. The Laguna corner was in the shade, the Buchanan team, which was increasingly looking like the sacrificial offering at a pagan festival, were brutally exposed. Buchanan could have redefined 'pallid', and his skin seemed to turn pink in seconds. Eddie Thomas insists there was a switch: 'We were first in the ring as the challenger and were heading to the shaded corner, but people got in the way and the next thing we knew Laguna had got there first. They were all smiling at us.' It was a great fight, voted the best of 1970 by the American Boxing Writers' club. Tommy, Buchanan's father, borrowed a parasol from a woman at ringside and was able to offer his son some relief from the blazing Caribbean sun during the minute breaks. It ended in a downpour. A full set of seasons had touched the ring, and it was a proper finale for Buchanan and his bruises. The decision was tight, a split vote, but it was fair and Ken Buchanan was the new WBA lightweight champion of the world. Laguna's men were distraught, Buchanan's party ecstatic. The smiles would soon fade.

The Board refused to acknowledge Buchanan as WBA world champion because they had an exclusive alliance with the WBC. They had warned him he was in breach of their rules for accepting the fight, the same breach that had persuaded Cooper to quit a year earlier. It was a stand-off that was simply preposterous. Buchanan flew back to Edinburgh, wearing a giant sombrero, and expecting a reception; six people, including his wife, Carol, and infant son, Mark, were waiting for the skinny man with the swollen face and the sad hat. Solomons cheered Buchanan a little when he called later to say that the men at Madison Square Garden wanted him on a bill. The news was as incongruous as the sombrero had been at arrivals that morning. Buchanan had started the year with a loss in Madrid, then fought for the exclusive pleasure of the silent members at another of the West End's private clubs and now, with the WBA's gold trophy on the kitchen table, he had an offer to fight at boxing's holiest of temples, Madison Square Garden in New York City. 'It was all a bit difficult to take in,' said Buchanan.

To end a ridiculous year for Buchanan, he was booked on Muhammad Ali's undercard that December. He was not given an easy fight and he was not impressed when he realized he was facing Donato Paduano, an unbeaten Canadian welterweight. Paduano was 10lb heavier than Buchanan at the scales, which is madness. Buchanan was the lightweight champion of the world and he was at the Garden fighting a welterweight. It was a tremendous risk. An hour before his fight there was a knock on his dressing room door – it was Angelo Dundee, Ali's long-suffering trainer. 'Can we share this room?' he asked. 'My guy's not been given one.' That is how Buchanan's year ended, sharing a room in the bowels of boxing's sacred building with the greatest fighter on the planet. 'He was a cool guy,' said Buchanan.

In the Garden ring, Buchanan won with a brilliant display of boxing and received a standing ovation; the Garden had a new fighter and the homeless Buchanan had a new boxing home. Ali stopped Oscar Bonavena in the fifteenth and last round with just fifty-seven seconds left – it had not been easy against this famed playboy from

Argentina. He was eventually stopped by a bullet, fired at close range by a strong-arm felon, hired for the kill by the owner of a Reno, Nevada brothel who was upset that his wife was having an affair with Bonavena. 'The guy shot the wrong one,' said Reg Gutteridge, for decades the voice of boxing on ITV commentaries. Gutteridge always backed the boxer as the innocent party.

In August it had been the turn of another British boxer to pack his bags and go on the road. Chris Finnegan had gone to the Mexico Olympics and won a gold medal at middleweight, but gold medals meant very little in those days and Finnegan turned professional behind closed doors at the Hilton Hotel, in London's Mayfair, late in 1968. He fought eight of his first fourteen fights on shows at private clubs like the Anglo-American Sporting Club. One night in 1969 he beat Brendan Ingle, a year or so before the great whispering guru from Dublin would locate full-time to Wincobank on the grubby outskirts of Sheffield where he created a boxing centre and crafted a boxing philosophy that nearly fifty years later still produces world champions. 'I never drank, but Chris had a few pints after,' said Ingle. At the end of August Finnegan went to Valby in Denmark to fight Tom Bogs for the European middleweight title. It was a risk, and it nearly worked. Finnegan broke Bogs' nose, cut him above both eyes and chased the Danish pin-up for fifteen rounds. 'I took Finnegan too lightly,' Bogs admitted. The comedy was provided by the German referee, Herbert Tomser, who delivered a ludicrous scorecard that read: four rounds to Bogs, none to Finnegan and eleven even. Six years later Tomser took charge of an Ali world title fight in Munich.

In September a piece of history had unfolded during an ugly night at the Empire Pool when Basil Sylvester Sterling, better known as Bunny Sterling, became the first immigrant black boxer to win a British title. Sterling stopped Mark Rowe, an enormous ticket seller from London's border with Kent, on cuts in round four to become the British middleweight champion. Rowe complained bitterly and there were disturbances at ringside – a polite way of saying that a few lunatics tried to invade the ring to do to Sterling what their highly trained pal had failed to do. Sterling and his trainer, George Francis, would continue to get hate mail for years. 'I was called just about everything under the sun for helping a black fighter to become a British champion: I was a nigger lover, a traitor,' said Francis. 'Never bothered me, I laughed at their ignorance.' Sterling had won sixteen of his previous twenty-seven fights and was a veteran of the neglected circuit of private clubs, bottom of the undercard fights and foreign jobs; he was soon to be at the very core of the stable – an outlandish but still-used expression – Francis was putting together in north London. Francis was a pioneer, a fearless and respected man.

Joe Bugner was a big lad from Hungary, a survivor of a hazardous migration from the bloody streets of his homeland, and by 1970 he was a heavyweight prospect; blond, funny, and smart in the ring. Sadly, he was a boxer and not a banger, and the public prefer their heavyweights to bang people over. He was just 19 when he had the first of his nine fights in 1970. By the end of the year he had spent some time sparring with Ali, had fought thirty-one times in total and had lost twice, including getting knocked out on his debut in 1967 when he was only 17. Bugner would dominate the seventies and provide a few laughs in the eighties, and even more in the nineties. At the Royal Albert Hall in January 1970 Bugner had his first real test when he beat Johnny Prescott over eight rounds.

At the Empire Pool, Wembley, in early May it was the start of John Conteh's truly incredible journey when he won the senior Amateur Boxing Association title at middleweight. Conteh was 18, and in July he won the middleweight gold at the Commonwealth Games in Edinburgh. 'It's hard for me to even remember what I was thinking back then,' said Conteh. 'I look at pictures of me and ask: "Was that me? Was that really me?" It was so long ago.' During the next decade Conteh would go from the smiling cargo in the arms of a dozen Playboy bunnies – a defining image that haunted him – to being restrained on the floor of a toilet in an Atlantic City hotel. In the middle, somewhere, he would make a bold claim to be recognized as Britain's best boxer.

The Contenders

There was a betting frenzy at the Royal Albert Hall on a Tuesday night in late April when Alan Rudkin, fresh from back-to-back world title defeats in 1969, was defending his British bantamweight title and aiming to add the vacant Commonwealth title against Johnny Clark. The shrewd thinking of the experts and gamblers – there was never a shortage of either at the RAH on fight night – was that Rudkin had left too much behind in the losses and that Clark, who had fought at the Albert Hall seventeen times in twenty-seven fights, was unbeaten and would be too fresh. It was a classic, and ended in round twelve. Rudkin was still champion; Clark would fill the glorious hall a few more times.

In the summer a British boxer could pick up a payday on the road when the season slowed. Cardiff's charismatic and dapper Eddie Avoth went to California in June to fight Mike Quarry, brother of Jerry. Avoth had defended his British light-heavyweight title in April, winning by disqualification when he was blatantly butted by Young McCormack, and then went ten rounds with Quarry, who was unbeaten in twenty-one fights. 'I had to go, the fight was offered and I always needed the money,' said Avoth.

Olympian John H. Stracey had eight fights at welterweight in the year and won them all.

From the Notepad

In April, *The Ring* magazine, the so-called bible of boxing, ran a feature on the future of heavyweight boxing and it included two European Young Lions. The Americans were George Foreman and Ken Norton, both of whom would win a version of the world heavyweight title, and alongside the pair were Coventry slugger Danny McAlinden and the Basque iron-man Urtain. There was no mention in the piece of Bugner.

In October another Bunny, Bunny Johnson, who would make his own British history a couple of years later, was a paid sparring partner for Cooper before the Urtain fight. 'He's class that Cooper,' said Johnson. 'It's very enjoyable boxing with Henry. I like him because he doesn't take liberties, yet you have to earn your money. And, at this particular time, I need the dough.' Johnson would join the other Bunny and Francis in north London. In December, Cooper won the BBC's Sports Personality of the Year for the second time – the first person to do it – and that was an unexpected close to a year that had started with the balding idol in retirement.

Jimmy Tibbs had four fights in 1970, won them all and walked away from boxing in March. He would become one of the most respected coaches over the next five decades. Before that there was a stint in prison after a shotgun went off, his car was bombed, and he found the Lord. 'Fighting eight rounds at the Albert Hall is a picnic,' Tibbs remarked.

1971

'There's one who can't take a punch and the other big girl's blouse who can't give one.'
Janet Dunn, wife of Richard Dunn, previews a heavyweight fight

'Joe never deserved the scorn of the public. He did nothing wrong.'
Reg Gutteridge defends Bugner

AT THE END of January the fight between Henry Cooper, the British, European and Commonwealth heavyweight champion, and Joe Bugner was formally announced. It made the news. Harry Levene, the promoter, paused between puffs on a cigar to answer questions, but refused to disclose the purse. 'It's between myself, the fighters and the income tax man,' he said. It was reported to be £60,000 in total. Jim Wicks, Cooper's manager, insisted 'Enery should get a minimum of £45,000. 'I want fifteen for each of 'Enery's Lonsdale belts for fighting him,' he said.

Bugner had come through ten rounds a few days earlier at the Royal Albert Hall against former British title challenger Carl Gizzi, who lost a title fight to Jack Bodell in 1969. It was a routine outing for Bugner, memorable only for a fabulous assault by Janet Dunn, wife of heavyweight contender Richard, who was not impressed before the first bell: 'There's one who can't take a punch and the other big girl's blouse who can't give one. I'll let you into a secret: Richard told me I've got a bigger dig than Gizzi.' She went on to explain that Dunn, who would one night in 1976 fight Muhammad Ali, would ban her from 'bingo for at least a week' if he found out what she had said. Bugner found out, and he never forgot.

The most infamous fight in British boxing history took place on a Tuesday night in March at the Empire Pool. Cooper was 36, nearly 37, and Bugner had turned 21 three days earlier. Cooper had first won the British heavyweight title in 1959, had dropped Cassius Clay in 1963 and had lost a rematch for the world title with the man then known as Muhammad Ali. Cooper was adored, he bled for the British public; a double BBC Sports Personality of the Year winner, he was a sacred fighter even before his confirmed martyrdom at the end of the fifteen rounds with Bugner. There was as much hate in the air that night, air thick with the smoke from 10,000 punters, as there was love.

Harry Gibbs, the referee, had spent the war as a prisoner in Camp XXB in Marienburg, Poland, after his capture at Dunkirk. He was a former fighter, an amateur coach that had once had a young Cooper in his England amateur team, but he was best known as one of the world's highest-profile referees: 'Next to honesty, aloofness is the quality a good ref needs most.' Even before that torrid night with Cooper and Bugner, Gibbs had as many enemies as fans. He was not universally liked in Bermondsey. He went to see both of the boys before the fight. The Cooper visit was simple: two old pros from south London nodding and talking, veterans in each other's company. Then Gibbs went to see Bugner. He looked at the blond fighter, not really his type of fighter, and then started growling. Gibbs: No hitting on the break, no hitting on the back of his head, leave his kidneys alone and no foul blows. Bugner: Fuck, Harry, am I allowed to touch him? Gibbs: Don't be cheeky, son. It was a wonderful remark.

Just minutes later, it started. Bugner in light blue shorts and Adidas boots. Cooper in black boots and dark blue shorts with a white trim. Gibbs in a bowtie. Their pristine burgundy Baileys gloves had started to darken by the end of the first round. The odds on outsider Bugner, so commentator Harry Carpenter said during that first round, had dropped. The gambling faithful at ringside, who were thick at Wembley that night, were hedging their bets; a real fight was on, and the nation was gripped. The old champion needed to land his 'ammer, as his left hook was known, on Bugner's chops. They jabbed and jabbed like the two brilliant pros they were. They had fought a combined total of seventy-three fights; Cooper had been in seventeen major title fights. Cooper was cut for the first time in the third. The pace never dropped, and it was fast. At the end of round ten Wicks told his fighter, 'You're not being busy enough – he's going to nick it.' Cooper responded. Bugner came back, and it went the full fifteen rounds. Cooper looked at Gibbs for his hand to be raised in victory, Gibbs looked away. Cooper thought to himself: 'Cor, stone me.' He never said a word, he had too much pride to bleat. Wicks tried to get to Gibbs. Carpenter famously uttered the deathless words, 'How can they take a man's belt like that?' Gibbs stopped Bugner from walking to his corner and quietly raised his hand – the new champion, the winner by just one round.

Back in the packed dressing room, Cooper sat down and in front of the invited boxing writers put an end to his career: 'Well, gentlemen, that's me lot.' He never fought again and finished with forty wins from fifty-five fights.

Bugner asked the gathered writers a simple question that he regrets: 'What 'appened to the 'ammer tonight?' He said it in a heavy imitation of Wicks, a man that had delighted the paper boys for nearly two decades with an endless seam of priceless quotes. The aftermath was brutal on Bugner. It was still an issue when I managed to persuade the pair to sit and talk in 2007. The tension never faded during the twenty-minute confrontation and Bugner was shaking his head when I returned after walking Cooper to his car. 'I was treated like the man that shot Bambi's dad back then and it's not changed,' Bugner said. 'If I had known about the stink I would never have fought him, and I tried to tell him that.' Cooper claimed in later years that he was not upset or angry with Bugner, and that Gibbs was the man he hated. He seemed angry with Big Joe when they came together. Cooper and Gibbs never spoke again until, finally, in the early nineties they met and shook hands. It was not a reconciliation, just a quick act. Gibbs had decided to sue Cooper for comments made in the boxer's autobiography. 'I took him to court and won,' Gibbs said. 'I didn't do it for the money, just to clear my good name.'

Eight days earlier in March there had been a truly bizarre cameo by British heavyweight Danny McAlinden on the undercard of the Fight of the Century at Madison Square Garden, New York. Joe Frazier narrowly beat Ali and McAlinden outpointed Muhammad's brother Rahman over six rounds. A brief appearance in *The Ring* magazine the previous year had obviously worked for Danny Mac, who would be involved in some tremendous slugfests.

Bugner was back in action in May at Wembley, retaining his European title against the German Jürgen Blin on a split decision. 'The Cooper fight has taken a lot out of Joe,' said Andy Smith, his manager. Bugner was 21, he had been attacked relentlessly in the press, and the Blin fight was his thirty-sixth of a career that started when he was just 17. 'Joe never deserved the scorn of the public,' said Reg Gutteridge.

Bugner lost his British, Commonwealth and European heavyweight titles in September, when he was outpointed over fifteen rounds by Jack Bodell. It was a betting shock, but Bugner was exhausted. The fight was his ninth in twelve months; eight had been at the Royal Albert Hall or Empire Pool and four, in less than six months, had gone the full distance. 'I lost fair and square,' admitted Bugner. It had been six months since he beat Cooper and it would be just seventeen months before he met Muhammad Ali for the first time.

Bodell, fresh from beating Bugner, was back at the Empire Pool six weeks later, in November. His fight with Jerry Quarry, arguably one of the five best American heavyweights of the seventies, lasted just sixty-four seconds. Quarry had been warned that Bodell was awkward and some wit in the press corps asked him about it after the fight. Quarry looked up, smiled and replied, 'Awkward? Well, he sure fell awkward.'

The Quarry fight was possibly too soon after the Bugner encounter, but seventies heavyweights just got on with it. Bodell was back in the ring just thirty-one days later, on 17 December in Madrid. It was a gruesome schedule, by any standards. He was defending his European title against the rock-lifter, José Urtain. This time the broad-shouldered Spaniard with a hundred strongman records to his name blasted poor Jack in two rounds. Three hard fights in just ten weeks is brutal testimony to the bravery of the boxers and the ruthless streak of the men that made them fight and paid them the money. Bodell would fight just once more before leaving the sport for a quiet life in Swadlincote, a man without a moan and far more than just a chicken and pig farmer (which he never was) and awkward brute (which he was). He was, as we say, a proper handful.

Back in February in Los Angeles it was all going wrong for WBA lightweight champion Ken Buchanan. He was due to defend his title and add the vacant WBC version in a fight with former champion Mando Ramos. In sparring, two fillings were cracked and needed replacing. It was a four-day sparring break so this was crucial time lost at a critical moment. Buchanan also hurt his knee in a freak sparring accident; the fight was in real jeopardy. Then Ramos was pulled out with severe venereal disease and Rubén Navarro, who was suspiciously ready and primed, was slipped in at short notice. Buchanan never did it the easy way. He did get $60,000, but had to avoid some classic tricks. A woman called his room and offered to visit, there was a blatant attempt to get Buchanan to drink from a tainted bottle, and before the water trick a Mexican was discovered under the ring apron hiding in an attempt to eavesdrop on the talk in the Scot's corner. 'Best of luck with that,' Buchanan said. In the opening round Buchanan was over from a sneak punch, but at the end of fifteen dirty rounds he was a clear winner. Both titles were his and this time hundreds were waiting at Edinburgh airport. (Ramos, incidentally, did get clean and won a version of the world title in 1972.)

In May Buchanan had a non-title fight at Wembley and stopped his opponent in eight rounds. In his hotel after the win, the fight fixer at Madison Square Garden, Teddy Brenner, proposed a rematch with Ismael Laguna at the Garden with $100,000 as the prize. Buchanan was a happy boy.

There was a pure Hollywood moment in New York in September when Buchanan fought that lucrative rematch with Laguna. A total of 13,211 traipsed through the turnstiles to watch the adopted Scotsman, a boxing artist who mixed the ingredients that the city's fight fans adored. Buchanan in his tartan shorts ruined Laguna with educated punches and won comfortably after fifteen rounds. In the one-minute break at the end of four, Buchanan sat down with a severely swollen left eye. There was no way he could fight the next eleven rounds with the eye closing and Laguna knew it, sensing that the injury could end the fight and he would regain his title. In the corner, Buchanan looked up at Eddie Thomas. The Welsh maestro produced a razor blade and cut a small incision at precisely the right point in the swelling; the blood oozed out, the swelling instantly reduced, and Laguna's chance was gone.

The cut later required eleven stitches and became infected. Buchanan met with Jarvis Astaire, a key member of the small team of boxing people that became known as the Cartel, one day in London after the fight. Astaire took one look at the ugly cut and immediately directed Buchanan to an expert in Harley Street, where the injury was lanced, cleaned and fixed. The London doctor found some alien nylon gut stitches in the foul wound: the doctor in New York that inserted the original stitches is described more like a drunk vet than a doctor tending a world champion. He had asked Buchanan's father to sit on the boxer's legs, told Eddie Thomas to hold his head, then inserted the stitches without a painkiller. 'He treated me like an animal,' said Buchanan. Eddie had saved the fight, Jarvis might have saved the Scot's career.

On the undercard at the Garden was another kid from Panama of just 20 called Roberto Durán. He met a solid pro and it lasted just sixty-six seconds. Durán was now unbeaten in twenty-five. There were plans for a fight with Buchanan even before the lights went out over the historic ring that night. Durán had been promised Buchanan and watched the Scot retain his title with an indifference that would make him such a lasting attraction. The result of Buchanan–Durán, like Bugner–Cooper, is still discussed nearly half a century later.

At the World Sporting Club, hidden in the depths of the Grosvenor House Hotel in London's Park Lane, a British and Commonwealth title fight took place in late January on a Sunday, the first on that day since 1929. It was always going to be entertaining, which makes its location even more annoying. There was a simple explanation, according to promoter Jack Solomons: 'The club lost money on the show, but I wanted to get a title fight for the members.' Old Jack, forever loyal to the men that bought his fight tickets, delivered Cardiff idol Eddie Avoth, with his light-heavyweight belts, against Chris Finnegan, the man that travelled to Mexico in 1968, narrowly avoided being sent home for being drunk when he went out before the boxing started, and then won the Olympic gold medal. Freddie Hill trained Finnegan above a pub in London's Lavender Hill – yes, they did all go downstairs for a few pints of Guinness after sparring, and at this early stage of his fighter's career he was defending him against suggestions that an occasional pint was harmful. 'You see, Chris is a bricklayer,' Hill explained. 'He needs fuel. There is nothing wrong with a glass of Guinness. You have to put coal on the fire or the fire goes out.' Finnegan stopped Avoth with just forty-eight seconds left in the fifteenth and final round. Avoth had been in a car crash five months earlier and received twenty-seven stitches to his face, which was not an excuse, just a fact. 'I want a return,' Avoth said. Hill shook his head in despair at the mention of a rematch: 'I must admit I expected Avoth to be better.' The trade paper the *Boxing News* called it 'one of the greatest domestic light-heavyweight title fights'. There is no recording of the polite applause the brawl so obviously deserved. Solomons had delivered for his private punters.

The following night, just a short stroll down Park Lane at the Hilton Hotel, the first European title ever to be contested in a private club took place; the venue was the Anglo-American Sporting Club. Cuba's former world champion José Legra, who was exiled to Spain after Fidel Castro banned professional boxing, simply knew too much for British featherweight champion Jimmy Revie and took the verdict after fifteen bloody rounds. Legra had lost his title in 1969, was still only twenty-seven, and the Revie fight was his 134th. He looked like an old man of fifty. Relics like the Cuban regularly haunted rings in Britain during the decade.

In June, July and August there were just eleven promotions in Britain. In June the British welterweight champion, Ralph Charles, travelled to Geneva and lost his European welterweight title when he was stopped in seven by Roger Menetrey. Charles had won the title on the road in Vienna the previous November. He defended his Commonwealth belt a few months later in Brisbane and ended the year retaining his British title at the Royal Albert Hall, in December. It was a sickening schedule.

In March 1972 Charles was finally, after forty-two fights and nine years as a professional, given a world title fight. The career of Charles, like those of so many sixties and seventies British champions, was difficult, and he was matched hard on the road: there was very little protection for even the best British boxers in overseas fights and they travelled as the designated losers. Charles could bang, he stopped or knocked out the last sixteen men he beat, he was from London's East End, but still he had to go on the road for title fights. He did get home advantage for his world title fight with José Nápoles, but it was not enough for Charles, who remains one of the decade's enigmas.

In August, in front of 12,000 at a bullring in Bilbao, it was Alan Rudkin's turn to fight against the odds, the sun and the crowd. Rudkin, the British champion, was defending his European title at bantamweight a long way from home and the civilities that can protect you in a British ring. Rudkin had lost in world title fights in Tokyo, Melbourne and Los Angeles in the sixties; in Bilbao he dropped a fifteen-round decision in the Plaza de Toros to unbeaten Agustin Senin. Rudkin was over four times against the local idol and it still went the full punishing distance. There is a case to be made that Rudkin's career was one of the hardest ever in British boxing history, certainly in terms of just how good he was and how good so many of his opponents were. 'I never had it easy, I had to go away and fight the very best,' Rudkin said. 'I was the underdog so many times. The Senin fight was normal, I got treated that way a lot.' In his fiftieth and final fight, which took place in December, he was once again matched as the loser. He defied the odds and went out a winner.

The Contenders

John Conteh decided that fighting for lamps, electric sleeping blankets, medals and pride was wasting his time and he turned professional. He had won two British amateur titles and a gold medal at the 1970 Commonwealth Games in Edinburgh, but his attempt to win a European amateur title in Madrid in June 1971 had been a farcical disaster. Conteh had been drawn against a fat and balding Austrian called Richard Kolleritsch and had lost. 'That was my lot, I was going pro from that moment,' Conteh said. His debut was, as so often happened, buried on a private night at the National Sporting Club inside the Café Royal, just off Piccadilly Circus. Conteh won in fifty-six seconds.

In May, Finnegan got a crazy draw in Germany for the European light-heavyweight title.

John H. Stracey won six and drew once to end the year unbeaten in eighteen.

From the Notepad

Tickets for the Fight of the Century in New York were priced from $150 (about £62) down to $20 (close to £8) for the cheapest. I know liars that claim to have been there. It was possible for British fight fans at the time to pay just £3 for dinner, boxing and cabaret at venues like the Cat's Whiskers in south London. It was at that delicious joint near Brixton that a fighter called Clarence Cassius was beaten by Bootle hardman Harry Scott just a few days before Ali, formerly known as Cassius Clay, lost to Frazier. It was also the venue where Frank Bruno, a few years later, would enjoy a quick knockout victory as an amateur. Bruno had to pretend he was 17 and a senior, because nobody believed he was still a junior boxer of 16. It was a ruse to get him fights, but it got him a ban. Bruno boxing in the same decade as Cooper seems weird, though he would eventually on one wet night in 1987 fight what was left of Joe Bugner.

The delights of the sporting clubs that dominated the British boxing scene in the early seventies never made any sense. Some of the very best fighters of their generation fought behind closed doors for the pleasure of men eating and smoking and often looking on with glorious indifference. The journalists covering the fights also had to dress accordingly, and this was not something limited to the seventies. In 1993 I was banished to a BBC camera position, located in a tiny secret room with a view high in a wall above the dinner guests, when I arrived for a world title fight at the St Andrew's Sporting Club in Glasgow without a tuxedo or kilt. The promoter, Tommy Gilmour, had warned me, but I thought he was joking. He was not.

1972

*'It's like being hit with a scaffolding pole with a glove on the end of it,
and I know a bit about scaffolding poles.'*
Chris Finnegan on fighting Bob Foster

*'I saw this little mob with guns as I was coming back from a run
and I ducked away and got on the phone to the security.'*
Terry Spinks remembers the Munich Olympics

IN JUNE, KEN BUCHANAN left Edinburgh to return to Madison Square Garden for his third fight at the New York venue since winning the world title. His tartan shorts were starched, but being a star in the fight capital was lethal and there was no chance of an early night.

The man in the opposite corner had been stalking Buchanan, watching his fights, and had fought on the Scot's undercard the last time he was in New York. Roberto Durán was unbeaten in twenty-eight, Buchanan had lost just once in forty-four, and their fight attracted 18,821 paying customers on a Monday night. The gate reflected the quality and the ticket revenue was $225,000, which was a record for a lightweight fight; it was the type of record that boxing people adored and fighters bragged about. The bones of the deal had been done after Buchanan's last fight in the Garden ring; he was promised $125,000. 'There were other, more deserving contenders but the Garden came up with the money.' Buchanan was ever practical. The Garden wanted Roberto.

24

The fight was hard from the opening bell. Durán dropped Buchanan in the first with a right cross after the Scot's jab fell short. It was like that until the thirteenth round, punishing for both with some terrific action. Round thirteen was simply brilliant. After a minute Durán was warned to keep his punches up. He didn't listen, and Buchanan didn't complain. The borderline body shots continued, with a few elbows and plenty of Durán's head in Buchanan's busted-up face. The American commentator was talking about a rematch, the fight was not for the squeamish. As the thirteenth drew to a close, Durán had Buchanan back against the ropes and then, in rapid succession, three things seemed to happen simultaneously: the bell's long ring started, Durán connected with a very low right hand, and then his right knee landed where the illegal punch had connected. The bell finally stopped trilling. One, two, three and ouch. Buchanan's protective box had been dislodged and the boxer was in agony, over on his side and then his back. Cornermen jumped into the ring. The crowd were cheering and jeering and screams of 'foul' fill the air. It was toxic at that charged moment and very confusing. Buchanan regained his feet after twelve or thirteen seconds, but the ref had not been counting, so that ruled out a knockout verdict.

The stricken boxer was helped back to his corner and there was concern and crazy activity as Buchanan's people, which included his father, Tom, and New York's Gil Clancy, worked to revive their boxer. Johnny Lobianco, the ref, went over to his corner and appeared to wave the fight off; and then the warning buzzer for the fourteenth sounded, and as the crowd stood for another round of the classic, Lobianco went to Durán's corner and raised his hand.

There was mayhem in the ancient venue. Nobody seemed sure what had happened or why, but about a dozen people clambered over the ropes and fell on Durán in relief and joy. Buchanan was desolate. The referee gave an interview in the chaotic ring inside two minutes of the fight finishing, something that is still shocking to watch. The punch was late, after the bell, he concluded, adding that it is impossible to be hurt by a low blow when wearing a protective cup. It was a dazzlingly dumb comment, and untrue. The ref had simply decided that Buchanan was in no condition to continue. He finished his interview, and that was that for Johnny Lobianco.

'I was hit low and I have no idea if it was a punch or his knee – I was looking at his face, I don't know what hit me,' said Buchanan. 'I told the referee that I would be able to come out for the fourteenth round, but he refused to listen.' Buchanan was losing on all three of the scorecards.

Nearly fifty years later, Buchanan still remembers the punch/knee and the two contracts for a rematch – a fight he wanted, but one that never happened.

Buchanan's night was over, his cherished title gone to the unbeaten Panamanian, known as Hands of Stone, who was just 21. At the end in the packed Garden ring, an illuminated square divided equally between rapture and heartache, Buchanan simply bent forward, his head down over his thighs to ease the pain and hide the tears.

Durán would go on to feature in some of boxing's greatest fights before finally retiring in 2001, nearly thirty years after his foul-filled triumph. Durán did make his peace with Buchanan at some point in 2008 during one of the Panamanian's many speaking tours of Britain. At one gig, Durán praised Buchanan for 'having big balls' and the Scotsman laughed and said, 'Aye, well, you'd know – you've had a good feel, son.' Buchanan was not finished with the Garden.

There was a return fight for Chris Finnegan against the German Conny Velensek in February in Nottingham. In the original fight, which took place in Berlin in May 1971, there was a fair amount of slapstick and farce when a drawn verdict was announced. Mickey Duff, part of Finnegan's corner, knocked out a German reporter. Finnegan said it was the best punch of the night, but the real comedy came when Velensek climbed through the ropes. 'All week the geezer had a full toupee on, a fine head of hair,' said Freddie Hill, the boss of his own Lavender Hill mob. 'And then he stepped through the ropes and I turned to Chris and said: "Fuck me, who's the bald geezer?" It was not funny in the end.' Finnegan won the European title over fifteen rounds, and had three more fights before getting his chance at the world title.

'It's like being hit with a scaffolding pole with a glove on the end of it, and I know a bit about scaffolding poles,' said Finnegan after losing this world light-heavyweight title fight to American Bob Foster at Wembley in September. It was over in the fourteenth round, Finnegan down at the end of a truly memorable scrap. It was voted *The Ring* magazine's Fight of the Year for 1972, proudly placed between Muhammad Ali and Joe Frazier in 1971 and Frazier and George Foreman in 1973. It mattered being *The Ring*'s Fight of the Year. Finnegan was only the third British boxer to challenge for a world title in the seventies.

On the Finnegan–Foster undercard there was a warning for John Conteh, who was unbeaten in eleven at heavyweight (at which weight he began his career). Conteh dropped a disputed decision over ten rounds to novice American Eddie 'Big E' Duncan. It was not a real setback, just a loss, and at the time every decent fighter had losses on his record. More importantly, a defeat made no difference to the fans at the time because being unbeaten was not seen as a necessity for either commercial success or glory in the ring.

It is hard to believe, but Finnegan was back in title action in November only seven weeks after his fight with Foster. He lost on cuts in the twelfth round of a European light-heavyweight defence against Germany's Rüdiger Schmidtke at Wembley. Conteh won on the same night to keep the pressure on an inevitable fight with Finnegan. Six months later and Conteh, down at light-heavyweight, would fight Finnegan.

It seemed impossible to keep Alan Rudkin down. He had his fiftieth and final fight at the Albert Hall in late January when he met south London's Johnny Clark, the man that was meant to beat him when they met for the first time in April 1970. The first meeting was considered the best British fight of 1970. There was nothing in the rematch. The first had ended in the twelfth with Clark totally exhausted; this time, at the end of fifteen rounds, Rudkin took a narrow decision to win the British and Commonwealth bantam-weight titles. He was 30, and that was his lot. He retired to Liverpool, a city where being a boxer is still hard currency. He ran a few pubs, including the iconic The Vines, known as the 'big house'; the pub was eventually taken back by the brewery. In 2010 he was found on the street at three a.m., just a short walk from his favourite pub; he died in hospital twenty-four hours later. He was 68, a forgotten crafts-man, a pure boxer and one of the greatest British fighters never to win a world title. It is possible that he holds that elusive crown. He certainly deserved the verdict when he lost on a split decision to world champion Lionel Rose in 1969 in Melbourne. 'That's the sport, Lionel was a lovely guy,' said Rudkin.

Evan Armstrong once bred a wild rabbit with a pet rabbit – a rarity in the rabbit-breeding business – and it led to a certain fame on the agricultural circuit. In 1971 he won the British featherweight title one hard, anonymous night against London boy Jimmy Revie behind closed doors at the Grosvenor House. Armstrong had lost nine of his previous forty-one fights. He was not precious cargo, just a relentless fighter from Ayr. His career had started without any noise but after seven straight wins he fought one Thursday night at the Ice Rink in Paisley; it was 1964, and Sugar Ray Robinson, the best fighter ever, lost on points at the top of the bill.

When Armstrong fought, a distinctive and mildly disturbing red mark would appear above his left eye. It was a submerged scar from a bike crash on ice when he was 15. Armstrong had fractured his skull in the accident and the blood-red smear surfaced whenever he was in a real fight – and he was often in real fights. Rudkin had stopped him in a British bantamweight title fight in 1969, he had beaten pin-up kid Revie for the featherweight version in the summer of 1971, and lost over fifteen rounds for the Commonwealth version in Australia in late 1971. In February he was matched with José Legra, the Cuban living in Spain, for the European featherweight title at the Royal Albert Hall. Legra, a crafty, well-aged veteran, simply knew too much for Armstrong. Both Legra and Armstrong are lost to history, two men that walked one-way into the distance when they quit.

The road to the Munich Olympics took a detour for Alan Minter at the London ABA finals, held at the Royal Albert Hall in late March.

He was stopped on a cut by Frankie Lucas, a member of the Sir Philip Game club in Croydon, south London. The fight was at middleweight, and Minter had won the ABA title at middle the year before, but he was offered a place in Munich at whatever weight he picked. He opted for light-middle. Lucas won the title at middleweight and would be overlooked, though his dreadful omission that summer, when the GB selectors sent the light-heavyweight champion at middleweight, would be eclipsed by the Commonwealth Games fiasco in 1974. The selection process for some of the nine British boxers for the 1972 Olympics was both comical and insulting. Six of the nine were from the London championships, only two had won the ABA title, and one of them, the Lynn club's Billy Knight, fought at a different weight.

In Munich, Mick Carney, the chief coach at the Fitzroy Lodge gym in south London, took charge of the Canadian team and West Ham's Terry Spinks, a gold medal winner in Melbourne, was in charge of the Korean team. Incidentally, Carney had three boxers (more than any other club that year) in the ABA semi-finals, including lightweight Nevell Cole who won the second of his three national titles. Cole did go to Munich. Twenty years later Carney discovered David Haye at the Fitzroy Lodge and had him from the start (at one point Haye was forced out of the sport for a year with growing pains). Carney, who worked for over fifty years alongside Billy Webster in the railway arch near the British war museum, was awarded the MBE in 2003 and was still in the gym just a few weeks before his death in 2011.

The ABA semi-finals were held in Manchester at Belle Vue in April and two quite brilliant 17-year-old featherweights won. Vernon Sollas from Edinburgh and Kirkland Laing from the Clifton club in Nottingham reached the final in May at Wembley. As professional boxers they would each win British titles and have a combined total of sixteen proper championship contests in careers with relentless twists. One fought until he was 40 and the other quit at just 22.

At the ABA championship in May the decision in the

featherweight final went to Laing. It was tight. 'I think Laing himself is a bit astonished,' said the BBC's boxing voice, Harry Carpenter. Laing wanted to go to the Olympics. He had no chance: he was too young. The selectors picked Sollas, and that made no sense, but there was a ridiculous twist or two to come. Laing was forgotten and a Repton fighter called Billy Taylor was nominated from nowhere to have a box-off with Sollas. The Sollas/Laing/Taylor debacle was not an isolated scandal. Larry Paul, who would go on to become the first British light-middleweight title holder, won the amateur version on that night at Wembley; Paul was overlooked, dropped in silence to make way for Minter's place after the Crawley boxer decided to fight at the lower poundage.

In June at the Double Diamond Club in Caerphilly, Sollas, the losing ABA finalist at featherweight, had to fight Repton's Billy Taylor, the London champion at bantamweight from the year before, for a spot in the British team for the Munich Olympics. Sollas won a difficult fight, and there was no mention of Laing, the man that beat Sollas in the ABA final the previous month. Sollas then missed two training camps and was dropped. Taylor was back. However, on 12 July the squad was named and Sollas was selected. There was a lot of screaming, shouting and threats. Laing was still overlooked and held his voice. A week after the final selection, Sollas broke into a parked car, nicked a few items and was arrested. He ended up in court, was fined forty quid and waited for the news he dreaded. 'I knew it was coming, I knew the Olympics were over for me,' he said, and he was right. The teenage Scot was dropped and Taylor, said to be on holiday in Clacton, was contacted and told he was going to the Olympics; he was one of three Repton boxers, each selected from nowhere, named in the GB team. Laing had to just sit in forced silence. 'I was ready, I told everybody that, but they never gave me a chance and I knew they would never pick me,' Laing said. It was cruel and inexplicable, but expected at a time of abuses. Laing had, in fairness, lost a fight ten days after the ABAs to Tommy Wright, the winner from the year before. Wright was never considered either. It should never have been taken into consideration as a one-off eliminator, but it seems it was. When Taylor put on his Olympic blazer he found a name tag stitched in: Vernon Sollas. It was not funny, not even for Taylor, who was a funny man.

The nine picked for Munich were: light-fly Ralph Evans (Waterlooville); fly Maurice O'Sullivan (Roath Youth); bantam George Turpin (Golden Gloves); feather Taylor (Repton); light Cole (Fitzroy Lodge); light-welter Graham Moughton (Repton); welter Maurice Hope (Repton); light-middle Minter (Crawley); middle Knight (Lynn). Just two were champions that year at their weight, a fact that remains barely believable.

The tournament started in August, ended in September, and was interrupted by the infamous bloodshed. Much was made of the security in place before the terrorists invaded, but a large British boxing contingent, swollen by the jobs given to Carney and Spinks, had no trouble getting in and out of the athletes' village. Kenny Lynch, the singer, was said to have used a pass allocated to a female gymnast to slip in and out to watch the boxing, which is probably true.

There were many outstanding performances from the final team and three – Turpin, Evans and Minter – came back with bronze medals. Minter was judged harshly in his semi-final against the West German Dieter Kottysch, losing 3-2 in a real bad decision. Minter had won three times and Kottysch won the final; Minter had his first professional fight six weeks after the Olympics finished. Turpin also lost a controversial 3-2 decision to the eventual winner, the Cuban Orlando Martínez, but his exit never received anything like the sympathy that Minter's departure generated. It was also the Games when the Cubans arrived, winning their first three gold medals and topping the table. However, the real story could be the seven medals won by sub-Saharan African fighters from Uganda, Nigeria, Niger, Kenya and Ghana, which is a total that would now be a miracle.

Joe Bugner won the European heavyweight title again in October when he bludgeoned old rival Jürgen Blin in eight rounds at the Royal Albert Hall. Bugner knew a fight with Ali was a possibility and squeezed in two more wins before the end of the year. He would fight Ali in Las Vegas the following February.

The Contenders

In March, Ralph Charles was stopped in round seven when José Nápoles, the WBC and WBA welterweight champion, met him at Empire Pool. Conteh moved to eight and zero on the undercard and Buchanan had another non-title fight, and would have yet another, this time in South Africa, before the Durán fight in June. 'There was no chance of just sitting and waiting for world title fights, I had to stay busy and stay earning,' Buchanan said.

Danny McAlinden, the Coventry heavyweight who fought on the undercard of the Fight of the Century, blasted Jack Bodell into defeat and retirement in two savage rounds. It was a typical British heavyweight performance and McAlinden was a wild and vulnerable champion; at the end of his career thirty-six of his forty-five fights had finished before the last bell. McAlinden had five more fights before risking his title in a behind-closed-doors first defence against Bunny Johnson in January 1975. 'I had no idea why he kept me waiting so long,' said Johnson.

From the Notepad

British boxing has hundreds of chance, odd encounters, nights and days when boxers are connected somehow. In December a coachload of teenage fighters from London's Tower Hamlets, part of the East End with a rich fighting tradition, went on a journey to fight a Welsh select. Two men met that night, both boys of 16 at the time, and both would have a tremendous impact on the boxing scene. One joyous, one tragic. Charlie Magri boxed for the Arbour Youth club and Johnny Owen was from Merthyr Tydfil, a place with a burden to fight as deep and ruinous as the filthy streets that surrounded the Arbour Youth in Stepney. Magri won, stopping Owen that night in Wales; eight years later, on another night, at the Empire Pool, the pair sat talking after each had won his title fight. Magri was the European flyweight champion, Owen the British bantamweight champion. There was no super-fly then, the pair were not separated by a division. 'We should fight,' Owen said. Magri agreed. Three months later Owen was dead.

1973

'*The dark, handsome and trendy character from Liverpool.*'
Harry Carpenter introduces John Conteh

'*It was a great fight between two black men in Alf Garnett country.*'
Des Morrison on his British title fight at Shoreditch Town Hall

'I WANT THAT man, give me that man,' demanded Muhammad Ali at the Royal Albert Hall in January. Ali removed his shirt, climbed up on the ring apron and continued shouting and pointing at Joe Bugner.

A few minutes earlier Bugner had finished fifteen rounds with Rudi Lubbers, one of my favourite heavyweight names, to retain his European title. Ali was shopping at ringside, looking for somebody to fight, looking for somebody to get him ready for his inevitable rematch with Joe Frazier. There was no date for the Frazier–Ali fight and Frazier had first to beat George Foreman in the Sunshine Showdown in Jamaica, scheduled for later in the month. Once that was done, a rematch could be made and it would be boxing's richest fight. Wrong: Foreman destroyed Frazier and changed the shape of the division. The veteran *Evening Standard* reporter Wally Bartleman predicted the win, the only British writer to do so. The following morning at breakfast in the blinding sun by the pool, Wally received a standing ovation when he popped down for his boiled eggs. He was in a suit and tie, always appropriately dressed. As he was nodding, shaking hands and smiling, he walked headfirst into the pool. Reg

Gutteridge, ITV's voice, wasted about a second before saying, 'Wally, you predicted the result, but you ain't Jesus; you can't walk on water yet, son.' Wally, who hired me to file results from amateur boxing shows in the early eighties, told me that he just kept on walking once he hit the bottom of the pool.

Ali had been talking about fighting Bugner since the pair had sparred a couple of years earlier. A fight was made for Las Vegas at the Convention Center just twenty-nine days after the Lubbers fight. 'I had to take it, it was a fight with Ali and I wanted it – I was ready,' said Bugner.

Bugner had a row with Elvis Presley just before the fight. Bugner had been 'working like a dog' (his words) to prepare for the fight. Ali had one defeat in forty-one and was considered a great; Bugner was 22 and had won forty-three of his forty-eight fights. He was right, he had worked like a dog to get where he was. Elvis and Ali had been friends a long time, and Ali had been an Elvis fan since he was a kid in Louisville. Elvis presented Ali with a specially designed and constructed robe with 'People's Choice' written on the back. The flowing, full-length and full-collared white robe, with typical Elvis sleeves, was weighted down with rhinestones and jewels. Several pounds of stones were removed before Ali wore the thing. However, the robe (which now lives at the Ali Center in Louisville, Kentucky) became a big story in Las Vegas that week with Ali's facilitator Gene Kilroy spinning the cloth relentlessly.

During the week of the fight Bugner and Ali were invited to Elvis's suite in Las Vegas. It was there that Ali was given the robe. Bugner asked Elvis where his robe was. Elvis, surrounded by his legendary flunkies, told Bugner he had to earn it first. 'I told him that I would beat Ali and that he could get fucked, and believe me, nobody spoke to Elvis like that. But I didn't care, I was just a kid.'

Bugner was cut in the first round. Ali did what he had to do to win over twelve rounds on points. It's an entertaining fight to watch, a reminder of just how good Bugner was. Ali knew that. He told everybody at the time and he would also go on Michael Parkinson's television show and defend Bugner. 'Joe Bugner will be the champion a couple of years from now,' said Ali. 'It will be Bugner's time when I'm gone.' Mickey Duff, who organized a trip for 1,500 British fans to the fight, thought Bugner had 'a fairly good big-time temperament'. Certainly nothing seemed to upset him, and very few things seemed to make him angry. 'I showed I belonged in the ring with Ali. I'm ready now, nobody scares me.' The problem was that Bugner, for all his size and credentials, did not scare anybody himself.

It was Ali that convinced John Conteh to drop down to light-heavyweight. Conteh won on the Bugner undercard and Ali told him he was 'too pretty to be a heavyweight'. It was a good line, and true. 'Ali told me that I was not big enough to be a heavyweight and he was right. I made the right decision,' Conteh said. On the Ali bill Conteh, who was just 7lb above the light-heavyweight limit, had stopped Terry Daniels in seven rounds. Daniels had lost a world heavyweight title fight to Frazier a year earlier. Conteh was mixing in the right fighting pool, but was never going to be big enough to have a hard fight with a heavyweight.

Bugner was fighting at the very highest level, something that was often neglected. 'I went the distance with two of the greatest heavy-weights ever in less than six months and still some people complained,' he said. 'I hit Bugner with shots that *no* man had any right to take,' said Joe Frazier in London in July after one of the finest fights in Britain of the seventies. Frazier beat Bugner over twelve rounds, every one as intense as the other.

The last round was a 180-second slugfest, with Smokin' Joe's left hook landing and Big Joe firing back with right hands of his own. The pair, standing temple to temple, whipped in vicious punches and the referee, Harry Gibbs, was poised less than two feet away. There was no break, no breather in the brawl. The noise at Earls Court was quite incredible, and Reg Gutteridge on the ITV microphone was breathless. 'This is a tremendous show by Bugner, no doubt. There are people who might argue that Frazier has lost his punch, but why should they take the credit away from Bugner?' Bugner had been down in the tenth and hurt; Frazier thought it was all over. 'Joe hit me with a beautiful right cross and I went down,' said Bugner. 'He thought I would stay down, he wanted me to stay down. I got up.' At the final bell, barely audible amid the screams, the pair kept throwing punches and Frazier's man, Yank Durham, jumped between them. Bugner was still glaring when Gibbs, the sole arbiter on the night, raised Frazier's fist in triumph. Frazier finished the fight with his left eye nearly closed, Bugner's right eye was also purple and swollen.

Frazier tried to dismiss how hard the fight had been, weaving the suffering into a larger narrative about getting ready for another fight with either Foreman or Ali. In January Foreman had crushed him and taken his world heavyweight title, and in his next fight he would lose on points back at the Garden to Ali.

'I was sick for two months after the fight,' Bugner told me. 'My kidney and liver were bruised and I was pissing blood for two weeks. That is what fighting, I mean really fighting, a man like Joe Frazier does to you.' Bugner would, however, meet two more opponents in 1973 and end the year having had five distance fights, with a total of sixty-four rounds. He was still only 23 and had been in the ring fifty-two times, which remains a set of figures that will never be broken.

In January, Ken Buchanan had fought far from the capacity crowds at boxing's spiritual home when he challenged Glasgow's Jim Watt for the British lightweight title at an exclusive sporting club in a hotel in the Scottish city. Buchanan won clearly over fifteen rounds in one of his rare appearances in a British ring. Six years later Watt won the world title, and by that time Buchanan was past his best, though still fighting for the European title. Watt hired Buchanan as a sparring partner for his last world title fight in 1981, and that was close to the start of the freefall for the man that had salvaged British boxing's pride when he won the world title in 1970.

In March, Conteh stopped Germany's Rüdiger Schmidtke in the twelfth to win the European light-heavyweight title. Poor Rüdiger was dropped in the sixth and took a shellacking. Chris Finnegan, the British champion, had lost to the German and a fight with Conteh was instantly inevitable and desired. 'Conteh was the most talented fighter I was ever involved with,' claimed Mickey Duff, but Finnegan was never complimentary about Conteh's head and expressed doubts about it before their fight, in May at the Empire Pool. Three belts – British, Commonwealth and European – were on offer; the winner would also move a fraction closer to a world title. Finnegan had been there: his world title chance had gone and the memory of Bob Foster taking him out in the fourteenth round was still too fresh. Conteh was just 21, a golden amateur with a smooth look in the gym and ring. Harry Carpenter introduced him as a 'dark, handsome and trendy character from Liverpool', a glorious anachronism that I never grow tired of hearing. He was popular with women, but still some way from the man he thought he was when he was held aloft in triumph by a dozen wary-eyed Playboy bunnies. Finnegan drank Guinness, prescribed by his old-school trainer Freddie Hill, and never traded on the gold medal he had won in 1968. It was a proper clash, a very British affair.

Conteh entered the three-roped Empire Pool ring first, chants of 'Finnegan, Finnegan, Finnegan' clearly audible. 'I have not heard a night quite like this in a London ring for a long time,' Carpenter said. Finnegan joined Conteh in the ring, and the referee Sid Nathan brought them together for the slow-motion formalities in the middle, the boxers accompanied by their cornermen all wearing starched short-sleeved seconds' jackets – items of comfort for fans of the boxing business that have long since vanished and been replaced by gaudy T-shirts stained with ads for hotels, plumbers' merchants and financial services. Nathan's final words were lost. It was a real fight, and Conteh took the decision and the light-heavyweight titles. Conteh had three more fights, and wins, before the end of the year.

Conteh's friend Bunny Sterling, his running and swimming partner from Parliament Hill Fields, was still gliding under the radar in defences and challenges for various titles all over the globe. He had lost once in Canada and three times for the Commonwealth middle-weight title in Australia. He had also been stopped in Paris for the European version in a brutal fight with the French matinee idol Jean-Claude Bouttier. One of his British defences had been at a sporting club in Solihull. 'It was a hard business, very tough for me,' said

Sterling. In April at the Royal Albert Hall, in a rare big-show appearance, he repeated a win over Kent wonder boy Mark Rowe to retain the title. Rowe retired after the loss. The top of the bill, incidentally, was south London's Johnny Clark, the bantamweight who was fighting at the gorgeous hall for the twenty-fifth time in thirty-eight fights. Clark, the British champion, won the European title that night.

There was a bloody problem for Alan Minter in June. He had turned professional after winning a bronze medal at the Munich Olympics the year before, a victim of a bad decision – people called it his 'unlucky bronze'. That summer at the Royal Albert Hall Minter was in control against Don McMillan, a true grit bruiser from Glasgow, when he was cut over the right eyebrow; the fight was stopped in the eighth and final round and Minter lost for the first time in twelve fights. Minter was in front and McMillan had been dropped three times. McMillan had lasted until the eleventh round of a British middleweight title fight against Bunny Sterling in January and was not an easy touch. The Crawley fighter's eyebrows came so close to ending his career: over the next twelve months he lost three more fights because of cuts. In most pictures of Minter fighting he is snarling, his gumshield stained, the blood smeared all over his face and head. He actually looks like he is smiling, and he probably was. He was a man that loved to fight, an uncompromising, unapologetic boxer.

In December, Minter lost on cuts for the third time in six months and the second time in exactly six weeks to Jan Magdziarz, the son of Polish emigrants with a wild head of ginger hair. The three-fight series with Magdziarz – they met for a final time in October 1974 – is a blot on Minter's record that is mystifying considering what he went on to achieve. In the first encounter, in late October 1973, Minter had been in front when a cut near his right eye forced a stoppage in round three. Minter dominated the December rematch, winning all six of the completed rounds and dropping Magdziarz twice. 'He's a brave boy and he's still taking it,' Harry Carpenter said at the end of the fifth. The pair had been in each other's faces before the first bell. In the sixth round the old wound opened. Carpenter said he thought it was the fourth time he had seen the cut bleed, which confirms

Minter's frailty even in victory. At the end of the sixth Danny Holland, the man that patched and repaired Henry Cooper's eyebrows during the sixty-second break, went to work with his magic swabs and adrenalin mix. The ring-card man in a light-blue full-length little number walked his mirthless circuit and then the bell sounded for the seventh round. Minter stayed on his stool, the fight was over. In their third and final fight the referee, Harry Gibbs, threw both of them out for not trying. Minter had been eleven and zero, but by the end of 1973 had drifted to sixteen fights with three defeats, which hardly look like the raw stats of a man on his way to the unified middleweight championship of the world. Magdziarz, who was from Eastleigh in Hampshire, is something of an enigma. He was unbeaten at the time of the second Minter win, but went on to lose ten of his next seventeen fights, including several gruesome encounters with good men, and then walked away.

In September a new weight division was officially sanctioned when Larry Paul won the inaugural British light-middleweight title in Wolverhampton. The division's parameters eased the pain of losing weight on all small middleweights: they could now drop from 11st 3lb or 11st 4lb down to a safe 11st and not have to somehow lose up to a stone to make the welterweight limit of 10st 7lb. The amateurs had introduced light-middle in 1951; the European title had been fought at the weight since 1964, and it had first been used in world title fights by the WBA in 1962. Paul had won the ABA title at light-middle in 1972, had turned professional in January, and after nine months and seven fights he knocked out Bobby Arthur in round ten. Arthur, incidentally, was just one pound above the welterweight limit, which is typical of the time when much less emphasis was placed on boiling down to a weight. Men tended to fight at a weight they could maintain and, unlike modern fighters, not make the weight for just the sixty seconds they stepped on and off the scales. Boxers were lean in the seventies, some like Johnny Clark looked skeletal, but they were not manufactured to compete at a weight that was both dangerous and unrealistic.

Bunny Johnson had sparred with Henry Cooper; he had been a

professional since 1968 and had patiently waited for an opportunity. In October he won a final eliminator for the British heavyweight title when he knocked out the former paratrooper Richard Dunn in the tenth. It was Johnson's forty-first fight, but his forty-second would not be for the British title; Johnson had to wait until 1975 to make history. The heavyweight champion was Danny McAlinden, and he went nearly three years between title fights. McAlinden was beaten twice during the period by Americans. Johnson kept busy. 'I knew that my time would come, I'd been patient for a long time and I just kept waiting,' he said.

The light-welterweight division was dragged out of a four-year hibernation in November when Des Morrison and Joe Tetteh fought for the vacant British title – the first time two black fighters had fought for a British title. The old light-welterweight title had been held by Vic Andretti before it was abolished in 1969 (the same Andretti would take Nigel Benn to the world title in the nineties). Morrison outpointed Tetteh over fifteen rounds at Shoreditch Town Hall in London's old East End and said at the end, 'It was a great fight between two black men in Alf Garnett country.' Morrison was from Bedford but had been born in Jamaica, and Tetteh was born in Ghana. Morrison would go on a mad run of hard fights, starting a few months later with a loss in Denmark, and is one of the most underestimated champions from the seventies. Tetteh was the man that taught John H. Stracey the tricks of the boxing trade during sparring sessions at the Royal Oak, the gym above a pub in Canning Town that Terry Lawless called his base. Lawless also listened when Tetteh spoke. At the time of the Morrison fight Tetteh was supposed to be 31; he had fought seventy-five times in fourteen different countries. Mr Tetteh was a terrific fighter, lost to history and long overdue some respect. He died in 2002, aged 60.

The Contenders

In Calais in December two men that would go on to fight Minter met in one of those weirdly arranged fights that litter the often exotic landscape of the seventies. Trevor Francis, from Basingstoke, lost on points to the Luxembourg-based Congolese slugger Shako Mamba. In 1974 Mamba was the winner of the only supporting contest when Ali knocked out Foreman in the Rumble in the Jungle. A month after the win in Kinshasa, Mamba lost on points to Minter in Munich.

It took popular welterweight John H. Stracey five years to finally win a British title. It was revenge for Stracey against Bobby Arthur: in October 1972 Arthur had won the vacant British welterweight title when Stracey was disqualified in round seven. There had been some low blows, some a bit after the bell, and that was it; the rematch was different, and Arthur was stopped in the fourth round. Strace, as he was known, sold tickets and had a loyal following, and that is why he never fought on any of the bills at the private clubs in London that the men in charge of the sport ran.

From the Notepad

In 2016 Jan Magdziarz, looking like a man of 30, not a veteran of too many ring wars, was part of a barber shop quartet on the south coast. He looked so young, I thought it was his son.

Thirty years after Watt and Buchanan had their British title fight, there was a celebratory dinner back at the hotel in Glasgow. Watt asked why there had not been a rematch and Buchanan, as spikey as ever, came over, hit the table with his two hands and said to Watt, 'And another thing, why didn't you ever fight Durán?' There was a silence, a tense stand-off, before Watt replied, 'Because I'm not fucking mad.' I believe that makes it 1-1 between the pair.

At the European amateur championship in Belgrade, Nevell Cole, from the Fitzroy Lodge in Lambeth, lost when local fighter Marijan Beneš broke his nose with a butt and then cut him with a punch after the bell. The Yugoslavian referee never said a word. That was how difficult it was for a British amateur in the seventies. Beneš won the title.

1974

'I knew from the very first punch in a fight if I was going to win and I also knew that if I was going to lose, then Christopher would be in trouble because we had been having some real wars in the gym.'
Kevin Finnegan

'That's the trouble with boxing: there are too many amateurs trying to do a professional job. They think that all you've got to do to be a trainer is flap a towel and shout "Last ten", but in fact training is the most difficult and skilful job in boxing.'
Danny Holland, legendary cutsman and fight fixture

JOHN CONTEH GOT his world title fight, and British boxing needed him to win.

At the end of the summer Conteh revealed that he had a fridge in the back of his Toyota. 'The champagne is chilling for when I win the world title.' He switched his training camp from the British Boxing Board of Control's gym in Haverstock Hill, north London, to the velvet-draped walls of the Café Royal for the last three weeks before his October fight. There was nothing bigger than this encounter with Argentina's Jorge Ahumada for the vacant WBC light-heavyweight title.

In May, Conteh had stopped Chris Finnegan in their triple-title rematch. Finnegan had a wound on his scalp above the left ear, and it was Conteh's head that had caused it. 'It's a sport for big boys,' Conteh maintained. There were very few apologies in the seventies.

Conteh prepared for Ahumada with frozen swims in the ponds at Parliament Hill Fields in the morning, then slept, and finally switched to the West End. I bunked off school to make the same journey, just to watch him train and feel part of a massive event.

The Argentinian had chased the great Bob Foster and left with a draw. The fight was in Foster's hometown. It was a lucky escape, Foster retired, and he relinquished his WBA and WBC belt. Conteh–Ahumada was for the WBC title. It was a stylish masterclass in the end, and Conteh was the clear winner, the first British world champion since Buchanan's painful loss to Roberto Durán in 1972. It was a triumph, the Toyota's fridge was emptied, and the post-fight party was at the Playboy club. His entourage would remember it for him.

But the fight changed Conteh. The final rounds had taken an invisible toll on the British boxer. Conteh was only 23, a kid with the brightest of futures, but the fight whisperers, the people that separate boxers from their loyalty, were out in force. A boxer is most vulnerable to verbal infection in the hours after a win. The morning after the fight he arrived at promoter Harry Levene's office in Soho and, according to Mickey Duff, he was screaming, 'You don't know what it's like in there!' Long after the fight Conteh sat with George Francis, probably in their favourite café near the entrance to the Fields where my auntie Annie worked. Conteh told Francis that the last rounds had been like being in a tunnel, a dark tunnel, and that he could not see light at the end. There was enough despair in Conteh's words to serve as a terrible warning for the fury of his future problems.

Bunny Sterling had known Francis from their days at the St Pancras amateur boxing club in Kentish Town, and he was also Francis's first British champion. In February, Sterling lost his middleweight title to Kevin Finnegan at the Hilton Hotel. 'I don't respect him,' said Finnegan. 'He kept me waiting nearly two years and if he's not happy with the money he's offered, then he should just throw in the title.' Finnegan had moved in for two weeks with Freddie Hill at his trainer's council flat in south London. There was a pie and mash shop across the road, and a pub attached to the flats. Finnegan was not taking any chances. Sterling had once broken

Finnegan's nose in a sparring session. The fight for the British title went the full fifteen rounds, Sterling looking like an old man at times, which in boxing years he was, and at the end Finnegan's hand was raised. Sterling was only twenty-six that night but a veteran of forty-six hard, hard fights, often as the avoided man.

It would be a great year for Finnegan, and with each win he would move closer to his dream of moving out of his own council flat in Hayes to a bigger place. Finnegan was a painter – Hill's gym in Lavender Hill was packed with his work. However, he fancied sculpting and needed a bit more room. 'He can't fight a lick, but he's a bloody good painter,' joked Hill. There were a lot of laughs when Hill and the two Finnegans were about.

It was a night of boxing wonder for Finnegan and John H. Stracey in Paris on a Monday at the end of May. The pair were both fighting for European titles, both were solid underdogs, and both won their bouts. It was the sweetest of nights. They had to beat French boxing heroes, a duo still talked about in reverence over forty years later. I don't think the French have ever replaced the pair.

Finnegan at middleweight was fighting Jean-Claude Bouttier, a loser of just five of his seventy-one fights. Bouttier had been dropped three times but gone the full fifteen rounds with Carlos Monzón for the world middleweight title eight months earlier in Paris. The Argentinian was untouchable, having stopped five of his seven defences, including Bouttier in their first fight. Monzón would retire in 1977 after another six defences. Finnegan became the only European ever to beat Bouttier and it was with a subtle, understated masterclass. The scores were tight, the verdict right. Finnegan relinquished his British title in September to concentrate on European and potential world title fights. Duff always maintained that Kevin was better than his brother Chris, but it made no difference. 'I'm always in Christopher's shadow. I understand it, but it does piss me off,' said Kevin.

Stracey stopped Roger Menetrey in the eighth round, breaking the Frenchman's heart in that gentle way that John had of piling the pressure on. Menetrey had gone the full fifteen rounds with world welterweight champion José Nápoles less than a year earlier. Stracey had sparred with Nápoles two years earlier when the Mexican, who was really a Cuban, had stopped Ralph Charles in a world title defence at the Empire Pool. Duff had a plan for Stracey and Nápoles, but the timing had to be perfect.

Frankie Lucas never meant to snub Princess Anne at a reception. He was in New Zealand to win a gold medal, not shake hands with members of the royal family. The slight happened at a function a few days before the first bell at the Commonwealth Games in Christchurch, in January. Lucas was not angry with the royal family, just angry with the men that had not selected him to box for England at the Games. Lucas had won the ABA middleweight title in 1972 and 1973; in 1972 he had been overlooked for the Olympics by the same selectors that were ignoring him again. Lucas had stopped Alan Minter on a cut eye in the London championships in 1972, but he did lose a bad-tempered return just before the Olympics. There would never be a third fight. 'When Minter won the world title, Frankie just started to cry and left the room,' Al Hamilton, a friend of mine, told me. Lucas was accused of having an attitude problem; there had been incidents at international events, a match in Amsterdam. He was a bit surly. I got his autograph one night outside Manor Place Baths, near the Elephant and Castle, and he nodded, signed, and went back to his patois. He wasn't a problem to me, he was just a teenage fighting god in south London. The Commonwealth Games selectors, in an act of horrific cowardice, went for Liverpool's Carl Speare, the man Lucas had beaten in the 1973 final. So it was heartbreak again for Frankie, and that is where the disgraceful incident should have ended. Instead, it became a teary fairy-tale.

A man called Ken Rimington, a policeman from south London, was on the committee at the Sir Philip Game club in Croydon where Lucas did his boxing. Big Ken was not impressed when his boxer was snubbed again and he formed the St Vincent and the Grenadines Amateur Boxing Federation, lobbied successfully, somehow raised the money and sent Lucas to New Zealand (the Scottish team helped with some of the funding in return for sparring, which must have worked as their welter and light-middle both reached the final). Lucas, by then 20, was the only member of the St Vincent team and carried the flag of the country of his birth at the opening ceremony. Lucas had left the Caribbean island when he was nine to join his mother in Croydon. Speare and Lucas both won twice and met in the semi-final. It was inevitable, joyous for Lucas and embarrassing for the thick-skinned blazer brigade that ran amateur boxing at the time: Lucas won and reached the final. Speare was an innocent player in the disgrace.

In the final Frankie had no chance, sorry. He met Julius Luipa, a Zambian who was trained by exiled Cubans. The African had been the devastating, cold-eyed main attraction in Christchurch. So far two of his three opponents had been knocked out cold. Lucas, with his distinctive afro, was fearless from the opening bell. The neutrals, led by his new Scottish friends, cheered his entrance. Lovers of a lost cause they were, but they also knew that crazy Frankie from Croydon would not go down without a struggle. Their faith was justified and it was one of the most memorable fights of the seventies. In the opener Lucas was cut, and each hurt the other; in the second it was just savagery. Lucas had such belief, such desire, he wanted only one ending. 'I came for the gold, I'm getting the gold,' he told the BBC's Des Lynam.

'Frankie had to take him out or he was going to get stopped because of the cut,' said Roy Chapman, the coach at Sir Philip Game's, and now the national coach for St Vincent. Lucas knocked out Luipa in that second round; the ring lights caught his afro in one picture and for a moment it looked like a halo was hovering above him. One probably was at that moment, though it never troubled him again. Luipa tried to get up, the Cubans banged the ring apron, Lucas watched, people watching on TV hollered, and Lynam loved it: 'Luipa is over. I don't think he is going to get up. He tries to get up. He's shaking. The referee counts to ten and Frankie Lucas, the man from St Vincent, dropped by the England team, wins a gold medal!' It was satisfying, scandalous, and just about the last high in the life and very troubled times of Frankie Lucas who, when he turned professional, joined the group of fighters, mostly black or mixed-race, gathered together by George Francis in north London.

In June the third European under-21 championship took place in Kiev. The previous two had also been behind the Iron Curtain, first in Hungary in 1970 and then in Romania two years later. British boxers, mostly labourers or apprenticed kids, had to beg for time off work if they wanted to compete. There was, at this point, very little chance of returning with a medal of any colour. There were eleven weights and before the championship in Kiev Eastern Bloc boxers had won all twenty-two titles, eleven of them going back to the Soviet Union. Nothing much would change in Kiev. Charlie Magri, who had won his first ABA title in May, lost in the final – a massive achievement for the kid. Kirkland Laing, overlooked for the Olympics in 1972, had gained over a stone in two years and was now at welterweight. He won a bronze, and featherweight George Gilbody also won a bronze. Seven Soviet boxers won gold and all the winners were again from the Eastern Bloc. 'Kirk's loss was the only bad decision for us,' said Kevin Hickey, the coach that served for decades in charge of amateur boxing. It was Hickey that Kirk had told in 1972 that he was ready for the Olympics.

In 1973 there had been a plan to launch the first world amateur championship, with New York, Montreal and Havana as contenders to be host. In August 1974 it was opened by Fidel Castro in Havana, which was the right location: the Cubans had won three gold medals, their first boxing golds, at the Munich Olympics in 1972. The fourteen-day event has taken on mystical qualities over the years. It was the start of a revolution in amateur boxing, the brilliant harbinger of the great summer conflicts during the next few Olympics. It remains a hard, hard event to win, arguably the most difficult title in what was then known as amateur boxing. The wait for a British finalist lasted twenty-seven years, and the first British winner was Frankie Gavin, from Birmingham, in 2007 at the fourteenth staging of the competition.

At the inaugural championship two Irish boxers, Davy Larmour and John Rodgers, were sent, but England, Scotland and Wales decided against packing off any sacrifices to Havana. Graham Moughton, who had represented Great Britain in Munich, was working in Bermuda at the time and easily switched allegiances for a brief appearance in the vest of the exclusive holiday destination. Moughton was an amateur boxing survivor, a highly respected breed sadly in decline by the end of the decade; a year earlier he had lost on points in New York at the fabulous Felt Forum to Sugar Ray Leonard.

Future world champion Leon Spinks took a bronze, the legendary Jamaican Mike McCallum left with nothing. History-making Yugoslavian Mate Parlov, who would become the first ever professional world champion from the Eastern Bloc, won a gold. The Ugandan Ayub Kalule, who would be based in Denmark, and Wilfredo Gómez, from Puerto Rico, at bantamweight, also won gold. Gómez was just 17 in Havana that summer but was a teenage veteran having fought at 15 in the Munich Olympics. The Cubans won five gold medals to emphasize their status as the world's top amateur boxing nation. At this point no boxers had defected and none considered it. The boxers were Fidel Castro's chosen heroes.

Little Johnny Clark, a seemingly irreplaceable attraction at the Royal Albert Hall, relinquished his British bantamweight title when the offer for a defence fell below what he wanted, and he was then, in August, forced to retire with a detached retina in his right eye. Clark was just 26, had been winning and losing title fights for four years, and had fought twenty-seven of his forty-three fights at the Kensington landmark venue. He was the European champion when he was made to quit.

It was Ken Buchanan's turn once again to hand back a title when he relinquished his British lightweight championship in September. Buchanan was left with no choice when a deadline set by the British Boxing Board of Control for him to defend against Jim Watt clashed with a planned European defence in France. ('I had beaten Watt once, the fight made no sense,' Buchanan remarked.) Buchanan won the European title in May in Italy and was nominated for a world title fight against Rodolfo González. It never happened, and González was beaten by Guts Ishimatsu in Tokyo. Buchanan would be next for

Ishimatsu, and his December European defence against Leonard Tavarez was an essential warm-up. The Parisian excursion was over in round fourteen when Tavarez's corner threw in the towel. Next stop for Ken, who won his world title in San Juan, Puerto Rico, would be Tokyo. Buchanan was an exile at that point and just four of his previous twenty fights had taken place in a British ring.

In December, John Conteh relinquished his British light-heavyweight title. He ended the year in elite company as a world champion next to Muhammad Ali, Roberto Durán, Carlos Monzón, José Nápoles, Antonio Cervantes and thirteen others. Several British champions awaited disasters, difficult fights and obscurity – a mixed bag of realistic expectations at the highest level. Maurice Hope and John H. Stracey were just edging clear of the pack, and Alan Minter, with his dodgy eyebrows, was at the fringes. Joe Bugner was still heavyweight-at-large, the European champion and a genuine top five fighter. The lean years were over.

The Contenders

There was a rare and final cameo as British champion for flyweight John McCluskey. The Scottish boxer had won the title in 1969 and this was only his second defence; Tony Davies lasted 125 seconds at the Top Rank Suite in Swansea. Davies retired for good after the fight, but McCluskey had two more bouts and quit in 1975. A close look at McCluskey's record reveals just how hard it was for unfashionable fighters in neglected weights in the seventies. He won and lost the Commonwealth title in Australia, failed three times overseas for the European title, and had to meet the very best bantamweights in Britain just to get a living. In late 1977 Charlie Magri saved the British flyweight division and won the British title in his third fight. McCluskey was long gone by then.

Maurice Hope had mostly put together a professional record compiled in secret after turning professional nearly a year after the Munich Olympics. Hope was with Terry Lawless at their outpost in the East End, a gym now starting to fill with quality fighters. In

November, Hope travelled to the Black Country – not a feared location on Donald Trump's new axis of evil – and stopped Larry Paul to win the British light-middleweight title. It was his eleventh fight and only the fourth in a public venue. Hope was three years away from a world title fight, but he was part of an expanding group that was poised to change the face of British boxing.

In March at the Royal Albert Hall, surrounded by Stracey and Minter, Pat McCormack stopped Des Morrison to win the British light-welterweight title. McCormack had lost twelve fights before that night and would lose two more on the road, one in Norway and one in Denmark, before dropping a decision and the British title to seven-fight novice Joey Singleton in November. He is part of a seemingly endless list of boxers that win the British title, lose it and never in any way cash in.

From the Notepad

In Denmark they knew McCormack as the Animal, a brawler with a packed bag ready to go on the road. He never wore bandages and once had a drag on a cigarette during the break between rounds. He loved fighting there. He was also a fixture at Manor Place Baths in south London. 'Pat was one of boxing's genuine marvels,' said Paddy Byrne, the iconic fight fixer and boxing face.

There was a curfew at the European under-21 championship in Kiev which amused the English team, who still devised ways to get out and meet local girls. 'All the women were blonde and had gold teeth,' said Clinton McKenzie, a member of Sir Philip Game.

'Those were the greatest days, the hardest days, and I never appreciated them – I thought they would never end,' Conteh told me one day in 2004 as we sat and went through his career.

1975

'*In Mexico City they pulled a few strokes; one geezer tried to break my hand when he shook it, and in the sparring they followed every punch with their nut. One of them cut me and Lawless went mad. He cleaned it up and told me to go and knock the bastard out. I did.*'
John H. Stracey on the days before fighting José Nápoles

'*It was all a long time ago; he's changed and so have I. Anyway, you can't really plan a fight, you have to turn it on and fight, or run, or box and fight.*'
Kevin Finnegan before his first fight as a professional with Alan Minter

THE MAIN BULLRING in Mexico City was packed with 30,000 when John H. Stracey met José Nápoles for the welterweight world title. Stracey was the heavy betting underdog after travelling 12,000 miles to fight Nápoles in December. Nápoles had made thirteen defences during twelve years as champion. He was the great Nápoles, make no mistake. But Stracey was a Bethnal Green boy to his core, and he had the right attitude.

'I was homesick right up until the moment I got in the ring,' said Stracey. 'I clapped Nápoles when he came to the ring and the Mexicans liked that and I thought, this ain't so bad. A few seconds later I was over. They had not even got down the steps. I knew then it was going to be a hard night.' Stracey had sparred four rounds with Nápoles when he was in London for his defence against Ralph Charles in 1972. 'I knew how good he was, don't worry about that.'

Terry Lawless had taken a long time to agree the fight with Mickey

Duff: 'You always had to argue to get Terry to take a fight, always.' In July, Duff had been ringside to watch Nápoles beat Armando Muñiz over fifteen rounds in the Mexican capital. He had phoned Lawless to tell him that the time was right. 'Are you sure?' Lawless replied. Duff did the deal right then but it took a couple of weeks to persuade Lawless to take Stracey to Mexico. 'I was regretting it in an instant and praying "please, let him last the round" when John went over in the first,' said Lawless.

Stracey got up, fought back, silenced the crowd, dropped Nápoles, closed his eye, and in round six the fight was stopped by the Mexican referee. 'Stracey was consumed with the desire and the will to win and my guy was knocked out,' said Angelo Dundee, who watched in disbelief from the Nápoles corner. 'Stracey was a gritty Londoner.' In 1993 I went to the same bullring with Dundee to watch a bullfight, which did not impress the American. He was still stunned by the Nápoles loss. 'It happened in one night, in one fight: my guy became an old man in that fight. I liked Stracey, he was a nice guy.'

Nápoles never fought again and in the late nineties was skint, performing karaoke for pesos and charging people a few dollars to sit and reminisce. He is arguably the greatest Cuban fighter in history and only stayed in Mexico because Fidel Castro banned professional boxing in Cuba.

'Only he and I and the referee know just how damn hot it was in there,' said Muhammad Ali after his heavyweight title fight with Joe Bugner at the Merdeka Stadium in Kuala Lumpur in June. Ali ended up on a drip, Bugner ended up under immense pressure. 'The coverage of that fight tipped me over the edge – it was fifteen rounds and 118 degrees under the ring lights and I got bloody crucified,' Big Joe said. 'I refuse to accept that I gave anything less than my best and it's a miracle we could move under those conditions, let alone fight.'

The problem for Bugner was the timing of the fight: it was at ten a.m., and that meant it was hot by the time the pair were deep into the championship rounds. It also meant – and this is the main reason for his dissection by the gathered media – that he could go in the hotel pool, in the sun, surrounded by friends and family that after-noon. 'I was bloody stitched up, it's that simple,' insisted Bugner. 'A lot of my friends had come to the fight and my body was aching all over; getting in the pool made sense.' Ali, remember, was, under Gene Kilroy's guidance, at the hospital on a drip after being examined for exhaustion and dehydration. Bugner was in a pool with a drink. 'I was not celebrating, but some of the British press got the idea that I was having the time of my life.' (Bugner had been paid $500,000, Ali $2.5 million.) Bugner has always maintained that it was a couple of British photographers who bought him a drink when he got in the pool and then got the shot they wanted.

Two incidents, one before and one after, define the fight for me. A few days before the opening bell the boxers selected their gloves. Ali was then told that the gloves would be kept under lock and key at the local prison. 'How can you put my gloves in jail? My gloves ain't done nothin' . . . yet.' It was quality stuff. In the bad-tempered aftermath at the conference, Bugner, still sweating and coming to realize that lasting fifteen rounds with Ali was not going to be enough to make the press happy, got a bit upset. 'Who would you lot have me fight? Jesus Christ?' It was an immediately unfortunate choice of opponent for the frustrated and increasingly angry Bugner. In the press row was Hughie McIlvanney, then of the *Observer* and a sacred soul in our business: 'Joe, it's interesting that you have picked a man with bad hands.' There was nothing more to say, and Bugner was soon back at the pool, adding a perceived arrogance to his perceived pacifism. Bugner was still only 25 and he took sixteen months out, but he remained slighted for the rest of his boxing life. Ali never forgot what happened in the ring that morning either and would defend his friend for a long, long time. I always think of Ali's passionate defence when I hear idle chat about Joe Bugner's ability. It's simple really: if Ali was so great, then how did Bugner go the distance twice – a total of twenty-seven rounds – with him if he was so bad? Ali praised Bugner until the end.

Eddie Futch, hailed now as one of the greatest trainers in the sport, was in London in March with his light-heavyweight Lonnie Bennett, an American felon with convictions for shooting. Bennett was also highly ranked by the WBC and had beaten Eddie Duncan, who had taken a slim decision over John Conteh. Angelo Dundee thought that Bennett would beat Conteh for the world title. It was not a simple defence and rumblings of Conteh's discontent continued. 'Why should I take all the punches in the ring and the promoters take the biggest slice of the profits?' Conteh said. The fee for the Bennett fight was £33,000.

The fight at Wembley ended in the fifth with Bennett cut. Conteh's life away from the ring was about to escalate out of control and threaten to ruin his life in the ring. Over the coming months the madness of King John Conteh intensified. There was a plan to fight in Uganda and Conteh was in Kampala for two weeks; the bout never happened, but he did receive an advance of £18,000 and he got to swap war stories with Idi Amin, a former heavyweight and noted butcher. There was a fanciful plan for a truly big fight with middle-weight champion Carlos Monzón. It was a fight that could have defined the age had it ever taken place.

Between Amin tales, Monzón schemes and his own hectic life, the situation was messy. Then it turned litigious. The next few months were hellish for Conteh and the men he had once trusted. 'I want to talk to John Conteh,' said Don King, as part of his pitch for the WBC light-heavyweight champion. 'I can make that kid two million pounds in two years in the States. He has everything going for him: looks, personality and a lot of ability.'

What Conteh did not have when he flew to America for an August fight with Willie Taylor in Scranton, Pennsylvania was George Francis. The pair had been close since Conteh turned professional in 1971, but Conteh had launched legal action against George and the Board on the grounds that his earning potential would improve if he was self-managed. He had also initiated proceedings against Duff, his matchmaker, and Harry Levene, his Wembley promoter. In ten months, Conteh had won the world title, defended it, and fallen out with everybody from his past.

It gets worse.

The Board temporarily banned Conteh, and the WBC ordered him to pay a fine of $35,000 and decided that Duff was owed compensation. King got his man with a fifty grand offer – dollars, not pounds – for the Taylor fight. The relationship never lasted. 'John had slender hands and that was something that George understood and he wrapped his hands very carefully and in a special way,' said Duff. There was no George in the changing room at the Catholic Youth Center in Scranton that night, the hands were not bandaged correctly, and Conteh suffered a nasty fracture to his right that kept him out of the ring for fourteen months. He won over ten rounds but it was a hollow victory for John, and it must have been a terrible fight for George to read about.

The passport king of British boxing, Ken Buchanan, went to Tokyo in February for a difficult fight against Guts Ishimatsu, the WBC lightweight champion. Buchanan had won the world title in San Juan, defended it in Los Angeles and lost it in New York. He was often a man at war with himself, which worked both ways. In Tokyo there was an early problem when he got a thumb in the eye from a planted sparring partner, a man hired with just one aim. It was a deliberate foul and Buchanan was told not to spar or train until the trapped air behind the eye had gone. He asked for a delay of a week, it was denied. All boxers fight with injuries and at some point have to make a potentially life-changing decision to fight or withdraw: Buchanan was fearless, the fight was on. There was also the oddest of verbal exchanges at a press conference, and Ishimatsu's blunt words surprised Buchanan. 'He had a right go at me, told me I would need a gun for a knockout. It never felt good in Tokyo.'

On the night, in front of 9,000 people, Buchanan was boxing behind his educated jab, mindful of the eye injury, and it went well until the bell to end the fifth round. 'He hit me on the eye after the bell and that was it – I had just the one eye, the left, and I had to go on like that. The ref warned him, but it was too late. The damage was done.' It went the full fifteen; two judges had it by a slim margin for Guts, the third, a Japanese judge, went by nine rounds for his country's idol. Buchanan was desolate.

The summer was messy. In July, Buchanan, in his first fight since losing to Ishimatsu, travelled to Sardinia to defend his European lightweight title in a football stadium against the local fighter. It was a risky assignment. Buchanan had severe double vision after he was thumbed in the eye again, this time by the referee, in round seven. In his corner, Freddie Hill was concerned, but in the twelfth Giancarlo Usai was stopped. The Italian had taken a beating. His fans were not impressed and in the riot that followed Buchanan's father, Tommy, was hit with a brick (the wound required seven stitches) and one of the ring lights exploded on the boxer's back. The eye damage was serious and Buchanan believed he would not pass a Board medical check; so, with no rumours of a rematch with Roberto Durán being discussed, Buchanan retired. 'I said then that I would only come back if Durán or Ishimatsu gave me a world title fight in Scotland – that was never going to happen.' He did return, in 1979, but in the meantime his life had been both complicated and heartbreaking.

It was over seven years from the time Jim Watt first fought for the British title to the night in Glasgow when he won the world title – the type of ancient apprenticeship that stayed in the seventies. Watt is possibly British boxing's most patient man.

In January, he won the vacant British lightweight title at the St Andrew's Sporting Club in his Glasgow hometown. He stopped a man called Johnny Cheshire in seven, dropping him twice in the sixth. Watt finally switched his management after a loss in late October on the road in France, and his days in obscurity were nearly over. He had been with Glasgow manager James Murray since 1968, he had made only one appearance on a big London show in twenty-nine fights, and fifteen of those, including both of his British title fights, had been in front of the patrons at various private sporting clubs. His anonymity was a scandal and his new manager Lawless, with his partners who included Duff, was determined to change it.

There was a bit of history at the Grosvenor House in the middle of January when Bunny Johnson became the first black British heavyweight champion after stopping Danny McAlinden in the ninth round. McAlinden was making the first defence of the title he had won in the summer of 1972. Both weighed well inside the modern cruiserweight limit, a weight division that was not adopted by the British Boxing Board of Control until 1985. Johnson was not finished with the history books. 'I never think about what could have happened and what should have happened – I just think about what did happen,' he told me one afternoon in Birmingham in late 2014. Johnson is regal and respectful in retirement, an ambassador for a business that leaves too many of its old men still living on past glories, bitter and twisted.

Lawless announced that he had signed Kirkland Laing. 'I've never had a more talented fighter in the gym,' he said. It was never an easy arrangement: Kirk was difficult and brilliant. He was also a solid 11st 4lb, which was over two stone heavier than Vernon Sollas, the kid he had beaten in the 1972 featherweight ABA final when the pair were just 17. Sollas, weighing exactly 9st, won the vacant British feather-weight title at the Royal Albert Hall two weeks after Laing went over. It was his nineteenth fight, a rematch with south London's Jimmy Revie, and it was controversial. Revie had beaten Sollas in an eliminator the previous March, but in the return Sollas was ruthless and hit Revie when he was down in the fourth round. Revie's corner-man Dennie Mancini, a fight figure across six decades, screamed and moaned, which is something that Dennie did quite a lot whenever he got near a ring. The decision stood. 'I always wanted to be somebody,' said Sollas. He was just 20, he lost the title in his first defence, and he was just 22 when he fought for the last time. In that final fight, at the Civic Centre in Wolverhampton in 1977, he was unconscious for a long time, perhaps as long as fifteen minutes, before being taken to hospital for observation. Sollas recovered, and trained a few fighters in the nineties. There was something lasting about the brief career of Vernon Sollas, a vulnerability in life and boxing that has endured. But his is a sad boxing story and it was all done and dusted by the time he was in that ambulance in Wolverhampton.

In April, Laing won his first professional fight at the Albany Hotel in his hometown Nottingham. He took care of Joe Hannaford in the second round. His career didn't come to an end until 1994 when he lost to Bristol's Glenn Catley, who would go on to win a world title. Laing weighed 156½lb for his debut, and fifty-four fights and nineteen years later he weighed 156lb in his last fight. His career and life were chaotic, brilliant, frustrating, and it had all come so close to ending violently when he fell from the fourth-floor balcony of a council block in Hackney in 2003. He was rushed to the Royal London Hospital in Whitechapel, in a coma and close to death. There was a report that Laing was dead; I also had a call telling me that he had been pushed. He had just recently been part of a police swoop on crack houses in the area but was not charged. I'd made a short film with him for the BBC a few weeks before the fall and it took two days to track him down. It cost £250, a packet of cigarettes and a six-pack of Special Brew to finally get him to meet in a park. 'He looks like a black Father Christmas,' a fella who was drinking in a small group had told me during my search. A former boxer called John Zeraschi, who in 1975 won the ABA light-welterweight title, had agreed to broker the meeting, and it was he that had set out the terms: 'Nice few quid, a couple of beers, and get him some snout.' Kirk arrived with his European title belt and we started drinking and talking. He had a story to tell that day in the park.

In June in Britain there was a fight that made no sense and a skirmish that made every sense. At the Royal Albert Hall, Chris Finnegan met Johnny Frankham for the vacant British light-heavyweight title. It was a hard fight, a war, and both ended bruised, cut and weary. The referee raised Frankham's hand at the end of the fifteenth round. It was tight, debatable, and at ringside other fights started. Finnegan's wife Cheryl was in the middle of the punching mob and had to be restrained. As the disgruntled punters thumped each other, Frankham's baby boy was passed from hand to hand into the ring from the seats – the most dangerous baby in town.

Bunny Sterling and Maurice Hope had clashed at a nightclub in Croydon. Nothing unusual about that in the seventies, but the pair had both been British champions; Hope was still the British light-middleweight title holder. Hope wanted to fight Sterling, and the totally unnecessary and predictable scrap took place for Sterling's old British middleweight title, which was vacant, at the National Sporting Club, a deep velvet enclave inside the Café Royal, in early June. They both struggled to be attractions during their careers, that is the harsh truth, and it was another odd fight to hide for private viewing. It ended in round eight, with Sterling just too big. Hope would defend his own title in September and get a long-overdue shot at the world title in 1977. Hope and Sterling were a breed apart, united in a fight one night that still makes no sense.

Finnegan got sweet revenge over Frankham in October to win the British light-heavyweight title, but a detached retina meant that the 1968 Olympic champion was forced to quit. He had a glorious philosophy on boxing: 'If I'm boxing nice and cool, and making the other geezer miss and look like a clown, dancing around and popping away, then I'm living it. But if I'm taking a bit of stick there's no pleasure in that. I'm not a masochist. I wouldn't say I like smashing people's heads in. I just like making them miss. Mind, I wouldn't lose any sleep over it if I hurt them a little.'

The Contenders

In November the first of three fights between Kevin Finnegan and Alan Minter took place at the Empire Pool. The pair fought forty-five rounds in total, most were hard to call, and Minter got all three decisions.

The British middleweight title had been relinquished by Bunny Sterling, a man convinced that he would get a world title shot, which never happened and was never likely to happen. Sterling finished his career with five more fights, winning the European title and losing three on points, and all were overseas.

In September Bunny Johnson, conceding 25lb, dropped a decision to Richard Dunn and lost his British heavyweight title at Wembley. In 1974 Dunn had been stopped in three consecutive fights, and by Johnson himself in 1973. There was an endless possibility in the seventies of being recycled. A man just had to be bold.

From the Notepad

There is an asterisk for lovers of both the film and boxing worlds at the end of January when Ray Winstone, who boxed for east London club Repton, won the London Federation of Boys' Clubs class C under-67kg final. It was Winstone's crowning glory as a fighter. He was the Daddy that night at the Café Royal.

Johnny Cheshire was another Repton boy, a good little fighter, but he liked a bit of aggro and a bit of loving. 'When I turned pro I had it too easy and I was mixing with celebrities,' he said. 'It wasn't the ideal start, but I enjoyed myself.' He had been the ABA champion, a beautiful boxer to watch, he'd gone to the Olympics in 1968, where he lost to the eventual silver medallist, and he had a swell East End following. His life away from the ring kept getting in the way of the boxing, though. He managed to mix both on a couple of occasions and was disqualified for being, as he once said, 'spiteful'. After he was thrown out of the ring, the fighting continued in the dressing room and he was fined £50 by the British Boxing Board of Control. 'It was worth it, that was a proper row,' he said. The title fight with Jim Watt was the last hope for Cheshire. He never fought again.

1976

'I'd like to be able to box full-time. It's up to the promoters. I have to give up jobs to train for fights and then look for another job when the fight is over. It's a hard way to fight.'
Phil Martin, former light-heavyweight turned Moss Side trainer

'When I came from Ireland I had only my boxing gear and the clothes I stood up in and people helped me. Now it's my turn to help the kids and put something back into a great sport.'
Brendan Ingle, the Whispering Guru of Dublin, on his life in Sheffield

JOHN H. STRACEY was the world welterweight champion, and that was something for British boxing to celebrate. A proper homecoming was planned and Stracey was booked to make the first defence of his WBC title against American Hedgemon Lewis in March at Wembley. The Union flags were being ironed.

Lewis had been stopped by José Nápoles, he arrived in London with the actor Ryan O'Neal as his manager, and he managed to upset Stracey from the start. 'I never liked him, never liked his attitude, never liked the way they were all looking at me – I fucking beat Nápoles, this geezer got stopped by him,' Stracey said. Lewis had also lost on points over fifteen rounds to Nápoles.

It was a truly emotional night, ending in the tenth, and then the singing started. 'Maybe it's because I'm a Londoner . . .' Stracey was belting it out, draped in a flag with a smile of pure bliss on his soppy face. It was just that type of night. Harry Mullan, who would go on to edit *Boxing News*, said, 'Stracey seems to have claimed the Union flag as his own personal symbol.' Stracey was just 25, yet the Lewis fight was his forty-eighth. It was to be Lewis's last, and Stracey would only fight three more times.

It's possible that a fighter called Henry Rhiney from Luton was conned one afternoon in June. Rhiney had been sent to spar with Carlos Palomino, a Mexican-born Californian and the next opponent for Stracey, at the Duke of Wellington gym in Highgate. Rhiney did a job on Palomino, reported back, and there was calm in the Royal Oak gym as Lawless fine-tuned Stracey. There was talk of unification fights, a fight with Roberto Durán, even fights with middleweight Carlos Monzón and Britain's Dave Boy Green were progressing nicely. Palomino had drawn with Lewis and Stracey had ruined Lewis. The press backed the Bethnal Green idol, the flags were out, the song sheets printed. Duff, however, had some concerns: 'Palomino's people were too confident. I knew them, and that was not their style. That worried me.' A veteran Los Angeles trainer called Jackie McCoy had spoken to Duff in the ring. Duff was in his tuxedo, smiling. 'I told him we were here for the title, not the money,' said McCoy. 'It was ten grand, bad money even then. Mickey knew then.' It was instinct, and Duff was right.

Stracey hit Palomino three times after the bell. Palomino was patient, digging in short hooks to the body, and in the twelfth round it was over. Stracey survived the first knockdown but was in agony from the second body shot. 'I'm sorry, I was hoping for a better knees-up,' Stracey told the crowd. In tears, he was led away, but not before one final tender moment when he gently touched his green WBC belt which had been placed round Palomino's waist. Stracey had two more fights left; Palomino would make seven defences before losing a split decision over fifteen rounds to the unbeaten and brilliant Wilfredo Benítez in 1979.

In Kuala Lumpur, when Muhammad Ali fought Joe Bugner, the gloves were put in prison. In Munich, when Ali fought former paratrooper Richard Dunn, there was an attempt to put Ali in a hypnotized state.

A man called Romark, a tabloid regular in Britain, had been flown to Germany to improve Dunn's chance of winning the world heavy-weight title. Romark did confront Ali at the hotel, and Ali fell on the floor laughing when Romark told him he was 'doomed'. Norman Giller, a publicist and author of a hundred books, had to turn away. 'Angelo Dundee looked at me and said: "Who is this nutter?"' Giller recalled. 'I was lost for words.' Romark worked on Dunn in private, telling the Yorkshire lump that he had 'fists of iron'. Dunn was a straight man and Romark was humoured. 'He was a donut, that's what I call him.'

Dunn was not even meant to be in Munich to fight Ali. He had knocked out the German champion, Bernd August, to add the European heavyweight title to his British and Commonwealth belts. He was meant to lose; August was meant to be fighting Ali. The German promoters should have walked away then. Ali arrived in Munich, saw the state of play, and took a $100,000 reduction on his $1.5 million fee (Duff maintained that Ali was getting $3.3 million) the night before the fight. The Ali reduction helped buy two thousand tickets for American military personnel. 'I blame Dunn for this mess – if he hadn't knocked out August, this place would be a sell-out,' said Dundee.

Dunn did claim that Ali had spies watching him train, and that was probably true. This fight happened so fast, it's likely that Dundee, Gene Kilroy and Ali had no idea who Richard Dunn of Bradford was. Ali had beaten Jimmy Young twenty-four days earlier and Dunn's win over August was only six weeks earlier. Ali also had a ridicu-lously swollen entourage of fifty-four in Munich and they were all looking to do something to justify their room service tabs, phone calls and outrageous spending during their stay at the elite Bayerischer Hof. After the fight Ali called everybody together in his suite and tried to get angry about the bill; he failed, and abuse of his hospitality continued. 'He could never say no,' said Kilroy.

'I'm just going to help Richard make his final drop,' Ali promised before the fight. Dunn was led to the ring by members of the 1st Parachute Regiment, which is hard to believe, to earn his $175,000.

Dunn was stupidly brave, dropped five times and stopped in the fifth. A photographer from Leeds called John Varley, the man who took the picture of Pelé and Bobby Moore swapping shirts, snapped Dunn in the shower, sitting, boots still on, his head on his knees and a bottle of beer in his hand. It was not a funny image.

The knockdowns were the last of Ali's career. This is the fight when Ali gave the gloves to either Duff or Giller to be auctioned at a Chris Finnegan benefit. Inside the gloves, written long before the first bell on a piece of paper, was a deathless prediction: Ali wins, round five. There is another version of this story where Ali has written in both gloves. Finally, there was a bit of magic.

I like a story, a nice ending, but I refuse to believe that Romark emerged after the fight in tears and grabbed Dunn by the shoulders: 'Richard, I let you down, I'm sorry. I made your fists turn into iron – but I forgot about your chin.' That's a quote too far, but I like it.

A man called José Sulaimán ran the WBC from a citadel in Mexico City. His patience with his light-heavyweight champion John Conteh was running thin. 'He's a nice young man, but he is making a lot of bad decisions,' said Sulaimán. Conteh's last title fight had been in March 1975, then he'd broken his right hand in a non-title fight in August; finally, in October 1976, he was ready to defend his title. The venue was Copenhagen, the promotion a disaster, and the opponent, Álvaro Yaqui López, a real threat. Conteh had damaged the hand again, but knew that if he pulled out Don Sulaimán, as he liked to be known when people kissed his pinkie ring, would have him stripped. Conteh was still in dispute with the people that had given his career direction (though he had built a bridge back to George Francis), but now, guided by a separate set of voices, he was at last in some type of shape. The López fight went the full fifteen, which is no shock: the Mexican went the full fifteen the following year with Victor Emilio González, the Argentine that held the WBA version. Conteh won, kept his title, and any dreams left stayed alive.

He lost outside the ropes. His brother Tony had put in place a convoluted deal where John was expected to make £100,000 for the fight. He never did, receiving in the end anything from two grand to twenty grand: there is no science attached to calamities like this in the boxing game. He fell out with Tony. The demons grew louder in Conteh's head.

Joe Bugner ended his sixteen-month exile in October and was matched with Dunn at Wembley for the British, Commonwealth and European heavyweight titles. Dunn and his wife, a free-talking bingo fan, had been highly critical of Bugner during his long absence. 'I'm back to shut a few people up and get a bit of respect,' said Big Joe. Both boxers had lost their previous fights to Ali. 'I told everybody that Ali would walk right through Dunn and I will do the same,' said Bugner. There had been a picture in the paper of Dunn flushing a picture of Bugner down a toilet and it was said to have upset Joe's mum. It was a bold act from Dunn and aggressive talk from Bugner, both unusual for the day.

The crowd knew their role, and they screamed and hollered when Harry Gibbs, the referee, pulled the boxers together before the fight. Bugner was angry. Dunn was dropped heavily in the sixth second with a sickening right hand. He jumped up, was caught again and again, then another right sent him down after thirty-one seconds. He was up too quick, but this time survived for over ninety seconds as Bugner caught him with big looping left hooks and right crosses. Dunn was dropped for a third time from a left-right combination and jumped up at ten; Gibbs waved it off and Dunn tumbled comically to the canvas. There was some laughter at ringside, but not in Bugner's corner. The time was officially 2:14 of round one. Bugner embraced Gibbs at the end and the veteran third man smiled. Bugner weighed just 226lb for the bout, lighter than in any of his remaining twenty-three fights over the next twenty-three years. Bugner was a legend, make no mistake.

The ABA finals were in April and five of the eleven winners would make it on to the plane for the Olympics in Montreal. Charlie Magri was the pick; the triple champion was followed and pursued from Wembley that night. 'There was too much pressure on me for the Olympics,' Magri said thirty years later. He was right.

In July a squad of seven British boxers flew to Canada for what is considered the greatest Olympic boxing tournament ever to have taken place. It was Cuba v. America, the battle of the amateur powers. It ended with Cuba winning three golds, America five, and the pair facing each other in three finals – the American boxers won all three. It was the last Olympics where the Americans beat the Cubans.

Middleweight Dave Odwell beat a Moroccan and lost to a Yugoslavian; light-middleweight Robbie Davies beat an Australian and lost to a Venezuelan; welterweight Colin Jones beat Ireland's Christy McLoughlin and lost to a Romanian; light-welterweight Clinton McKenzie beat an Italian and a Puerto Rican but lost to eventual gold medallist Sugar Ray Leonard; lightweight Sylvester Mittee lost to a Romanian. Bantamweight Pat Cowdell won against Poland, Puerto Rico and the Philippines but dropped a close one to Gu Yong-Ju from North Korea, who won the gold; Cowdell came back with a bronze medal. Flyweight Magri had a walkover in the opener and was knocked out by Canada's Ian Clyde. It was a shock, a disturbing finish for the British boxer who turned 20 at the Olympics. Also at flyweight, Belfast's Davy Larmour had two walkovers before losing to America's Leo Randolph, the eventual winner, in the quarter-finals. Magri had beaten Larmour at the European championship in 1975 and won a bronze medal in Katowice. 'I got up too fast from the knockdown, but I still think I could have continued,' said Magri. He was not given the chance, and it was correctly stopped in the third. Magri then had to suffer for a week as a tourist in a city he didn't want to be in and at a tournament he'd believed he was going to win. Not easy. I've seen it a few times and it can break a boxer's spirit. (Colin Jones, by the way, was just 17 in Montreal; he would wait over a year before turning professional.)

Four of the five American gold medallists won world titles. Howard Davis, the lightweight champion and winner of the Val Barker Award for best boxer, came to Scotland in 1980 to fight Jim Watt for the world title. The final at light-welterweight between Sugar Ray Leonard and Andrés Aldama of Cuba, who had stopped or knocked out all four of his opponents, was unforgettable. Leonard boxed brilliantly and won clearly.

Cornelius Boza-Edwards, from the Fitzroy Lodge in south London, was selected to fight for Uganda but an African boycott ended his Olympics early. Boza had lost to Cowdell in the ABA championship, but would win a world title in the eighties. Boza had joined his guardian Jack Edwards in Harrow in 1974. The pair had met at the Kampala boxing club in Uganda when Bosa, as he was then known, was just 10. 'Boza was so good, so strong, that when he was fifteen we had to upgrade him to senior – he was too dangerous for the kids,' said Edwards, who worked in Uganda for sixteen years. In 1957 he had been the referee when Idi Amin lost to Les Peach for the Ugandan heavyweight title. Jack had also been in charge of the Ugandan boxing team at the Commonwealth Games in Edinburgh in 1970 when they won three golds and two silvers. In Britain, Jack took Boza to the Lodge and handed him over to Mick Carney and Billy Webster. I met Boza there at some point in 1975. All he wanted was a Capri; he got much more. His professional debut was in December at the Hilton Hotel on London's Park Lane. He won in six rounds. The journey to the Capri was on.

There had been some bloody problems for Alan 'Boom Boom' Minter – a ring moniker that mimicked his guttural shouts as he threw punches. He had lost, been cut several times, and been disqualified for not 'engaging'. He fought six times in 1976, beat good men, and still had to wait until 1980 for a world title chance. He stopped five of those good men and had a rematch with Kevin Finnegan, which was considered the British fight of the year.

Finnegan and Minter II was at the Albert Hall in September. It was hard again, the full fifteen rounds, and Minter took the slenderest of decisions and won the Lonsdale belt outright. It was a classic seventies fight, and a classic series in many ways: two good boxers, both stuck waiting for a world title shot in a long line that at times looked endless; the options were limited and to stay busy and keep earning they were left with no option but to fight each other. This situation lasted into the eighties, but was finished by the nineties when the best fights between the two best British boxers were invariably for a version of the world title. They did their business differently in the seventies.

In October Maurice Hope was in Rome on a difficult mission. He stopped Vito Antuofermo with just twelve seconds left in the fifteenth and last round to win the European light-middleweight title. Antuofermo, who was born in Puglia but based in Brooklyn, won the world middleweight title less than three years later, defended against Marvin Hagler, and finally lost it to Minter on a split decision. He also played what he looked like, a mobster, in the *Sopranos* television show. Hope's win is just one of the bewildering fights from the seventies and eighties that have inexplicably remained under the radar. Antuofermo had won the European title earlier in the year when he beat Eckhard Dagge in Berlin; Dagge then won the WBC light-middleweight title and Hope was his next opponent.

The year ended with John H. Stracey beaten and just Conteh as a British world champion; he was standing next to Roberto Durán, Pipino Cuevas, Wilfredo Benítez, Alexis Argüello, Carlos Zárate, Alfonso Zamora, Saensak Muangsurin, Carlos Monzón and the heavyweight champion Ali. It was a rare time to be a boxing fan.

The Contenders

In the eighties and nineties Phil Martin changed the face of boxing in Manchester when, from the ruins of a torched supermarket, he created Champs Camp in Moss Side. Martin lost on points for Chris Finnegan's British light-heavyweight title to Tim Wood in April. He would take his own fighters to British titles twenty years later and would remain a boxing activist until his death at just forty-four in 1994. His premises are still there, twenty-five years after he took over the abandoned building.

Maurice Hope might have won in Rome, but Rhiney, the kid that sparred with Palomino in the sweltering summer, won the British welterweight title at Caesar's Palace – yep, the one in Luton. He also fought at Neptune's Palace – the one in Caister-on-Sea. Rhiney had made a career on the continental circuit, often getting a draw if he won clearly and losing without complaint. Rhiney stopped Cardiff's Pat Thomas, who would train WBO super-featherweight champion Barry Jones in the nineties, in the eighth. Thomas was over twice and, three years later, would win the British light-middleweight title. A defeat meant very little in the seventies; Conteh, Minter, Bugner, Hope and Stracey had all lost in learning fights.

From the Notepad

In late January at the Café Royal in the London Federation of Boys' Clubs finals, there was a double act that would have cost a lot of money to see as professionals. At Class A under-63kg Lloyd Honeyghan from the Fisher won, and in Class C under-60kg the winner was Terry Marsh. Both would win world titles in the next twelve years. However, the real star on the night was Davey Armstrong, the Class C under-75kg champion. Armstrong stopped most of his opponents as an amateur and is a permanent fixture on any list of great young fighters that never made it. Armstrong plunged deep into the dark side after a short pro career – prison, shot in the face – and he remains notorious. 'I've never known anybody quite like him,' said Terry Lawless, his manager. He was shaking his head at the time.

In January at the Royal Albert Hall, Minter stopped Trevor Francis in eight rounds. Minter was one of three world champions that Francis met in the last nine fights of his career. He never got a British title fight, losing to three and drawing with two other champions. In 1997 he was in the corner when his son Dean won the British super-middleweight title. Sadly, in January 2017, Dean was diagnosed with terminal cancer.

George Gilbody lost to Tommy Hearns at Wembley when the ABA drew 5-5 with the USA. Gilbody, who won five ABA titles, pushed Hearns all the way. 'When Tommy beat me he lifted me up in the ring,' Gilbody told me in 2005. 'When I met him again [Hearns fought in Manchester in 1999] he couldn't remember me. I gently reminded him and he remembered.'

In 1976 the number of active professional boxers in Britain reached four hundred for the first time in the seventies.

1977

'Joe could really fight and if you weren't on your game, guess what, you got an ass-whuppin'.'
Ron Lyle, feared contender and convicted killer, on Joe Bugner

'Green nutted me three times in the first round. I don't think he'll beat Palomino unless he nuts him.'
John H. Stracey

THERE IS NO doubt that March is one of the most remarkable months in British boxing history. This year, two world title fights, a vicious confrontation in London, and a bizarre twelve rounds in Las Vegas. There was blood and lots of it, controversial decisions, and accusations of apathy. It was a truly crazy month.

The fights started in John Conteh's hometown at the Liverpool Stadium. There had been a scare when the forty-five-year-old venue was initially ruled out with doubts over the building's maintenance. 'They ain't coming here to use the toilet, they are coming here to see me fight,' said Conteh. There was some American television money and Conteh was getting paid a total of £117,000 – his highest payday to that point. ITV planned to screen the fight at eleven p.m., which was a delayed slot, and they paid £40,000 for the rights, which was a British record at the time. There was talk of fighting the Argentinian Miguel Ángel Cuello, his number one contender, but in the end it was the American Len Hutchins. There was a full house of 3,800 at the stadium: Conteh the world champion was coming home and the promoter, Manny Goodhall of Blackpool, was forced to apologize to the fans that could not get a ticket. The touts made a killing, and the best face-value tickets were £30. There were ring-card girls holding up the rounds It was an event.

Hutchins had been stopped in twelve rounds by WBA champion Victor Emilio Galíndez, the rock-jawed rival of Conteh, and he could fight, make no mistake. Conteh was quite brilliant, dropping and stopping Hutchins after just sixty-five seconds of the third round. Hutchins had a gash by the side of his left eye, a wound from the opener, and when he scrambled up from the knockdown at seven or eight it was called off. It was not a very gentlemanly fight. Jerry Quarry, the top-ten heavyweight from California, was ringside for CBS-TV and he was disgusted with Conteh's headwork. 'We both went in with our heads, and that happens,' Conteh said. 'It could have been me with the cut, and as far as I'm concerned I won the fight with the left hook.'

Conteh left the ring knowing he had sixty days to defend against Cuello, his mandatory, or risk being stripped. Bob Arum won the purse bid for the fight and picked Monte Carlo on 21 May. Conteh was getting $200,000, Cuello $65,000, and the trade paper *Boxing News* started to advertise a three-day package for £89. A bad clock was ticking for Conteh.

Ten days later it was Maurice Hope's turn in a world title fight against Eckhard Dagge in Berlin at the Deutschland Halle in front of 10,000 Germans. Hope had waited, beaten the right people, and had a good chance of winning the WBC light-middleweight title if the fight was fair. It was not. At the end of fifteen rounds one judge went for Dagge, the referee, Harry Gibbs of Bermondsey, went for Hope, and the Italian judge scored it a draw. It meant Dagge kept the title. 'I'm sorry, but I don't give the verdicts,' Dagge told Terry Lawless in Hope's corner. 'It was a real hometown decision, a shame,' said Lawless. 'I won it from the start to the finish,' said Hope. The British press agreed with him. It was a world title fight without British cameras, a time so distant to the modern world that it is barely comprehensible.

Hope asked the British Boxing Board of Control to assist him in getting a rematch, but Dagge had a commitment to fight Italian-Australian Rocky Mattioli. They fought, Rocky won in five, and Hope had to wait two full years before Mattioli gave him a shot. Incredibly, Hope went back to Germany to defend his European title, a slender decision, just seven weeks after the draw in Berlin. There seems to have been genuine optimism after the Dagge fight, but ultimately all the empty talk about taking less money, to defend the title in London to avoid the risk of another hometown verdict in Germany, was forgotten. Hope, as expected, took the risk so many world-class British boxers took in the seventies. He had no choice: he had to fight to earn a living.

A Sunday afternoon show in March at Caesars Palace in Las Vegas between a felon and the British heavyweight champion was never going to be a bigger attraction than a mile-long buffet of prawns the size of chickens and lobster as hefty as a small lamb. But Joe Bugner against Ron Lyle was a serious fight, live in the UK on ITV at ten p.m.; the winner was slated to fight George Foreman, and the winner of that would get a crack at Muhammad Ali – or rather another crack, as all three had failed against him. The Vegas scrap still had intrigue.

The plan collapsed when Foreman was dropped, battered and beaten over twelve rounds by Jimmy Young in Puerto Rico three days before the first bell in Las Vegas. Foreman was taken on a stretcher from the dressing room to hospital, hallucinating and making deals with his God. He had an epiphany that evening in his bruised, bloody and delirious state and was, within months, on the road with a bible in his hand. He remained road-bound, waving his bible and proselytizing, until a comeback in 1987. Foreman regained the world title in 1994 and there was talk once again of a fight with Bugner. Madness for sure, but then Big Joe did continue fighting until 1999.

Bugner had not boxed since beating Richard Dunn in October 1976 and that had been his only fight since the loss to Ali for the world title in Kuala Lumpur in June 1975. Bugner was stripped of his European heavyweight title before the end of January for not fighting the Spaniard José Manuel Urtain, instead agreeing terms to meet Lyle. Bugner had broken a bone in his right hand when he knocked out Dunn and could not have fought. He was also looking at making just fifteen grand for the defence, which was planned for Bilbao, and that was not enough. 'It's a liberty, I loved that belt,' said Bugner. There were also problems with his first marriage, and a great strain had been placed on his relationship with Andy Smith, his manager and coach. Bugner turned 27 during the week of the fight, an age when a heavyweight should still be considered a baby. Big Joe had not been a child in the heavyweight world for a long, long time.

It was a bad fight to watch, a hard fight to survive. Lyle was given the split decision at the end of twelve mauling rounds. Mickey Duff at ringside had tried repeatedly to lift Bugner, make him try just a bit more. It was frustrating, and even Smith struggled to justify the performance: 'There really are no excuses.' Bugner's shattered body told a different story. 'It took me six months to recover from the Lyle fight,' he said. 'I ended up in hospital in an ice-tank to ease the internal bleeding.' The medical report failed to dampen the criticism, and even Henry Cooper joined the abuse: 'Bugner must decide: quit or have a go.' Lyle, like Ali, came to Bugner's defence. 'Joe could really fight and if you weren't on your game, guess what, you got an ass-whuppin'. We had a hard fight that day in Vegas,' Lyle told me in 2010. Bugner always considered it the most severe beating he took, which is strange as most people consider it a boring fight.

Lyle had been beating Ali for ten rounds, he dropped Foreman twice in a thriller, and had come off the floor to knock out Earnie Shavers, often considered the heaviest puncher of the seventies. In prison for manslaughter in the late sixties he was stabbed and lost thirty-five pints of blood. Ron Lyle was a real fighter.

In defeat, Bugner felt isolated. A threat to strip him of his British title unless he defended against Billy Aird in Liverpool in May was the least of his problems. His marriage was over and he was depressed, drinking heavily and flopping in cheap hotels. He was lost to boxing at just 27. But six months later he would meet the fearsome Marlene.

The month ended with Dave Boy Green fighting fallen idol John H. Stracey for the right to meet Carlos Palomino for the WBC welterweight title. Green was, oddly for the time, unbeaten in twenty-three fights, and had prepared with Bugner in Las Vegas for a time. The pair shared Andy Smith's managerial and training skills. Stracey had had to watch as Green deserted the light-welterweight division, moved to welterweight, and was then spoken about as Palomino's next challenger. 'I was a bit pissed off about that, to tell the truth. I wanted the rematch, I wanted the belt back.' It was over ten rounds, no titles were available, but a date with Palomino on 14 June was the prize.

The fight was most certainly not for the squeamish that night at Wembley. Green, who was known as the Fen Tiger, had travelled with a horde from Chatteris in Cambridgeshire, and Stracey had his usual cockney hard-core in the crowd of 10,600. Some experts believed it was the best fight in a British ring for twenty years. In the opening round the referee, Harry Gibbs, stood back as the pair put the nut in. The butts were flying. Green had struck first; Stracey retaliated and Green dramatically pulled back. Gibbs did finally intervene, grabbed Green and, in his distinctive voice, which belonged with rations, smog and hardship in a different epoch, told him: 'Oi, cut out the acting.' They both knew they were in a fight. Stracey's left eye had started to swell and mark by the bell to end the first. Nobody was sitting at Wembley that night. It came to an end when Gibbs waved his arms to signal it was over with just eighty seconds left of the tenth and last round. Stracey's left eye was closed, he could not see Green's big right hands. 'It was anybody's fight,' Gibbs said at the end. Presumably the winner of the last round would have won the fight on his scoring as the sole arbiter.

'Green nutted me three times in the first round,' said Stracey. 'I don't think he'll beat Palomino unless he nuts him.' There were tears again in a British ring. 'I wanted to pull John out three rounds earlier, but he wouldn't let me,' said Terry Lawless. It was the last time the pair would work together. They never even spoke again before Lawless died in 2009. Stracey, at 26, would have just one more fight. 'We all realized that John was finished,' said Duff, who with Lawless, Royal Albert Hall promoter Mike Barrett and financier and boxing fan Jarvis Astaire had established a cartel to control their interests in boxing. It was a legal working arrangement, but it would get tested in court.

May was a terrible time for Conteh. He pulled out of his WBC defence against Cuello in Monaco at short notice. The WBC stripped him. An American called Jesse Burnett was put on a plane on a Wednesday and on the Saturday Cuello, who was in Monaco waiting for Conteh, was the new champion when he survived a knockdown to stop Burnett in the ninth round. There was a dispute over the potential quality of the film and the Americans had concerns, threatening not to pay if the sound and picture quality were poor. Conteh walked out on the fight during the uncertainty. He was drinking, still listening to the last person to put a thought in his head. He was just 25. Bugner was gone at 27, Stracey finished at 26. The trio were harsh proof that boxing took a toll on talented men who sacrificed everything in real fights.

In June, Green started as slight favourite with the paper boys when he met Carlos Palomino at Wembley for the WBC's welterweight title. Palomino had made one defence since stopping Stracey. 'Palomino has improved twenty per cent,' said Duff, which is the type of equation that boxing people consider science. Green was caught and knocked out cold in round eleven. 'I still say it was the way he fell and not the punch that caused the knockout,' Smith insisted. 'Dave got caught with his feet in line.' Three years later Green would get another world title chance.

Alan Minter went on the road in early February, a fight in Milan against Italian Germano Valsecchi. It was a bad night for the local lad and Minter won in five rounds on what was a relatively safe mission to a dangerous land for British boxers. Still, Minter was taking absolutely no chances and recruited some minders to travel with him, stand outside his dressing room and look as mean as possible. Reg Gutteridge, who was on the trip, took a quick look at the boys and remarked, 'They had faces that were well lived in.'

Also in the travelling party was south London publican, fight face and promoter Beryl Cameron-Gibbons. She was, according to Reg, 'obviously well beveraged on arrival'. Gibbons had been landlady of the Thomas A'Becket pub, a boxing retreat for decades, in London's Old Kent Road for sixteen years. The gym upstairs and its ring had been home to the finest fighters ever to visit the city, but more than that it was where fighters and fight people gathered. Getting to train at the Becket was like being asked into some type of inner sanctum, a step back in time. At ringside in Milan, as Reg and the press corps sat down for their work, Beryl appeared and looked like she had been 'poured into a lace dress and some was spilling out'. There was a lot of Beryl to contain, but she was certainly a pioneer as Britain's first female promoter. There is a glorious tale about Beryl, her fake boobs (which she admitted to), Lord Longford and an associate of the boxing twins Reg and Ron Kray. It seems that one night there was a charity function at the Becket and Beryl arrived in a full-on see-through shirt. Longford was stunned, but villain Tony Lambrianou defended the outfit and said she was 'a smashing girl – everybody loved Beryl'. Everybody except the boyfriend that beat her up one night. 'I went to shoot him, but I think he emigrated,' remembers Lambrianou.

In April there was another setback for Minter. In March he had been stripped of his British middleweight title by the Board. A request to go through with a European title fight in May, and then defend the British title at the end of May, was refused. It was a ridiculous decision. 'He was proud to be the British champion and he never fiddled about with it in the clubs, he defended it in the public eye,' said Doug Bidwell, his manager and father-in-law. Minter and Bidwell found out in the press. In the ring at the Albert Hall in April, Minter was busted up by Ronnie Harris, who had won a gold medal at the Mexico Olympics. It was over in the eighth with Minter cut over both eyes and grotesquely so on his lip. Harris had arrived unbeaten with a record of either sixteen, twenty-one or twenty-three wins. It was probably the latter. The loss scuppered any European plans and ruined a world title eliminator against Bennie Briscoe in the summer;

the winner had a world title fight in September back in Monaco. Minter would, instead, have to wait until March 1980 for a world title fight.

The Harris fight was bloody, even by Minter's standards. 'We are not butchers, but we didn't retire Alan – I thought he was going to win,' said Bidwell. Harris was marginally in front when the referee, Sid Nathan, called it off at the end of eight rounds during the sixty-second interval. Duff and Barrett disputed the decision to import Harris. 'I never made that fight, I was away in America, and I was furious about it,' said Duff. 'Harris was in the "Who Needs Him" club, and we certainly didn't need him.' Barrett had made the match, stuck by the decision and refused to change it when Minter was promised the world title eliminator. 'How could I call it off?' Barrett said. 'He [Harris] had a contract.' Thinking like that never made it out of the seventies.

After the Harris loss, Minter went to Monaco in July and beat the great Emile Griffith. It was a strange outing, an odd fight. Griffith had been a superstar in the sixties, had won and lost world titles at welterweight and middleweight, and lived a spectacular double life as a very active gay man. Sweet Emile wore hot pants and lipstick and fought alongside towering transvestites in New York street fights throughout the sixties and seventies. His final fight was against the young Englishman. Minter won on points, and even with the loss on cuts and the victory in Milan, he still had two hard title fights before the end of the year.

The first one was just seven weeks later, in September. Minter met a Frenchman called Gratien Tonna and had to travel to Milan to defend his European middleweight title against him. Tonna was a hardman. In March he had been shot in the left arm; the bullet had exited and lodged in his throat. Two of his companions outside the bar in Paris at six a.m. were also shot. Tonna was discharged from hospital – his 'musculature' had saved his life – and he travelled back to Marseille with the bullet still in his throat. He had just been given an eighteen-month sentence for reckless driving after an incident the previous summer when he had hit and killed a policeman.

There was blood – it was a Minter fight – but it was also hugely physical. Minter chased Tonna, responded every time he was caught, and was in control when suddenly the referee jumped in after seventy seconds of the eighth. The ref never even took a look, but he had gone over to Minter's corner at the end of the seventh. There was a gash across Minter's brow, but it had not got any worse and the skilled corner had it under control. It was another setback.

In a year when Minter seemed to be at the centre of just about everything, he had one final title fight, in November, when he regained his old British championship from Kevin Finnegan. The fight completed a trilogy of fifteen-rounders, with Minter the winner every time. 'I do feel like he is my brother,' Minter said at the end of a hard year, the type of year that makes a champion.

It had been an exceptional year, and there was one exchange, between Duff and Bugner in Las Vegas, which serves as a perfect footnote. Duff said to Bugner in the dressing room after the Lyle defeat, 'The name of the game is money.' Bugner replied, without a pause, 'Yeah, and being able to count it.'

The Contenders

At the top of the bill when Charlie Magri had his first pro fight was Jimmy Batten, retaining his British light-middleweight title against Larry Paul. Batten went the distance with Roberto Durán in 1982 and is another of the fine list of British fighters that never got a world title shot. In October 2016, the 25th to be precise, I had a call to tell me that Jimmy had just been diagnosed with Parkinson's. He'd beaten Paul exactly thirty-nine years earlier.

Just forty-two days after his pro debut, in early December, Magri won the vacant British flyweight title. It was his third fight, and the weigh-in was at the Odeon Cinema in Leicester Square. Magri beat Eltham's Dave Smith, who had won seven fights; he was dropped seven times and finally stopped in the seventh. Smith's bravery will never be forgotten by anybody inside the Royal Albert Hall that night. Magri never made a defence, but ten years later the Board gave him a Lonsdale belt to keep.

There was a popular, punishing win by Kevin Finnegan at the end of May when he regained the British middleweight title against Frankie Lucas. The fight was over in the tenth with Lucas cut over the right eye. Finnegan was the sentimental favourite, a boxer's boxer. Lucas was having just his tenth fight. 'Nobody wants to fight Frankie and you've got to take the chance when it comes,' said Duff.

From the Notepad

In Liverpool on Conteh's undercard there was an odd cameo by Montreal gold medal winner Leon Spinks. The fight with Bolton's Peter Freeman lasted just eighty-six seconds. It was Leon's second, and eleven months later he beat Ali for the heavyweight title. 'He was a wild man, that is for sure,' said Conteh.

There was a truly infuriating bureaucratic disgrace at an amateur show in Yorkshire just before Christmas. A local pro promoter called John Gilpin was ringside and he had donated a nice few quid by sponsoring bouts, which was the way shows survived. At some point, with two boys in the ring and gloved up, Gilpin was invited into the ring to take a bow. There was an immediate flurry at ringside and the OIC (official in charge) abandoned the show because of a regulation breach: nobody with a professional licence was allowed in an amateur boxing ring. Harry Mullan, who had written about amateur boxing before graduating to Las Vegas nights, was not impressed: 'Not all professional fight people are cheque-book-waving gangsters.' As Reg Gutteridge might have said, 'Oi, not so much of the cheque-book waving.'

1978

'He had the crowd, the title, the officials, a layer of plastic over his eyes, the government and just about everybody on his side. And he was a gifted boxer. Me? I couldn't wait to start fighting, that's how mad I was.'
John Conteh on fighting Mate Parlov in Belgrade

'I've known Johnny since he was a baby and he's never been out with a girl in his life. He's dedicated to his boxing, he doesn't bother with girlfriends.'
Dai Gardiner, manager, on Johnny Owen, the Matchstick Man of Merthyr Tydfil

JOHN CONTEH WENT behind the Iron Curtain to Belgrade to fight for the world title in one of the toughest missions for a British boxer. Conteh met Mate Parlov at the Red Star Belgrade football stadium in front of 40,000, packed in for the homecoming of their national idol, the pride of Yugoslavia (in 1999 he was voted Croatia's Sportsman of the Century). 'I knew I would never get the decision in Parlov's backyard,' said Conteh.

The fighters had taken separate roads to their meeting; Conteh had been on an Ali undercard in Las Vegas when Parlov was away behind the Iron Curtain winning his second European amateur title. Men like Parlov and hundreds of fabled Soviets and silky Cubans never turned pro, never stuck their noses in the professional business. Parlov was the pioneer, and that night in June was the first real professional test of the West v. the East. It was stacked on Parlov's side.

Conteh had been ringside in Milan in January to see a bit of history when Parlov became the first boxer from the Eastern Bloc to win a professional world title. Parlov had won the Olympics in 1972, the inaugural world amateur championship in 1974 and the European championship twice. As an amateur he had lost just thirteen of his 323 fights and he knew how not to get hit. Conteh watched the towering, rock-eyed southpaw knock out Miguel Ángel Cuello with a tap on the side of the head in round nine. Parlov was a sight, a punch-perfect operator, and Cuello, who looked like a pudgy waiter at a pool party, was finished long before the last shot landed. Parlov had broken Cuello's spirit with simple textbook boxing and then finished it when it was safe. The Klitschko brothers Wladimir and Vitali would adopt the exact same tactics over twenty years later during their reign as heavyweight champions.

The job was made harder on the night. 'I looked over and I couldn't believe it,' said George Francis. Parlov had entered the ring with a synthetic skin across his eyebrows. His cornermen had complained about Conteh's use of the head and they had taken the drastic action to avoid losing on a cut. A boxer can smear his eyebrows in Vaseline, often treated with a drop or two of adrenalin, but plastering on a fabric to form a protective membrane is against the rules. Except in Belgrade on a warm summer night when the mighty southpaw hero takes his robe off and is cheered like the homecoming hero he is. 'I didn't know whether to laugh or cry,' said Conteh. 'Cuts happen in our business, we are all big boys and we get on with it. Not Parlov, he was having none of it.'

The fight was a cruncher, the type where every punch seems to jar, every hit leaves a mark. The square-jawed brute from Yugoslavia kept on sticking out his long, accurate southpaw jab, a punch cultivated in a thousand lonely hours of preparation at training camps through-out the Eastern Bloc during the compilation of his 323 amateur fights. In the eighth round Conteh was deducted a point for use of his head and that meant one point off the final tally of the three judges. In the fifteenth and last round the referee took a point off again, this time for illegal use of the elbow. It was another point off Conteh's score and an extra safety cushion for Parlov. The decision was a split, amazing in many ways, and Parlov retained his title. Conteh deserved the vote, and without the deductions he would have regained his WBC light-heavyweight belt. He has remained gracious in defeat, which is impressive.

At some point over the summer Conteh reached an uneasy peace with Duff and his old promoter, Harry Levene. In September he was back on a Wembley bill, stopping American Leonardo Rodgers in seven rounds. A sign of Conteh's turmoil was glaringly obvious when he came in on the scales at a career-low 168lb, which in modern boxing is super-middleweight; Conteh had started as a heavyweight. On his undercard future world champions Maurice Hope and Cornelius Boza-Edwards had wins. The show was not a success, however, and Duff announced that Conteh's drawing power was over. It was a troubling time for the fallen idol and a few weeks later, at about three in the morning, he crashed his Rolls-Royce into six parked cars in London's Piccadilly. He was drunk, he was high, and there was nothing he could do about it. 'It was about destroying everything that I had achieved – that is what can happen to an alcoholic,' said Conteh. Immediately after the crash in the heart of the West End he attracted a large audience; they cheered and jeered as Conteh emerged, wobbled, and was then met by the police. It was nowhere near the bottom: just a few years later and Conteh could be found with the dossers at Euston station, passing back and forth their poison. He was an alcoholic, he was using cocaine, and he was 27 years old. He'd also injured his damaged right hand in the smash, guaranteeing that he would never be a fully fit two-handed fighter ever again. But he did, amazingly, have one more truly great night left in him.

In July, Minter was in Italy fighting Angelo Jacopucci for the vacant European middleweight title. The fight, like all of Minter's scraps from the early trio with Jan Magdziarz to the bloody brawls with Finnegan, was hard from the start. The eleventh ended with both boxers marked. In the twelfth a short southpaw right hook made Jacopucci's knees buckle and Minter chased him, connecting cleanly a dozen times. The final left sent the Italian down and he folded over his legs with his shoulders and head dangling between the bottom and middle rope (the rings had three ropes at the time, not four as they have now). He was counted out, the full count of ten, with his head slightly moving, probably as a result of Minter still skipping from foot to foot during the count and causing a slight vibration in the ring. The handlers jumped in at ten, and Jacopucci was soon on his feet, smiling and pulling faces to friends at ringside. They embraced for photographers, two scarred men. Minter was the champion of Europe again.

After the fight Minter and Jacopucci met at a restaurant and had a drink. Later, Minter saw the Italian after he'd left the restaurant. 'He was leaning over a bridge spewing up, but I thought he'd just had too much to drink,' said Minter. Jacopucci collapsed soon after that final chance encounter, was taken to hospital, and died three days later. He was 29. The defeat to Minter was his third in thirty-six fights and two years earlier he had beaten Bunny Sterling to win the European title.

'I'm not a killer – I was there to win, not to injure,' said Minter. 'I was just doing my job and it was hard that night. I remember, going into the twelfth, both my eyes were closed and I had trouble seeing, but I just tapped him and he went down.' The Italian doctor working at ringside that night, Ezio Pimpinelli, was found guilty of second-degree manslaughter in January 1983 for failing to take proper action. He was given an eight-month suspended sentence and ordered to pay the boxer's widow £10,000 in compensation. 'I sat down after I found out about his death and I asked myself about fighting on,' Minter revealed. 'I thought, it was him, but it could have been me. I knew then I would continue. There is one thing, and I'm not bragging, but I wanted Jacopucci's children to be able to say that their dad lost to a champion and not just some mug.' It's a last word that explains a lot about what motivates boxers.

'You'd come round a corner and there would be two or three boys taking a position to open up on the army,' said Charlie Nash. He was talking about the difficulties of doing roadwork in Derry in the seventies. Nash was not just a witness, he was a victim, and in 1972 his younger brother William was one of fourteen Derrymen killed by the British army in the atrocity known as Bloody Sunday. Nash's father Alexander was shot in the arm as he went to try and help his son. 'I'm angry about what happened, but nothing can justify killing,' Nash said. He was a dedicated pacifist.

At the Munich Olympics, Nash was cruelly denied a minimum of a silver medal when he was disqualified in the quarter-finals against Poland's Jan Sczepanski, who went on to win the gold after a bye in the semi-final. 'It happened, that's the way the amateur sport works.' In February 1978 Nash won the vacant British lightweight title, Jim Watt's old belt, when his fight with Johnny Claydon was stopped because the referee had Nash ten points clear after twelve rounds. It was a mercy stoppage, a bizarre conclusion to a one-sided professional fight. Nash never adjusted his style for the pro game and was a smart boxer, a defensive master. Claydon never stood a chance that night in Derry.

The blood flowed in Boston in March when Kevin Finnegan fought a young Marvin Hagler for five grand. Hagler at the time was just 23, an avoided fighter and a local. The fight was over at the end of round eight with Finnegan's face marked with splits, gashes and bruises; at the time Hagler was up by just one round. Finnegan had cuts over both eyes, his forehead was cut, and his left cheek had a two-inch wound. 'His cheek was open almost to the bone, he couldn't have carried on,' said Mickey Duff, who was in the corner with Freddie Hill. The doctor had come over to inspect the wounds and call the carnage off. Well, that was the idea, but he shocked Hill and Duff when he refused and told Finnegan: 'Get out there, son, and give this son-of-a-bitch a whupping.' The corner was stunned and pulled Finnegan. 'I never wanted to do it, I knew the stick Kevin would give me if I pulled him out,' said Hill. 'I had no choice, the cheek was hanging off.'

The crowd of 5,300 at the Boston Garden saw Hagler hurt in rounds six and seven and Finnegan keep fighting as the blood formed a complete mask over his face. Finnegan required twenty stitches to stem the blood flow and left Boston with a promise to Rip Valenti, the promoter, to return for a rematch. The fans loved that, and he was back seventy-two days later for more. Hagler was still over two years away from winning the world middleweight title at Wembley.

Hagler cut Finnegan again in the May rematch, again at the Boston Garden. The wound on the left cheekbone opened, which was not a shock. 'The bad cut was the one-inch break at the corner of the scar on Kevin's cheekbone,' said Duff. Hagler won in the seventh and Finnegan never moaned about Marvin's head. 'It's a big-boys sport and I'm not going to cry over a few clashes,' he said. 'It happens – it just seems to happen to me a lot.' Hagler was the same, cut from different cloth. 'Finnegan is the toughest man I ever fought,' he said. Finnegan was a truly battle-scarred veteran at that stage, but he had some big wins left in him. Duff always considered him a better fighter than his brother, Chris. Even in a decade when so many deserving British boxers never got near a world title it is surely close to criminal that Kevin Finnegan went his entire career without getting a chance to become a world champion.

Johnny Owen fought seven times in 1978 and remained in virtual obscurity even after winning and defending the British bantam-weight title. He would have been remembered alongside Evan Armstrong, Pat Thomas, Alan Richardson and Dave Needham had he not fought for a world title with such fatal consequences in 1980. In April, at the Leisure Centre in Ebbw Vale, Owen retained his British title when he stopped Wayne Evans, who had left Wales when he was six for England's south coast. The resistance was slowly battered out of Evans and in the tenth he slid to the canvas.

There was agony and odd ecstasy in the dressing rooms after the fight. Evans wept in pain as his sodden bandages were cut from his swollen hand. It was a purple mess, and he knew the damage would never fully heal. All boxers know their physical faults, even if they never mention them. Owen was known as the Matchstick Man and people doubted he had the strength to be a fighter; some doubted that the skinny kid with the mop of dark hair and enormous ears *was* a fighter. In his dressing room Owen told his trainer, Dai Gardiner, not to put anything on a slight abrasion under his left eye, which in boxing is called a mouse. 'Leave it, please, it shows I'm a fighter.' Nobody who ever saw Owen in the ring ever doubted that.

It was the end for former world champion John H. Stracey in May when he finished with a win at the Michael Sobell Sports Centre in north London. Strace stopped Frenchman Georges Warusfel in the ninth, and he never fought again. He was 27 and had been a pro for nine years. He had split with Duff, Lawless and the rest of the legal cartel that had run his boxing career; he stopped because he was weary. 'I had too many fights too quickly: three world title fights in six months – too much,' Stracey said. 'Palomino never hurt, I just had nothing that night. A hundred and thirty amateur, fifty-one as a pro – I was ready to retire when I did. I'll be all right.' He tried a few things away from the ring and not all of them worked but he still gets a living talking at dinners, and more than that he remains a gentleman. 'You know what, you can't have regrets in this business,' he told me in 2010. Perhaps the last word on Stracey's career should go to Duff: 'I don't think Palomino or Green would have beaten John in his prime.' That is good enough for me.

Wee Barry McGuigan was only 17 when he won the Commonwealth Games gold medal at bantamweight for Northern Ireland in August out in Edmonton, Canada. His final was tight, a majority over Tumat Sogolik from Papua New Guinea. The weight above was won by another boxing baby, 20-year-old Azumah Nelson from Ghana. The pair would be featherweight world champions at the same time eight years later and unfortunately never fight.

Also at the Games, Joe Awome from Woking won gold at heavyweight; he turned professional the following year, signing a high-profile contract with Duff. He lost three of his twelve fights, all of which finished inside the distance, and he quit after fourteen months to concentrate on his work with The Jam. Awome worked with the band from the early days. He died in 1995 at forty-one on the operating table while having a brain tumour, which was benign, removed. In December 1995 Paul Weller played a benefit night for Awome at the Empire in Shepherd's Bush.

Joe Bugner's British and Commonwealth titles were on the line at the Royal Albert Hall in October when Billy Aird, who was meant to fight Bugner the previous year in Liverpool, and John L. Gardner were matched. John L. was part of the Terry Lawless team at the Royal Oak in Canning Town. He was local, from Hackney, an east London boy, and he entered the ring with just one loss in twenty-seven. Aird was fresh from losing a European title fight over fifteen rounds in Spain; he had fought hard men in eliminators, tough men on the road, and even lost to Conteh back in 1972. Gardner stopped Aird in five rounds. Sadly, over the next five years there would only be four fights for the British heavyweight title.

John Conteh was the only British boxer to fight for a world title during the year and he finished stumbling, drunk and injured after a seven-car crash that he caused. World champions like Wilfredo Gómez were defending their titles in Thailand and Japan, and most of the other world champions seemed like distant figures. We had their pictures on the walls in the gyms, but that seemed like the closest anybody in the British game would get to men like Gómez, Pipino Cuevas, Antonio Cervantes, Eusebio Pedroza and Carlos Zárate. However, over the next three years – 1979, 1980 and 1981 – British boxers would be in twenty-two world title fights. British boxing's dark ages were truly coming to an end.

The Contenders

Henry Rhiney, the British welterweight champion, went to Dornbirn in Austria, and Nottingham's Dave Needham, the British feather-weight champion, was in León, Spain. Rhiney punished Joseph Pachler and won in round ten; Needham was busted up in five by unbeaten Roberto Castañón and retired with a gash on his cheek. In 1970 Needham had won a Commonwealth Games gold medal and had been in and out of title fights, winning the British bantam and feather titles, since 1974. He was not known as a puncher – he stopped just ten of the thirty men he beat – but in the summer of 1977 he had finished the career of Vernon Sollas with a sickening knockout. Sollas was unconscious in the ring for as long as twenty minutes. After Castañón he had five more fights, four for titles, and then walked away from the sport.

In September at Wembley, but this time at the newly built Conference Centre, Jimmy Batten retained his British light-middleweight title when Tony Poole was forced out with a badly damaged nose in the thirteenth round. It was considered the fight of the year. Batten was knocked out in a European title fight back at the Conference Centre two months later. It was a gruelling schedule for British champions in the seventies, with a lot of non-title fights, difficult European fights, and seldom a sniff of a world title. 'That world was very different to the boxing world today,' Batten told me in 2011. 'I don't want to sound like somebody that lives in the past, but take a look at what we had to do. It was fucking hard graft.'

From the Notepad

Joe Bugner was seemingly lost to the sport in 1978 and 1979 and never threw a punch; he was gone and forgotten in boxing. Bugner had met and would, in November, marry his soulmate, Marlene. She was a grand Australian dame. He would also fall out with his manager and trainer Andy Smith. Their relationship had been tempestuous for too long, and after Smith and his family attended the wedding, which took place in Santa Monica, California at Gatsby's, owned by Frank Sinatra, they had a harsh conversation on the phone. Smith told Bugner, 'You owe me.' Bugner passionately disagreed. The pair never spoke again, and Bugner regrets not going to Smith's funeral when he died in 2005. At the wedding Tom Jones was best man, but banned from singing. 'I didn't want him upstaging me,' Bugner explained.

Needham died in Thailand in 2008, estranged from the boxing world. In 2009 I did a one-man show in Nottingham and I asked the audience how Dave Needham was. 'Not good,' I was told. 'He's dead.' It got an awkward laugh – probably the highlight of the show.

1979

'Nine times out of ten I'm in the ladies. I do my best to watch it;
if Jim does his best, that's the best we can ask for.'
Margaret Watt on her fight-night routine

'It's my formula, the secret is the tannic acid in the tea leaves.
I told the doctor, but I was not telling that fucking limey or
the yoyo from the Commission.'
Adolph Ritacco, cornerman, defends his secret potion for cuts

JOHN CONTEH WAS involved in one of the bloodiest and most savage
fights of the decade when he met Matthew Saad Muhammad in
Atlantic City in August. He had left Belgrade with nothing the
previous summer, had fought three times since without distinction,
and was in with the new WBC light-heavyweight champion known
as 'Miracle Matthew'. Conteh was getting $300,000, but he fought
like the money never mattered.

In April, Conteh had boxed behind closed doors at the Anglo-
American Sporting Club in Mayfair. He drew over ten rounds with
American Jesse Burnett, who had lost a world title fight two years
earlier. Conteh was recovering from booze binges and a serious loss of
direction. He was dropped twice but Harry Gibbs, the ref, scored it a
draw. It's possible that British boxing was the only place in the world
where a British referee would have gone against a former British
world champion fighting on home soil, and in need of a win in a fight
a long, long way from the public eye. The Burnett fight was in many

ways perfect preparation for the brutality of the Muhammad fight.

Muhammad was cut so severely above his left eyebrow in round five that it looked like the fight would be stopped and Conteh would be champion again. In Muhammad's corner, veteran cutsman Adolph Ritacco quickly applied his secret coagulant (which turned out to be roasted tea leaves) to his fighter's brows; by round nine the bleeding had stopped. A black rind was now visible where the gash had been, and this provoked George Francis to go over and confront Ritacco at the end of round nine. 'It was a joke, I was fuming,' said Francis. The pair squared up, Ritacco threw a punch at the 'fucking limey', they were kept apart, and the title fight continued with the visible substance solidly wedged in place. In round fourteen Conteh was dropped twice – heart-breaking knockdowns. He beat the counts, and survived the fifteenth to lose a slender decision. It was a last stand that defied logic, a simply incredible effort by Conteh. It was not quite the end for him, but the final acts of his professional career are not for the squeamish.

Maurice Hope had been the victim of a mugging by the judges when he'd first fought for a world title back in March 1977. Hope had left Berlin that night with a draw, the WBC light-middleweight champion Eckhard Dagge had driven home with the belt in his car. There was a lot of talk about a rematch, getting Dagge to London. Ringside that night was the Italian-Australian Rocky Mattioli. He thought Hope had won and was relieved it was a draw because that meant he got to fight Dagge. He did, he won the title with a stoppage in five rounds, he made two defences, and finally he agreed to fight Hope in March 1979. The only problem was the fight was in San Remo, in a circus tent, and Mattioli, who was based in Melbourne, was born in Italy. It was a tough gig; Rocky was a banger.

And then, bingo, Hope took less than fifteen seconds of the opener to slot home a perfect looping southpaw left behind Mattioli's guard and the champion was over, falling heavily. Hope won every second of the fight from that point; two years of rejection was the ideal motivation to silence a raucous mob, who turned on Mattioli after about six rounds. Rocky quit at the end of the ninth. 'They've packed it in,' bellowed Harry Carpenter. Hope sank to his knees as Terry Lawless, his aide Frank Black and then Hope's friend Jim Watt surrounded him. In a decade of change, Hope became British boxing's first black world champion. He had been born in Antigua, and the Caribbean nation rewarded him with some land.

Mattioli complained about his broken wrist, insisting it had snapped in the first round when he was knocked down. 'He was looking for the decision to be changed, but I told them, had he not been dropped, he wouldn't have hurt the wrist,' said Mickey Duff. Mattioli did get a rematch at Wembley the following year; the wrist was healed, the loss was quicker.

A man called Mike Baker was found for Hope's first defence of his WBC light-middleweight title, and if ever there was a British fighter that deserved a break and an easy fight it was Hope: he had won and lost title fights in Rome, Berlin, Hamburg and San Remo, battling top fighters. He got it at Wembley in September, and Baker was crushed in seven rounds. Baker's high ranking was a surprise at the time, though he had entered the ring fresh from a stoppage of Stanley Blyth, who had a record of one win and two defeats. Notorious lawyer Edward Bennett Williams, who had a stake in the ownership of the Washington Redskins at one time, carried out legal work for the WBC and Don King; his other clients included the gambling tsar Frank Costello, a Mafia mobster whom Williams saved from deportation, fight fan Frank Sinatra and extinct union boss Jimmy Hoffa. 'We knew he had a complimentary WBC ranking, but there was always a chance that Baker could fight,' Duff said. There was no chance. Hope deserved his touch.

It was just forty-four days after Hope's win in the San Remo big top when he travelled to Glasgow for the extended fairy-tale career of his friend Jim Watt. In 1972 Watt had lost a British title fight, and had lost again in 1973 for the same title. He was a wilderness fighter for most of the seventies, with the patience on both sides of the ropes that distinguishes every one of the successful fighters from that decade. There was no such thing as a rush job; boxing was a trade, and it often seemed like an eternal apprenticeship until close to the very end when an opportunity often arrived. Watt was matched with Colombia's Alfredo Pituala for the WBC lightweight title in April at the Kelvin Hall in his hometown of Glasgow, a fight made possible with a lot of help from the local council. Roberto Durán had just vacated the unified belt; Pituala was also the number one contender for the WBA version. Watt was 30, had been a professional for eleven years, had lost seven of his forty fights, and he walked to the ring with a knowing and nervous look on his face. This was his fantasy, a world title fight and 10,000 people making more noise in a British arena than anybody present had ever heard before. Harry Mullan, my first editor and friend, was stunned by the sound. 'You'd have to be a zombie not to be affected by that atmosphere,' said Watt.

There was a presentation of the WBC belt to Hope, and then the fight started. Pituala was dropped in the seventh, battered in the tenth and eleventh, and stopped in the twelfth. Watt was way out in front at the time. The Scot was champion, Britain now had two world champions, and a fighting fortress had been established; the same city would surround world champions Ricky Burns and Scott Harrison over twenty-five years later. 'The crowd beat me, not Watt's punches,' said Pituala.

It was Watt's turn for a defence in November, and he never lost a round against Roberto Vásquez from Texas. In the ninth, after a belting, the ref finally stepped in. A crowd of 2,500 at the Kelvin Hall had kept their hollering at a pitch that can win fights from the start. Vásquez was 21, ten years younger than Watt, and had got the chance because of a shock stoppage of highly touted Hawaiian Andy Ganigan. Watt was merciless, jabbing and picking his punches with a coldness that many forget the Scot possessed. Watt had looked serene before the fight when he was putting his gloves on in the ring and he fought with a conviction shaped by a decade on the road, ten years in long fights behind closed doors with men willing to gouge, butt and foul their way to the bell or the changing room. Little Roberto looked sickened at times by the slow beating.

At the start of March in the bullring in Almería, Johnny Owen lost on points in the last European title fight to go the full distance of fifteen rounds. It was a tight decision: one judge returned a draw and the other two had it by just one round for the Spaniard, Juan Francisco Rodríguez. It was a bitter end to an ugly few days in Spain. Rodríguez had failed to make the bantamweight limit but had been allowed to box; the British Boxing Board of Control's inspector on the night, Harry Vines, had protested in vain. A substance was then rubbed on Rodríguez's gloves which caused Owen's eyes to burn. Vines went to the Spaniard's corner to complain but was bundled by the police back to his seat with a gagging order.

The farce in Spain happened just months after Mate Parlov defeated John Conteh in Belgrade with his eyebrows covered in a synthetic shield. The boxing business could be openly lawless at the time, very dangerous and edgy for a fighter on foreign soil without the necessary backers. Alan Minter certainly travelled with a few lively people. The men in charge of Parlov, Mattioli and Rodríguez had all pushed it, tried it on in some small or big way. Thirteen years later, in 1992, Nigel Benn needed some heavy people to help him escape a vicious mob after he won the WBC super-middleweight title on the outskirts of Rome.

At the Royal Albert Hall in April one of the most memorable and savage fights of the seventies took place when Frankie Lucas met late-replacement Tony Sibson for the vacant British middleweight title. Kevin Finnegan had pulled out and Sibson, who had turned 21 the day before, was drafted in. Lucas had not mellowed with age and was as angry now as he had been when shafted by the England team selectors before the 1974 Commonwealth Games. 'Nobody wanted to fight Frankie, nobody,' said Duff. The beautiful hall was vicious that night, its plush corridors echoing with the faithful. The pair came together for instructions from the referee at the start, and Lucas pushed his head into Sibson's face. They were kept apart, just. Lucas was known as the Wildman of Boxing. The men in the game also knew he was a bully in the ring and could be broken – but to break him a boxer had to survive some nasty rounds. Lucas cut people, he got cut, he dropped people, and he left you hurt. Sibson was a little bit stupid (being fearless can do that to a boxer) in the nicest possible way, and very brave, and that made the fight so memorable. They just stood and delivered, two men fighting with no agenda, no excuses. Both were hurt – Lucas was badly cut over the right eyebrow – and Sibbo was taking risks. In round five Lucas was dropped, sent crashing on to the canvas by two desperate right hands. The ringside was mayhem. 'He's up too soon,' screamed Carpenter. 'Here comes the new British middleweight champion and Lucas doesn't know where he is. The underdog from Leicester, twenty-one yesterday – today comes the real birthday present.' It was called off in the fifth. Lucas would fight just one more time. Sibson had a date later in the year with the veteran Finnegan, a night that would remind people why boxing is called the sweet science. There had been no science in the Lucas fight, just emotion and aggression.

On the first day of May, Charlie Magri won the European flyweight title when he outpointed Franco Udella over the new championship distance of twelve rounds (for European title fights) at Wembley. The fight had been made when Magri went to San Remo to watch Hope win his world title. Udella had been the WBC's light-flyweight champion in 1975. Magri was still four years away from a world title fight, but he had missed out on a chance when Mexico's Miguel Canto was beaten. Gibbs, the globetrotting docker and referee from Bermondsey, had told Magri he would beat Canto. Too late: Canto lost the world title in March and Magri had to wait. He fought again that month, just twenty-eight days later at the Royal Albert Hall, against Freddie González and was dropped in the opener, but stopped the Mexican in the third. After that scare the press reminded their readers that Magri had been dropped and stopped at the 1976 Olympics, which seems fair enough. 'They started to think I was chinny,' said Magri.

Muhammad Ali was in London for the Royal Albert Hall show and took part in a couple of exhibition bouts, including sharing the ring with John L. Gardner, who was the British heavyweight champion. There was a disastrous plan for Gardner to fight what was left of Ali in Japan. It thankfully never happened, much to Duff's consternation, and that cost Gardner a big payday. 'Ali has made money for boxers all over the world and now he's making money for me,' Gardner said when it was announced in December 1980. Ali was due to get £1 million and Gardner £200,000 for the abortive fight. The great man did fight one more time, the pitiful ghost appearance against Trevor Berbick in the Bahamas in late 1981.

In 1976 a shocking documentary about prison life in Yorkshire had been shown on British television. It was disturbing for the time, packed with unpleasant men, their flabby minders and their rat-eyed friends. At the very heart of the doc was a man called Paul Sykes, a father, thief and bully, a notorious thug and a known pest in the Wakefield area. The cameras caught him lifting weights, swearing at screws and promising to win the British heavyweight title. He was released the following year and turned professional, at 31. 'I'm not a violent man but I am an expert at violence,' said Sykes.

There was interest in a fight with the British champion Joe Bugner, but Big Joe was a retired celeb in LA and by the time Sykes had fought a few times the champion was Gardner. In September 1978, Sykes raised his profile when he kept on hitting an unconscious American called David Wilson as he draped over the ropes. The Yorkshireman was dragged off snarling. In June 1979, the fight with Gardner was made for the Empire Pool. 'I will knock him out and then have seven hundred and fifty birds like Bugner,' said Sykes. The British champion had lost just once in thirty fights, Sykes had won six of his eight bouts. He could fight and he was popular, but 'smashing bouncers' had cost him too many of his good years. 'They all loved him,' said Tommy Miller, a manager and trainer with about fifty years of experience. 'Gangsters, petty villains and the police always bought tickets to watch Paul.'

At Wembley on the night it was a truly horrible mismatch. The referee needed to stop it long before Sykes turned his back in round six. The daddy of a dozen prison yards was ruined – a tough capitulation for a man once dubbed Britain's Hardest Man. Sykes was soon back in prison, and in 1990, when he was 44, it was calculated that he had spent twenty-one of twenty-six years behind bars. He died, living rough, in 2007, a heavyweight footnote and a cautionary warning to any loudmouth hard men.

In November, Kevin Finnegan came back from nowhere to put on a masterly display and beat Sibson over fifteen rounds to win back the British middleweight title. In the previous eighteen months Finnegan had lost four times, including twice to Marvin Hagler in Boston, and he had been winning and losing title fights for five hard years. It was one of the hardest careers of any British boxer in the seventies, and it was not finished yet. In 1980 he would have three European title fights – a win, a draw and a loss – in three different countries.

In September there had been ugly scenes at the Civic Hall in Wolverhampton when Nottingham's Dave Needham retained his British featherweight title against Warley's Pat Cowdell, a bronze medal winner from the 1976 Olympics. On the same bill as Finnegan's resurrection, Cowdell and Needham did it again, and Cowdell won. It is possible that this early November night was the last in Britain when two fifteen-round fights went fifteen rounds. Cowdell would box for nine more years and get two world title fights.

The world title plans of Dave Boy Green took a mad fall in June in Denmark against the veteran Jørgen Hansen. Green was 6-1 on with the bookies, defending his European welterweight title, and he forced Hansen to touch down in round two. Green and his corner were all smiles at the start of the third; the fight ended a couple of minutes later after Green was sent tumbling heavily twice, once face first. It was sudden.

In Nabburg and Stockstadt, two German towns briefly on the boxing map, Frank Bruno won twice for Young England against West Germany. Bruno fighting in the same week as Ken Buchanan, both in real fights and not novelty comebacks, seems like the odd passing of a baton. One a veteran, a man that started the seventies by winning the world title, and the other a big kid with heavy fists who ended the decade knocking out a German heavyweight. The parliament of British boxing was ready to open for a fresh decade, the old, the new, the ugly, the clearly lunatic and the golden all polishing their combinations.

The Contenders

At the start of April it was Kirkland Laing's chance to end his period of transition and move from fighter with promise to champion. Laing dropped Henry Rhiney nine times in total at the Arden Sporting Club, near Birmingham, before the end in round ten. Laing was the new British welterweight champion. Rhiney was paid just £2,600 for the loss; he had been paid £70,000 when beaten by Green a few months earlier. Laing had been known as the Whispering Welterweight by Terry Lawless. This ring moniker would get upgraded to the Gifted One, which he was. He was also close to impossible to control, contain and manage.

Buchanan ended his first year back in the ring by falling short in Copenhagen in a European lightweight title fight against Charlie Nash early in December. 'I thought I'd done enough,' said Buchanan. 'In the end I just got my money and got on with it. I knew by then the business was unforgiving.' Nash relinquished the title and agreed terms to fight Watt for the WBC belt.

From the Notepad

In May there was a mad amateur fight at the Café Royal in front of the silent diners. There had been whispers about the meeting, and on the day it was finally confirmed I travelled from the Fitzroy Lodge gym in Lambeth to the fight. I have no idea now, nearly forty years later, why there was such a fuss. In the ring, boxing over three rounds of three minutes, was Repton's Colin Derrick and Tottenham and District's Lloyd Morgan. Both had lost in their ABA final the year before. The fight had an edge to it, a feel of the underground, a sense that it was very special so few knew about it. Morgan won on points. They each turned pro, but that night was their night, and those of us crowded high above the chandeliers were part of some type of boxing brotherhood. It is odd that I still hold that 24 May date. It's written down; it passes from diary to diary.

When Green lost to Hansen, a friend of mine called Mohammad

Ali was on the undercard. He was from Ghana, based in north London, and cleaned shops for a living. Mighty Mo ended the year 4-4. I always thought he was about fifty, but it turns out he was only about twenty-two when I knew him.

In December the promoter Jack Solomons died. It was Solomons, with flair and style, who helped create modern boxing with fights like Sugar Ray Robinson against Randolph Turpin in 1951 and the first Cassius Clay and Henry Cooper fight at Wembley Stadium in 1963. Solomons had fallen out with the British Boxing Board of Control, and left just 1p to the Board from his boxing fortune.

The programme adverts for fights at the Royal Albert Hall included some gems. There was an invite to the Northumberland Arms, a pub just off the Walworth Road in south London, with a 'Top Ladies' Darts Team'. There was also an invite on the back to join Gary Duff, son of the promoter, matchmaker and international fight fixer, at the Spotted Dog in Willesden for a two-hour 'show with over 300 famous fights on 16mm film with sound'. The entry was a pound, and it was the only way to see ancient and modern greats.

1980

'Why you fucking about with that? Get a licence.'
Reporter Wally Bartleman to Frank Warren

'He does a better Howard Davis than Howard Davis does.'
Terry Lawless on Kirkland Laing's ability to mimic other boxers

ON A SUNDAY in March at Caesars Palace in Las Vegas Alan Minter's long wait for a world title fight came to an end.

It had been a troubling few years for the Munich Olympian and the scars ran deeper than the jagged marks on his eyebrows. Minter had killed Angelo Jacopucci, beaten Gratien Tonna in a bloody rematch, boxed the ears off fringe contenders and been ready for a world title fight for two or three years. 'Nothing came quick back then, you had to wait, and sometimes it never came at all,' said Minter. He had been promised the fight in July 1979. The unified world middleweight title was the prize, the Italian-American Vito Antuofermo was the champion, and Minter was his number one contender. Antuofermo had retained his title with a drawn verdict over Marvin Hagler the previous November. 'How the hell have I gotta fight my number one contender twice? How is that fair?' asked Antuofermo. Hagler had moaned that he deserved a rematch.

The fight could have been fought in an alley, and it's a miracle they both went fifteen rounds without bleeding out. Antuofermo closed Minter's early lead and it was torrid going into the last few rounds.

Vito had done the same with Hagler, mauling and brawling his way back into the fight. The decision was a split for Minter, which divided the ringside, the bookies, the experts and the fans. However, the real problem was the final score of British judge Roland Dakin: he gave Minter thirteen of the fifteen rounds. The Las Vegas judge went for Minter by four rounds, the Venezuelan for Antuofermo by two rounds. 'Dakin scored the fight like a Minter fan and that must not be allowed to happen again,' said Bob Arum, Hagler's promoter, who was still screaming about bad judges in Las Vegas over thirty years later. Dakin, in his defence, said that Vito was not hitting with the correct part of the glove. The rematch made sense.

In June, Antuofermo arrived in London. The Italian Bomber was marked when he landed, fresh from some secret sparring in Italy. It took him about ten seconds at the Empire Pool to try and butt Minter. The atmosphere was frightening, a sign of what was to come in Minter's next fight. 'The whole place is exploding with patriotism,' said Harry Carpenter. Minter boxed beautifully against the Wildman and cut him over the left eye in round one and over the right eye in round two. There was, no exaggerating, blood everywhere, and Minter smiled at his legal butchery when the bell went to end the second. Minter was brilliant, his timing quite sensational. In Las Vegas it had been a fight, at Wembley it was a bloody massacre. A man called Howie Albert performed tiny miracles during the sixty-second break with his magic swabs to keep Vito swinging and in the fight round after round. Minter stayed calm, slicing his punches across his opponent's brow with intent. Antuofermo tried a playful tap at the end of round five, Minter never responded. In 1976 Maurice Hope had stopped Antuofermo with just twelve seconds left in the fifteenth in their European title fight in Rome, Vito finishing that fight cut over both eyes and exhausted. It looked certain Minter would do something similar. Carpenter was asking where was the 'humanity in letting a man continue with cuts like that'. Albert kept working away, Minter kept hitting his man. In the seventh the ref called for an inspection of Antuofermo's multiple wounds by the British Boxing Board of Control's doctor. It looked all over, it should have been all over, and Minter raised his hands. It was not over, and with about a minute left in the round the bloodbath continued. It was barbaric. The corner finally called it off at the end of the eighth round. Minter remained middleweight champion of the world and the only unified title holder in the increasingly splintered business of boxing.

His year was not over, and the end would not be pleasant.

In September, Marvin Hagler arrived in London, settling down and training at Freddie Hill's gym in Lavender Hill. In another part of south London at the Thomas A'Becket, Minter was putting in the hard work. They were scheduled to meet at the Empire Pool, Wembley for the unified world middleweight title. The previous November Minter had stalked the casino floors in Las Vegas when Hagler had challenged Antuofermo for the title. The draw was harsh; it meant Hagler had to wait, and Minter left the desert city knowing he would get his crack. At Wembley, Antuofermo was ringside working for Italian television. It was a particularly nasty atmosphere long before the first bell. Kevin Finnegan, twice a loser on cuts to Hagler, had maintained that Hagler had said to him 'I don't touch white flesh'. Hagler countered, denied the charge and said he never shook any of his opponent's hands before a fight. Minter then claimed that Hagler had been unable to look him in the face when they were introduced in Las Vegas. Finnegan did a series of interviews, attacking Hagler. 'I hate him, he's a bully, he's arrogant, and I rate him one of the dirtiest boxers I ever met.' Minter stood accused of saying that he did not intend 'to lose to a black man'. There are several versions of this, all said to have come from the same conversation. In the one that appeared in the *Daily Mirror* in August, Minter claimed he had said 'that black man'. It was not pleasant, but it pleased morons, and many bought tickets and beer; reliable writers talked about punters having cases of beer. There was a 'rancid smell of racism' in the air, as Carpenter remarked.

The fight was in many ways over after about thirty seconds when a Hagler jab opened up a cut under Minter's left eye. In the second and third rounds, one above that eye and one next to his right eye were opened. Minter tried to fight his way back – the second was sensational – but Hagler had been constructed over hard nights against many dirty, desperate men fighting in front of their fans; he stayed calm and stayed nasty. In round three the referee took Minter to his corner for an inspection, the smeared blood was wiped away, and Doug Bidwell, his manager, trainer and father-in-law, nodded to the referee to stop the fight.

The first bottles and cans started to land in the ring three seconds later, their spray forming shining arcs under the ring's neon lights. Hagler's people quickly formed a human shield over him as he sank to his knees; people were getting hit with missiles from all sides as they bundled him through the ropes. Reg Gutteridge was clipped by a hardback copy of Minter's autobiography, which he threw to the ground in disgust. (Copies of the forgotten book now sell for over fifty quid on Amazon, something that would have tickled Gutteridge.) Carpenter took a bottle on the head. It was very frightening. 'Marvin beat the shit out of him, and when they finally stopped the fight because of the cuts, they went crazy and started throwing bottles,' said Arum. Hagler made it back to the dressing room, surrounded by police. Antuofermo grabbed American boxing writer George Kimball, who covered Hagler like a religion, by the arm and started to lead him to safety. Some fool hit Vito with a bottle; the fighter turned and connected with one shot to take the guy out clean. 'It was perhaps the best punch Vito ever threw,' said Kimball.

Minter was paid $480,000, he needed fifteen stitches to close his wounds, and his world title days were gone, buried under a fusillade of bottles, heavy debris and shame. And one unwanted autobiography.

'It was one of those punches that you see coming and then a split second later you are on the floor,' said John Conteh after losing his rematch to Matthew Saad Muhammad in March. Conteh was over five times in round four, leaving the referee no option but to call a halt. Muhammad caught him on the ears, gloves, top of the head and side of the chin. Conteh sounded fine, but he was disturbingly distant when sweet old Reg Gutteridge got to him in the ring for an interview. Reg had doubted the power of the American's punches, but had added that he was not the one 'taking them, Conteh is'. Muhammad received a record for a light-heavyweight title fight of $448,305 and Conteh was paid $366,795 for the loss. Before the rematch Muhammad's cornermen Adolph Ritacco and Nick Belfiore were suspended for using an illegal concoction to close Muhammad's left eye in the first fight.

Those are the raw facts, this is the story of the fight. Conteh went through some type of breakdown, having arguments with himself during the rounds. There were crazy conversations going on in his head, and each time he went down those conversations continued and intensified. He was not fit to box, not fit to be risking his life in a boxing ring. 'I never wanted to be on the floor in that fight, I kept thinking I should be out drinking champagne,' said Conteh. 'It was like I was not there getting hit.' After the fight, and after drinking for a day, he had to be tackled and restrained when he was running naked down the hotel corridor by George Francis, his long-suffering trainer, manager and friend. Francis tied him to a bed with sheets and Conteh fell into a deep sleep. Francis just sat there in the dark, within touching distance of his greatest fighter, now sleeping peacefully on the very edge of a lethal abyss.

On the Monday after Conteh's loss, Dave Boy Green was matched with welterweight world champion Sugar Ray Leonard in Maryland. It was an improbable and historic fourth world title fight, three of them in America, involving a British boxer in one month. The Fleet Street pack had been on a long jolly, and in 1980 a travelling three-week press corps was a handful. They had an easy night with Leonard, the Olympic golden boy and rent-a-quote machine. Green had been in some gruelling fights and knew how to beat Leonard; he chased the American for every second of the fight until the end in round four. 'I just prayed that he would get up and was not dead,' said Leonard. He never celebrated. The doctors fanned Green with a towel, a magic towel. The rush to lift Green up from his unconscious position was obscene. Green was placed on a stool, his head still rolling crazily, his eyes a cartoon blur, and people tried to talk to him. Leonard was announced as the winner and still he never celebrated. 'I have never been so scared,' he said. The final left hook was the best punch Sugar Ray ever threw. Leonard received $1.5 million for the fight and admitted that he wanted to hurt Green after the British boxer had pushed him and put his head in his face during the introductions. 'I asked Davey once why he did it,' said Leonard. 'He told me it was an attempt to "intimidate me". I told him that backfired and all he did was piss me off.'

After the fight there was another knockout when the historically well-connected Angelo Dundee, Leonard's chief second, was hit and dropped by Pepe Correa, an irascible character, who had worked with Leonard in Maryland for years. A mob summit was called, according to legend, and Correa was spared. Fifteen years later Pepe, the street guy, took over the training duties for Lennox Lewis. The man known as the Blade had not mellowed. I liked his reign, it was mental.

The Gifted One, as Kirkland Laing was known, was paid nine grand for his British welterweight defence against Colin Jones. It was his highest purse to date. He had sparred at the Royal Oak with Green before the Leonard fight, which was ideal preparation for Green. 'Kirk was as close to Sugar Ray Leonard as anybody in this country's ever been,' Green told Laing's biographer Oliver Jarratt. Green's pressure was also good for Laing before the Jones fight. Laing liked to spar and often that is all he would do. 'Nah, man, the training is boring,' Laing said repeatedly. There had also been an altercation in the gym and Lawless had banned him for a bit: a sparring session with Jimmy Batten had continued after the bell and the pair had had to be separated as they kicked and hit each other on the floor. 'There were times when I hated him and times when I loved him,' said Batten. Meanwhile, Jones had hired a fighter called Achille 'Speedy' Mitchell from Coventry as a sparring partner. Mitchell knew Laing well, never liked him and was an ostentatious ringside guest, splendid in a fedora, shades and a velvet number with about ten inches of collar. It was a flashy show that would irk Kirk. It was more than just a visual ploy: Mitchell stayed in a guest house near the gym in Wales for a month.

It was all Laing for eight rounds. The score was something like six or seven rounds to him with one even; Laing was dancing his way to the win. 'After about nine rounds Colin tears you apart,' Mitchell had said before the fight. In round nine a right connected and Laing's gumshield flew out, ending up in the third row of seats. Laing stumbled, glaring and scared, tried to grab the ropes; he was hit with an elbow, more rights, and then a succession of short left hooks. It was stopped, it was over. 'I knew he would go,' said Jones. Laing was broken, kept behind a closed door by a clearly rattled Lawless. 'How could I lose to a man like that, how?' Laing asked his friend Dave Armstrong, another Hackney fighter from the Lawless stable. Armstrong was a face, Laing was more fool than rogue. 'There was nothing we could say to him, he was totally gutted,' said Armstrong.

At the start of March the euphoric embrace at the end of Jim Watt's second defence of his WBC lightweight title, between the boxer and Terry Lawless, summed up the relief at the win. Derry's Charlie Nash was caught with inch-perfect left crosses three times in the fourth and final round to end a short but thrilling night in Glasgow's Kelvin Hall. Watt had been dumped heavily in the opening round from a short right, which caught him slightly off balance and clearly hurt him. Watt took over in the second, had Nash cut and broken by the end of the third, and then viciously closed the show. It was the first time two British boxers had fought for a world title since 1949. The pitiful lament of Northern Irish gold-medal-winning heptathlete Mary Peters, at ringside that night, can be heard over the commentary in the final seconds: 'Oh Charlie, oh Charlie.'

'Jim who? What's his name? Jim who?' asked Howard Davis Jr when he arrived in Glasgow for his WBC lightweight title fight with Watt in June. Davis, who had won the gold medal and the Val Barker trophy for best boxer at the Olympics in Montreal, had fought just thirteen times. In 1974 he won the inaugural world amateur championship in Havana, breaking the stranglehold of the Cuban hosts and the Soviet system. He turned pro on $185,000 per fight – more than the other American gold medal winners Leonard and the Spinks brothers Michael and Leon. He was a gifted, teetotal, vegetarian maverick and looked confident when he entered the ring in the wet and wind and cold at Ibrox, the home of Watt's team Rangers. The weather kept the crowd to 12,000, a disappointment. Watt was a few days away from 32, but he had hardened even further during the lucrative twilight of his world championship months. It was a real fight and Watt retained with a tight but clear unanimous decision. Davis was criticized, which seems harsh considering how tough Watt was, how inexperienced Davis was, the location and the bad conditions. Duff had secured home advantage with a big purse bid, which he personally delivered to José Sulaimán's WBC office in Mexico City. He won the bid, Watt fought in Glasgow, and the Davis team of Dennis Rappaport and Mike Jones, known in boxing as the Wacko Twins, were sick. The Wacko act did their best in Glasgow to undermine the show, complaining about everything, but had to sit, wet, miserable and in increasing silence, as Watt jabbed their investment to defeat. Davis never won a world title, which remains one of boxing's great mysteries.

The fighter himself, his dad, his grandma, his corner, American television broadcasters and some neutrals were screaming after Watt stopped the American Sean O'Grady. The bloodbath took place back at the Kelvin Hall in November. The O'Grady bunch had arrived in force, and they moaned and moaned. There was even a claim that a death threat had been phoned in. (O'Grady had posed in a Celtic shirt, so the death threat was probably true.) It was a third successful WBC lightweight title defence for the Scot in 1980. Watt was nearly ruled out in the ninth with a cut, and in the eleventh and twelfth rounds a gash on O'Grady's forehead was inspected. Ringside guests covered their faces when the boxers were above them on the ropes: the blood was flying everywhere. O'Grady was blinded by his own blood, swinging wildly and being hurt by the spiteful champion. The referee ignored the towel from O'Grady's corner before finally ending the mess in the twelfth. 'Watt should have been thrown out for butting,' screamed Pat O'Grady, the boxer's ex-fighter dad. Pat was also his son's matchmaker and he had managed to get his son a record of seventy-three wins in seventy-four fights, with sixty-five ending quick. The cut, which needed eleven stitches, saved O'Grady from a potentially more punishing loss. Watt was in front on all three score-cards when it ended. It was his last win as a boxer.

There was another world championship rematch in July when Rocky Mattioli met Maurice Hope for the WBC light-middleweight title at the Conference Centre, Wembley. Mattioli's broken wrist had healed, he went a few more rounds, but Hope stopped him in the eleventh. Hope was a long way in front at the time and had boxed a perfect fight, destructive at times to break Rocky's will. Arthur Mercante, the American referee, intervened just before it became uncomfortable to watch. The Americans, led by Howard Cosell, loved it. 'Maurice Hope is giving Rocky Mattioli a tremendous beating, a tremendous beating,' Cosell told his flock. Three British boxers, all southpaws, had retained world titles in the space of just thirty-five days and they had all won with fine exhibitions of the noble art.

At Wembley in the last few days of November it was Hope again. He had survived the surgeon's knife, been ripped off in his first world title fight in Berlin, and was now being mentioned alongside Sugar Ray Leonard. There was $700,000 on the table for the Leonard fight; Lawless asked for a million; Leonard moved on, and had his rematch with Roberto Durán the night before Hope's latest defence. Hope had been in that mix. The Durán–Leonard fight from the early hours of that morning was shown on screens – six of them – after the boxing. It was a messy experiment, it never worked. In 1980 it would have been easy to avoid the result from the 'No Más' fiasco.

Hope won comfortably against a stone-faced fighter from the seemingly endless line of tough Argentinian boxers. Carlos Herrera went the full fifteen rounds and gave Hope a real test in a purist's outing. Life was about to get even more difficult for Hope.

Two boxers met each other again at Wembley in June, but not in the ring. Johnny Owen retained his British and Commonwealth bantamweight titles against previously unbeaten John Feeney, and Charlie Magri stopped Italian Giovanni Camputaro in his European flyweight defence. After their wins the pair sat chatting, and agreed they should fight. But first Owen had a fight planned in Los Angeles.

On 12 September at 2.15 p.m. Owen and his father Dick arrived in California for Owen's bantamweight world title fight against the Mexican Lupe Pintor. They shared a room at the Gala Motor Hotel in a part of Los Angeles that only the brave, the homeless and the addicted knew. The tiny travelling party of Welshmen, refugees from a tough but gentle lifestyle in Merthyr Tydfil, were in alien territory, and at the Olympic Auditorium in Little Mexico a sell-out of 10,000 Pintor fans awaited their arrival in the ring. It was full to capacity, possibly overflowing illegally on the night. It was that type of place. In Owen's dressing room the noise of the crowd chanting 'Lupe, Lupe, Lupe' was a distant, disturbing rumble. Owen, Dick and Dai Gardiner, his manager and chief trainer, were joined by the rest of the fight corner, Ken Bryant and Nat Nicholls. Owen, as is common with boxers in big fights, was the calmest man in the room. The walk to the ring was difficult. The crowd's hostility was not a pantomime of noise. 'Johnny had no nerves at all and I was a very proud man,' said Dick.

The Merthyr Matchstick Man, a fighter so improbably slim that he wore his bruises like a badge of honour because they proved he was a fighter, was trailing on all three scorecards when the fight ended at 2:25 of round twelve. Owen had been swallowing his own blood from a cut inside his bottom lip from round five, he'd been over heavily in the ninth, and dropped twice in the twelfth. The final knockdown is the single most disturbing image in British boxing history; I have watched it back for you, so please avoid it. Owen was out cold on the blood-stained canvas, and the fight to save him started immediately. Somebody tried to revive poor Johnny with smelling salts. There was no resuscitation equipment, no trained trauma personnel. The stretcher was ancient, Johnny's body placed on it like an equally ancient peaceful sacrifice and then raised by the men chosen to carry him from the ring for the last time. Dick was one of the bearers – it was the only way to stay close to his beloved son; it was also the only way to get the boy from the ring. Dick had $300 stolen from his pocket and was, along with the other men carrying the boxer, splattered with empty beer cups filled with urine. The cheers and jeers of the Little Mexico faithful were relentless as the shattered Welsh party pushed their way to an ambulance.

The body of Johnny Owen was first operated on at the Lutheran Hospital on Hope Street at 11.30 p.m. on 19 September. The first operation was four hours long. He was in a coma, and the vigil on Hope Street started. Two days later his mother, Edith, arrived at her son's bedside. Dick and Edith remained there until his death on 4 November. Owen was 24. In Mexico City, the tiny fighter Pintor wept. In 2002 he would finally meet Dick.

Bunny Johnson completed a unique double when he won the British light-heavyweight title. He had been the British heavyweight champion and a pro since 1968. Johnson had struggled against all sorts of prejudice and taken just about any fight on offer. In the summer of 1979 he had gone behind bars in America to fight James Scott, a celebrity prisoner whose fights were screened live on American television. Johnson was paid $20,000 for the experience and was pulled out at the end of seven rounds. 'Scott was a very rude man,' Johnson told me one afternoon in 2015 at one of Ron Gray's boxing lunches in Birmingham. At the time of the Scott payday, Johnson should have fought for a world title or two.

Dennis Andries was cut from the same unfashionable cloth as Johnson. Andries had ducked and dived his way from Harry Griver's notorious Colvestone club in London's East End, turned pro in boxing's backwaters and first been matched in a non-title fight with Johnson a year earlier. Johnson won that, but the novice survived the distance. 'Dennis is a fierce young man, fierce and fearless,' Johnson said.

They met in February under the twinkling lights of a Staffordshire dance palace and Johnson defended his British title for the last time when he beat Andries over fifteen rounds. Johnson had five more after the Andries win and they were all overseas. He finished in Brisbane in September 1981, his fourteenth loss in sixty-five fights; he weighed 184lb, just 4lb more than he had weighed for his debut in 1968 and 16lb inside the modern cruiserweight limit. He would have ruled the earth in the cruiserweight division had it existed when he was fighting. Andries did finally get some breaks and won a world title.

In December, Frank Warren promoted his first professional show as a Board licence holder. He had been putting on shows under the auspices of the NBC, lively shows featuring the old, the young, the faded and the notorious. It was Wally Bartleman, the hero of the first George Foreman and Joe Frazier fight, who pulled him to one side, grabbed his arm, leaned in close to his ear and said, 'Why you fucking about with that? Get a licence.' Warren listened to the old journalist. He was given a licence the first time of asking, but Nipper Read, a prominent Board member and often credited with capturing the boxing twins Ron and Reg Kray, resigned. The main event at the Bloomsbury Crest Hotel, near Russell Square in London, was world-ranked Philadelphia light-heavyweight Jerry Martin. In May, Martin had gone behind bars at Rahway prison, New Jersey, to inflict the first loss on James Scott, the prison celebrity. On Warren's show Martin stopped American Otis Gordon in seven. 'It was terrible, a boring fight, but I was off, it was the start,' said Warren in 2011.

The Contenders

John L. Gardner defended his European heavyweight title twice, once at the Royal Albert Hall and once in Italy. Big John stopped Lorenzo Zanon in five rounds in Lombardia; nine months earlier Zanon lost a WBC heavyweight title fight to Larry Holmes in six rounds. 'I never got a sniff at a world title,' said Gardner.

At the old Empire Pool, Wembley at the start of May a couple of future world champions won ABA titles. Terry Marsh, once of St George's in Stepney, won at welter representing the Royal Navy, and at just 18 Frank Bruno beat Rudi Pika in a nine-minute brawl. Bruno turned pro after the win with Terry Lawless and Mickey Duff but would not be cleared to fight until March 1982. Pika was five months younger than Bruno and also turned pro. He won thirteen without loss on Duff shows, but personal problems led to him walking away after a win over Glenn McCrory in April 1986. Three months later

Bruno lost a world title fight. Pika, a neglected product of the Cardiff docks, committed suicide in 1988 when he was 26. Eleven months later McCrory won a world title.

Kevin Finnegan won the European middleweight title in Paris, defended in Munich and lost it in Italy. Tony Sibson then won it from Matteo Salvemini in London. The European title was always considered a legitimate belt to hold and one that was often difficult to keep.

From the Notepad

It has become a legend, some think it is myth, but the Night of the Tijuana Tumblers actually happened. It took place at the Royal Albert Hall in October when four Mexicans were flattened in a total of just seven rounds. All four of the hapless imports, often referred to as Mexican Road Sweepers, had losing records. The winners were Dave Boy Green in two, Charlie Magri in one, Jimmy Flint in two and Cornelius Boza-Edwards in two. Flint never had a world title fight, but the other three had ten in total. Señores Mendez, Castro, López and Torres never had a chance.

The Wapping Assassin, Jimmy Flint, was still moaning about Pat Cowdell's tactics in 2016. 'I came to have a fight, I wanted to have a fight – he never wanted to know,' Flint said. Cowdell retained his British featherweight title when he beat Flint at the Royal Albert Hall in February. Flint was a major part of Ron Peck's outstanding film *Fighters*. The documentary was first shown on Channel Four in 1992. Flint's performance in his mum's front room is brilliant.

1981

'You're not going to win on the floor, son. You've got to get up to win it.'
John Coyle to Colin Jones, after the Welshman had been hit low

'Ali has been making money for fighters all over the world and now it's time for him to make some money for me.'
John L. Gardner on his planned fight with the Greatest

MAURICE HOPE WENT out to Las Vegas in May to defend his WBC light-middleweight title against Wilfredo Benítez of Puerto Rico. It was a money fight.

Benítez, 22, had first won a world title at light-welter when he was 17, and had added the welterweight version when he beat Carlos Palomino. His only loss in forty-three fights was against Sugar Ray Leonard. Hope accepted the fight for £270,000 and travelled out to the Caesars Palace Sports Pavilion, an ugly building that was in the shadow of the hotel (twenty years later it was demolished and replaced by a sprawling pool area, including, briefly, a topless 'continental experience').

Hope was in his sixth world title fight, his fourth defence of the belt. The fight was tight for about nine rounds; Benítez had a good sixth, Hope had a good ninth. In the tenth, it changed. Hope was dropped by a right, which thankfully landed on the side of his cheek and not flush on his jaw. The flash knockdown was close to the bell and Hope looked a forlorn figure as he sat during the minute-long reprieve. The eleventh was hard for Hope, but he survived and walked back to his corner, very slowly, when the bell sounded. He was a broken and beaten man.

Hope lost two teeth in the twelfth when Benítez caught him with a sickening right hand and sent him down, flat on his back, for the full count. He was out, hurt bad, and the smelling salts and desperate words from Terry Lawless at first had no effect. He did finally wake and insisted on walking to the ambulance and not going out on a stretcher. 'Please, don't do that to me, man.' Benítez celebrated throughout these disturbing moments, with Hope in the ring hurt, and then he mocked the British champion at the press conference. Benítez was a great boxer but a rotten human. Hope spent the night in hospital, where one of the visitors was Jim Jacobs, manager of Benítez and the man that guided Mike Tyson to the world title a few years later. Lawless took the loss bad. The following day, after an all-clear from the doctors, Hope married his long-time partner, Pat, at the Imperial Palace on the Vegas strip. It was just across the road from Caesars, and Lawless was the best man. Hope had just one more fight.

In June the setting was Wembley – the Arena now and no longer the Empire Pool – for Jim Watt's fifth defence of his WBC lightweight title. Alexis Argüello was the man in the opposite corner and it was a technical, ultimately gruelling and gripping fight. Watt was cut, bloody, swallowing blood and badly marked by the Nicaraguan's accurate punches. He was also dropped in the seventh. Argüello, like Benítez, was going for a third world title, and he had to fight every second of the forty-five minutes of boxing. The final embrace is a reminder of what should happen when two good fighters conclude their business. Lawless towelled Watt's face during the wait for the verdict, and he knew. Watt also knew. He was a true fighter, an honest man, and that was his last fight. Jim Watt won thirty-eight fights and lost eight times, including three debatable decisions on the road, three by cuts and once in a British title fight to Ken Buchanan.

'He was a good boxer with a good heart,' Argüello said. 'He wanted to prove to his people that he was a good champion, and he did.' The victor's life ended in a mess, his wealth confiscated by the Nicaraguan government and his reputation hurt by painful comebacks. He did finally return to his homeland and became mayor of Managua, but drugs, corruption and the memory of his great nights in the ring haunted him. In 2009 he shot himself through the heart.

In the summer of 1980 Mickey Duff had taken a risk with Cornelius Boza-Edwards, the kid from Kampala who lived in Harrow and had boxed for the Fitzroy Lodge as an amateur, and agreed a ten-round non-title fight with Argüello. Duff had believed in Boza for years, talked about his progress and predicted hard, hard fights before he became a champion. He was his matchmaker, so he had some say in his prediction coming true. Argüello was the WBC super-feather champion at the time. Duff pulled Boza out after seven rounds. 'It was the fight that made him,' Duff said. It was shown live in America on ABC. Argüello complained that Boza was so tough he had hurt his hands hitting his head.

Argüello vacated the title, Rafael 'Bazooka' Limón had won it, and in March 1981 Boza was his first defence. It went the full fifteen rounds at the Civic Center in Stockton, California. Boza was the world champion, and he looked like a world champion in his white boots and white shorts with the letters CBE on the black trim. He fought like one of the exotic names that held world titles and he'd beaten a slick Mexican called Bazooka. He did an Ali shuffle and called-in Limón in round fourteen. In round fifteen the pair put on a fight that defined the dictionary definition of toe-to-toe. It was a truly great round. Boza had started in 1976 at the Anglo-American Sporting Club in Mayfair, but he was never going to finish there. Boza was Las Vegas. After the final bell he paraded around the ring on the shoulders of George Francis while Duff got busy and tried to get an idea of the score. There was a dreadful delay before Boza was given a tight unanimous decision. He then got on Duff's shoulders. And it was only at that point that the penniless refugee from Idi Amin's Uganda cried. 'It was all a dream, all a dream,' said Boza.

The venue for Boza's first defence was the Showboat Hotel and Casino, never one of the gambling city's best retreats. It was the type of place where old women sucked on their last cigarette, invested their last quarter and dragged their oxygen tanks through a battle-field of one-armed bandits like they knew they were on a death mission. It was the right place for Boza against California's Bobby Chacon. It was called off by Chacon's corner at the end of round thir-teen. He was severely cut over the left eye; Chacon had been told before the bell for the thirteenth that he only had one more round. Boza was in front, but he had been wobbled; Chacon, a former champion at feather, was dangerous. 'He hurt me in the ninth, I felt my legs go,' said Boza at the end, his accent a bizarre mix of Duff and other London fight figures. 'I just had to stand there and prove to him that I was the champion.' The pair would meet again in 1983 in a fight considered the best of the year by *The Ring*. Chacon made a career out of truly exceptional fights and it cost him his life. He died in 2016 and had been suffering from dementia for too long.

The end of Boza's reign as world champion, a mad period of just over five months, came at the end of August in Italy, of all places. Duff was a wise boxing man, a genius at fixing fights at the right time, but he got it wrong with Boza's second defence. He talked about Boza being like a son and he was probably telling the truth. In Tuscany, Boza was stopped by Filipino Rolando Navarrete, who was a durable fighter but not in the same league as Limón or Chacon, in five rounds. Boza was flat in the ring, dropped twice, and would never win a world title again. His short reign, and the loss the previous August to Argüello, is one of the most brutal sequences of fights by any British boxer. Limón beat Navarrete the following May, and Navarrete had been extremely fortunate in his first defence when an early end to a round saved him after being knocked down. Navarrete did have a beauty of a nickname: he was known as the Bad Boy from Dadiangas.

In 2016 Boza was living in Las Vegas and working as part of Floyd Mayweather's Money Team. 'I still miss Mickey,' he told me in 2015.

The Laing–Jones rematch was fiery. The Welshman was dropped by a low punch in the eighth round and was given twenty-six seconds to recover, adjust his foul protector and have a little count. John

Coyle, the referee, gave Laing a talking-to and then the fight continued. Laing landed another suspect punch, a right on the left hip rather than a groin foul, and this time there was a thirty-eight-second gap to allow Jones to get his breath back. The infringements, the referee's lectures and the bad blood between the pair since their fight the year before incited a volatile crowd. 'I've not seen scenes like it for years,' said Henry Cooper at ringside. The British and Commonwealth welterweight titles were the prize that April at the Royal Albert Hall, but Colin Jones against Kirkland Laing was never about leather and gold belts. They disliked each other, they were different fighting beasts, and round eight of their rematch was shocking. Coyle decided not to disqualify Laing and had a word with Jones: 'You're not going to win on the floor, son. You've got to get up to win it.' Harry Gibbs, the ex-docker, World War Two prisoner and no-nonsense referee of the seventies, would have been proud of that line.

In round nine Jones took control, digging in borderline left hooks to the body and pushing Laing back. Laing had prepared like he had never done before, sparring with Maurice Hope, who had a world title defence in May, at the Royal Oak. 'The loss hurt Kirk, he could never work it out, and for once he was motivated,' said Lawless. In the ninth, Laing was fading, gasping for air, before a perfect left hook dropped him heavily. Laing landed on his side, rolled over, somehow got up and then fell back into the ropes. His fight was done – Laing beaten in the ninth again, a repeat of the loss from 1980. Two years later Jones would get a world title chance; the following year Laing would beat Roberto Durán in a non-title fight in Detroit.

Peter Eubanks, the brother of Chris, ended 1981 with a professional record of four wins and five defeats, one of the wins against previously unbeaten Barry McGuigan in August. 'It was a hometown decision,' insisted McGuigan. 'He was brave but I beat him from pillar to post.' McGuigan's unbeaten record was gone, finished at two. There was a rematch, in December in Belfast, McGuigan won, and in 1985 he fought for a world title. Eubanks – there was another boxing brother called Simon, Peter's twin – fought until 1991 when he retired, leaving the sport after thirty-five fights, including fourteen wins, the most high-profile of which was that eight-round decision over young Finbar McGuigan at the Corn Exchange in Brighton. 'Honestly, his own fans howled at the decision,' added McGuigan. The fighting Eubanks twins never had any fans.

Alan Minter had let his scars heal, returned with a win on points at Wembley in March, and then dropped a split in Las Vegas to Mustafa Hamsho in June. He was facing the end. The last rites on a brilliant career were read when he met Tony Sibson at Wembley in September for the European middleweight title. Minter had won the same title four years earlier in Italy, Sibson had just defended it in Spain in May. Minter was 30, had a face that had been stitched closed dozens of times and a career that had been tarnished by the comments about Marvin Hagler. Sibson was 23. It was another torrid, emotional night with trumpets, flags and a crowd ready for a fight. They still loved Minter. A light-beam from the sky illuminated each boxer's entrance. Sibson struggled to look at his hero during the introductions and with his long hair he looked so young. They had sparred, Minter had paid.

Sibson was just too fast, his punches looping in behind Minter's high guard. The first and second were quality rounds; Minter with his sharp counters looked good, but he was not hurting Sibson. In round three a left hook hurt Minter early and then another left hook dumped him on his hands and knees. He jumped up too quick, was caught with a vicious right uppercut that turned his body, and then a final left hook dropped him for the last time in his career. It was over. Minter sat on the canvas, his nose split, a smile on his face. Sibson looked a little bit embarrassed.

At the Royal Albert Hall in November it was the end for Dave Boy Green. It was not a happy ending. Green was stopped by Reggie Ford at the end of the fifth and during the usual cleaning up, comforting, celebrating melee in the ring his manager and trainer, Andy Smith, took the microphone and told the punters that it was Dave's last fight. Green, realizing too late what was happening, turned and said, 'You bastard.' The applause of the crowd drowned out the boxer's complaint. Green's turn on the microphone was tearful. He was 28, had won thirty-seven of his forty-one fights. Ford entered the ring having won eight and lost seven with one draw, and returned to the old venue the following February to beat Laing, who was a late replacement for Hope. Laing and Green, incidentally, met four times as amateurs and Green won three of the four. Kirk always wanted a fight as a professional with Green.

In December, Pat Cowdell travelled to Houston, Texas to fight Mexico's Salvador Sánchez for the WBC featherweight title. Sánchez had lost just once in forty-three fights and was fresh from a stoppage win against Wilfredo Gómez in Las Vegas; Gómez was unbeaten in thirty-three fights at the time and considered one of the world's best fighters. Cowdell entered the ring having won and lost the British title and with medals at the Olympics, the Commonwealth Games and the European championship as an amateur. Cowdell was the only British boxer considered as a candidate for the inaugural world championship in Havana back in 1975.

In Houston, against crazy odds and at the end of a bad year for Britain's best, Cowdell lost a split decision to Sánchez, surviving a last-round knockdown. It is one of the fights that is forgotten when Cowdell and the eighties are discussed: too many people remember his 144-second knockout loss to Azumah Nelson in another world title fight in 1985. It is harsh on Cowdell. Nelson, by the way, was stopped by Sánchez with just seventy-one seconds left in the fifteenth and last round in Madison Square Garden in 1982. One judge had Nelson in front. One day in 1994 at Nelson's home in Accra, Ghana, I sat and watched his fight with Sánchez. 'Mickey [Duff] was telling me not to try too hard, can you believe that?' he told me. 'I could have won that title if I had just known a bit more.' Duff was a fixer for the Garden and evidently the kid from Ghana, having just his fourteenth fight, was not meant to mess with the grand plans for Sánchez. It made no real difference, and just five months later, at the age of 23, Sánchez died in a crash. He left behind a floating asterisk which is attached to any other choice as the best Mexican boxer. Nelson is Africa's greatest fighter.

Bunny Johnson had been fighting in Australia throughout the

year, winning two and losing two, and in December he was stripped of his British light-heavyweight title, which he had last defended in Staffordshire in February 1980. Johnson's final fight was a loss to Steve Aczel in September. Johnson was a genuine pioneer for black fighters in Britain, the first black British heavyweight champion, a man that had to wait patiently for eligibility to fight for the domestic title and a man so cruelly denied even one world title fight. How, in late 2016, he has still not managed to receive recognition from the Queen is one of boxing's deepest mysteries. Johnson finished with fifty-five wins from seventy-three contests. He fought in now extinct heavyweight competitions where the prize money was measured in guineas, on a Muhammad Ali undercard, behind bars at a maximum security prison, and in British venues so obscure they are now wiped from maps, and he left the sport without any sense of bitterness at never getting the opportunities he deserved.

The Contenders

It was nearly the end for Ken Buchanan in January when he lost a final eliminator for the British light-welterweight title to Steve Early in Edgbaston. He had three fights left under the British Boxing Board of Control's regulations, he lost the lot, and then it turned bad.

Also in January, Lloyd Honeyghan won his second fight and finished the year five and zero; at the Royal Albert Hall the same week Mark Kaylor had a simple win and ended the year ten and zero. Kaylor was popular, an ABA champion in 1980 from West Ham, and nine of his first ten fights were at either the Albert Hall or Wembley.

One of Conteh's old opponents had another crack at the British heavyweight title. Billy Aird, a future publican at the boxing boozer Thomas A'Becket in the Old Kent Road, had lost to Conteh in 1972; in March 1981 he lost over fifteen rounds to Gordon Ferris for the vacant title. He had lost to John L. Gardner for the same title in 1978. Aird had had his first eliminator for the British heavyweight title in 1973. They were certainly patient lumps at the time. Conteh always insisted that Aird had one of the two best chins he ever hit. The other belonged to Jorge Ahumada, whom Conteh beat for the world title in 1974.

From the Notepad

Terry Lawless, Mickey Duff, Jarvis Astaire and Mike Barrett had their successful cartel flying. Duff called it 'an incoming sharing agreement'. Frank Warren had been a licence holder less than three months and he was determined to expose and then break the cartel. 'It was just wrong, nobody could get a fair deal,' Warren said. The British Boxing Board of Control disagreed and declared the arrangement legal. 'Duff did every possible thing he could to keep me from being a success,' Warren added. 'I did every possible thing I could to make him lose sleep. As soon as I got him ranting and raving I was happy, and it was easy to get him ranting and raving.'

'The Viking' was Steve Foster, and he had his first fight in February. He finally quit in 1999 and his fans, who wore plastic horned hats, sent a burning barge down a canal in Salford to celebrate his retirement. He once lost when he was so drunk he could barely stand, but he beat some very good fighters and fought a great boxer for a world title in 1997. 'I only started because I needed a few quid, it just went a bit mad from then,' said Foster. His son Stephen Jr also fought for different versions of the world title.

1982

'The Durán fight was the only one where I gave up drugs and concentrated.'
Kirkland Laing

*'The selectors got it wrong, I would have won gold in Brisbane. It's just
one of the things boxing teaches you – it teaches you to be patient
and to expect some idiot in a blazer to try and ruin your life.'*
John Hyland on not being selected for the Commonwealth Games

IT HAD ALL started for Ken Buchanan at the National Sporting Club in London's Piccadilly in 1965, and that is exactly where it ended in January. He lost for the fourth time on the spin when, having accepted the fight at three days' notice, he was beaten over eight rounds by George Feeney.

Ken needed the money. The Ken Buchanan Hotel in Edinburgh had been lost in 1980, money had been taken from the boxer, and he had been duped by two people. In 1981 he had started accepting fights in desperation; Feeney was his last official outing with a British Boxing Board of Control licence. Buchanan had started the modern British boxing revolution in 1970 on a stormy hot afternoon in Puerto Rico when he won the world title. 'I said a few words and that was it,' Buchanan claimed when asked about his last fight. He deserved better. In 1983 he was back on the pirate circuit at a nightclub in east London and then York Hall, Bethnal Green. Buchanan was skint, the cash was welcome. He beat two good men in Johnny Claydon and Jimmy Revie, both quality professionals like Buchanan. He split three grand with Claydon in their fight at the Palais in Ilford. Revie had been the British featherweight champion and Claydon had lost a British title fight to Jim Watt. Buchanan won both and walked away again. In 2016 he admitted that he had started to take a pad and pen with him everywhere he went to help with his memory.

Brendan Ingle wanted Herol 'Bomber' Graham to be an attraction away from the bright lights of the big city and the men that operated their cosy cartel of legal convenience. Graham, who was from Nottingham originally, was the first proper product of the Ingle gym in the Wincobank area, a hill with houses on the outskirts of Sheffield; Johnny Nelson, Naseem Hamed and then Kell Brook followed during the next thirty-five years. Brendan, the exiled Dubliner, was still whispering away in 2016, still crossing the road from his house to the ring in the gym. In early 2017, at the special wake for Dennis Hobson Sr, Ingle was receiving guests at his table for hours. 'He gets tired, but he is doing OK,' said Amer Khan, who was known as Killa Khan and retired unbeaten after thirteen, one of the many fighters Brendan had from a child to a man. Killa was thirty-five that night, a fireman, but he still spends time with the man that changed his life.

Graham had won the British light-middleweight title in March 1981, stopping Cardiff's Pat Thomas, and defended in February against Stoke Newington's Chris Christian; in between he'd added the Commonwealth version – all in fights at the City Hall in Sheffield. 'We sold out on the shows in Sheffield and everybody did their bit to make them a success,' said Graham. 'I wanted the best deals for the fighters,' said Ingle. 'I spoke to everybody, I took the fighters every-where, and this upset Duff and a few others.' On the night Bomber beat Christian he was unbeaten in nineteen and still only 22. When he finally quit in 1998 he was rightly ranked in the top three British boxers never to win a world title. Graham tried and tried but he was too often invisible during his career, disgracefully overlooked by domestic boxers and some on the international scene. He also made a few bad decisions, like all boxers.

The wait for Frank Bruno to have his first professional fight ended in March. His previous fight had been in the ABA finals, against Rudi

Pika in May 1980. Bruno had spent the time getting ready under the watchful eye of Terry Lawless in what was surely the longest training camp in history. Bruno had also required surgery on a damaged eye, which is something Lawless and his partners had not factored in when they signed him. Getting the eye fixed, which cost about £5,000 in total, was, so Duff said, a 'business expense'. Bruno, so the Board doctor had said, was short-sighted in his right eye and had a rare weakness in his retina. There were two places where Bruno could have an operation to fix it: Bogotá and Moscow. Bruno went to Colombia at 19 on his own to have the operation, which was a success. There has always been an alternative version to this story, one that will never be printed. Anyway, Bruno's eye was now good enough for him to get a licence. All he needed was an opponent.

A man called Johnny Bos, a fight fixer, matchmaker and lunatic from New York, was selected to find the men Bruno would beat. 'I'm looking for a guy with a pulse, but not much of a pulse,' Bos would explain when asked how he selected opponents for his clients' fighters. In 2001, when Audley Harrison turned professional, his team (which is a loose term) also hired Bos, who was still operating under the same strict guidelines. Bos was a delight.

Lupe Guerra was found. 'He went over from a punch I don't remember throwing,' Bruno said. It lasted less than two minutes. The Mexican took three counts before the end and the diehards at the Royal Albert Hall had a new hero. On the same night former world champion Cornelius Boza-Edwards won the European super-featherweight title with a brilliant display to stop Spain's Carlos Hernández, and unbeaten Mark Kaylor made it thirteen in a row, but it was all about Big Frank. Just thirteen days later, at the end of March, Harvey Steichen survived until the second round at Wembley Arena, the old Empire Pool: Bruno was in business. In his first twelve months Bruno would have thirteen fights, with a total of fifteen knockdowns, and they ended in the following rounds: 1, 2, 1, 4, 2, 1, 2, 2, 1, 1, 4, 3 and 2. 'Terry told me that it would get harder and that they would not all fall over,' said Bruno. Lawless was right, but the first scare didn't come until 1983. In the ring at either the Albert Hall or the

Arena he stood to attention each time he sent a Bos import sprawling; the punters loved it, loved every concussive second. Bruno was a devastating puncher, and that should never be forgotten.

We knew he could punch, but the quest to find out if Bruno was more than just 'a happy, smiling black dude from Wandsworth' was also on.

In May, Joe Bugner appeared from nowhere in a ring in Dallas opposite Earnie Shavers. Bugner had not fought for nearly two years, Shavers had shared a ring with some of the best heavyweights from the seventies: he had survived the full fifteen with Muhammad Ali, knocked out Ken Norton, and twice pushed Larry Holmes. The Shavers–Bugner fight is one of the most overlooked fights from the eighties. Shavers was 36, Bugner still only 32, and this was always going to be a brutal encounter: both men talked boldly about winning and getting another shot, but they probably knew that was not the truth.

Bugner caught Shavers in the first and the Acorn, as he was known, had to hold. Bugner's jab had not deserted him, but Shavers had the right hand that every fighter envied and he caught Bugner clean with about twenty seconds left in the round; then, as Bugner tried to hold, Shavers hit him low with a left and then connected with a right uppercut. Bugner went down on his knees, got up, shaken, and survived until the bell. In the second Shavers went looking for the finish. Bugner pumped out his jab and there was a clash of heads after one exchange. Big Joe had a cut over his left eye and the fight was off. Shavers grabbed Bugner in a beefy headlock and told him, 'We'll fight again, man.' They never did, and Shavers never got the big last fight he wanted. Bugner moved back to Britain and did a deal with Frank Warren, fighting twice in London before the end of the year.

At the start of May at the ABA finals Jimmy McDonnell, the 'Camden Caretaker', won at lightweight, Chris Pyatt from Leicester took the title at welter, and Crawford Ashley was the winner at light-heavyweight. The trio would have a total of nine world title fights in the next fifteen years. Harold Hylton won the heavyweight division

– the first time it had not been the heaviest division – when he beat Horace Notice in the first round. It was the first defeat for Notice, from the Nechells club in Birmingham, after nineteen wins and it would be the only loss of his boxing life. In the ABA final a year later Notice stopped Hylton in the first. There was one more outing as an amateur before turning over and Notice was the only winner when England lost 9-1 to the USA in July 1983. Notice then turned professional, won the British heavyweight title in 1986, and was forced to retire with an eye injury after sixteen straight wins in 1988.

In June, Asymin Mustapha was killed in the ring by Barry McGuigan in front of the indifferent diners at the World Sporting Club in London's Grosvenor House Hotel. Mustapha fought under the name Young Ali and he was knocked out in round six. 'He fell down on his face and I looked over at the corner,' said McGuigan. 'I could tell they knew he was hurt. They carried him out on a table.' The boxer went down in the wrong year: no paramedics were in attendance, the nearest neurological unit had not been alerted, and in the lottery for his life that followed the knockout, the young Nigerian lost. McGuigan was in his changing room when he was told that his opponent was seriously hurt – he had previously been told that the kid was up, waving to the crowd. He had been lied to, probably to keep him from being upset. McGuigan was an emotional fighter.

Young Ali had an operation to relieve the pressure on his brain. He remained in London for two months and was then transferred to Nigeria. He never recovered, he never waved to the fans, and on 13 December he died. It is likely that he would have lived if he had been injured after 1991 when the first of the serious and meaningful emergency medical procedures were introduced by the Board. In 1982 he had no chance. In 1985, when McGuigan won the world title, he dedicated the victory to Young Ali. It was the first thing he said when he was interviewed: 'I made my mind up long before the moment to dedicate the win to Young Ali.'

There is no record of Kirkland Laing dedicating his most significant win to anybody. In September, a long way from Hackney and the London gyms, Laing arrived in the ring at the Cobo Hall in Detroit to fight Roberto Durán. It was a Duff move, a brilliant piece of matchmaking. Durán had stopped Ken Buchanan for one world title, beaten Sugar Ray Leonard for the welterweight title, knocked out a horse to impress a girl and win a bottle of brandy, and decked an angry female fan after another fight. The Hands of Stone, as he was known, was vicious. When the fight with Laing was announced there was criticism of the Board for allowing Laing to risk his life in such a potentially dangerous mismatch. There was outrageous talk of another 'Johnny Owen'. Kirk never listened, this was his chance. 'The Durán fight was the only one where I gave up drugs and concentrated,' he said. At the Colvestone gym, the ancient and now lost boxing pit that was run by taxi driver Harry Griver, Laing prepared under the watchful eye of Joe Ryan. A teenage Michael Watson was one of his sparring partners. 'Durán was the only fighter that Kirk ever feared,' said Ryan. Durán had lost to Wilfredo Benítez over fifteen rounds in his previous fight and at the same time Laing had been outpointed over ten rounds by Guyanese survivor Reggie Ford, who had entered the ring having won nine but lost seven.

Laing won, and won clearly, over the ten-round distance. One judge gave it to Durán, but that was a joke. It was an entertaining fight and Laing had to stand at times and take the Panamanian's best shots. At the end both looked stunned. Duff started to plan a glorious future for Laing; Durán was in dispute with Don King and ended up with Bob Arum. It looked that night in Detroit like Durán was finished – well, that was the thinking. Nine months later, after a win against Jimmy Batten in Miami, he knocked out previously unbeaten Davey Moore at Madison Square Garden to take the WBA light-middleweight title. Kirk was missing, Duff was turning down offers. Laing's first fight back was twelve months after the Durán win and it was in Atlantic City. It was a disaster: he was knocked out cold by Fred Hutchings in the tenth round and spent four days, according to Ryan, recovering in hospital. The Board suspended his licence. A few weeks later Durán made $5 million in a title fight with Marvin Hagler. Laing took fourteen months out and fought again in

November 1984, by which time the victory in Detroit meant absolutely nothing.

London's Bloomsbury Crest Hotel was heaving for Bugner's British ring return in October. It was Big Joe's first fight in Britain since knocking out Richard Dunn in one nasty round in 1976. It was only his fourth outing since that night at Wembley. Bugner stopped Winston Allen in the third. 'I'm here to get the respect back, I'm here to win the world title,' he said. It was too early to talk about Bruno; that dialogue would come later, and they would eventually fight in 1987. Bugner biffed over Eddie Neilson back at the Bloomsbury venue in December; it took him five rounds, and four months later it took Bruno just three rounds. There is nothing quite like comparing results for fuelling a rivalry. Soon, at any venue where Bruno or Bugner fought there would be a mildly comic chant of either 'Bruno, Bruno' or 'Bugner, Bugner'. The fans always clearly chanted the name of their boxer in the seventies and eighties. The thick smoke in the venues, the three tiny ropes and the lack of emergency medical care I will never miss, but those heavy chants will remain forever cherished by anybody that was there. Big fights felt like big fights.

The Commonwealth Games in Brisbane ended in October and all nine members of the English team returned with a medal. Jimmy Price and Chris Pyatt won gold. There were medals for Scotland's Joe Kelly and the Northern Irish duo of Roy Webb and Tommy Corr, who also won a bronze at the world championship in Munich in May. Once again Kenya and Nigeria dominated, winning three golds each.

In November two young fighters, each draped in contrasting cloths of expectation, made their debuts. Errol Christie won in Coventry and Duke McKenzie started anonymously on an undercard at Wembley Arena. They were the sons of West Indian immigrants and both grew up in strict households surrounded by brothers that boxed. McKenzie was born six weeks before Christie, and they started their journeys just five days apart. They were truly amazing journeys for both, and they ended in very different places.

Christie had only lost three of his eighty-two contests as an amateur and had won a record ten domestic titles. In 1982 he went to the European under-19 championship in the East German city of Schwerin and beat a Russian in the semi-final and an Italian in the final to win gold, which remains a rarity for a British or Irish boxer. He was put under intense, previously unknown degrees of pressure to turn professional. He was a superstar at the time, his passage to glory apparently guaranteed. However, there were disturbing tales, hushed whispers of problems in sparring back in Coventry, the two-tone city he defined in the bloody and violent eighties. Christie was managed by a man called Burt McCarthy, a veteran of the management business, a gentleman and a man to be treated with the utmost respect. Errol won his debut in the third and was back in action three weeks later at the Bloomsbury Crest on the Bugner undercard. He won in three again. He was the chosen one, make no mistake.

Little Duke won in the second round on a night when his big brother, the irrepressible Clinton, had a routine stoppage, Frank Bruno, his former clubmate at the Sir Philip Game in Croydon, won for the ninth time, and future opponent Charlie Magri was also victorious. Magri would win a world title in his next fight four months later, and by then Duke was in Las Vegas with Cornelius Boza-Edwards under the watchful eye of his manager, Mickey Duff. 'Duke was a very good professional throughout his career and a pleasure to manage,' Duff said. He always had a soft spot for little Duke.

The Contenders

George Feeney won the British lightweight title in the fight after beating Buchanan when he stopped Ray Cattouse in round fourteen at the Royal Albert Hall.

Roy Gumbs defended his British middleweight title in Liverpool, stopping Glen McEwan in the thirteenth round. Gumbs was a couple of years away from becoming the first British licence holder to fight for the world super-middleweight title.

Colin Jones and Charlie Magri both won European title fights overseas. Magri had a nice two-round job in Spain and relinquished the flyweight title to focus on the world title. Jones went to Denmark and also had a two-round stoppage to win the welterweight title. He also relinquished to concentrate on securing a world title. It would be his next fight.

From the Notepad

In 2014, the year Duff died, McKenzie was a loyal visitor to the nursing home where the great boxing icon was living out his last days. 'It breaks my heart, Steve. I hate seeing him this way. He doesn't know who I am.'

'Nobody could have prepared me for turning pro,' Errol Christie said. 'It happened so fast and I just had to keep fighting. I never had a break, a real break. It was just boxing all my life.' There is a famous ITV promotional picture of the station's talent outside a grand house; there are hundreds of familiar faces and right at the very back, top-less and waving an enormous Union flag on a pole, is Errol. He was a star.

'I would take Herol to the working men's clubs and ask if anybody thought they could hit him,' said Ingle. 'Then I would tell them that Herol couldn't hit them! They all put the gloves on and loved it and they came out for the fights. Nobody ever hit him, never.'

1983

'Mickey Duff told me once that it takes three years to make a fighter and ten seconds to ruin one.'
Johnny Bos on his special relationship with the British promoter

'Touch me again and I'll drop you right here.'
Marvin Hagler to Tony Sibson at a press conference in Boston

LITTLE CHARLIE MAGRI had been waiting far too long when he finally got his world title fight. He had been topping bills, selling out venues and fighting eliminators most of his career and after thirty fights and seven years as a professional he was ready.

In an emotional night at Wembley in March, Magri stopped Eleoncio Mercedes on cuts to win the WBC flyweight title. It finished in round seven and he was leading on two of the three scorecards. Mercedes had won the title on a split decision over fifteen rounds the previous November in a brawl with a Mexican called Freddie Castillo. The belts were still hard to win. I have often heard people dismiss Magri's win over Mercedes, but the Mexican-based Dominican Republic fighter had done all that was asked, had won fights in foreign backyards. In 1983 there was no WBO or IBF alternative, no toxic dilution of talent, the WBA had not yet splintered their tarnished title and there were certainly no walkovers at world level. Some champions were much better than others, but they were all to be feared, and Magri had already lost fights he was meant to win. In

1983 British fighters with padded unbeaten records did not get to fight for world titles against petrified imports.

Mickey Duff and Terry Lawless had moved cleverly to get Mercedes in London, offering him £80,000 to make it happen. Duff had worked some magic with the WBC to keep Magri in contention – the type of deal and double deal that greased the boxing machine in the eighties. Magri made about £20,000 for the fight. But it was not about money for Magri that night at Wembley. 'It was the hardest fight I ever had, a real war from the start,' he said. Both were cut, but it was worth it. At the end, with Mercedes being led away beaten and slashed, it was Harry Carpenter who called Magri 'Champagne Charlie'. 'I liked that, liked the sound of that: "Champagne Charlie",' said Magri. The reign would be brief.

In September he defended his title for the first time and it all went painfully wrong. The setting was Wembley again and this time he was in control, leading on two of three scorecards and drawing on the third after five rounds. The Filipino Frank Cedeno had won and lost regional and domestic titles and looked perfect on paper for Magri's first defence. Magri was getting £60,000, his highest purse, but the preparation had not gone smoothly. He'd been diagnosed with something called a 'blind boil' in his right ear and given tablets, which left him groggy during the week of the fight. 'I was weak at the weigh-in, I felt like I had nothing,' said Magri. It ended in the sixth, with Magri over three times. He ended up in hospital, getting the boil fixed. Cedeno was knocked out in two rounds four months later when he made his first defence of the WBC flyweight title. Magri was 27, close to the end, and would get one final world title chance before a brutal, pitiless conclusion to his career in 1986.

Frank Sinatra opened the Centrum in Worcester, Massachusetts and in December 1982 13,577 tickets sold out in twenty-four hours for Marvin Hagler's defence of the unified world middleweight title against Leicester's Tony Sibson. It was billed as a 'blue-collar championship' by the American press: both Sibson and Hagler had worked on building sites as hod carriers. The fight took place in February and it was a problem for the WBC because the

Mexican-based sanctioning body had reduced their title fights to twelve rounds from fifteen rounds at the start of the year; the WBA had stuck with the true championship distance. José Sulaimán, an expert dance master at the negotiating table, nimbly found a compromise in his head to allow the best middleweight in the world to fight the WBC's mandatory challenger. 'The fight was made before our rule change,' Sulaimán explained.

Hagler was on an unbeaten run of thirty before the fight, his machine just starting to attract the attention he deserved. Hagler was 28, but a recently discovered birth certificate claimed he was 30; the two-year difference had allowed him to fight men when he was still a boy during his amateur career. Sibson was 24 and getting $537,000 for his challenge. Hagler was pocketing $1.1 million. It ended in round six with Sibson over twice and cut in a couple of places. Hagler had the cheek to say that Sibson was dangerous with his head. It was not the straightforward massacre the scores (all heavily in Hagler's favour) and blood suggest. Sibson went at Hagler and the champion put on a boxing class, switching from orthodox to southpaw to confuse and then break Sibson's resistance. Both the knockdowns in the sixth came from punches thrown in the orthodox stance – Hagler is a southpaw. 'Tony is a dangerous fighter, he hurt me in the first or second – why would I take any risks with him?' said Hagler. 'I wanted to break him down slowly. I have to finally start giving myself some credit.' Sibson would get two more world title fights, Hagler would get the respect that once eluded him. He is now considered one of the best middleweight champions in history.

At the Convention Center in Reno, Nevada, Colin Jones started as a 6-1 underdog against unbeaten Milton McCrory for the vacant WBC welterweight title. The odds dipped as the travelling Welsh followed their hearts and put a few dollars on their man, but it still looked like a difficult job at long or short odds. Jones had twice beaten Kirkland Laing, lost just once on a disqualification, and in the fight before Reno, in November 1982, he had won the European title in Copenhagen. McCrory was from the Kronk gym in the dysfunctional city of Detroit. He had backing, the men with power in and near his corner. Jones took the fight to him, hunting the body and not show-ing any respect. McCrory admitted he had taken it too easy. The verdict came at the end: one judge for McCrory, one for Jones and one even. 'It was a bitter pill to swallow at the time,' said Jones. It was tight, but McCrory could have edged it. There had to be a rematch. Sulaimán ordered both boxers to rest for forty-five days, then to set a time limit on a deal being reached with Don King, the promoter of the first fight. Eddie Thomas, the manager and mentor, and Jones agreed a deal quickly; Jones would get £450,000 for the rematch and McCrory would get to fight at home once again. In 1983 men fought for the heavyweight title and received less money. It was a fine deal. 'I went back to America for the money,' said Jones. 'If I hit him on the chin in London it will be the same as hitting him on the chin in the States.' He was simply not interested in getting home advantage and getting paid less money. I like that honesty in a fighter, and he was right: Las Vegas in August it would be.

In Belfast they queued for hours for the best standing position at his fights, and in the violent, dangerous and divided city he was fast becoming a hero to both sides in the ancient conflict. Barry McGuigan was a Catholic, his wife a Protestant, and his fans united each time the neon illuminated his craft in the ring. The Ulster Hall was filled to capacity in April when he won the vacant British featherweight title in two rounds against Vernon Penprase. McGuigan had worked on the technicalities of his trade during a long camp with former world champion Ken Buchanan. The pair had shared a room at a guest house in Bangor, McGuigan sleeping at night as Buchanan tapped away at an old typewriter, putting down on paper, in the dim light of the double room, the story of his life in the ring. A sponge like McGuigan could learn a lot from a man like Buchanan. And he did.

McGuigan won three more times before a European title fight at the King's Hall in November. It was a big fight, the crowds immense, and the feeling across the city of Belfast was that the world title was just a fight or two away. It was actually eight more fights and over eighteen months before McGuigan's night of unforgettable glory.

The pavilion behind Caesars Palace in Las Vegas was the venue for the Cornelius Boza-Edwards and Bobby Chacon rematch. It was made for Chacon's WBC super-featherweight title, the belt Boza had defended against Chacon two years earlier, but the WBC withdrew recognition; the bout went ahead as the People's Championship. It won the *Ring* magazine Fight of the Year award; Chacon had done the same in 1982. In May, Chacon and Boza-Edwards put on one of the most memorable fights of the eighties. Boza was down in the first, second and twelfth and final round. Chacon was over in the third and won on points. It made no difference that Sulaimán's gang in Mexico City had bowed to dumb pressure and refused to sanction the fight. It was just a simple, brilliant fight between two men who repeatedly gave too much in the ring. When it was over Chacon would need forty stitches to close his facial wounds. Chacon's wife had repeatedly asked him to give up boxing. Concerned about his health, she'd begged him to stop, and when he was away from home for a fight in March 1982 she called him and asked him not to fight. He refused. She killed herself that night and left him with three young children. He fought the next day for $6,000, insisting on it after the promoter tried to cancel the show; ten months later he won the world title. 'I will get married to boxing now,' Chacon said. The Schoolboy, as he was known, died in September 2016 and had long been a prisoner to dementia. They threw away the mould when Bobby Chacon was made. Boza-Edwards was inconsolable when his great rival died.

On the night that Magri beat Mercedes there was a low-key London debut on the undercard for unbeaten Herol Graham. He won easily, and in May was back in his beloved Sheffield winning the vacant European light-middleweight title on a show promoted by his manager and trainer, Brendan Ingle. The promoter, for the record, was actually Brendan's wife, Alma. In October, Graham was back in London at the Royal Albert Hall for a one-round job and then in December travelled to France to retain his European title. 'It's hard to do a deal with Brendan,' said Duff. 'Every time you agree something he takes his fighters off and they are on another bill, promoted by somebody else.' It would be six more years, a move up in weight and eighteen more fights after the European win in May before Graham got a world title fight. It remains the longest wait by a genuine British contender, a shameful series of delays, and Graham had stopped smiling long before the first of his three world title fights.

After two more stoppage wins in London on Frank Warren shows it was time for Joe Bugner to go back on the road. He was not quite Aussie Joe yet – that would come in the next few years. Bugner was at the Sands Casino Hotel in Atlantic City in June to fight Joe Frazier's son Marvis. Bugner was 33 and had fought sixty-seven times, Frazier was 22 and this was his tenth fight. Bugner lost on points after ten rounds and it was not even remotely close. 'It was odd looking over at Joe in the corner and then looking at the son,' said Bugner. Marvis was not Joe, he never fought like his father, and that caused a few tactical problems. Joe had done his best to make Marvis fight like he had. It was a bad move, but Marvis was a devoted son and tried to throw looping left hooks instead of boxing, using his movement and skills.

Las Vegas in summer is a harsh and cruel place for a boxer, any boxer. In August they fry eggs on the rooftops of limousines, suck all day on ice and pity anybody that has to go out in the afternoon sun. Colin Jones met Milton McCrory at 2.39 p.m. – the time at the first bell – in a car park at the Dunes. The start time was kind for the people on America's east coast and brutal for the Welshman. It was not a lot easier for McCrory, a Detroit dweller familiar with the very harshest of winters. It was 105 degrees under the ring lights – a sapping battlefield for two men. Jones had trained away from the air-conditioned hotels at Johnny Tocco's filthy pit of a gym. It was a place where the walls ran with water in the summer season and the ground was slippery with sweat, blood and tears.

King had erected a twenty-thousand-seat stadium in the car park but only two thousand seats were taken. He had attempted to get Jones to take $100,000 less. That never worked out for him and Jones got his full guarantee. There was also a move to get the weigh-in switched to the night before, which would have helped weight-drained McCrory.

Sulaimán then came up with a bright idea to eliminate a draw and tried to introduce a rule that would have made the judges pick a winner if another drawn verdict was returned. The idea was rejected the night before the fight.

Jones was over in the opening round, a sneaky left uppercut slicing through his guard and forcing him to drop to his knees. He was not hurt, just stunned, and he winked at Eddie Thomas, who insisted it took Jones three rounds to recover fully. McCrory never went in search of a quick win. Jones did recover, and McCrory was in deep trouble in the seventh, reeling, stumbling and looking like a beaten fighter during the minute break. Jones was aware of the heat, conscious of the sudden shock a body could suffer in such extremes, and held back in round eight as the American clutched to hold and sucked in the hot air to survive. However, McCrory had a terrific last round, and then it was left to the judges to deliver heart-breaking judgement in the sweltering afternoon.

'They could meet five or six times and every one would be a thriller and there would never be a clean-cut winner,' said Manny Steward, the creator of the Kronk and McCrory's trainer. Harry Carpenter on the microphone at ringside for the BBC thought McCrory was a clear winner. King, Steward and the rest of McCrory's gang were not so confident. Half the ringside guests were topless in the heat as the pair stood toe-to-toe – literally – in the last three minutes, right until the bell and the ring invasion. Both boxers were lifted on shoulders; both boxers could barely sit up straight. It was a special fight. One judge for Jones, one judge for McCrory, and just one point separated the boxers in each score. It was a split decision and the final decisive score was for McCrory, and it was too wide. It was not a robbery, but Jones could have got it. 'It was a bad decision and I will ask for a rematch,' said Thomas. 'Lucky I was sharp all week because they have tried it on with the money and the weigh-in.' Jones never got any-where near McCrory again, but he did get another world title fight two years later.

A little bit of history was made in Hull in December when Broad Street's Rod Douglas boxed for England against West Germany and his opponent, Manfred Zielonka, wore a head guard. It was the first time that had ever happened in Britain. Douglas won, and England won 8-3. In 1989 Douglas nearly died after a British middleweight title fight with Herol 'Bomber' Graham.

The Contenders

In October Jimmy Batten walked away from the sport after losing a vacant British light-middleweight fight to Prince Rodney at the Royal Albert Hall. Batten was still only 27 and had won forty of his forty-nine fights. After boxing he acted, and was a comic and compère. 'I had to stay away from the game,' he said. 'I wanted to fight, but I knew it was over.'

Promises had been broken, deals had collapsed, and in November John L. Gardner, with Darkie Smith in his corner, fought for the last time. He was stopped in two rounds by Liverpool's Noel Quarless on a Warren show at the Bloomsbury Crest. It was the first time in thirty-nine fights that a European boxer had beaten him.

Quarless slugged his way through a nine-year career – he lost the three fights following the Gardner win – and twice met world heavyweight champions at York Hall, which might just be a bizarre British record. He beat John Tate in 1988 and in his final fight Lennox Lewis stopped him in two rounds at the East End venue in 1990.

From the Notepad

'I was told that there was some damage before the Roberto Durán fight,' Batten whispered to me one night in the winter of 2016 at the Globe, a real London boxing pub. 'I was told that I had brain damage.' In November 1982 Batten went the full ten rounds with Durán in Miami. It was the last of five fights in America, and in January 1983 he was back on familiar ground topping a bill at York Hall in Bethnal Green. 'I never told anybody about the scan I had in America, I couldn't, I had to get a living,' said Batten. 'I was offered the Durán fight before Kirk [Laing] got it and he was beatable then. When I was offered it later in the year I was told it would be a mistake to take it. I went ten rounds with a good Durán and it was the best mistake I made.'

There was a short period in 2014 when Herol Graham was loading delivery trucks for a supermarket chain in north London and getting paid eight quid an hour. 'It's not been easy,' he said in 2011. 'I never had the breaks and now I have to do what I can. I want a gym. I know I can give something back.'

In his office Johnny Tocco had Polaroids pinned to the wall of him and Sonny Liston, casual poses at barbecues. Tocco hated all talk of Liston and drugs. 'Sonny fucking hated needles, loved kids,' Tocco told me. In Tocco's world, inside his palace, Liston was a god, a perfect ferocious fighter that posed with small children, smiled and drank beers at anonymous garden parties. It was no wonder that Colin Jones loved the sweat box and prepared there for the second McCrory fight. 'It was a real gym, no fancy stuff, no posing,' said Jones. A few years later it would be Mike Tyson's chosen gym. Johnny and his gym are long gone now. He died in 1997, though the gym continued with his name above the door after his demise. Las Vegas does not surrender its memories easily.

Gardner never got a world title fight and never got the fight with Muhammad Ali he was promised by Harold Smith, the man who embezzled $21,305,705.18 from the Wells Fargo Bank and spent it on promoting fights, paying fighters and entertaining fight people. The FBI were able to account for all but seven cents of the vast sum. In 1981 Gardner's manager, Duff, was paid a deposit of $350,000 by Smith for the Ali fight. Smith was arrested a few weeks later, and Duff immediately declared the money from the empire of deceit to the FBI investigators. They let him keep it, Duff gave evidence at the trial, and Gardner never got a penny of the deposit. He never got the breaks he deserved. Big John had been British and European champion. In retirement he survived a savage knife attack from a very dangerous man. 'My guts looked like cauliflower, I was trying to hold them in,' Gardner told me in 2014. The man that attacked him was killed in another knife fight when he was released.

1984

THERE WAS NO glamour at the start, no rich nights and high expectation, but somewhere between obscurity and desire Dennis Andries won and lost the world title three times. He came from nowhere, did his business over nineteen years, and then slipped with ease into the background.

In January Andries won the British light-heavyweight title, outpointing Tom Collins over twelve hard rounds at the Lyceum Ballroom in London's Strand. Andries had lost title fights to Collins in 1982 and Bunny Johnson in 1980. Those fights had been over the longer, harder and far more draining fifteen-round distance. Andries was 30 when he won the British title, it was his twenty-sixth fight, and there was talk even then that he was five or ten years older. 'This old man nonsense is OK,' said Andries in 1995. 'It started early and I have never bothered to shut people up, I just keep it going. I heard I was forty when I was thirty and fifty when I was forty. Age doesn't matter. I've seen guys washed up at twenty-four. One bad beating can make you old overnight.' Andries pulled a regular stunt in the eighties when he would drift in and out of a pro gym, look poor and convince people that he was out of shape, and it would get him fights. At the same time he would be training five days a week at the Colvestone, the lunatic and ferocious gym that Harry Griver ran in east London.

In April he beat Collins again – it was their fifth and final fight – and he kept on winning until in April 1986 he fought for the WBC light-heavyweight title.

Nearly a year after losing to Marvin Hagler for all the middleweight belts, Tony Sibson took a bad fight in Atlantic City. In January, Sibson was stopped by Dangerous Don Lee, an avoided southpaw, in eight rounds, and just six weeks later he was in Paris fighting for the European middleweight title. Sibson beat Louis Acaries over twelve rounds for his old title and in November would bring the slim European belt to the ring for a triple championship fight with Mark Kaylor. Sibson won and left with Kaylor's British and Commonwealth titles.

The brief and mad career of Jimmy Cable is one of the oddest from the eighties. The Orpington boxer, who fought for the Fitzroy Lodge as an amateur, had a ridiculous seven months of action starting in February when, against the odds, he won the vacant British light-middleweight title after twelve rounds against Nick Wilshere. Six weeks later he was back in the Royal Albert Hall ring to face an unknown American called Buster Drayton. Cable was done in the first, left stunned in the ring.

There was no time for lengthy inquests: six weeks later he was in France fighting for the vacant European light-middleweight title. Cable was dropped three times by Said Skouma and given a standing count, but he rallied, dropped Skouma in the tenth, and again before stopping him in the eleventh. It was over five months before Cable was paid by the French promoters. He took a four-month break to heal, then went to Munich and lost the European title on points to Georg Steinherr to end the seven-month period of action. 'I just kept taking the fights that were being offered,' Cable said in 1993. 'It was the money – how could I say no?'

The story of David 'Bomber' Pearce is not pleasant. He was a heavyweight caught between the weights as a boxer and after failing a brain scan in 1984 his life declined. In September 1983 he'd won the British heavyweight title in the last scheduled fifteen-rounder, stopping old rival and fellow Welshman Neville Meade in nine rounds. Pearce could have been a real star.

In March he was in Limoges, France, to fight for the European heavyweight title against Lucien Rodriguez. A year earlier Rodriguez had gone the distance in a world title fight with Larry Holmes. The Casablanca-born fighter lost every round to Holmes but he was on his feet at the end. There was a problem for Pearce before the fight when he claimed that he had been forced to spend a night on a park bench or at the airport, depending on what version you want to believe. This upset his manager, Burt McCarthy, who pointed out that he had given Pearce the money to get a hotel room. It was messy, just like Pearce's life in many ways: the big kid from Newport was one of seven brothers and six became professional boxers. Pearce dropped Rodriguez heavily in round eight for two long, long counts. In London or Cardiff, the European title would have been his: Rodriguez took thirteen and then seventeen seconds to get up. The big Frenchman was never short of heart and he survived the round, went the full twelve, and got the nod. In August Pearce was still waiting to be paid his £20,000 purse by the French promoters and he also claimed he was owed a percentage of the television fee.

Pearce and McCarthy split after the fight, the news of a failed scan forcing Pearce into an exile he never enjoyed. He was offered fights on both the unlicensed and bare-knuckle circuit. He sensibly refused, but did fight again in America in 1990 when he was stopped in eight rounds. There was talk, rumours and invented tales of offers to fight some of the very best Americans – Leon Spinks and Buster Douglas – at the time. Instead, Pearce returned to Wales and lived alone, battling epilepsy and his demons from the ring. He was found dead in his flat in May 2000, at the age of 41. His hearse needed a police escort when he was buried. He was adored, known as the Rocky of Newport.

I have one disturbingly dark memory of Pearce. It was early 1985; the scan news had broken and shattered him. He was livid with something that Harry Mullan, the editor of *Boxing News*, had written and he arrived at the offices, just off Great Portland Street, to clear the air. Mullan and Pearce were behind the thinnest of closed doors. Pearce screamed, the entire office shook, and Mullan listened, occasionally talking in a murmur I could hear but not understand. A sobbing Pearce left the office soon after and Mullan closed the door and sat in silence. Pearce was 24 at the time. It was no way for a man's career to end.

James 'Bonecrusher' Smith was unbeaten in his last thirteen fights when he was picked to test Frank Bruno at Wembley in May. Bruno was still only 22 and unbeaten in twenty-one, with all twenty-one ending early and only the one wobble, when Floyd 'Jumbo' Cummings had hurt him in October 1983; Bruno recovered, then bludgeoned Cummings in round seven.

There was a good house on the night, a real buzz in the air. Bruno boxed sensibly, like he could, using his jab and not taking risks. At the end of the ninth round he stunned Bonecrusher with a right cross. Bruno was way in front; Bonecrusher was marked and trailing when the bell for the tenth and final round was tolled. It went wrong quickly. Bruno missed with a big right, was countered and hurt, and then hit with a dozen punches before a sickening left hook dropped him heavily to the canvas. Bruno had stood, taking every punch flush, not trying to hold before the final left hook. It happened so fast. He landed heavily on his side, rolled over, and was pulling himself up, using the ropes as an unforgiving ladder, wide-eyed and delirious but determined to continue. The veteran referee Harry Gibbs reached ten and Bruno staggered into the arms of Jimmy Tibbs before Terry Lawless and Frank Black joined the sad huddle to lift him lightly from destruction to the corner stall. An odd silence swallowed the ringside, where too many members of the press nodded the 'I knew, I told you so' look. That seems harsh. 'The Bruno story is virtually over,' said Harry Carpenter. That seems ridiculous.

Bonecrusher went on and won and lost world heavyweight titles, took Mike Tyson twelve rounds and fought until 1999. He never got lucky against Bruno, he was a good fighter, and he did what good fighters do when they have a gap.

On the Bruno undercard another Lawless fighter, Mark Kaylor, was bludgeoned in seven rounds and dropped five times by Philly fighter Buster Drayton – the same man that had ruined Cable a month earlier. Mickey Duff, a long-term partner with Lawless in their perfectly legal cartel, agreed a deal with Drayton; in 1986 he won a world title and in 1987 he defended it against Said Skouma; Cable at that time had become a loser, an old name for hire, and would join the pirate circuit.

It was left to Bruno, shattered, bruised and barely able to talk, to persuade Lawless to continue. Lawless was not used to setbacks, and with both Bruno and Kaylor ruined he threatened to quit the sport. Bruno talked him round. That dressing room was pure theatre with water all over the floor, discarded bandages, bloody towels crumpled in piles, tearful loved ones and, in the middle, on two chairs, Lawless, with his head in his hands, being comforted by Bruno. 'I reminded Terry what he had said to me about it being a long journey and I reminded myself that a lot of great fighters had lost and then gone on to win world titles. I was not going to walk away after one loss.' It is too easy to forget how honest Bruno was.

In July the Los Angeles Olympics started without the Cubans, the Russians and most of the Eastern Bloc fighters. The British team consisted of all twelve of the ABA champions from May. The American boxers won nine of the gold medals, but Evander Holyfield was a loser when he was disqualified for hitting New Zealand's Kevin Barry after the bell. Earlier Holyfield had stopped Taju Akay from the All Stars club in north London. Akay was representing Ghana but would win the British cruiserweight title in 1987 when he boxed as Tee Jay. There was just one medal for Britain when Bobby Wells, whose father Billy had fought in the 1968 Olympics in Mexico City, won a bronze at super-heavyweight. Wells had lost in the domestic

ABA quarter-finals in April to Keith Ferdinand, but Ferdinand had withdrawn. Wells had stopped Gary Mason in the third round to win the south-west London divisional title in March; Mason would go on to win the British heavyweight title as a professional. Wells had just five fights as a professional but was back in the Olympic ring in 2012 – as a volunteer at the London Games.

Little Charlie Magri returned to the ring for just one fight in 1984, a job in Sardinia in August against a local fighter for the European flyweight title. Magri was not happy, but it ended in the first with Franco Cherchi badly cut. The crowd were a bit upset and filled the ring with debris. Magri was then promised a world title fight at good money, which failed to arrive. The following year he agreed a deal to fight for a world title on a Frank Warren show. It was a blow to the cartel and their long-established ability to deliver their boxers world title fights. Warren had been promoting less than three years and he was providing a much-needed rivalry to the cartel's solid hold on the British boxing industry.

There was a horrible setback for Errol Christie in September. He was still a boxing baby of 21, unbeaten in thirteen, when it went wrong for the first time. Christie had just fought in Las Vegas: he had sampled the other life, the one that was warm, wealthy and far removed from the Coventry streets he had prowled as a young, angry black man. He had also spent some hard time in Detroit at the Kronk, the fighting house that Emmanuel Steward had built in the ruined city. It was an unforgiving place. The sparring sessions could destroy a man. Christie and Andy Straughn, who travelled with him, had to fight hard each day, but they were young and stupid enough to enjoy it. Christie admitted to me that the return to London, after his time in America at the Kronk gym, left him deflated. Straughn and Christie also shared a flat in south London and keeping it going had left the pair skint.

The fight at the Britannia Leisure Centre in east London against a Belgian with a wild mop of blond hair was meant to be routine. 'I was not up for the fight,' Christie confessed. 'I looked at him and knew I'd win.' José Seys, meanwhile, had looked at Christie and asked:

'Why is this small man fighting me?' Christie was 8lb lighter, but Seys had a massive frame, the body of a cruiserweight, even if he was inside the light-heavyweight limit. Seys was one of the ugliest south-paws I had ever seen, a fighting nightmare. He had just lost in South Africa to Piet Crous, who won the cruiserweight world title in December.

At the Britannia it was all over after forty-six seconds of the first round. Christie was dropped twice. Seys could not believe what had happened – a feeling shared by the people in the Christie business; Burt McCarthy, his manager, looked in shock when he climbed through the ropes to comfort his boxer. Christie was wild-eyed, oblivious to the calamity. 'I should have beaten him, even with the size difference,' he said. 'I had to think about things after that loss. I had never stopped training. I should have had a break coming into the pros. I ignored what my body was telling me.' McCarthy and Warren brought Christie back with two one-round blow-outs before the end of the year.

In January there had been bold talk of Christie fighting Mark Kaylor, a fight that collapsed when both suffered shock defeats and were dropped a total of seven times. It would be memorably resurrected in 1985. In May the Board had ordered a final eliminator for Kaylor's British middleweight title between Christie and Herol Graham. McCarthy sensibly destroyed that plan by pointing out Christie could make more money elsewhere, and he also questioned Graham's eligibility. 'Why should he [Graham] be granted a final eliminator in his very first fight since giving up the light-middleweight title?' Nobody wanted to fight Herol.

The Contenders

The real main event at the Britannia when Christie lost was the British light-welterweight title fight between Clinton McKenzie and Terry Marsh. It went the full twelve, and Marsh took the title. He would go on to win the European and the world title. He would also stand trial for shooting Frank Warren and he was acquitted.

Seys was back in a British ring twenty-eight days after beating Christie. He was picked gently apart and stopped in six by Herol Graham. The win moved Graham to 29-0, but he would have to wait another five years for a world title fight, which is one of British boxing's great injustices. It is often casually remarked that Graham was not a banger, preferring to run, pile up points and not take any risks. The raw statistics, however, have never endorsed that fantasy. Graham won nine times between Seys and his world title fight and he stopped or knocked out eight of the nine men.

Lennox Lewis boxed for Canada at the Los Angeles Olympics, lost before the medal stage, and in October was in Bletchley to stop Bobby Wells in three rounds. The team result was 6-6. There was also an odd cameo in October by another future world champion when Mike Tyson, representing the USA, fought at the Tammer Tournament in Tampere, Finland. 'He was just a big kid,' said Chris Blake, the English representative at welterweight who won a silver medal. As a pro Blake was stopped in one round for the British light-welterweight title by Lloyd Christie in late 1987.

From the Notepad

Jimmy Cable finished his boxing life fighting on the unlicensed circuit as part of the United Boxing Organization's dysfunctional franchise. The UBO was a governing body created by a man called Reg Parker, whose requests for a British Boxing Board of Control licence were always rejected. Parker ran his empire from an office above a World of Leather showroom in Eltham. Jimmy Cable was his greatest fighter. 'I took home more for some of those fights than I got for beating Wilshere at the Royal Albert Hall,' Cable remarked.

'I'm from a hard country, a hard place where you get to think like a man and do man things by the age of twelve,' Andries said. 'I just got on with boxing like I got on with life.' Andries fought a total of fifty-three rounds with Tom Collins, which is a raw statistic that no modern fighter would ever be able to replicate.

1985

*'I knew how good he was, how dangerous, and when it started I
realized that everything I had been told was true. Still, I caught him,
I went for him – I had to have a go.'*
Charlie Magri on fighting Sot Chitalada

*'While they are in the hall they are Barry McGuigan United. The old
prejudices will come to the fore soon enough in plenty of cases but I'll tell
you this – the wee fella could walk up the Falls Road or the Shankill Road
any day and not a man or woman would lift a hand to hurt him.'*
Barney Eastwood, promoter

BARRY McGUIGAN HAD to take a massive risk before fighting for a world
title, and Belfast fell silent when he met Juan LaPorte at the start of
the year. The Puerto Rican was a former world champion, still only
25, and very dangerous. After ten rounds he suddenly became an old
man in the ring. Some had dared to say he was shot and a safe option;
he was none of those things before the first bell at the King's Hall.
LaPorte had lost his WBC featherweight title eleven months earlier
on points to Wilfredo Gómez and in 1982 had lost on points over
fifteen rounds to Eusebio Pedroza for the WBA version. Five years
after losing to McGuigan he would drop another decision in a world
title fight, this time to Africa's greatest fighter Azumah Nelson.
LaPorte was not shot.

In the ninth round McGuigan was hit so hard he thought he was
in a childhood toyshop. But at the end the ref, Harry Gibbs, raised

Barry's hand with a clear score of 99-97 and LaPorte, who had been in Belfast for two weeks, was left to shake his head. 'We knew Barry was good, but not this good,' he said.

The world title talk started, and a month later, after a European defence at Wembley, the deal was reached with Pedroza, who was in London. It took McGuigan's manager Barney Eastwood and his fixer, Duff, all night after the fight at Wembley to agree the terms. It was set for June, but it was sealed in the King's Hall that February with the LaPorte win.

The eighth of June is a night that nobody in British boxing will want to forget, for it was a fight that defined more than just a decade. At the end of fifteen rounds in front of 26,000 people at Loftus Road in west London the hand of Barry McGuigan was raised into the air. He was the world champion. It was a formality, and Pedroza, who was making the twentieth defence of his WBA featherweight title, put his sore lips close to McGuigan's ear and told him, 'You will be a great champion.' McGuigan, close to exhaustion, crying and hugging everybody within reach, dedicated the win to Young Ali, the boxer he had killed in the ring back in 1982. I marvelled at that gesture and still do over thirty years later. How did Barry find the composure to ignore the moment, seal himself away for thirty seconds and do something like that? Stunning. Then there was pure bedlam as the crowd swarmed closer to the neon lights above the ring. They were cheering, boozing and crying as they edged glorious inch after glorious inch closer to their idol. These men, and some women, had been there from the start; they were veterans of the fights in Belfast; they'd collected the names of the men their man had broken. They were fighting men, often divided by violence in a city they loved, but each of them united behind wee Barry and his fists. They had believed, kept him going in rounds thirteen, fourteen and fifteen, rounds when a smile distorted his face as he traded jabs with one of the best modern champions, a man blessed with such skills that he remains a great today. He knew then, long before the final bell, that he was part of something that would never be forgotten.

The day of the fight had started in chaos at the weigh-in, which took place at the Odeon in Leicester Square. Pedroza had hopped on and off the scales and Barney Eastwood was fuming, threatening to become a one-man riot. 'Get him back on, get him back!' Eastwood ranted. There was a real impasse. Barney talked of pulling the fight. Pedroza had probably had to lose 20lb in the eight-week camp and Eastwood was right to demand a clear view of his weight. He never got it, the boxers both made weight, and the other wait was on.

The London streets seemed to be packed with boxing fans. At dusk they were inside QPR's ground, filling the night sky with noise. McGuigan entered the ring to the *Rocky* theme, his father, Pat, then sang 'Danny Boy'. People openly sobbed – grown men. A dwarf dressed in boxing kit tumbled like a fool in the ring – a demented leprechaun, just to add a touch of vulgarity. The robes were removed, the last smears of Vaseline swiped across brows, and the bell sounded.

Pedroza was smart, a master of the black arts and capable of timing an impossible punch perfectly. McGuigan was simply relentless. In round seven he caught the Panamanian and the champion was down. In the ninth and the eleventh Pedroza was hurt. At the end of the ninth it looked like his cornerman/manager Santiago Del Rio stuck a white tube up his boxer's nostrils, which jolted his head back. The potential illegality was lost in the euphoria later. McGuigan was the new champion.

After this there is one solitary moment, one of few in McGuigan's life, when he wakes up sore all over and goes for a sauna on his own. Nobody is there, and he starts to shadow-box. It is the last moment of a once private man, the final sweaty seconds before Barry McGuigan emerges and becomes public property.

Pedroza was beaten but McGuigan now had just ninety days to agree terms and fight his number one contender, Bernard Taylor. The American would have won gold at the 1980 Olympics if there had not been a boycott. He had lost just nine of his 489 amateur contests and was unbeaten in thirty-four as a professional, with one draw, over fifteen rounds against Pedroza. It was a hard first defence, so strict that in modern terms it is difficult to comprehend. The fight was made for King's Hall in September. In the run-up McGuigan had concerns about the way he was living. He was constantly in demand. Everybody had a 'when I met Barry' story. Taylor was not the knock-over job other fighters get, and finding a balance was a task.

On fight night the venue played a critical role. Taylor blamed the smoke, the heat and the noise for his loss. It was a terrific performance from McGuigan to slowly punish the American and force him to quit. It was waved off during the break between rounds eight and nine. 'I might not have knocked him out, but I would have beaten him up in the ninth,' said McGuigan. It was an odd way for a quality fighter to end a world title fight. Pedroza had taken a much more sustained and painful beating, and in 1986 McGuigan would come close to redefining bravery in a losing fight. But McGuigan deserved his break. In December he had another win when he collected the BBC's Sports Personality of the Year – the first boxer to do so since Henry Cooper in 1970 and the last before Lennox Lewis in 1999.

'I will fight Barry McGuigan anywhere in the world, I'm not afraid of the crowd,' said Azumah Nelson in Birmingham in early October. Nelson was in town to meet local boxer Pat Cowdell in defence of the WBC featherweight title. Cowdell had won five European title fights and was unbeaten in eleven since losing that fifteen-round split decision to Salvador Sánchez for the same belt in 1981. Sánchez had stopped Nelson eight months later, then died in a crash, and Nelson had eventually knocked out Wilfredo Gómez to win the title in 1984. Nelson had silenced Gómez's Puerto Rican faithful in San Juan on that occasion, and that was impressive. He was serious about fighting McGuigan in Belfast. The fight with Cowdell was at the NEC and it was all over after 2:24 of the first round. Nelson was clinical.

'I knew how Pat Cowdell fought,' Nelson told me in 1994 during a series of lunches at his house in Accra. 'I thought he would run. He obviously didn't get good advice. Why did he come to me? I was ready to chase him. I waited for him to make a mistake and when he did I said "Goodbye".' Nelson seemed genuinely shocked at Cowdell's tactics. He was also angry that his fight with McGuigan never happened.

Above left: Chris and Kevin Finnegan put Freddie Hill in a belt harness at their gym in south London. I grew up with this picture on my wall.

Above right: Henry Cooper and Spanish strongman José Urtain at the end of their one-sided brawl for the European heavyweight title. It was an easy night for Cooper.

Below: No smiles from our 'Enery after losing a tight decision to Joe Bugner. It was Cooper's last fight and he never forgot it.

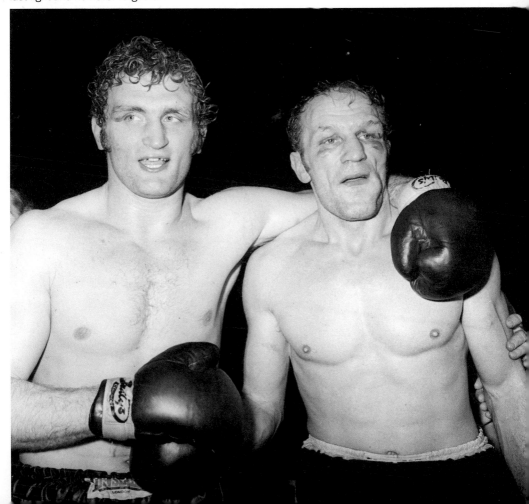

Above: Jim Watt and Ken Buchanan fight for the British lightweight title at a private club in Glasgow. Buchanan won a technical feast of a fight after fifteen rounds.

Below: John Conteh embraces Chris Finnegan in the Wembley ring after winning their first triple-title clash in 1973.

Above: Richard Dunn is down from Bunny Johnson's punches at the Belle Vue in Manchester. The venue is gone; Johnson is too often ignored.

Left: John Conteh traps Jorge Victor Ahumada on the ropes in their vacant WBC light-heavyweight title fight. Conteh won and it hurt in all the wrong places.

Below: Alan Minter beats Vito Antuofermo in their Wembley rematch to retain his undisputed world middleweight title. Minter was bloody and gutsy.

Above: John H. Stracey hides his damaged left eye behind a towelling hood after losing a bloody and bad-tempered fight with Dave Boy Green.

Below: Jim Watt roars at the crowd inside Ibrox Park after retaining his WBC lightweight title against Howard Davis Jr. It was a masterclass.

Above: Andy Smith applies a soothing hand to the dazed Dave Boy Green after his round-eleven loss to Carlos Palomino for the WBC welterweight title.

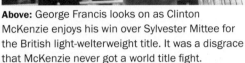

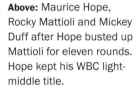

Above: Maurice Hope, Rocky Mattioli and Mickey Duff after Hope busted up Mattioli for eleven rounds. Hope kept his WBC light-middle title.

Right: Cornelius Boza-Edwards needed just four rounds to stop Carlos Hernández for the European super-feather title at the Royal Albert Hall.

Below: Tony Sibson had no fear of Marvin Hagler when they met near Boston, but Hagler retained his undisputed middleweight title in round six.

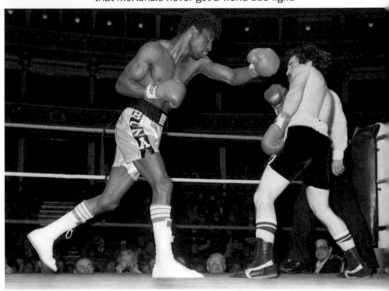

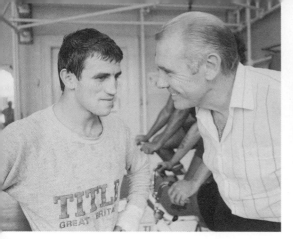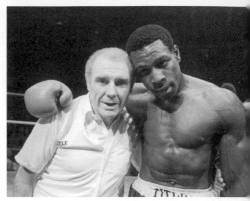

Above left: Charlie Magri and Terry Lawless at the Royal Oak gym when they were still friends. (**Above right**) Lawless also fell out with Frank Bruno, but guided the heavyweight brilliantly for most of his career.

Right: Pat Cowdell won and lost titles during twelve years at the top. He is always overlooked.

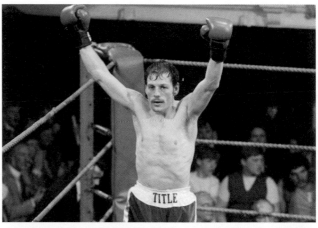

Below: The fright on the face of the guy in the hat tells the real story of the street fight between Errol Christie and Mark Kaylor. It was nasty, not hype.

Above left: The sanctioned fight between Christie and Kaylor was packed with hate and action. Both were on the canvas before the classic ended in round eight.

Above: Barry McGuigan's moment of triumph and reflection after that amazing night at Loftus Road in 1985.

Left: Glenn McCrory was known as the Rocky of the North East.

Below: Dennis Andries was either thirty-two or thirty-five and had been a professional for nine years when he beat J. B. Williamson for the WBC light-heavyweight title.

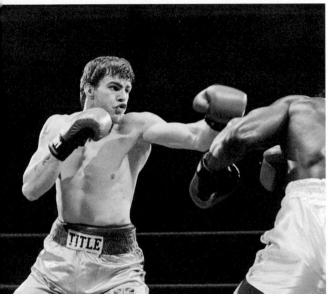

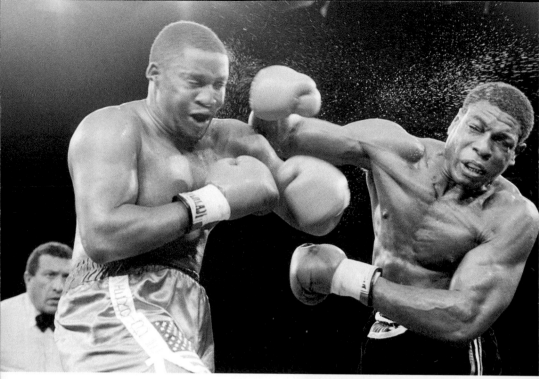

Above: Frank Bruno was heroic under the stars at Wembley against Tim Witherspoon in their WBA heavyweight title fight. Too many people forget how good Bruno was before losing in the final seconds of round eleven.

Right: The brilliant Herol 'Bomber' Graham was unbeaten in thirty-six fights when he stopped Mark Kaylor. Nobody wanted to give Graham a chance.

Below: Lloyd Honeyghan and Mickey Duff are all smiles after a shock victory against Donald Curry in Atlantic City that proved to be another landmark moment in British boxing history.

New Year's Eve in Seoul was horrible for Tottenham's Roy Gumbs and the start of January was not going to get any better. Gumbs was stopped in round two of his IBF super-middleweight title fight by Chong-Pal Park in what was his fortieth fight. 'It was a different world out there,' said Gumbs, who had lost his British title to Mark Kaylor in a bad-tempered brawl in September 1983. 'Nothing was like anything I had ever seen before or eaten before. It was difficult.'

Gumbs was the first licensed British boxer to fight for a super-middleweight world title; he would be followed into the ring by Chris Eubank, Nigel Benn, Richie Woodhall, Joe Calzaghe, Carl Froch and James DeGale. It has become the British weight. The Gumbs–Park fight was only the third world title at the new weight. Incidentally, the first champion was Murray Sutherland and he had been born in Edinburgh, but based himself and fought in America.

In January in Perugia, Lloyd Honeyghan pulled off a win just as impressive as Maurice Hope's against Vito Antuofermo in Rome in 1976. Honeyghan was unbeaten in twenty, the British champion at welterweight, and for five years he had been predicting his rise to greatness. He had made a few enemies, and was eventually evicted from the Terry Lawless gym at the Royal Oak in Canning Town, finding managerial sanctuary with Mickey Duff. 'Terry threw him out and I asked, "Are you mad?"' said Duff. 'He told me that if I liked him so much I should sign him, and I did.' The fall-out was after the fight in Italy. Honeyghan was up against the European welterweight champion Gianfranco Rosi, who had lost just once in thirty-three fights. Honeyghan stopped Rosi after fifty-nine seconds of the third; Rosi, it should be noted, went on to enjoy two reigns as world champion and made eleven defences the second time. Honeyghan would have his glory night in 1986, but the Perugia win was special, a rare winning diversion in a European stronghold.

The fury was disturbingly familiar at the NEC on the outskirts of Birmingham in late January when Colin Jones was rescued from his own bravery against Donald Curry and then forced to witness the stupidity of some in the crowd of 11,500. Fights took place in the high seats, plastic bottles and other debris filled the ring, and once again a brilliant American was pelted with hate and rubbish as he left a British ring. Curry retained his IBF and WBA welterweight titles when Jones was ruled out by the ringside doctor after thirty-six seconds of the fourth. The Welshman required eight stitches to mend his nose; his pride would take a little longer to heal; it was possible he'd remain scarred for life. 'I'm so ashamed and disappointed,' Jones said. 'I feel so stupid that it has been stopped like this. I had so much fight left in me.' Unfortunately, so did the extraordinary Curry. 'Jones wasn't nearly as strong as I thought he would be – it was easy, I'm the best in the world,' he said. Harsh words, but a fair assessment of the brief, bloody and technically brilliant fight. There had been hopeful but ultimately misguided talk all week in Birmingham about Curry's struggle with the scales. The fight game's hangers-on had earned their keep with whispered tales of Curry fasting his way to the limit and looking drained in sessions, and even the boxer had hinted that it would be his last fight at welterweight. Each dispatch seemed to improve the meagre chances of Jones winning. When it was done and Jones had been sliced and hit with clinical punches that echoed with a distinct crack through the cavernous arena, a sound that only the best can make when they are connecting, it was time for reflection. 'I suppose I ought to retire,' he said. He did, but not before a solitary tender moment when he bent over and kissed one of Curry's world title belts. It was the final boxing kiss of a man that had been training since before he was 10, had fought at the Olympics, won the British title, and twice before come so close to a world title. He was just 25, another worn-out young fighter finished far too early. Jones was just a year younger than Honeyghan, but in fighting years it seemed like they were separated by decades.

At Alexandra Palace in north London in February, Charlie Magri met Sot Chitalada. It was not the fight you have heard it was and it was probably not the fight you remember. Magri was pulled out by Lawless at the end of the fourth and Chitalada kept his WBC flyweight title. Two of the scores after four competed rounds were even, with two rounds each, and in the second round Chitalada was staggered by a right cross. Magri put the Thai champion under pressure and was, by the end of the fourth, starting to get hit and hurt. Magri also had a bad cut over his left eyelid. It was a good stoppage, but it was an even better fight.

It came so close to never getting made. Magri was still with Lawless and Duff, but Frank Warren offered him the one final chance, settled on £40,000, which was his second highest purse, and delivered Chitalada. The Thai was rumoured to be on £100,000. The deal was done in Magri's sports shop in Bethnal Green at a meeting attended by Lawless, who sulked and refused to speak, and Warren with his matchmaker, Ernie Fossey. 'It was a comedy, but we got the deal done,' said Warren. Chitalada was a kick-boxer who had converted, and he stepped into the ring with Magri having lost just once, a world title fight at light-flyweight in his fifth of eight outings. He would win and lose world titles until 1992, but Magri had just two fights left.

In October a press conference at a casino in London's Russell Square went violently wrong, and boxing was in the spotlight. The routine announcement of a long-overdue fight between Mark Kaylor and Errol Christie ended with the obligatory photographic face-off. The pair disliked each other, and for the face-off nobody stood between them. Vicious words led to a fight, they grappled and fell over, and every action was captured by the expectant photographers. Christie claimed one thing was said, Kaylor denied it. The pair were splitting £82,500, which was a record fee for a non-title fight in Britain, and the final eliminator was big news. It was a real story at a time of horrible racist unrest and most of the apologies sounded insincere. A few days later there was a cosmetic handshake – an undeniable necessity that looked fake – and then the business of selling the fight continued. It was not a publicity stunt, trust me. There was real hate on both sides. Kaylor was white and with Lawless and Duff; Christie was black and part of Warren's business. A lot of stereotypes were in play and the fear of trouble on the night was real. On 21 October, Wembley Police Commander David Polkinghorne wrote to the Board advising that the fight should be postponed. 'The two boxers have already inflamed a volatile racial situation,' he said.

It went ahead. They met at Wembley Arena on 5 November. A

special security team was hired by Lawless, the details of which were wisely concealed from the press: Lawless had agreed a deal with Cass Pennant, famously a member of the West Ham United firm; he was very big and black and connected. 'I had a meet with Lawless at the Royal Oak gym and he told me that boxing was on trial,' he confirmed in 2010. 'I knew where the trouble would be and I handpicked some men – my men knew who the troublemakers were. We played the respect card. The police were not happy, but we were straight in at the first scent of trouble.' Pennant joined me on the twenty-fifth anniversary of the fight in my BBC London studio. I had Christie there, and Kaylor on the phone from his home in Chino, California.

Kaylor: Errol, I have so much respect for you. I'd like to apologize.

Christie: I never had any qualms with you, we were just two fighters.

Kaylor: Why were we allowed to get nose-to-nose? Somebody never did their job.

Christie: You are right. It was all going well and then (turning to me) he called me an ugly black bastard.

The fight started underneath a wild noise that drowned the bell, and twenty seconds later Christie was down. He was up and hurt, up too quick and surely too hurt to survive. A firecracker sounded a few seconds later. Christie held and then threw his own punches and two minutes later Kaylor was dropped. Kaylor landed one after the bell and Gibbs, the old cockney stevedore, went and told him off. In the third round Kaylor was down again from a sneaky right, but Christie was forced to hold on the bell. 'It's like a fight on the cobbles, which is where they started,' Harry Carpenter reminded everybody. Nobody could hear the bell to end the fourth and punches were thrown. It was all over in round eight when Kaylor connected with a right and then a left hook and Christie dropped face first. He seemed to nod at Ernie Fossey in his corner, then he crawled to the ropes and was counted out as he tried to climb up. Kaylor tried to celebrate, was quietened by Jimmy Tibbs, and then went to comfort Christie. There was no trouble and Pennant's firm in their Keep it Cool shirts had helped. Christie manager Burt McCarthy kissed Kaylor in the ring melee and tried to lift his boxer. 'That was the worst performance I've seen from Errol Christie,' agreed McCarthy when Carpenter asked a loaded question. 'Mind you, it's possible that Mark Kaylor would have done that to the best version.'

Back in the studio, after I had played some commentary, Christie was smiling: 'You know what, Mark? We were both born too early – that fight would be worth one million each now.'

There was nothing Kaylor could say to that. Christie was right.

A week after the fight, the Board fined the pair for the press conference brawl: Kaylor £15,000 and Christie £5,000. It was over, but not forgotten.

The Contenders

Cowdell had eight more fights after losing to Nelson. He won, lost, won and lost the seemingly cursed British super-featherweight title, all four title fights ending inside the distance. The super-featherweight division had first been introduced in 1968 but had existed for only two years and four fights before being dropped by the British Boxing Board of Control. In January 1986 it made a comeback and fourteen men won the title in a seven-year period before one, Neil Haddock, managed to make one successful defence.

In April there was a classic domestic title fight at the Dolphin Centre in Darlington between a man from west London and a boxer from Birmingham who was known as the Greek Tank. They fought to a standstill for Honeyghan's vacated British welterweight title in that distant venue, making the journey difficult for their fans. Rocky Kelly is convinced he trained wrong, Kostas Petrou is convinced he would have won no matter how Rocky trained. It was finally called off after 1:09 of the ninth and Petrou was the new champion. Kelly would be involved in a death fight in 1986 and get another British title opportunity in 1987. Petrou lost the title in his first defence in September to Sylvester Mittee, who defended his Commonwealth welterweight title on the Darlington undercard. At the end of the eighties the Kelly–Petrou encounter was rightly considered one of the very best British fights of the decade.

The main event when Kaylor beat Christie was Camden caretaker Jimmy McDonnell winning a European title at super-feather. 'That night was unbelievable,' McDonnell told me in 2010. 'It was a pleasure to box in that atmosphere, and when Mark walked out he was so calm. "See you in a minute," he said. I was stunned he could be that cool.'

From the Notepad

McGuigan rightly considers the LaPorte fight his best performance. 'You are on your way to a world title, it was a pleasure to watch tonight,' said Sugar Ray Leonard, who was a pundit at ringside in Belfast.

Cornelius Boza-Edwards, the former world champion from Kampala, Harrow and Las Vegas, was convinced that McGuigan would have won a fight with Nelson. 'Azumah is a heavy hitter but I go for Barry on points,' he said. 'He would be too busy.' The debate lasted for years.

In 2015, Roy Gumbs was working for a sports consultancy firm in Dubai, offering boxing training sessions for businesses. 'I was there at the start, no hometown fights for me – I had to go and try to win the title the hardest way possible.'

1986

*'I knew Nigel and knew how dangerous he was. I fiddled for a round
and then that was it; you don't need any other details. I won a round,
he won the fight.'*
Wendell Henry (Repton) with the bare facts from his fight with Benn

*'They keep coming through the door at nine or ten or eleven and we keep
making them into boxers. It's all they know, they come here to change;
it's a way of life straight away for them.'*
Tony Burns on the Repton conveyor belt

THERE WAS A stark lesson in glory, hype and pain for Barry McGuigan in his second defence of his WBA featherweight title in February. The fight took place in Dublin, the first in the city for sixty-three years, and a sold-out crowd of 6,000 were witness to a real struggle. The figure was more like a guess – the venue was packed.

Danilo Cabrera from the Dominican Republic was just 22, a late replacement plucked from the gym during the final stages of preparation for a fight of his own. It was not just any fight: he was getting ready for a grudge match with his bitter local rival Manuel Batista for the national title. They were one each after two fights; the third was coming before the call came in from McGuigan's people. That makes Cabrera the worst type of substitute – unknown, and in great shape.

There was the usual emotion before the first bell. It was a second homecoming. The Irishman was in front on all three scorecards when the fight was finally stopped after 1:40 of the fourteenth round.

McGuigan had a free shot as Cabrera tried to retrieve his gumshield and that was the end. In all fairness, McGuigan had just looked to the referee to stop it; when the third man held back, McGuigan let go. Cabrera had sliced a wound in McGuigan's cheek, which later required six stitches to close, and taken the Irish idol's best punches. He had also backed McGuigan up, put him under pressure and made a lot of people think again about some of the more outlandish claims they had made after the two world title wins in 1985. He was described as 'jaded', 'one-paced', 'unimaginative' and lacking 'snap, sparkle and variety'. You needed thicker skin to be a British world champion in the eighties. Cabrera, as the saying goes, fought out of his skin and McGuigan was clearly drained by the whirlwind of events that had so thoroughly altered his life over the previous eight months or so. I would argue that no British boxer in history had ever had to face the same levels of expectation, craziness and celebration that McGuigan found himself a prisoner to when he beat Eusebio Pedroza. He also had his enemies, too many envious people in the boxing business that hate others having success.

The fight had first been halted at the end of round eight after McGuigan had dropped Cabrera and had him trapped on the ropes. The referee, Ed Eckert, seemed to save Cabrera from McGuigan's fists and right then nobody could have complained. However, the bell had sounded. Cabrera's cornermen were volatile in the extreme as they pointed out to the referee that the round was over when he had stopped it. As they complained, the ring filled with smiling people, and it was lucky that McGuigan's gloves were not immediately cut off. There was mayhem, the ring was cleared, and the bout started again. Incidentally, in his next fight, for the WBC featherweight title, Cabrera was stopped in ten rounds by Azumah Nelson. Cabrera said that Nelson would beat McGuigan. It was an empty statement because less than twenty-four hours later came McGuigan's denouement in the desert.

There are so many tales about that day in June when McGuigan lost his WBA featherweight title. The facts and fictions have blended into one long disturbing narrative, a tale that has priests in tears at ringside, McGuigan in hospital, a Panamanian biting McGuigan's ear in desperation in the corner, and a kid from Texas leaving the ringside with his 15-year-old bride and the world title belt. It was that type of night.

McGuigan never wanted to fight Steve Cruz. The original opponent was Fernando Sosa but he was out with two detached retinas. Bob Arum, the promoter, found Cruz and he was hired three weeks before the fight. He worked for a plumbing company in Fort Worth, Texas. When he got the call about the fight he was outdoors in the sun, running a sewer line from the main line under the street to a new house. He was plucked from his wedding bed to share a room for three weeks with his trainer, Joe Barrientos. 'Steve was getting mean on us,' said Dave Gorman, his manager. 'He was missing his bride.' In Las Vegas the Texas team trained at Johnny Tocco's filthy gym, a pitiless retreat for real fighters.

McGuigan was in Palm Springs. The camp was not good. He was persuaded to change his mind and accept Cruz when his manager and mentor Barney Eastwood agreed to pay him an extra $250,000. They fell out after the fight and eleven months later, in May 1987, McGuigan and Eastwood would reach an agreement on the day of a High Court case. Their love ended somewhere between Palm Springs and the final seconds of the horror fight in Las Vegas. It was a night that ended with the Irishman exhausted, dehydrated, wrapped in a giant tinfoil shroud and being carted off to hospital for examination. He was not delirious, but he was broken.

The fight was unforgettable for the slow-motion quality of the last three minutes. It was played out under a sun that heated the ring to 130 degrees. Cruz had worked in that heat, McGuigan had never been to that burning hell before in his life. He claimed he had prepared in 125 degrees, sparring four-minute rounds in Palm Springs, which might have been a factor in his collapse. He was dropped in round ten, had a point deducted in round twelve, but was in front on two of the three scorecards going into the fifteenth and last round. There is a haunting picture of McGuigan staring at something that is not there as he sits in the corner. The picture is best viewed through your fingers as it captures a boxer's many sacrifices better than a blood-stained image of a broken face. It was in the corner that the Panamanian pulled, pinched and bit his ears. There was chaos in that unholy corner; delirium had invaded the glory of the fighting hero. Cruz had been a 9-1 outsider before the bell, before the rumours of unrest, before the cruel brutality of the last round. McGuigan had lost his legs and his head, but his desire kept him going in the last. He was sent tumbling twice, and that altered the scores in favour of Cruz. The old champion, just 26, watched as the American had his hand raised. The final scores were 143-139, 142-141 and 143-142. Had McGuigan gone down just once he would have retained his title with a draw. It was the end for Barry McGuigan. There was a rematch clause, one that Cruz was desperate for. The fight never happened, and Cruz lost in his first defence.

A man called Harry Holland, who had as many roles in boxing as he had walk-on cameos in *EastEnders*, took Rocky Kelly to Tenerife to train for a fight. It was billed as the Showdown of West London and took place in a hotel near Stamford Bridge in March. Kelly was fighting Steve Watt and the brawl ended in round ten, the last round, when the referee intervened. Watt walked back to his corner, and then it all started to go horribly wrong. He sat down, his head slumped, and panic started. He was rushed to Charing Cross Hospital in Fulham Palace Road and neurosurgeons removed a blood clot from the surface of his brain. He hovered in an induced coma, his family at his side. Kelly also visited. Steve Watt died on 18 March at the age of 27. The Kelly loss was his second in thirteen fights. Kelly was at his funeral and there was a sharp intake of breath when he threw a handful of gravel at Watt's coffin. It looked and sounded like an angry gesture; it was not. 'Rocky had great respect for Steve, that's why he threw it like that – he was throwing it like a warrior would,' said Holland. There was nothing gentle about Kelly. Three fights later, in 1987, he was back at the same hotel losing in a British welter-weight title fight to Kirkland Laing. The Laing fight was stopped too early, according to Holland: 'Rocky was hurt, but he knew where he was.'

It was business as usual for Holland and Kelly, but not for Watt's trainer/manager Dickie Gunn. 'I don't blame boxing, but I never want to see another glove.' Watt was a registered organ donor and his heart, liver and kidneys were offered for transplant. The modern statistics for death and serious injury in boxing start on that March night when Watt was beaten.

Dennis Andries was the old man of British boxing long before he was an old man. He was 24 when he turned professional, 30 when he finally won the British title, and in late April, at 32, he fought for the world title at Pickett's Lock in north London. Andries would win and lose the WBC light-heavyweight title three times in the next five years.

This first title win was against the reluctant J. B. Williamson and it was a tough fight to watch. 'The JB stands for Just Bad, and he ain't lying,' said Reg Gutteridge, the ITV commentator. Andries deserved the split decision win, everybody deserved a better fight. Williamson lost to George Foreman a couple of years later and ended his career on a run of eleven defeats. Andries would spend the next ten years in major fights. Sadly, London cabbie Harry Griver, the small growling man behind the old Colvestone gym where Andries trained, was in hospital on the night of the fight. Andries took the green WBC belt up the next day.

The Pavilion at the Alexandra Palace in north London was the setting for the first defence of the WBC light-heavyweight title by Andries in September. The two boxers were senior members of the British boxing business: Tony Sibson had first won the British middleweight title seven years earlier, in 1979, and Andries had been a professional since 1978. Sibson had a loyal following and they booed the British world champion when Andries arrived, which was a first. It was only the second time that two British boxers had contested a world title since 1949, the first being Jim Watt and Charlie Nash in 1980. The Hackney Rock, as Andries was often known, was too strong; Sibson was suddenly drained, weary and unhappy in the eighth. He was stopped in the ninth after being on the canvas four times. Sibson was shattered, not hurt, and howled in frustration at one point. It was his sixty-first bout and he would have one more world title fight before retiring. It was only the start for Andries.

There were two nights of extremes for the marvellous McKenzie brothers in May. There was a dismal and bad-tempered end to Clinton's vacant British light-welterweight title fight with Kirkland Laing's brother, Tony, at the Royal Albert Hall early in the month. McKenzie had first won the title in 1978. He had lost it, won it, lost it, and then came the Laing fight. He should have fought for a world title at some point between 1978 and 1986. In 1984 a fight with WBA light-welter champion Johnny Bumphus was agreed and then Bumphus lost to Gene Hatcher. McKenzie was involved in three *Boxing News* fights of the year. On the night against Laing it looked like McKenzie had won by five or six rounds; the referee, Roland Dakin, went heavily for Laing. 'I quit, that's it,' raged McKenzie. Laing was with Mickey Duff, the show was a Duff and Mike Barrett show, and McKenzie was with south London's Frank Maloney. 'That decision was a disgrace, a total disgrace,' remembered Kellie, as Frank was known in 2016 after a full sex-change operation.

Duke McKenzie had won the vacant British flyweight title in June 1985. Charlie Magri had retained his European version a couple of months later. They met in May at Wembley for both titles and Magri's wild, sell-out crowd went missing. The boy from Tunisia who had been raised in and adored by the East End of London was a lonely flat-nosed figure that night. Magri was dropped in the fifth and Terry Lawless launched a final towel of surrender to end his boxer's career at 2:05. Duke went on and won world titles at three different weights, but it was all over for Champagne Charlie.

In Magri's dressing room, as the backslappers came and went mostly in silent embarrassment, Lawless sat down for one final damning chat with the 29-year-old he had first taken under his wing ten years earlier. Terry the father figure hardened up as he started to talk in the harshest of terms. 'You are going to have to get up off your arse and go out and get a real job now,' Lawless told a stunned Magri. The little flyweight who'd delighted so many and generated so much never forgave Lawless for that brutal outburst.

In July at Wembley Stadium, a fixture that had no severe heat warnings attached, there was a heavyweight world title fight and another British boxing idol was left bruised, bloody and beaten. Frank Bruno was matched with Tim Witherspoon for the WBA version of the splintered title. It was the first fight in the ancient stadium since Muhammad Ali, then known as Cassius Clay, had met Henry Cooper in 1963. That was the fight with the knockdown, ripped glove and inventions (the gloves Cooper wore, with the split in the left, live in London as part of the Trevor Beattie Collection). Ali and Cooper were introduced to the crowd of 40,000. The bookies had Bruno as prohibitive 7-4 favourite, the papers had him crowned. It would, inevitably, get ugly.

It was a tight fight. All three judges had Witherspoon in front going into the eleventh, but a lot of shrewder judges had Bruno slightly ahead. It was a good fight, a hard fight. It was scheduled for fifteen and Bruno was starting to fade, to slow down. Spoon, as he was known, had arrived overweight and had not improved his appearance during a training camp of long meals and big laughs in Essex. However, he was a good heavyweight, a throwback fighter, raised taking punches inside Ali's camp and the Philadelphia gyms. He was a heavyweight fighter. He had no need for a six-pack.

Witherspoon had been looking for and landing his big overhand right from the first round. Bruno had been taking the punch, coming straight back with his own. A left hook from the American champion in round eight was absorbed; it was the type of punch that destroys the myth that Bruno had no chin. There was nothing wrong with Bruno's chin, it was just that his body shut down when he was tired and he left himself exposed. In the eleventh round Witherspoon buckled Bruno's knees with the big right. Bruno stumbled back to the corner post, was caught again, trapped, and then finished with a series of punches that only natural fighters can unleash. Bruno slumped, hands low, and took the punches before slowly sinking down, helped on his way by a few more clean punches. Nobody ever doubted Bruno's heart. He was bloody, dazed and crouched in the corner when Terry Lawless lobbed in a white towel. It was officially

2:57 of the eleventh when it was called off. There was some trouble at the end: two hundred chairs were thrown, twenty-seven were arrested and ten police were injured.

It was not a disaster for Bruno, it proved he could fight. However, Mickey Duff, his promoter, was not as kind: 'When it mattered, Bruno did not have the will to win.' The fight was shown on ITV at 9.30 the next morning and on the BBC later that evening. The rival broadcasters had, apparently, drawn lots for first screening rights. Bruno was only 24, and he would eventually win a world heavyweight title when he was 33.

The first IBF world title fight to take place in Britain was at Granada Studios in Manchester in August. The New Jersey-based sanctioning body was not yet recognized by the British Boxing Board of Control, but a compromise on working officials had been reached and the Board's secretary John Morris was ringside. The super-featherweight champion was Barry Michael, who had been born in Watford, but his family had left for Australia when he was a toddler. The challenger was Manchester's Najib Daho, who originally was a Berber from the mountain regions of Morocco. Daho had settled in Manchester when he was 15, but he was probably younger. 'I have no idea when I born, I was asked for date and I just give date,' said Daho, who had developed a powerfully confused accent by the time he was fighting. He turned pro at 17, was paid thirty quid for his debut, and entered the ring against Michael having lost eighteen of his forty-nine fights. 'He has a great record if you don't just look at it in terms of fights won and lost,' said Daho's promoter, Jack Trickett. 'You need to look at who he has fought, when the fight took place and what condition he was in, and how much notice he had.' In May, at the Free Trade Hall in Manchester, Daho had stopped Pat Cowdell in the first to win the British super-featherweight title. It was the win that secured the Michael fight. It went the full twelve and Michael retained comfortably. Daho lost a rematch to Cowdell in 1987, won the Commonwealth lightweight title in 1989, and died in 1993 in a car crash in Morocco. He was possibly 34 at the end.

Something odd happened in Atlantic City in September when

Lloyd Honeyghan, a big 7-1 underdog, stopped previously unbeaten Donald Curry in a savage one-way fight. There was talk before the fight that Curry had a $10 million offer on the table for a showdown with Marvin Hagler. Honeyghan had nothing to lose. The fight programme was a single sheet and fewer than a thousand people were in the ballroom at Caesars. Curry was defending his WBA, WBC and IBF welterweight belts, but it was not a big event. It was meant to be routine. Curry had lost just three times in over four hundred amateur contests, was on a run of twenty-five as a professional and was on the edge of the money fights. He had also been forced to lose 21lb in camp and would never fight at welterweight again. The fight was being screened in British cinemas at a cost of £20 per head. Honeyghan and Duff, his manager, had a big wager on victory. They each put $5,000 down. Duff won $37,500, Honeyghan marginally less because the odds had dropped.

Honeyghan had promised to 'smash' Curry all week, and it sounded like a desperate attempt to create some interest in a fight that was being ignored by the Americans. At the end of round six Curry stayed on his stool. He had a broken nose, a cut lip that needed a solitary stitch and a cut under his left eyebrow that required twenty stitches. It had been a horrible mismatch the wrong way round. Honeyghan and Duff celebrated in the ring, a jubilant display of relief and joy as Curry left for surgery on his wounds. At 1.30 a.m. Curry met with the press. 'My timing wasn't there,' he said. 'I was sluggish. I wasn't myself.' Curry would win a world title at light-middle in 1988. Honeyghan's life would never be the same again. 'Lloyd doesn't fight like a British guy, he's mean and nasty,' said ringside guest Mike Tyson, just 20 but only six weeks away from becoming the new world heavyweight champion.

The night before Honeyghan's win, in Miami Beach, Cornelius Boza-Edwards lost on points to Hector 'Macho Man' Camacho for the WBC lightweight title. It was not quite the end for Boza, but it was close. One judge scored the fight a shut-out, which seemed a bit harsh.

In November, Herol Graham stopped Mark Kaylor; Lawless pulled his fighter out at the end of the eighth round at Wembley. 'He's impossible to hit, and how can you beat somebody you can't hit?' asked Kaylor. Graham retained his European middleweight title, moved to 37-0, but was still two years away from a world title fight. The Kaylor stoppage was the fourteenth by Graham in his previous fifteen fights, a raw number that should have ended any talk of him being a light puncher. Graham was avoided by world champions, it's that simple.

Joe Bugner was back after a two-year break and won in Sydney in November. It was his second fight in three months. Bugner was 36 and convinced he could win a world title. 'Fighting Bruno would be a backward step for me,' said Bugner. 'I'm still in my prime.' His return was attacked by Bunny Johnson: 'He's in the foothills of middle age now. He was once the best in Europe and one of the best in the world – that prime was over ten years ago.' Bugner had a win over former world champion Greg Page in his next fight and then the attention did turn to Bruno. It was inevitable, all part of the glorious pantomime.

The Contenders

Jimmy McDonnell retained his European featherweight title at Wembley. It was the last title fight that Jimmy Mac won.

Chris Pyatt won the British light-middleweight title in February when he beat Prince Rodney, added the European version in September, and finished the year, like so many British boxers did in the seventies and eighties, with a stoppage win overseas.

Horace Notice went to the Isle of Man in April to beat Catford's Hughroy Currie for the British heavyweight title.

At the ABA finals at Wembley in May Nigel Benn won, Big Bad James Oyebola won, and there was a stunning one-punch knockout win for Daren Dyer. The Commonwealth Games were in Edinburgh in the summer and Oyebola finished with a bronze medal when he lost to London-born Lennox Lewis, who was boxing for Canada. Rod Douglas had lost to Benn in the north-east London divisional championship, but Benn had some problems, Douglas got the recall, and won gold.

From the Notepad

'Outside of my area nobody has heard of me,' McDonnell, the 'Camden Caretaker', told me. 'I'm the European champion. When Alan Minter was the European champion he was a household name.'

In August, after Douglas had won the Commonwealth Games gold, a full-page advert appeared in the *Boxing News*. It was, according to the wording, an official 'Put Up or Shut Up Challenge'. The small print in the bold advert promised to take every available ticket for the show if an amateur club would put on a fight between Benn and Douglas. 'I've not said a word,' said Douglas. In February at York Hall, after Benn had beaten Douglas on a majority decision, he had stood to attention at ringside when I interviewed him for London's *Evening Standard*. Benn had lost to Douglas the year before at light-middle. The third fight never happened and Benn turned pro the following January.

1987

'I know I should not be fighting any more, but I need the money.'
Chuck Gardner before fighting Frank Bruno

'There is nothing in our contract that says we have to like each other.'
Mickey Duff on his special relationship with Lloyd Honeyghan

LIFE WAS NEVER simple for Lloyd Honeyghan, and in January he dumped his WBA belt in a bin. Mickey Duff, his manager, claimed he never knew anything about the publicity shot. 'He did it because he had to do it,' Duff claimed. 'The WBC threatened to strip him, the WBA ordered him to fight a man he was refusing to fight.' It was alphabet soup politics at its very best.

It looked like Honeyghan had taken a stand against apartheid by refusing to fight South Africa's Harold Volbrecht, but that is too simple an interpretation. Volbrecht was one of the WBA's leading contenders, but he first had to beat Mark Breland, a gold medal winner in 1984, in a final eliminator before he got anywhere near Honeyghan. And that was never going to happen. Volbrecht, it turns out, was a decent fella, a man that fought in townships, had taken a stance against apartheid and, after being the white champion in the seventies, won the full South African welterweight championship, known as the Supreme title, in 1978. In early February at Trump Plaza Hotel in Atlantic City, Breland stopped Volbrecht in round seven to win the vacant WBA welterweight title.

Honeyghan was free to get on with his business and would have four world title fights during the year. In February at Wembley in front of 2,900 people Honeyghan defended his IBF version over fifteen rounds against his number one challenger, Johnny Bumphus. The WBC had reduced their title fights to twelve rounds, so they never recognized the fight, which meant that if Bumphus won he would not have taken home the WBC belt. Only the IBF bauble was on the line.

It was quick and controversial. Bumphus was dropped in the first, punched all over the ring, and looked like a beaten man as he stumbled back to his corner at the bell. At the start of round two, before the bell, Honeyghan had moved close to the Bumphus corner, and on the bell he launched an attack. The American was listening to Lou Duva – a man who had spaghetti-eating competitions in the fifties with Rocky Marciano, and a face shaped by decades in the boxing world – and was just starting to rise when Honeyghan struck. Duva was still in the ring when a wild Honeyghan left sent Bumphus down. The bell had sounded, but the referee, Sam Williams of Detroit, was stuck in no-man's land, seemingly unaware that a man of 10st 7lb wearing sparkling silver shorts had walked across the ring. Bumphus went down, Duva turned and started screaming, and Honeyghan celebrated. Williams called a time-out, dealt with the situation, calming Duva (who a few years later had a heart attack in the ring after another post-fight squabble), and then deducted a point from Honeyghan's score. Duff was standing on the ring apron, concerned that his man could be disqualified. The ref waved the pair on, the bell sounded again, and Bumphus never recovered; he was trapped on the ropes when the fight was stopped after fifty-five seconds. The moaning went long into the winter night.

The WBC wanted Honeyghan to defend their title and in April at the Royal Albert Hall he obliged, met their mandatory, and this time the men from the IBF refused to sanction the twelve-round fight. It was starting to feel like a silly game where the slick-suited fixers, hidden in their lavish distant bunkers of endless intrigue, attempted to manipulate their champions. The WBC's shorter distance saved Honeyghan his title.

It was a hard night for the Londoner against the unbeaten Maurice Blocker. Honeyghan looked wild at times, desperate, and kept lunging. The three officials scored it to the champion by seven, five and three rounds, which seemed generous – a ludicrous interpretation of the action in fact. It was tight at the end, Honeyghan was marked and exhausted, and the IBF's extra, and traditional, three rounds would have probably been too much. 'I lost forty rounds of sparring and that was my problem,' said Honeyghan, who had prepared in France. George Francis, the latest man in his corner, had struggled to hire men to spar. The win over Donald Curry was less than seven months earlier but that paradise moment had gone for ever. There was growing animosity between Duff and Honeyghan. Terry Lawless, remember, had discarded Honeyghan and challenged Duff to take him on. Duff had, and now the problems were developing.

Honeyghan's year continued with a date in the Marbella bullring in August against Gene 'Mad Dog' Hatcher in front of over 7,000. The stars were out, it was hot and sticky, and it ended after forty-five seconds: Hatcher was down for four and then backed up, hit with some hefty punches before sliding down on to the canvas. The ref was abysmal, a frozen witness to the violence, and Hatcher needed a few minutes before he was helped back to his stool. 'The ref didn't stop the fight – I did,' said Honeyghan. 'I stopped throwing punches. I just walked away, I didn't want to hit him any more. He was out cold.' The fight had been postponed for twenty-four hours and Honeyghan was a lot bigger; Hatcher had been a world champion at the weight below, and it showed. 'Honeyghan is a helluva puncher, but I still think he's an arrogant son of a bitch,' said Hatcher. Honeyghan was in an astonishing run of world title fights, but there were many who shared Hatcher's sentiments.

Honeyghan went for one world title fight too many in October when he met Mexican Jorge Vaca for the WBC welterweight title at Wembley. The mess at the end was a poor way to lose a title. In round eight a clash of heads, which was ruled accidental, left Vaca with a bad cut on his right eyebrow. The fight was stopped then and the referee instructed the three judges to add up their scores for the seven completed rounds but then to take a point off Honeyghan. It was a new WBC rule. The final scores were savage on Honeyghan: one judge went for him, the other two went 67-65 and 67-66 for Vaca. If there had been no deduction then Lloyd would have kept his title on a draw. The IBF declared their title vacant. Vaca needed fifteen stitches to close the wound and returned five months later for a rematch.

March was extreme for British boxers in world title fights, with one winning in an Italian circus tent and one losing in the very battered heart of a city in terminal decline.

Terry Marsh had been due to fight Patrizio Oliva for the world title in September 1986. He had first won the British light-welterweight title in 1984, the European version the following year, and in early March 1987 in Basildon a tent was erected in his honour. Marsh stopped American Joe Manley in the tenth of fifteen rounds to win the IBF light-welterweight title in front of a crowd of just under 6,000. Manley was over in the ninth, finished in the tenth. Marsh was Frank Warren's first world champion.

Three days later Dennis Andries met Thomas 'Hitman' Hearns at the Cobo Arena in Detroit for the WBC light-heavyweight title. Hearns was a Detroit legend, the Kronk fighter at the core of the only revival in the shattered city's modern history. This fight had been agreed in December 1986, and it never made any sense. Hearns had turned professional the year before Andries, in 1977, weighing 30lb less, and had won world titles at welterweight and light-middleweight. His 1985 fight with Marvin Hagler is often listed as one of the greatest ever to have taken place. Andries was still anonymous and had been booed into the ring before his first defence, which took place at a venue less than three miles from his house in north London. On the night in Detroit, 11,230 paid to watch and they left happy: Hearns was the new champion when it was finally halted in the tenth. It was not the massacre people think. Andries was down many, many times in a hostile fight. He was hurt, wobbled, and remained defiant. In round seven, after being over five times in the sixth, he chased Hearns all over the ring. That took guts and a bit of stupidity. He fought back each time until the end when he staggered to his corner, away from the ref, after the last knockdown; he was not surrendering, but he was finished. Andries could never surrender. Andries, at 33 and after thirty-seven fights, was only getting started in the pro game.

Dave 'Boy' McAuley would finish his career after just twenty-three fights in nine years. He developed and fought in the shadow of Barry McGuigan for a few years. He made five defences of his world title and that was a modern record; Jim Watt had managed four. He is too often overlooked, forgotten or relegated to some type of freak champion when lists are compiled. In addition to the statistics, McAuley was in outrageous fights that mixed blood, guts and heroics. In many ways he belonged to a different time.

In April at the King's Hall, Belfast, McAuley fought Fidel Bassa for the WBA flyweight title. Bassa was unknown, unbeaten in seventeen with thirteen ending quickly. He had won the title in Barranquilla, his hometown in Colombia, on points over fifteen rounds. The fight had been delayed when his opponent, the champion, Hilário Zapata, was assaulted by somebody at ringside. He was knocked out according to some reports and there was a twenty-minute delay. The atmosphere inside the iconic Belfast venue was not quite so violent.

There was a quick warning of Bassa's power when McAuley was down in the first thirty seconds. In round nine Bassa was dropped twice, both times heavily, and McAuley chased: a third knockdown in the round and the title would have been his under the WBA's rules. It was a brutal night for both boxers. If the fight had been under WBC rules and only twelve rounds, like Honeyghan's defence earlier in the month, the Larne man would have won on points. It ended in round thirteen when three rights connected and brave McAuley crumpled to the canvas as the towel came in. All three judges had him in front. 'He was very dirty and he kept hitting me with his head and thumbing me in the eye. I still can't believe how he managed to survive the ninth,' said McAuley, who had lost for the first time in fourteen fights.

The year had started for Herol Graham with his promoter Barney Eastwood offering Marvin Hagler a million dollars for a fight. It was not enough. Eastwood then promised to lobby the WBA to strip

Hagler for his continued refusal to fight Graham. It seemed harsh on Hagler, a man that had struggled, battled the odds, to get to the title, but the great bald one certainly had a blind spot with Graham. Hagler had been the unified champion for seven years, had made twelve defences and had a ridiculous payday finale planned at that time against Sugar Ray Leonard. Hagler was stripped of the WBA title in February and he lost a disputed decision to Leonard in early April.

Graham was back in the ring in May and still no closer to a world title fight. He was unbeaten in thirty-eight fights and during Hagler's reign he had stopped or knocked out eighteen of the twenty-four men he met. That is not the record of a non-punching runner. The May fight was against Sumbu Kalambay, and it was a disaster. Brendan Ingle, who had been with Graham from the start, had been pushed aside for Eastwood's choice, the mystery Panamanian Frederico Plummer. So many boxing trainers come and go, working in gyms that open and close like storefront churches, offering instant remedies. Ingle was gone, a sickened spectator to the horror. 'I'd have won that fight if Brendan had still been in my corner,' admitted Graham in 2011. Graham had tried to pull out and not fight. His head was in pieces, and during the fight he was trying to second-guess the instructions he was receiving by wondering what Brendan would be telling him. At the end of twelve rounds he lost by just one, two and three rounds. His European middleweight title was gone, but the real loss was the planned, schemed and dangled world title fight. Graham would have to wait another two years before finally, in his eleventh year as professional, getting a world title shot. Kalambay would fight for and win the vacant WBA title five months later. It was the first of the sad nights in Graham's career, one of the most remarkable and frustrating in British boxing history.

At the ABA finals in early May there was a rare double for Akay Isola's All Stars gym when lightweight Michael Ayers and super-heavyweight James Oyebola won titles. The pair would win British titles as professionals. (One night in the summer of 2007 a coward shot Oyebola in the head after a tiny dispute about a cigarette.) Mr

Akay, as he was always known, started the All Stars gym in his flat and on the balcony and hallways of his block in the mid-seventies when his son, Tee Jay, was refused entry at an amateur boxing gym on London's Harrow Road. Tee Jay told me, one night in Berlin, that he had been called a 'wog', had his pocket money stolen, and was then evicted. Tee Jay lost to Evander Holyfield at the 1984 Olympics and won the British cruiserweight title in 1986. He was always proud of what his father achieved. 'I had the sparring in the living room, skipping by the lifts, and every night more kids showed up,' said Mr Akay.

There was no fun in the sun for Frank Bruno in late June when his one-punch dismissal of Chuck Gardner after fifty-nine seconds of the first round in Cannes was condemned. Gardner was 33, he claimed he was 35, and nobody expected the fight to last. Terry Lawless, ever loyal to his fighters and partners, called it a 'quick, clean knockout', but others were less convinced. The head of sport at the BBC, Jonathan Martin, paid for the shambles and was quick to stick the boot in: 'It's damaged boxing and it's damaged boxing's image.' It was shown live on BBC. The match had been made by Johnny Bos, a genius at finding heavyweights. Big Frank did exactly what you are meant to do when a gift arrives in the opposite corner. Bruno was blameless.

In July there was celebration in Sydney when Joe Bugner beat former world champion Greg Page on points. On that day the kid from Hungary, the British heavyweight champion of infamy, became an Australian citizen. 'I wasn't going to let my country down – I never came to dilly or dally,' said Aussie Joe at the end. The following month Barry Hearn, the Essex accountant and snooker impresario, agreed a promotional deal with Lawless. In September, Hearn, Lawless and Mickey Duff, their other partner, announced that Aussie Joe was coming back to Britain to fight Bruno outdoors at White Hart Lane on 24 October. No baby steps for Barry, that's for sure.

'For five years I've listened to his insults,' said Bruno. 'Now I will shut him up.' Bugner arrived in London wearing a T-shirt that said 'We promise you blood, sweat and tears'. 'They used to call me a robot,' Bugner countered. 'But that's exactly what Frank is. I'll flatten him in five rounds.' Sadly, away from the pens and microphones of the media horde, Aussie Joe was having problems with his ex-wife. He had been divorced ten years. 'I needed more time, I tried to push it back,' Bugner said.

On the night over 37,000 people paid. There were some serious teething problems and Hearn later held his hands up and apologized in the *Boxing News* for the bad seats, skirmishes, dreadful stewarding, an atmosphere of intimidation and a few other problems. But it was a great event, and Bugner played the baddie role to perfection, pulling faces, threatening havoc at every turn. On the night there was a delay before he walked to the ring. He was said to be holding out for more money and he deserved every penny. Bruno won the fight, finally clubbing a reluctant Bugner heavily near the end of the eighth round. Bruno then manhandled him to the canvas. Aussie Joe hauled his considerable bulk up, Bruno rushed in, a towel of surrender sailed in, the bell sounded and the fight was over. The post-fight caper included Bruno repeatedly asking ITV's Jim Rosenthal 'Where's 'Arry?' Rosey was not impressed. And Bugner started to sell Bruno as a future opponent for the world champion Mike Tyson: 'Frank has the power to hurt Tyson. I hope he smashes Tyson's face in.' What a night that was. Bugner was not finished, and Bruno, well, he was still a boxing child.

After the circus tent there was the carnival, and for Marsh the first defence of his IBF light-welterweight title at the Royal Albert Hall in July would be his last. Marsh was getting £147,000 for the fight and at ringside was former WBC lightweight champion Hector 'Macho Man' Camacho. That fight could be made. Marsh had also talked about dropping down to lightweight, a verbal diversion that had attracted the attention of Barry McGuigan. It had been over a year since McGuigan, now managed by Warren, had lost to Steve Cruz in Las Vegas and he was talking about a return. 'I would like to meet Marsh,' the Irishman said. 'I could come in at nine-five, so he would have to come down a fair bit.' Marsh had also said the defence against Japan's Akio Kameda would be his last. That decision was taken firmly out of his hands in the next few weeks.

Marsh cut and dropped Kameda, forcing the Japanese boxer to quit at the end of the sixth round. It all started to go horribly wrong shortly after that. In September, Marsh was talking about wanting £500,000 for his next defence; he then gave an exclusive to the *Sun* announcing that he had epilepsy and would never fight again. Marsh had signed a deal to fight his leading contender, who strangely was called Frankie Warren, the day before the epilepsy story ran in the paper. There was, as expected, a bitter dispute with Frank Warren, and Marsh later claimed boxers were treated like 'slaves'. The ugly story rumbled on and ended in court.

The Contenders

At the end of March, with Mike Tyson at ringside, Bruno had ended an eight-month exile with a fifth-round stoppage of James Tillis in front of a small crowd at Wembley. Bruno would fight for the world title three more times, survive an eye operation, delight and infuriate the purists in equal measure, prop up pantomime stages and remain a fixture in the business for eight more years. His longevity is seldom praised; he finally won a world title thirteen years after turning professional.

It was the end for Cornelius Boza-Edwards in October when he was stopped in round five of a fight for the WBC lightweight title against José Luis Ramirez in Paris. Both Boza and Ramirez belong to a distant time. Ramirez, the champion, was having his 105th fight; it was Boza's fifty-third and final night in the ring. Boza was about sacrifice in the ring.

From the Notepad

'Duva is a licensed squealer,' said Duff at the end of the Honeyghan–Bumphus fight. 'I've never known him to lose a fight without causing a commotion.' The same could be said of Duff, and that is a great thing for a fighter to know.

'He [Duff] looks at me as a pawn, a commodity. I don't like him,'

Honeyghan said. Duff was not bothered by the comment. He wore an invisible overcoat which allowed him to work with people he hated, a traditional piece of clothing that all the very best boxing operators have to wear at one time or another. Duff responded: 'Fortunately, there is nothing in our contract that says we have to like each other.' A few years later Duff would add another gem to the list of his unforgettable quotes. He was asked about a fighter that had left him, and if he was shocked. He said, 'If you want loyalty, get a dog.'

After the Boza–Chacon fight in 1981, George Francis said, 'It's fights like this that make young boys into old men.' It was both a warning and a compliment. Fighters like Boza never worried about being old men. They just wanted to be remembered as fighters.

1988

'I want to give myself at least one private contest, maybe two, before
I start throwing punches in public. I think the other fella will be glad
of his head guard. I will wear no head guard and I will find out
again what it is like to be hit with the eight-ounce gloves.'
Barry McGuigan on his secret training tactic

'If I'd fought Bugner when I was, say, 31 or 32, I'd have knocked him out,
no bother, but I was an old man of 37 when I got him. Bruno would have
been no trouble either – I could always handle the big men. He's not a very
mobile fighter, or quick-thinking in the ring.'
Henry Cooper on British heavyweights

FIVE BRITISH BOXERS fought for world titles, in six fights at four different
weights, during an extreme year for the business.

It was the end for Tony Sibson in February when his third and
final world title fight ended in round ten. Sibson had lost to Marvin
Hagler in 1983, then Dennis Andries in 1986, and in Stafford he was
stopped in the tenth by Frank Tate for the IBF's middleweight title.
Tate was unbeaten in twenty-one at the time; Sibson lost for the
seventh time in sixty-three fights of a career that had started a long,
long way from the bright lights in 1976. He beat Alan Minter, Mark
Kaylor, and Frankie Lucas in an unforgettable fight at the Royal
Albert Hall in 1979. That Lucas fight remains one of the most savage
short brawls in British boxing history.

The King's Hall in Belfast was heaving once again in March when

Dave McAuley entered the ring for his rematch with WBA flyweight champion Fidel Bassa. McAuley had talked the year before about moving to light-flyweight, but he struggled with weight before the Bassa rematch, had his nose broken in the seventh, was dropped in the ninth, and lost a tight decision. Bassa had been lucky eleven months earlier when the fight was over fifteen rounds, but this time he was clever. McAuley wanted to retire, wanted to walk away and concentrate on being a chef at the family restaurant. It never happened, but he was unhappy with his manager, Barney Eastwood.

There was blood revenge for Lloyd Honeyghan three days later at Wembley Arena when the south Londoner stopped and dropped Jorge Vaca in the third to regain the WBC welterweight title. It was an ugly night in many ways. Honeyghan refused to shake hands before the first bell, pushed Vaca away, and then, to a deafening chorus of approval, set about assaulting the Mexican until a final right sent him down and out. A quarter of a century later, Honeyghan walks in and out of boxing shows in fur hats, fur coats and often with a walking cane. The look, the swagger makes people chuckle, but he certainly delivered on his big nights back in the eighties.

At the end of July Honeyghan retained his WBC welterweight title in Atlantic City at the Convention Hall, stopping Yung-Kil Chung of South Korea in the fifth; but the real fight was to impress the Americans on a bill when the WBA champion Marlon Starling also retained his title. The pair were matched, they disliked each other, but to be fair, Honeyghan hated all welterweights. Starling had won the title from Mark Breland in 1987. It would be a proper test, a serious world title fight.

The twenty-two-month exile ended in April at a pavilion pitched in the Alexandra Palace car park. Barry McGuigan had prepared for the fight after his extended sabbatical by sparring without a head guard and with 8oz championship gloves, not 14oz. The fallen idol was back at super-featherweight, under different management, and he looked anxious as he made his way to the ring. The crowd still adored him. Frank Warren, the new man in the McGuigan business, had IBF president Bob Lee at ringside. If McGuigan won, a fight with the IBF's super-featherweight champion Rocky Lockridge could be made. Warren had contractual options available on Lockridge. McGuigan sent Nicky Perez down twice in the fourth before it was called off. He was back, a bit older, a bit slower, but still a big attraction.

Some nimble legal attention had had to be paid before McGuigan stripped for combat. His relationship with Eastwood was now completely over. Warren had paid Eastwood £200,000 to finally relinquish his stake in McGuigan's future. Eastwood said a few unkind words before the Perez scrap. McGuigan would not retaliate. 'Things went wrong but an endless slagging match won't do anybody any good,' he said.

In June, over 14,000 watched him win in four again, this time at Luton Town's ground against Francisco Tomás Da Cruz. There was a final outing in December when 12 million watched on ITV as McGuigan stopped Julio César Miranda in eight. It was a tough fight – too tough. McGuigan was cut over both eyes, his right hand was damaged, and it was a struggle. McGuigan was worried that he had not finished the Argentinian in the third when he had been dropped. It was a sign, and McGuigan knew what it meant; he considered it 'a poor performance'. It wasn't by ordinary standards, but by McGuigan's standards it was. The Clones Cyclone had just one fight left and it was not going to be pleasant for him.

On the McGuigan bill in April, Nigel Benn won the Commonwealth middleweight title when he stopped the Ghanaian Abdul Umaru Sanda in round two. It was Benn's seventeenth consecutive stoppage win. 'The fight that the people want to see is [Herol] Graham v. Benn and everything else is just second division material,' said Frank Warren, Benn's promoter. Benn had one more fight for Warren – and it was not against Graham – before leaving to be promoted by Frank Maloney and Terry Marsh. There was a pit-stop in the High Court to break away from the contract with Warren. The pair would work together years later.

Benn was back, free of his contract with Warren, at the end of October as the main attraction on a non-televised show at the Royal

Albert Hall. The Hall's long-term promoter and one-time member of the original boxing cartel, Mike Barrett, joined with Maloney and Marsh – the latter addition sure to irritate Warren – in order to promote the oddity. There was a promise of a £25 VHS recording of the action. Benn had Ambrose Mendy, a figure from boxing's fringes – an uncharted destination that has been his home ever since – as his 'commercial representative'. The fight was a blast: Benn was over in the first and seemingly gone in the second before delivering a single-punch knockout to beat Anthony Logan.

In May it was meant to be the end for the latest East End golden boy when Mark Kaylor was knocked out by Tom Collins, an ageing beast of a fighter from Leeds, for the European light-heavyweight title. Nearly eighteen months later, Collins travelled to Australia for his first world title fight in what was his forty-first appearance as a professional.

It was the end that May for Pat Cowdell. The man from Warley in the West Midlands had won four ABA titles, an Olympic bronze in 1976, a Commonwealth Games gold, a bronze at the European amateur championship, and, arguably, should have been sent to the inaugural world amateur championship in 1974. As a pro he took the great Salvador Sánchez to a split in their world title fight over fifteen rounds in Texas, lost to Azumah Nelson in another, and won British and European titles at two weights. He beat Cornelius Boza-Edwards in the ABAs, and his British title win over Jimmy Flint, the Wapping Assassin, in 1980 was a pure masterclass. He has to be considered one of the elite British boxers of the modern era.

In July it was announced that Frank Bruno would fight the undisputed heavyweight world champion Mike Tyson at Wembley Stadium on 3 September. The date would get moved to 8 October and then to 22 October before the deal collapsed. Donald Trump was Tyson's adviser at the time. 'I have put together a team of experts to look at Mike,' he said. (That sounds familiar.) Away from the ring, Tyson injured his right hand in an altercation with Mitch 'Blood' Green outside Dapper Dan's clothing store in Harlem at 4.30 a.m., and then was knocked unconscious in a car crash. There was a claim that it was a suicide attempt, denied by Trump. Tyson was in freefall. Bruno had not fought since beating Bugner.

Eight British boxers were picked for the Seoul Olympics, which started in September and ended in utter turmoil and disgust in October. The GB selection was from the start a controversial process of elimination, inclusion and heartbreak. Only four of the twelve ABA champions from the finals in May were selected. There was not one box-off, but Richie Woodhall and Neville Brown were in opposite sides of the draw at the Canada Cup; Brown lost early and Woodhall won silver to secure the Olympic place at light-middle. Brown had beaten Woodhall in the domestic championship. Woodhall was exceptional at the Olympics, winning a bronze after losing in the semi-final to Roy Jones Jr. In the final, Jones lost to South Korea's Park Si-Hun in a fight that was considered at the time so controversial that the sport was close to being dropped from the Olympic programme. Oddly, it was not the one-way massacre it has been portrayed as since that night of infamy; Jones won, but Park was in the fight. At the Games, officials were punched, boxers sat in protest in the ring, two rings were used, it was mayhem. 'It was a comedy of errors from the first bell until the last, but a cockney-boy won the final gold and that ain't bad,' said Reg Gutteridge. Lennox Lewis, boxing for Canada, stopped Riddick Bowe in the super-heavyweight final. The London-born fighter would agree a deal with Frank Maloney and make his professional debut at the Royal Albert Hall in June 1989.

November was a cruel month for a pair of gym mates, men that had spent a lot of time together at the Royal Oak in Canning Town.

Horace Notice, the undefeated British and Commonwealth heavyweight champion, was forced to retire after suffering retina damage in both eyes. Notice lost just once as an amateur and never as a professional in sixteen fights. He had been due to make a career-high payday of £50,000 for a European title fight in Milan in September. Both Gary Mason and Bruno had been friends and sparring partners, and in 1989 a fight with Mason was a possibility. In January 1989 Mason won the vacant British title, and Derek 'Sweet D' Williams of

Peckham won the Commonwealth version the same month Notice was forced to quit. Notice is one of the forgotten men of the business.

The setting for Jim McDonnell's sad night was the Elephant and Castle Leisure Centre, a boxing hall that always had the smell of thick chlorine in the air from the wave pool; the venue had replaced Manor Place Baths for boxing in the south London area. McDonnell lost on points over twelve rounds to South Africa's Brian Mitchell for the WBA's super-featherweight title. Mitchell was hard and McDonnell never did enough – that's the simple interpretation of the fight. But it ignores the story behind Jimmy's odd performance. He was unbeaten in twenty-four fights, and had won the European titles at feather-weight. He regrets not pushing for a world title fight with Barry Michael, who had beaten Najib Daho for the IBF super-featherweight title in 1986. On the night of his world title fight at the Elephant, as McDonnell was getting ready to walk to the ring he was asked to sign a new contract by Lawless. There was a row, a threat to withdraw. The contract was not signed, the fight took place, and it was the last time McDonnell fought for Lawless and Duff. 'That was a terrible way to get ready for the biggest fight of my life,' he said. 'I never forgave Lawless for that.'

In late November and early December, Chris Pyatt, the former British and European light-middleweight champion, was close to losing his way but he fought and won three times in just over twenty days. At the time Pyatt had a criminal case hanging high above his head involving the robbery of a jewellery store in Leicester. Pyatt was eventually acquitted of all charges when he convinced the jury he had been sleeping in the back of the getaway car and was an innocent participant. He was a nap away from nowhere. He would win a world title before retiring in 1997 to train fighters back in Leicester.

In December there was news that Beryl Cameron-Gibbons, the landlady at the Thomas A'Becket and promoter from the seventies, was dead. She was remembered with much affection by the fancy that gathered for a light ale at her boozer. The boxers in the late sixties and seventies had genuine respect for her. She was not quite so popular with their wives and girlfriends.

It was also announced before Christmas that Bruno and Tyson would fight in Las Vegas in February 1989.

The Contenders

In early October, after twenty fights and six years as a pro, Duke McKenzie won the world title when he stopped Rolando Bohol in the eleventh for the IBF flyweight championship. Mickey Duff had worked his international connections perfectly to make the fight happen, and at the small hall at Wembley, the conference centre, McKenzie romped home easily. The Filipino was dropped twice in that eleventh round and the towel fluttered in. Duke had taken the chance his brother Clinton never had, and would go on to win world titles at two other weights, fail at a fourth weight, and retire a decade after the Bohol blitz.

In late April there was a cameo on a show in Hove when Chris Eubanks fought on the undercard of his older brother Peter. Young Chris, who was 21, was having his third fight in Britain after turning professional at just 19 in America and winning five times. The monocle and the act would follow; he would also drop the 's' from the end of his name.

Gary Stretch won the British light-middleweight title when he outpointed Gary Cooper in September. Stretch was in some interesting fights and then chaperoned Raquel Welch before making films. He was opposite Paddy Considine in *Dead Man's Shoes*. Considine made the truly excellent *Journeyman*, a boxing film with soul, in 2016.

From the Notepad

'I got involved in a street fight, and actually I was ashamed of myself,' said Benn after beating Logan. He also had to lose a pound to make the limit for the Commonwealth middleweight defence. He fought once more in 1988, a win in 126 seconds, and that made eight for the year ending in rounds 2, 2, 2, 1, 2, 2, 2 and 1. 'I don't like to hang about in fights,' he remarked.

At the end of Kaylor's loss to Collins it was left to Terry Lawless to deliver the living obit: 'Mark's always been a star. It's always the other fella that was "the opponent". I could never let him become just "an opponent" and that's what would have happened if he'd carried on.' I don't need to tell you that Kaylor did fight again, and in 1992 he was a central and tragic character in Ron Peck's film *Fighters*.

1989

'Those fellas are in a bad way, they have nothing left. They deserve medals. They've needed painkillers to stand up to the bruising Frank's given them.'
George Francis sums up Bruno's sparring partners

'I've watched it so many times that the video is on the blink. I kept rewinding the knockout and now the tape is stuck in the machine.'
Michael Watson on his fight with Nigel Benn

IN 1989, NIGEL BENN was christened the 'British Marvin Hagler', Frank Warren was shot in the stomach one dark night in east London, ten British boxers fought for world titles, and it was the end for Barry McGuigan. It was a relentless year of serious fights, upsets, heartbreak and mismatches. In many ways it was the first truly modern year for British boxing, a year when big events, fights that attracted thousands, never had or needed a significant belt of any colour to make the encounter credible.

Frank Bruno had not been in a fight for sixteen months before walking out to meet Mike Tyson in Las Vegas for the unified world heavyweight title in February. The fight had been twenty-one months in the making, but it took Tyson less than five rounds to leave his opponent in a mess. Bruno had stood and traded, and had hurt Tyson at one point. 'I had him in trouble, he had me in trouble; he was the better fighter on the night,' said Bruno. 'I learned one thing tonight, I think we all learned one thing: Tyson can be beaten.'

Over 2,000 Bruno fans were in the crowd of 9,000. In round one Bruno, who was paid $4 million, was down and was then hit flush as he was on one knee. It was after getting up that Bruno caught Tyson with the left hook that sent the American's legs into a hysterical boogie. Bruno was one punch from the Promised Land. In the end Bruno took punches that nobody had taken up until that point, and nobody would take in any future fight. His bravery, chin and heart were proved beyond any reasonable doubt in that Las Vegas ring. The big lad from Wandsworth returned a hero. He would not fight again for thirty-three months but the public's love for him would not diminish during that sabbatical.

Three weeks before the Bruno–Tyson carnival, Lloyd Honeyghan was fighting in the Sports Pavilion behind Caesars in Las Vegas. It was a ninth world title fight for Honeyghan and he lost his WBC welterweight belt when he was stopped by Marlon Starling in round nine. It was a nasty fight. Honeyghan took a beating, and was trailing on all three scorecards when it was finally halted after he had climbed up from a knockdown. 'He caught me on a nerve by the side of my head early on and every time he hit me it was like cutting me with a knife,' said Honeyghan. After the fight he failed a routine drug test for a painkiller called Lidocaine; it had been prescribed to help relieve the pain in his right hand. The Nevada State Athletic Commission fined him $1,500.

There was one British winner in a world title fight that February, but his win and his arrival back in London went virtually unnoticed. Dennis Andries had remained in Detroit after losing his WBC light-heavyweight title to Tommy Hearns. He had joined the Kronk family, the savage gang of fighters trained by Manny Steward and based at the Kronk gym in a part of Detroit that was closed. The city was dead; the gym was one of the few things left with a pulse in the lost wasteland. Andries had won five fights in the Kronk's gold colours before the world title opportunity; he had survived the wars and blood in the gym. He had also taken himself away from the British public in the twenty-three months since the Hearns loss.

Andries travelled to Miami and stopped previously unbeaten Tony

Willis in the fifth to regain the WBC light-heavyweight title. 'Dennis is a young thirty-five, he's dedicated and he lives the life. Forget age,' said Steward. After the win Andries went to Las Vegas to watch Bruno. The pair arrived back at Heathrow on the same morning but to a very different welcome: Bruno was cheered, interviewed, captured smiling in pain by the flashing lights of the cameras; Andries slipped in under the sparkling camouflage of his fighting brother's fame and jumped on the Tube.

'I do mind,' Andries said a few weeks later. 'But that's just the way it is. I was tired, but if anybody had recognized me I would have woken up.' That is just the way it is – Andries was right.

There was a $250,000 payday, in theory, waiting for him in a fight against Canadian pin-up Donny Lalonde in June. The fight never happened. Andries never had that type of luck. He had made less than $50,000 for the Willis win. As expected, Lalonde never agreed terms to fight Andries and the Canadian retired. In his place the WBC sanctioned a novice from Australia called Jeff Harding. He was not given much chance when he met Andries in Atlantic City in June for the light-heavyweight title. There was no perceived menace for Dennis: he had lost only to Tommy Hearns in twenty-two fights. Harding had fought just fourteen times. It was a modern classic. Harding was over in the fifth, Andries down twice in the twelfth, and the fight was stopped with just ninety-seven seconds left on the clock. Andries was in front on all three scorecards when it correctly ended. Harding had a broken nose, cuts, and was bleeding dark blood from the mouth when it was halted, but he was the victor. 'I want a rematch, anywhere, I will go to Australia,' said Andries. 'I know I can put right what I did wrong.' He would get his rematch.

The extraordinary career of Kirkland Laing continued in April with a fight in Italy against Nino La Rocca for the European welter-weight title. Laing had won the ABA title in 1972, cried when not selected for the Munich Olympics, first won the British title in 1979, beaten a good Roberto Durán in 1982, and was still waiting for a world title fight. He fought with a fresh cut from a sparring wound, a cut that meant he'd been able to spar for just four rounds in the final few weeks of preparation. It was an ugly maul and the Italian Ali, as La Rocca was known, won on points. 'I only lost if you count using your head, your elbows and having to also fight the referee,' said Laing. Kirk soon had a date with George Collins to defend his British welterweight title, and a purse of £18,600. The Collins fight did get Laing in the gym, which was increasingly rare. Collins suffered a rib injury and delayed the fight until November.

The wait was over for Herol Graham when he met Mike McCallum for the WBA middleweight title at the Royal Albert Hall in May. Graham had been the number one and most deserving challenger for over five years: he'd lost just once in forty-two fights. McCallum was dropped briefly in round five, and in round eight on a bad-tempered night Graham lost a crucial point for trying to throw the Jamaican. At the end of twelve rounds the split decision was in McCallum's favour; if Graham had not lost the point he would have won the world title. The inquest was horrible. 'I knew it was close, I thought I had done enough. Now I don't know what I'm going to do,' said Graham.

There had been a problem in his corner. Brendan Ingle had been restored, but his power was diminished by the presence of Graham's manager Barney Eastwood screaming instructions during the minute breaks. Graham had appealed to the British Boxing Board of Control to get rid of Eastwood, but the Board had sided with Eastwood and his contract. Graham had then been told by the WBA that he had to accept the Board's findings or risk losing his title fight. There was no happy compromise, just an undignified and unwanted intrusion in the corner, which was legal but ridiculous, by Eastwood. 'I tried to shut out Eastwood's voice and concentrate on Brendan's, but it was impossible,' said Graham after the fight. 'There was so much going on between Brendan and Eastwood that I was glad to get back out. With a calm corner – just myself and Brendan, the way we had both wanted it to be – then things might have worked out differently.' It is too easy to talk about heartache, it gets thrown about too often, but that night at the ancient venue was real heartache for Graham.

After the fight Eastwood met with the press and was critical of his boxer. Graham and Ingle both missed the post-fight conference.

In October, Graham defended his British middleweight title against Bow's Rod Douglas. It was the thirteenth British, European or Commonwealth fight for Graham; Douglas was having just his fourteenth fight, and it showed. Mickey Duff had never fancied Graham, never. He really believed that Ingle's protégé was ready to lose, was finished.

Graham banished Eastwood from the corner and the Belfast bookie retorted with one of the most dismissive comments from a boxing manager at any time and anywhere: 'What Herol Graham wants and what he does are not important. I will not let these petty things come into it. I am the manager and I will decide who goes in the corner.' It was a strained time, that's for sure.

Douglas was dropped twice and stopped in round nine. Nobody ever doubted his heart. 'Herol's in a class of his own and he will be fighting when he's forty,' said Ingle. It was masterful, Graham's twenty-fifth stoppage in forty-four fights, and the nineteenth in his last twenty-two. Amazingly, he continued to be considered a non-puncher.

Three hours after the fight Douglas collapsed and was rushed to hospital. He underwent surgery to have a blood clot scraped from the surface of his brain and made a fantastic recovery. Against all medical advice he had some full-contact kick-boxing fights and always wanted to box again.

Frank Warren's new venue, the London Arena, opened in May with a world title fight for Sammy Reeson, the inaugural British cruiserweight champion. Reeson was stopped in the ninth by WBC cruiserweight champion Carlos De León in the first fight for a world title at that weight to take place in Britain. Reeson was down twice in the ninth. 'It's a pity that I never had a world champion on the first night, but there will be other nights,' said Warren.

Reeson never fought again, and in 2011 he was collecting scrap – 'totting', as he called it – when a lintel above a garage shutter collapsed and injured his leg. He had to have it amputated below the knee. 'They did a twenty-two-hour operation to save my foot and it hurt; I told 'em to get the leg off and now there is no pain,' Reeson said in 2012. A total of three hundred stitches were used to make him better.

Duff finally agreed terms for Michael Watson to fight Nigel Benn. This was a tricky fight to make, involving lawyers, men without a Board licence and waiters with agendas. There was no venue, but the fight was sealed after a series of crazy meetings at a Greek restaurant in Stratford, east London. The fight was on for May, and it was an instant event.

The final destination for Benn–Watson was a tent pitched in Finsbury Park, a thirty-minute walk from Watson's home in Islington. It was a glorious carnival, but they were both serious fighters: Watson was number three with the WBC, Benn number four. Benn was unbeaten in twenty-two fights, all of them ending quick, and Watson had lost just once in twenty-three fights. Watson was twenty-four, Benn a year older. It was a great fight. Benn prepared with endless hours in a hairdresser's chair and many more in a private sitting with the woman. 'There was no pride in Nigel's eyes,' said Ambrose Mendy, the fighter's doppelganger and adviser. Watson stayed calm. 'Nigel was hitting me so hard, but he was hitting me in the same places and at the same tempo,' he said.

In round six a solid jab connected; Benn was over, and so was the fight. He did try to get up but was counted out. 'I've watched it so many times that the video is on the blink. I kept rewinding the knockout and now the tape is stuck in the machine,' Watson said. The following day his glory was savagely cut short when he watched in frustration as Benn went live on television talking about his future. 'I won the fight and there was Benn talking about America, winning world titles and giving me a rematch. I couldn't believe it.'

On the last day of May it was the last fight for Barry McGuigan. On the night at the G-Mex in Manchester, which was promoted brilliantly by Barry Hearn, McGuigan was the younger man – something that has been conveniently overlooked ever since. A fight with Jimmy McDonnell had first been mentioned in September 1986. McDonnell won in round four, his odds on a win in that round 50-1. McGuigan was cut above the right eye and it later required six stitches.

It was the end for the Clones Cyclone – he retired in his changing room – but he was not an old man. 'People still think I was part of some type of retirement fight for McGuigan and that he was an old man – I was the old man on the night!' said McDonnell in 2013.

After the win there was a setback for McDonnell when it looked like a fight with the WBC super-featherweight champion Azumah Nelson was unlikely. According to José Sulaimán, the dictator that ran the WBC, there was a problem. 'No way can he be ranked and considered for a world title fight until he has joined an official anti-apartheid organization,' he said. Poor José had failed to notice that the Camden Caretaker was ranked at fourteen. The Nelson fight took place in November.

McDonnell forced the fight for eleven rounds at the Royal Albert Hall and was winning on one of the three scorecards going into the last. But he should not have been in the ring in round twelve and that is the brutal truth. Nelson had closed McDonnell's right eye, closed it tight, and the referee, the doctor and Jimmy Mac's corner should have formed a merciful trinity and pulled him out. They never did and he was knocked out after 1:40 of the last round. He ended up in hospital; he was fine, just shattered and his pride bruised. As a trainer there is no way that McDonnell would send one of his boxers out under similar circumstances. He should have been spared the last round.

In a thirteen-month spell between 1985 and 1986 Glenn McCrory lost five times, was stopped in three of the fights, and conceded weight each time. He was not a heavyweight and, thankfully, with the creation of the cruiserweight division he had an alternative that did not include losing two stone to make light-heavyweight. McCrory started to train and work with American Beau Williford in Louisiana, losing weight and sparring with some dangerous men. He was also hired by Mike Tyson for certain fights. In 1987 he won the Commonwealth cruiserweight title, added the British in 1988, and in June 1989 fought Patrick Lumumba for the vacant IBF cruiserweight title near his home at the Louisa Centre in Stanley, County Durham. He walked to the venue on the night of the fight.

'I ate my way to heavyweight because being the heavyweight champion of the world was my dream,' said McCrory. That changed with the regular losses, but making weight was still a struggle, and for the Lumumba fight he had to go back to the scales twice. The official crowd was 2,300, and they packed the venue; the real figure on the night was a lot higher: every inch was filled with standing fans, there to watch their Rocky, a local hero, win a world title. Lumumba was crude, resilient and easily beaten on a night of raw emotion for McCrory. All three scores were wide for slimline Glenn as he completed his own fairy-tale at the age of 24.

McCrory retained his IBF cruiserweight title in October when he knocked out Siza Makathini after sixty-seven seconds of the eleventh round in a tent attached by tunnels to a leisure centre in Middlesbrough. Over 3,500 paid to watch the local idol perform. McCrory was a sincere story, from the dole queue to championship, the man that walked to his world title fights from his mum's house. He was also in demand, popular with female fans – and that was part of his inevitable downfall. It was also part of his attraction. I doubt if a nicer British boxer has ever won a world title.

There was a crazy end to a fight in September when former British light-heavyweight champion Tony Wilson met local boxer Steve McCarthy. Wilson was under pressure: he had lost his title in a shock to Tom Collins, he looked tense, and he needed a big win against McCarthy. Wilson's mum, Minna, had made the journey from the Midlands to Southampton to support her son. There was nothing happening for two rounds and then in the third Wilson was clipped and went over. He was fine. He got up but was trapped in the corner as the crowd stood and got behind their man. McCarthy was throwing everything he had at Wilson when he was struck from behind – Minna had entered the ring, slipped off a shoe and hit McCarthy on the back of the head with it. There was blood and utter confusion. Minna was ushered from the ring, the referee consulted with the Board inspector, and it was decided to continue the fight. Wilson, with Jimmy Tibbs in his corner, agreed to continue, but McCarthy was furious, refused, and then left the ring. The crowd got restless, and then Wilson's hand was raised in victory. McCarthy had deserted the ring, he'd forfeited the fight. The plastic glasses and bottles started to fly in from the seating as soon as Wilson's hand went up. Wilson took cover behind Tibbs, then left the ring to run a vicious gauntlet supported by James Oyebola, a 6ft 9in heavyweight, and genuine hardman Mo Hussein, a five-foot-nothing lightweight. It was bad: Hussein had a stab mark and Oyebola bowled over a few with his right hand. McCarthy rushed back to the ring and calmed the crowd. The pair did embrace in the dressing room afterwards. Minna was safely on her way back to Wolverhampton by then.

Jeff Harding returned to Australia after beating Dennis Andries and agreed terms to fight Tom Collins from Leeds, another hoary old man of British boxing. The end to the fight in Brisbane that October was a bit odd. After a two-round war, Collins pulled out when he got back to the corner. He said he had been hit in the throat and was concerned about his health. 'I couldn't breathe,' he added. His purse of £15,630 was held. 'What Collins did was a disgrace to boxing,' said Bob Arum. He later received his purse. It was strange because Collins had been involved in some brutal domestic fights for the best part of a decade. He fought nine more times and lost seven, including a world title fight in his hometown in 1991 when he was 35.

There was an easy night at the start of November for Larne's Dave 'Boy' McAuley in the first defence of his IBF flyweight title at Wembley's Grand Hall against Filipino Dodie Penalosa. Two judges were watching the fight and scored it 120-109 and 119-113 to McAuley. However, the IBF insisted on one of the judges being from the same country as one of the boxers, and the Filipino judge scored it 119-113 to Penalosa – one of the maddest scores ever returned by a judge at a fight in Britain. It's not even crooked, it's just crazy.

Two things happened in the last few days of November. First, a boxer called Ray Webb landed a final punch in the final second of the seventy-seventh and last round of sparring with Michael Watson. The punch broke Watson's nose and his fight on 29 November with Mike McCallum for the WBA middleweight title was off. In Watson's east London house he still has a tracksuit from the postponed fight framed and on the wall. They did meet in 1990.

On 30 November, in a side street in Barking, somebody with a handgun shot promoter Frank Warren two times in his torso at close range. The masked gunman fired the Luger .22 confident of a kill; Warren lost part of a lung and the bullet missed his heart by an inch. The assassin escaped, Warren survived. Warren was on his way to watch boxing at the Broadway Theatre and the show went ahead. Colin McMillan stopped Sylvester Osuji in the main event. Warren was in surgery when McMillan's hand was raised.

Warren had joked in an article in 1987 that 'boxing is supposed to be this big heavy Mafia number, but if that's the case why hasn't Mickey Duff shot me?' Duff did not shoot Warren that night in east London. Warren knows who tried to kill him. 'He was incompetent and that is what he has been his whole life,' he said. A court case did take place later.

The Contenders

Duke McKenzie had a soft-touch first defence in March, but three months later lost his IBF flyweight title to Dave McAuley. It was McAuley's third attempt. Duke was weight-drained and in 1990 won the European title up at bantamweight, an increase of six crucial pounds to these tiny men. McAuley had not fought for fifteen months; the points win was right and tight.

In December the rehabilitation of Nigel Benn continued with his second win in America. 'He's my English Hagler,' claimed Bob Arum in Las Vegas. 'Nigel Benn is changing the way America looks at British fighters.' Benn would soon be back in Britain in the fight and event and shock of 1990. The golden years were about to start.

From the Notepad

'I'm never going to fight again,' McGuigan said after losing to McDonnell. 'Boxing has been great to Barry McGuigan. This is the end for Barry McGuigan.' The plan, when he left the G-Mex that night, was for McGuigan to stay active in boxing and to work as Warren's promoter, leaving Warren free to manage the fighters. However, in June the Southern Area of the Board snubbed McGuigan when he applied for a promoter's licence.

'I was warned not to take Dennis on,' said the Kronk's Manny Steward. 'I was told you can't teach an old dog new tricks – but when I got him, he didn't know any tricks.' Andries was an enigma, even if he was ignored by too many in the boxing business.

1990

*'Horatio Nelson would have put up a better fight and he only had one eye
and one arm.'*
Reg Gutteridge with the final word on a bad world title fight

*'I don't know if I could handle the crowds anyway, if I was Bruno.
The man can't do anything.'*
Dennis Andries on his life and freedom as world champion

WHEN CHRIS EUBANK and Nigel Benn met in November in Birmingham
it was quite simply the fight that changed British boxing. It was so
intense, and the rivalry so bitter. It was a major event, but it had not
been easy to make.

In January there was talk of Nigel Benn fighting Roberto Durán
for a title that one of the magicians at the sanctioning bodies would
pluck like a rabbit from a hat. It never happened, and then in February
it was agreed that Benn would fight the WBO champion Doug DeWitt
in April. Benn had another win in January and that meant three
fights in America in the eight months since the Watson loss.

At the Circus Maximus Theater in Atlantic City, Benn stopped
DeWitt in round eight to become the first British WBO champion.
Benn had been dropped briefly in the second but took control and
sent DeWitt tumbling three times before the end. It was a breathless
fight to watch, the first of many WBO fights that thrilled beyond
their credibility.

'We do not at present recognize the WBO,' said the British Boxing

Board of Control's general secretary John Morris. 'I have written to congratulate him. He could defend in Britain and the WBO could provide officials, if they were recognized as judges and referees by a commission we recognized.' The obstacle was never an obstacle and since that April night the WBO has always found a home in British rings.

Benn injured his left hand, pocketed his £150,000 in wages with his good hand and talked of big fights in the future. He mentioned Sugar Ray Leonard, Tommy Hearns and Durán. 'They say they are all a bit too tasty for me, I disagree,' said Benn. He also had Watson on his mind, always on his mind. 'After the way I lost to Watson, a lot of people said that I was a coward because of the way the fight finished. I think about it all the time and it won't be settled until I have met him again.'

In May, Donald Trump came in with an offer for Benn's first defence against Iran Barkley. The Board refused to let Barkley fight in Britain because of retina damage and that scuppered a wild plan by Barry Hearn to put it on at Old Trafford. In the early nineties it seemed a big fight was being suggested just about every week by Hearn. His other 'big fight' announcement in May was an August fight for Eubank against McCallum at Brighton and Hove Albion's ground.

In August, Benn outraged America and it was truly very lovely. He met Barkley at the Grand Ballroom in Bally's, a Las Vegas casino across the strip from Caesars. The WBO middleweight title was their prize. Barkley had come down from 15st, had not boxed for one year, his dad had died the week before, and surgery had corrected a detached retina; but he had met Hearns, Durán and Michael Nunn in his previous three fights, all for the world title, and stopped the Hitman in the third round. Barkley was a big name, an attraction. Fifteen seconds after the first-round bell he was on the floor. Benn was then caught and hurt, then Barkley was down again, and, with the clock ticking, Benn sent the American down for a third and final time. The referee looked panicked. The WBO had a three-knockdown rule in place. Carlos Padilla looked outside the ropes for guidance as

Barkley stood on disco legs and then he waved it off as the bell to end round one sounded. Benn had clipped Barkley twice when he was over or staggering up from a knockdown, but the referee was at fault: he handled the fight like he was the third man with two gentlemen of the flyweight division, not two known brawlers of distinction. Barkley won a world title again and defeated Hearns one more time before becoming a bloated freak on the circuit, weighing over five stone more in some of his later fights. Benn had business in Britain.

Benn and Eubank had clashed so many times before the first bell at the NEC. Benn hated Eubank on sight, hated him from the outset, and that was the simple backdrop to their epic first fight. Harry Mullan described it as the 'most thrilling contest I have ever watched', and Mullan had been at ringside for twenty-five years at that point. The city of Birmingham was the world's fight capital that weekend. Every pub, club and restaurant was packed with fight people. Eubank was calm under Benn's verbal assaults, Benn was struggling with the weight. Eubank was also in a life-long struggle to shrink his body to the designated weight. He would eventually suck on freshly cut fruit for sustenance as that particular fight intensified. The crowd on the night knew they had paid for history. The ringside seats were a shocking £200.

It was tight, relentless and hard from the first bell. Every punch was hateful as their bodies were pushed long into a draining fight. In the eighth the Las Vegas referee, Richard Steele, ruled a Eubank fumble and stumble a knockdown: Benn had landed with a right behind Eubank's ear. Benn's left eye was grotesque by the start of the ninth and Eubank sensed the loss of his opponent's desire. It was finished after 2:55 of the ninth; Benn in Steele's arms, Eubank standing and screaming, the blood in his mouth a heavy reminder of what he had been through. One judge had Eubank in front, the other two went for Benn, and all three scores were identical at 76-75. There were no real excuses after the fight, just too many reasons for Benn's loss: Eubank was as good as some of us suspected. It was the launch of the WBO, and British boxing would never be the same.

Lloyd Honeyghan was cheered to the ring like a returning hero at

Wembley when he finally met Mark Breland in early March. Honeyghan's old WBA belt was the prize, the one he'd held for weeks back in 1986. The massacre lasted eight minutes and fifteen seconds, less than three completed rounds; Honeyghan was over six times, wobbled with every punch, and never troubled Breland. In defeat Honeyghan never made an excuse and simply ignored boos from the crowd. He still had five more years of boxing left – five years to move further and further away from his glory days.

Dave McAuley was untroubled in his second defence of his IBF flyweight title against Louis Curtis, the unknown member of the 1976 USA Olympic team, at the King's Hall, Belfast. It was a virtual shut-out. McAuley had had his wars when he twice lost in world title fights and nobody could begrudge him this easy night in the ring.

But the easy fights were always going to end for McAuley, and his third defence had a total of five knockdowns. In September, back at the King's Hall, it was Rodolfo Blanco's turn to try and wrest the IBF belt from the Larne man's grip. McAuley's previous two fights had been shut-outs; against Blanco the old spirit had to surface, and surface fast: McAuley was down twice in the second, once in the third and again in the eleventh. Blanco was dropped in round nine. McAuley took the decision and kept his title, but the Colombian would be back two years later. Before then there would be two more defences. There is no doubt that McAuley is overlooked.

Billy Hardy was declared the winner by a devoted flock of 1,400 at the Crowtree Leisure Centre in his hometown of Sunderland at the end of twelve rounds against Orlando Canizales for the IBF bantam-weight title in January. Sadly, fans don't get to decide, and the split verdict was for Canizales; it was close, but not a robbery. Hardy, who had been dropped in round nine, was in tears. He had nothing left to give and was shattered, sickened as he sat in the dressing room. 'What more do I have to do? I won the fight, I won the fight.' They would have a nasty rematch in Texas the following year.

The Johnny Nelson and Carlos De León fight for the WBC cruiser-weight title in Sheffield in March has never been forgotten. Promoter Barry Hearn called it 'a stinking fight'. He was telling the truth, others were not so kind. Reg Gutteridge was livid. 'Horatio Nelson would have put up a better fight and he only had one eye and one arm.' It was an inexcusable performance from both champion and challenger: De León was a better fighter than he was ever given credit for and Nelson, who was 23 that night, developed slowly into a proper world champion.

The end was nasty for Glenn McCrory a few days later. His blue-collar tale of dole queue to glory, of walking from his mam's kitchen to world-title fight venues, ended in round three. McCrory was caught with a perfect, wicked short left under his elbow by American Jeff Lampkin, and he took two steps back before dropping face first for the count. The crowd at the Gateshead Leisure Centre sucked in their breath, as stunned as their fallen man. This was real, not a movie, and McCrory was left weeping, his beloved IBF cruiserweight title gone. The next day he was in hospital getting his swollen liver looked at, and a few months later big Glenn split with Beau Williford and moved back to heavyweight.

April can be cruel, and Watson's delayed WBA middleweight title fight with Mike McCallum was truly brutal. Watson was stopped in the eleventh round at the Royal Albert Hall. He had been suckered all the way by the brilliant Jamaican, who at the time was not recognized like he would be in the future, and when he went down and out he was conscious but broken. 'I had nothing left,' Watson told me in 1990. Watson had been tipped and McCallum dismissed before the fight. 'I needed him the first time, when I was injured; I was sharper – that was my time,' said Watson.

In September, Watson initiated his split with Mickey Duff and there was a press conference to announce the arrival of a new adviser, a tool-hire millionaire from west London with a gold tooth who said that he had put together a deal worth £2.5 million in fights before the end of 1991. He seemed like a nice man, but we never saw him again. In the nineties I attended dozens of conferences like this. A million pounds, which is a significant pile, was once placed on a table – two bulky bank sentinels stood at either end – at the Bloomsbury Crest Hotel in central London. I was the only journalist present to record the million-pound offer, which was made to Eubank. I was at pie and mash shops, in churches, on boats and in lap-dancing clubs at ten a.m. as the quest for a unique press conference venue became ever more original; it was a search that often reflected a corresponding drop in the quality of the fight being sold. Proper promoters still preferred a casino, a fish restaurant or a boxing gym.

Paul 'Hoko' Hodkinson had already won the British and European title when he stepped in the ring to fight Marcos Villasana at the G-Mex in Manchester for the vacant WBC featherweight title in June. The last English world featherweight champion was Ben Jordan in 1898. Hoko was 24, an ABA champion from 1986, and in front on all three scorecards after seven rounds. But the scores made no mention of his left eye being closed and with that affliction he bravely went out for round eight, blind in that eye. He was dropped to his knees near the ropes, up at eight, bloody from nose and mouth, his face swollen. 'I can't see, I can't see,' he told the veteran referee Arthur Mercante. The fight was stopped with just two seconds left in the round, and the debate started about whether he should have been spared the eighth round. The decision to interview Hoko in the ring, with both eyes purple and closed and a trickle of blood falling from his nose, was poor. The fighter deserved better.

There was a terrible moment in February when the mercurial men at the WBC dumped Dennis Andries from their number one position and reinstalled the chameleon Donny Lalonde; it meant Andries would probably miss out on a revenge fight with Jeff Harding. Thankfully, Donny stayed retired and in July Andries–Harding II took place at the National Tennis Centre in Melbourne. Andries is incapable of making an excuse, but he did say that he crashed the weight before the first fight because Manny Steward was off on Tommy Hearns duty. 'It left me drained, and that is why I was so desperate for the rematch,' said Andries. In round seven Harding went down and out for the full count from a right cross. 'You can hit me with sticks and rocks and I will just keep coming,' said Andries. It was his forty-seventh fight, he was a minimum of 36, and had been a pro since 1978. He is British boxing's most remarkable man.

There was what passed for a triumphant homecoming for Andries in October when he broke Sergio Merani's jaw and retained his WBC light-heavyweight title. Merani was in front before he was cracked with a right uppercut and withdrawn at the end of the fourth. 'Anybody I hit with that punch either wobbles, drops or pops,' said Andries in the changing room at the Royal Albert Hall.

There is no dispute that French gypsy Jean-Maurice Chanet was a handful, and his fans probably even more of a nuisance. In May there had been a riot during the twelfth round of his European heavyweight defence against Peckham's Derek 'Sweet D' Williams. The round was stopped, riot police invaded the tent, which had been pitched in Foire du Trone, Paris, and there was a ten-minute break. The fight continued and Chanet won on points, his second win over Williams. In the scuffle, Horace Notice, former British heavyweight champion, was hit on the head with a chair. In late October Chanet was cut and stopped by Lennox Lewis in six rounds at Crystal Palace, losing his European heavyweight title. It was the first professional title for Lewis, who was having his fourteenth fight. 'Chanet was covered in ointment before the fight and I made him take a bath,' said Kellie Maloney, who as Frank Maloney guided the Lewis rise.

The Chanet win appeared to separate Lewis from Europe's best, but Mickey Duff had Gary Mason ready and willing. Duff believed it was an easy fight for Mason. First, Mason had to have surgery to re-attach a detached retina with a scleral buckle in his right eye. 'Horace Notice's retina went as well, worse than mine,' said Mason. 'Both of us had sparred hundreds of rounds with Frank Bruno. Frank had a habit of jabbing in a certain way, so that you caught his thumb a lot in the eye.' In November, Mason was given permission to fight and Duff started lobbying.

It was Herol 'Bomber' Graham's chance once again, this time in Spain against Julian Jackson from the Virgin Islands. Jackson too had retina problems and the fight was banned from Britain. 'I had no idea who Jackson was, but I was told he was as blind as a fucking bat,' Graham said. His vision was not great but he had managed to knock out or stop thirty-eight of the forty men he'd beaten. Barry Hearn had won the right to stage the vacant WBC middleweight title fight back in August with a bid of $223,000, beating Don King by $30,000 and Duff by nearly $50,000. It was meant to be in Monte Carlo but ended up at a plush venue in Benalmádena, Spain. Graham once described it as 'velvety'.

After three rounds Jackson had not landed a punch. His left eye was closed to a slit and the referee visited both corners to tell them that the fourth would be Jackson's last. The doctor in Jackson's corner was not happy. Graham only realized later that the ref had also spoken to the Virgin Islander. Jackson was punching wild, missing with shots in his desperation in the fourth. Brendan Ingle told Graham to move; Graham never listened and had Jackson repeatedly pushed back to the ropes. It happened, a last-chance right hand, and Graham was unconscious before he hit the floor with the sort of sickening thud that is impossible for Hollywood to recreate. He was out for five minutes, then collapsed again on the way to the dressing room and was made to spend a night in a Torremolinos hospital. 'It was a lucky punch,' said Graham. It only landed because he'd decided to try and finish the fight. Lucky maybe, stupid definitely.

The Contenders

In October the main arena at the Granby Halls in Leicester was full to capacity for Chris Pyatt's WBO light-middleweight title fight against John David Jackson. It was the first WBO title fight to be held in Britain and it was promoted by Frank Warren. Jackson was not given much hope, and when he came in 2lb 6oz over the limit his odds plummeted. It was a joy to watch in the end, a slick performance, and Pyatt was dropped in the eleventh before losing on points. Pyatt would win a world title three years later back at the ancient Granby Halls.

At the 31st National Schoolboy finals in Derby on the last day of March little Naseem Hamed won at senior under-48kg, future WBO super-featherweight champion Barry Jones failed the medical at senior under-51kg, and the most exciting fighter you have never heard of, Shaun Gray from West Ham, won in the first round at intermediate under-60kg. In May, at York Hall, Gray and Hamed added to their hauls and won junior ABA titles, Gray in fifty-two seconds in the first and Hamed easily on points, but against a vile backdrop of abuse. 'The crowd hate him,' I wrote.

From the Notepad

'Nobody will ever be able to take me out of the record books,' said Alan Levene. 'You lose fights, you don't lose records.' In October, Levene went to the under-19 world amateur championship in Peru and won a gold. He was the first British boxer to win any type of amateur world title.

When Graham was knocked out by Jackson there was an unwanted, but expected, nasty footnote from Barney Eastwood: 'This would never have happened if I had been in the corner; I would have told him to jab and stay away.' Ingle shook his head in despair when I told him.

1991

'Me and Frank have very different aims: he wants to be the world champion and I just want the money.'
Gary Mason on Bruno

'Boxing made me and boxing destroyed me.'
Michael Watson

THE END OF the Watson–Eubank fight at White Hart Lane in September will never be forgotten by the thousands in attendance and the millions watching live on television. Watson's suffering at the end and his miracle recovery gripped a nation.

There had been an ugly, bloody and disturbing end to Eubank's first defence of his WBO middleweight title in February. It needs to be said from the start that Eubank should have been disqualified when he butted Canada's Dan Sherry in the tenth round. It's really that simple. It was an unpleasant fight from the start. Sherry insulted Eubank during clinches, kissed him in the ear and, at the end of the fifth round, spat at the champion. In the ninth a terrific uppercut split Sherry's lip and did some real damage; in the tenth Sherry started to fade as Eubank put him under hostile pressure. And then it all went a bit crazy. Eubank was grabbed, turned, and was facing the wrong direction. Having been kissed by Sherry before, the champion threw his head back and connected with Sherry's forehead. The referee, Frank Santore, jumped in, touching Sherry as he did so, and the challenger went down on his knees. Santore deducted two points from Eubank's score. Sherry tried to get up, failed, tried again, fell through ropes, tried again, and it looked way over the top. Santore stopped the fight and the doctors jumped into the ring to inspect the Canadian. There was a lot of blood coming from Sherry's mouth. 'No way was he acting,' said Dr Tony Buckland. 'His right eye pupil was dilated and he was definitely concussed. I had to put an air shoot down his mouth – he had inhaled blood.' The split decision in Eubank's favour was announced and Sherry went off to get checked in hospital. 'There was blood and tooth chips in my throat,' said Sherry. 'My breathing stopped twice in the ring and once in the ambulance.' The right uppercut in round ten had done the real damage and Sherry's cornerman, Pepe Correa, had added to the carnage. 'I'm fucking human, I'm a human fucking being. I made a mistake, I fucked up: I never put the gumshield in,' he admitted. The ref refused to disqualify Eubank for the deliberate butt because the boxer had been 'constantly goaded'. It was a great escape for Eubank.

After the mess, Eubank insisted that Sherry had been faking it and his promoter, Barry Hearn, said it was 'the best performance I have ever seen outside of the theatre'. At the post-melee conference the next Eubank fight was announced. It was dubbed 'Beauty and the Beast', and it would become a real carnival fight.

Gary Stretch makes movies, but in 1988 he was the British light-middleweight champion. He was stripped of the title and spent some time in Las Vegas gyms before securing a world title fight as Beauty in this showdown with the Beast. The venue in April for the WBO middleweight title fight was the Grand Hall at Olympia in London. 'Eubank is ugly to look at and ugly of spirit,' said Stretch. 'Eubank has taken boxing's image down. I will restore it.' Stretch had fabulous media coverage before the fight. In the end, which was round six, Stretch was sent tumbling twice. He bravely regained his feet – his legs were gone both times – and was rescued. Eubank was too strong, it really was that simple. There is an old boxing axiom that perfectly tells the story of the fight: Eubank won ugly.

It had a working title of 'By Public Demand', and nobody was lying. Chris Eubank and Michael Watson was a sell-out with 11,000 inside at Earls Court in June. Eubank was defending his WBO middleweight title for the third time in the year. It was a tense fight; Watson was smart and Eubank was desperate at times. It is too easy to forget how raw, basic and determined Eubank the prizefighter was. Many of the rounds were tight, hard to score, and when it was over after twelve rounds there was a great divide. I had it for Watson by two rounds, others next to me had Eubank a clear winner. One judge had a draw, the other two went for Eubank. 'What have I got to do to prove I'm the better fighter?' asked Watson. 'I gave him a boxing lesson, I thought I won every round.' It was certainly tighter than that.

There were calls for an instant rematch. Watson lodged an official complaint with the WBO at ringside but Eubank had a tough mandatory in Gerald McClellan waiting and there was no chance of a rematch at middleweight. A McClellan fight was a dumb move on every level and would never happen.

'Watson was a test, a great test, and now I'm jaded,' admitted Eubank. He never got the rest he deserved, neither of them did. The following morning Watson met with a man called Alan Lacey, who had been in charge of Stretch's brilliant media offensive, in Islington. The meeting was five minutes from the council flat where Watson had grown up. Jon Robinson, a journalist and boxing official from Hackney, had put the meeting together, and a day later, 24 June, there was a Watson press conference at the Barbican Health and Fitness Centre. The national newspapers had filled their pages with the fight and the decision in that morning's editions. There was an appetite for Eubank. Watson put his case, asked again for a rematch. 'I deserve it, where can he go? Eubank is a very lonely man.' The dealing started. 'On the night I thought Chris Eubank won by three rounds, but I have studied the fight on video and now I believe it was a draw and that Michael Watson deserves another shot,' said Hearn, Eubank's promoter. The papers agreed.

In July, Eubank relinquished the WBO middleweight title and a fight for the vacant WBO super-middleweight championship was arranged: Eubank–Watson II at White Hart Lane on 21 September. A date that nobody present or watching on television will ever forget.

At 7.45 a.m. on the day of the fight Watson and Eubank went to the scales at the Grosvenor House on London's Park Lane. They had met in June for the middleweight title, but their rematch was made at super-middle – an increase of 8lb. At the real weigh-in the pair both came inside the 11st 10lb agreed weight; if either had been over the limit they would have been forced to pay a £50,000 forfeit. The early weigh-in was relaxed; the pair talked, waited, stripped and did their stuff. But five hours later, at the same venue, the nastiness returned when they had the 'official' weigh-in. They never liked each other, it was personal. Too personal, to tell the truth.

The fight was tight from the first bell. Eubank taunted Watson when they were close, and Watson was a bit too eager, too desperate, for revenge in the early exchanges. Over 22,000 people were standing for the fight, nobody was sitting. On ITV the audience figure was about to peak at 12 million viewers. Watson was in front after ten rounds. He was just too busy for Eubank. In round eleven – Watson still calls it 'the greatest round' – the pair pushed each other too far and too hard. Watson was hurt by a perfectly timed right and then Eubank, exhausted, was caught and, reeling, went down on one knee. At first Watson was stunned and just looked at his nemesis. It was a crazy moment, the pair exchanging looks of defiance, relief, pain and utter wonder. Watson was ushered to a neutral corner while Eubank regained his feet and sucked in air. The ref, a gentle giant of a man called Roy Francis, ordered the pair to 'box on'.

Eubank reacted just before Watson and twisted a long right upper-cut in under Watson's fists. Watson went down heavily, catching the back of his neck on the second-from-bottom rope. Now Eubank stood and watched, the fighters' roles reversed in less than ten seconds. Watson beat the count, staggered into Francis, and the bell sounded. The noise in the old stadium was astounding. 'I'm fine,' Watson told Jimmy Tibbs during the sixty seconds. He was not fine.

All Watson had to do was survive 180 seconds and he would be the new WBO champion at super-middleweight. And all Eubank had to do was connect with one punch and he would be the champion. Watson never threw a punch and Eubank never stopped throwing punches, and after twenty-nine seconds of the twelfth and last round Francis moved in. The boxing match was over, the fight to live was about to begin.

The fight had started at 10.09 p.m., and it ended at 10.54. Watson collapsed into Jimmy's arms. He was stretchered out of the ring at 11.08, rushed to North Middlesex Hospital by 11.22 and finally, at 11.55, diverted to St Bartholomew's for emergency surgery to scrape a blood clot from the surface of his brain. The ambulance rides were chaotic; Watson once told me that he sat up, knowing he was dead. At Bart's he was saved by Mr Peter Hamlyn. It was a medical miracle. Elton John sent yellow flowers when Watson was placed in a coma. His fight for life was now being measured in hourly instalments. Eubank was a broken man. Tibbs has never forgotten. The ref, Big Roy, took to his death in 2016 the pain of not knowing if stopping the fight earlier would have saved Watson from suffering an injury. (It would have made no difference.)

A few days after the fight it was boxing business as usual in Basildon, Essex, when Fidel Castro Smith stopped Ian Strudwick in six to win the vacant British super-middleweight title. Watson was still in a deep coma and I arranged for Eubank to make a midnight visit, using the tunnels under Bart's to avoid the press camp outside the main doors. So there I was in Basildon, working ringside and at the same time fixing for Eubank to sneak in to see Watson, my friend who he has left in a coma. It's a dirty game.

Mickey Duff bid £276,000 to win the right to promote Lennox Lewis against Gary Mason in their British and European heavyweight title fight at Wembley Arena in March. The fight was a throwback, heroic until it was over. Mason was unbeaten in thirty-five fights, ranked at four by the WBC, and the British champion; Lewis was fourteen unbeaten, the European champion, and number twelve in the WBC rankings.

Lewis was in control – too slick, too fast and too mean. At the end of the fifth the referee, the great Larry O'Connell, went to Mason's corner to look at his swollen right eye and assorted cuts. It went another round and it could have been stopped at the end of the sixth; Mason came out for the seventh knowing that with his facial damage it was his last. Lewis was pushed back, caught and trapped on the ropes before countering and hurting an exhausted and pitiful Mason. Larry intervened, and it was over. Lewis went on to become world champion while Mason had to defy the medics and box in back-waters in America with his damaged eyes. Mason died after a crash on a pushbike in 2011, and Lewis was at the funeral. 'I will never forget Gary's bravery at the end of our fight,' he said.

'I made a mistake,' admitted Duff. 'I made the fight because I didn't think Lewis was experienced enough as a professional to beat Mason.' There was a lot of betting surrounding this fight.

The rematch for Billy Hardy and Orlando Canizales took place outdoors in Laredo, Texas. Hardy had pushed Canizales close in the first fight for the IBF bantamweight title, losing a split in his home-town; the return ended in the eighth when Hardy was stopped. 'I will go away and cry and then I will be back – I know I'm world class,' said Hardy. It was 100 degrees in the ring, a sickening disadvantage for the Sunderland man. It was a different Canizales, happy in front of his 5,000 fans, and Hardy was cut, dropped in the third and knocked out in the eighth. There was no need for a count. Six years later Hardy would lose in another world title fight in ninety-three seconds, when he met Naseem Hamed. He also held British titles at two weights and the European featherweight championship.

Tom Collins had a fight in his local town hall when Leeonzer Barber arrived in Leeds in May for a vacant WBO light-heavyweight title fight. Collins lost every round and was stopped in the sixth. In the previous two years Collins had won the British and European titles at light-heavyweight. He had outpointed Dennis Andries at a sporting club in Southend-on-Sea in 1978 and his remarkable career was not yet over.

Also that May, Dave McAuley was on the canvas before he retained his IBF flyweight title against Pedro Feliciano in Belfast at the Maysfield Leisure Centre. It was his fourth consecutive defence and that equalled the British record set by Jim Watt. Feliciano was exactly five feet tall – a smaller opponent was on his way – and in round six he hurt and dropped McAuley; it was the only blemish in the comfortable win. Watt, by the way, beat three really good men in Howard Davis, Sean O'Grady and Charlie Nash in his quartet of world title defences, but McAuley's achievement deserves to be remembered. And Big Dave was not finished: he wanted Watt's record.

In September Soweto's Jake Matlala, who was also known as Baby Jake, was in Belfast to fight McAuley for the IBF flyweight title. Matlala was officially the shortest boxer in the world at 4ft 10in, though I think he was closer to 4ft 8in. He had been a professional on the South African club circuit, a workplace every bit as savage as the backstreet Mexican fight scene, and won thirty-three of his forty-three fights. He was really a light-fly not a flyweight – a difference of just 4lb – when he stepped through the ropes to meet local idol McAuley, a fighting giant of 5ft 7in and a four-year veteran of world title fights. It was over in the tenth. Matlala was saved from his own bravery, but he was not finished with British flyweights: he fought in Britain six more times, won world titles and kept on shrinking. Matlala was a pioneer and would become a close friend of Nelson Mandela, who insisted that Baby Jake was his favourite boxer. McAuley had now made five defences, and taken Watt's record. But he was coming close to the end.

Two years after losing his world flyweight title to McAuley there was a low-key but brilliant performance by Duke McKenzie in a WBO bantamweight title fight at the Elephant and Castle Leisure Centre. All three judges went for McKenzie by a shut-out, meaning they believed the boxer from Croydon had won every round against the champion Gaby Canizales, whose brother Orlando held the IBF version. Duke was often flawless, always neglected, and that night at the end of June in south London he was magnificent.

McKenzie retained his title in September at the Latchmere Leisure Centre, Battersea. Professional world championship boxing was on a tour of the truly exotic that weekend in London with fights in

Hammersmith and Battersea. McKenzie beat Mexican César Soto. It is a forgotten gem from the nineties, a classy performance by McKenzie against a fighter that eight years later would push Naseem Hamed the full twelve rounds, and who would still be fighting in 2011.

In Cardiff in September, little Robbie Regan and tiny Francis Ampofo – they were less than ten feet tall in total – fought for the British flyweight title. It was a renaissance for the small men of the ring and, in a division often neglected, three British flyweight fights took place in the year. Ampofo's smooth head tore lumps of flesh from Regan's eyebrows, and in round eleven of a genuine bloodbath the referee, Mickey Vann (an award-winning ballroom dancer in his day), had seen enough. Ampofo was the new champion and Regan was in hospital until three a.m. having thirty stitches woven into his left eyebrow. Vann had to throw away his shirt because it was stained with so much of Regan's blood. The two boxers met again in December, the eyebrow still dangerously raw, and this time Regan won on points and regained the title.

It looked like Dennis Andries was timeless. In his third reign, and aged 36, 39 or 41 – take your pick – he retained his WBC light-heavyweight title after twelve rounds in Adelaide against Guy Waters. It was a classic Andries fight from start to finish: close, gruelling rounds and a win on points for the Hackney man. Waters, who was born in London, would go on to lose a Commonwealth title fight in Dagenham in 2000. Andries, meanwhile, would meet his great Australian rival Jeff Harding for a third time, in September.

The old Hammersmith Odeon was raucous for that third fight. It was desperately close. One judge scored a draw, the other two went narrowly in Harding's favour after thirty-six minutes of fighting. It was hard, the type of fight in a venue with fine acoustics that sounded like a TV fight, a real *Rocky* without the sixty-nine unanswered left hooks to the eye. And Dennis was not yet finished.

The career of Frank Bruno was back on when he was given permission to fight again by the British Boxing Board of Control. Bruno had suffered a torn retina in his last fight – that nasty loss to Mike

Tyson in February 1989 – and had undergone surgery. The news was given to the press after a three-hour wait outside the Vauxhall head-quarters of the BBBC. Thirty minutes later, after a mad dash in any available car to avoid the taxi fare, there was a conference at the Cumberland Hotel, at the top of London's Park Lane. Mickey Duff was in bullish mood, dismissing cynics and promising the 'best Bruno yet'. Bruno still had to undergo a series of independent ophthalmic tests to satisfy the Board before he could fight, but he was back, make no mistake. Three days later Frank Maloney, the manager of Lennox Lewis, made Bruno an offer of £2 million to fight his man. Duff replied in typical Duff style: 'If they put the money in a letter of bank guarantee, I would certainly discuss it with Bruno.' Maloney, an apprentice jockey and publican in his time, shot back, 'If Mickey wants the money, I will deliver it in person.' Lewis and Bruno would eventually fight in October 1993, and that is another story.

The selection process for the man to fight Bruno was comical, and impossible to understand. Finally, John Emmen, who ran a bar in Tilburg, Holland, was selected. Emmen spoke six languages, had only fought three times in the last two years, and he was endorsed by John Morris, the Board's secretary: 'He's a character [Emmen] and a personality on the Continent, and if Frank needs a test at this stage, he's the right one.' Morris could have been talking about any street busker in any European city. Anyway, the Royal Albert Hall was heaving, expectant, on 20 November and even Harry Carpenter sounded at times like he was under siege. 'This is where the come-back begins,' uttered the silky commentator. Emmen, the Benelux champion, was introduced to boos; Bruno's reception was perhaps his best. The fight lasted three minutes exactly and everybody was happy. Emmen's wife and mother, who had Bruno sign their pro-grammes in the ring, were smiling.

It was not a funny fight. Bruno was missing with his heavy punches in the first minute or so and then caught Emmen on the ear, and down went the Dutchman. He toppled over again and, as he came to rest on a knee, Bruno connected with a sickening and illegal left hook. Emmen had the chance to dive on the floor and go for a disqualification, but instead bravely and stupidly struggled up, having clearly injured his left knee. Vann spoke to him, gave him a few seconds to recover, and then marched over to Bruno in a neutral corner and gave him a severe bollocking. Vann is possibly the only referee that would have risked his health and a riot to throw Bruno out. The Bruno diehards wanted a clean ending; they wanted their champion to have another chance at Emmen's chin and for the referee to let them fight. There was much hilarity and a lot of screaming from the ringside area. 'Oi, fucking get on with it!' somebody in Bruno's corner (probably George Francis) hollered at Vann. It did continue, and this time Bruno nailed Emmen with a perfect looping left hook and he was down and out. Bruno was definitely back. 'I was so anxious,' Bruno explained after the fight as we gathered round. 'I have apologized to him for the accident. He was ducking and diving and I just wanted to get him out of there.' Bruno went off into pantomime in Bristol after the fight. That's true, by the way.

Earlier that November there had been good news from the hushed corridors at Bart's when it emerged that Watson was out of his coma and had been placed in a recovery ward. I took him some boxing magazines one afternoon and he managed to pick out specific fighters, tapping gently on their pictures; it was a slow, draining process but it was the most encouraging sign yet. His bedside had been invaded by some of the finest C-list celebrities. His mother, Joan, was still holding constant vigil, with Sister June by her side. Only one photographer and one very senior and respected sports writer had crossed the line; they had tried to sneak in during the darkest of the coma days. I was stunned to see the award-winning hack pretending he was visiting a relative and sitting quietly reading in the ICU waiting room. When news of Watson's move from intensive care reached the media, Elton John sent more yellow flowers.

Watson spent his first Christmas after the fight in hospital. His recovery years were still a long, long way off.

The Contenders

June started with an odd WBO fight in Sicily when Joey Jacobs was stopped by Kamel Bou-Ali in round three. It was the first of many WBO title fights to involve a British boxer that happened without coverage and care. Jacobs had lost his British super-featherweight title in his previous fight and after the loss in Sicily he never fought again. He quit at 30 after just fifteen fights, including ten wins, and he is arguably the most anonymous British fighter to box for a world title.

In November, Tim Driscoll fought Maurizio Stecca, the bantamweight gold medal winner at the 1984 Olympics, for the WBO featherweight title in northern Italy. Matchroom, Driscoll's promoters, had arranged a truly madcap twenty-four-hour trip in and out of the Italian Lakes for about thirty of his faithful. Driscoll was pulled out by his corner at the end of nine rounds with a broken nose, cuts above his left eye and a swollen face. He fought just twice more and now trains boxers at the Fisher club in Bermondsey.

In October, Pat Barrett defended his European light-welterweight title against Racheed Lawal. There was an odd British heavyweight title eliminator on his undercard: Gypsy Johnny Fury, father of Tyson, was matched at the G-Mex in Manchester with unbeaten Henry Akinwande. It ended in the third, but Akinwande knew he had been in a scrap.

From the Notepad

'The bell sounded and Bruno's purple suede boots led his greased and bulging frame into the fray in pursuit of the immediately retreating Dutchman' – *Sunday Telegraph* report of Bruno's first-round blitz of John 'Flying Dutchman' Emmen. I like that line, it made me chuckle as I typed it.

'We have not seen the best of Frank Bruno yet,' said George Francis, the trainer, after Bruno's win.

'Don't, it's his living' – Dennie Mancini pleading with the referee,

Larry O'Connell, not to stop Mason from having one more round against Lewis in a clash of unbeaten British heavyweights.

'I just want to get Eubank out of my hair – I've had enough of him,' Watson said on the morning of his fateful world title fight at White Hart Lane.

'I've been the old man in this business since I was a young man,' said Andries, who started the year as the WBC light-heavyweight champion and was still fighting in his late thirties at the end of the year.

1992

*'I have studied Lennox Lewis and he throws a good elbow to the head,
his new punch. Derek Williams has the talent to win and I'm
here to make sure we see the talent.'*
Angelo Dundee before his guy, Williams, met Lewis

*'This is a hard game for kids nowadays, and if there's four world
championships to go for, that's great. We all deserve a chance to
be a world champion.'*
Pat Clinton on the modern business

IT WAS A year of extremes for Chris Eubank with five world title
defences of his WBO super-middleweight belt, controversial quotes
and often tedious fights.

Eubank beat South Africa's Thulani Malinga in February in
Birmingham. It was his first fight since the Michael Watson night
and there was a lot of scrutiny of the boxer. 'I never needed a shoulder
to cry on after the Watson fight,' said Eubank. 'I never knew softness
growing up.' Malinga was dropped in round five and lost a split
decision. It was an odd performance, and the South African was
underestimated. John Morris, general secretary of the British Boxing
Board of Control, wanted Eubank to take six months off. On
7 February, six days after beating Malinga, Eubank crashed his car
and killed a roadside worker. He was on police bail when his next
fight was announced.

In April in Manchester John Jarvis was knocked out in round

three. The American was the second replacement and 6,100 watched him go down at the G-Mex. Jarvis had fought just once in nearly two years and had lost that fight. There was some criticism, but Eubank was unrepentant. 'I don't owe the public, the public owes me, and if I had the fights that are being suggested I would have a very short career,' said Eubank.

There was talk of a fight with Nigel Benn, a hoped-for repeat of their brutal November 1990 fight. 'If Eubank doesn't agree to fight Nigel, the WBO might strip him of his title on June 27,' said Barry Hearn, who had guided Eubank's career since his return from America. Eubank wanted a fight with Benn, but he wanted it at a price: 'I will fight him but I must get 1.65 million pounds – that way I will clear a million after tax. That's my price.'

Benn was chasing Eubank hard and beat Dan Sherry in February but struggled against Malinga over ten rounds in May. Hearn secured Benn a fight with WBC champion Mauro Galvano but lost the purse bid, and Benn had to agree to fight in Italy. A date was tentatively set for October.

In June, Eubank won over twelve rounds in Portugal – the fight was dubbed the Bore on the Shore – when he met another American, Ron Essett. The outdoor event was spectacular, the fight forgettable. Eubank did exactly enough to win and not an ounce more. 'I don't care if they take away my title, I will just start again,' he said. 'I don't have to fight for the public's acceptance – I'm utterly indifferent to the public.' Eubank was attracting over 10 million on ITV. His Malinga fight had peaked at 13,028,000 viewers.

Defence number four was in Glasgow, against the punching post-man Tony Thornton in September. Eubank won on points. In November he met Juan Carlos Giménez in Manchester and it was another clear decision. There was an attempt to sell the fight as Justice Night for Giménez, but that flopped: Giménez was one of the two boxers that had vanished from the WBO's super-middleweight rankings in July 1991; the other was Italian Michele Mastrodonato. The pair were replaced at one and two by Watson and Eubank.

The Giménez win meant that Dave 'Boy' McAuley's record of five consecutive world title defences had been equalled. Eubank would break it and set new records in 1993 and 1994. McAuley, however, ended his sequence at five when he lost in Bilbao to Rodolfo Blanco on a tight, tight decision in June. It was, according to Barney Eastwood, 'trickery and thievery' that cost McAuley his beloved fly-weight title. He never fought again, leaving the ring after twenty-three fights, which included nine for world titles; he was knocked down a total of nineteen times in a brilliant career.

Duke McKenzie had three world title fights at two different weights – an achievement that would have been considered astounding in the seventies or eighties. In March, he retained his WBO bantamweight title when he stopped Wilfredo Vargas in eight rounds at the Royal Albert Hall in front of a small crowd. Two months later he lost it in just 116 seconds to unbeaten Rafael Del Valle, again at the Royal Albert Hall. He was dropped for nine, beat that count, and was then dropped again. McKenzie insisted after the fight that all was well with him – 'It's not the weight, there is nothing wrong' – so the blow-out was a mystery. He looked sickened by the shock loss. He had never previously been stopped or knocked down.

McKenzie gained 4lb and moved from bantamweight at 118lb to super-bantamweight's heady limits of 122lb, or 8st 10lb. He beat Peter Buckley, who at the time was having only his twenty-fourth of three hundred fights, and then in October, fighting a long way from the bright lights of the city at the Lewisham Theatre in south London, he beat Jesse Benavides to win the WBO super-bantamweight title. McKenzie was a three-weight world champion and some of the men he had beaten were good operators, potential champions in any epoch. McKenzie dropped Benavides in the tenth round, but it was a tight fight.

On the undercard in Lewisham a kid called Bradley Stone beat Kevin Middleton and the crowd showered the ring with £36 in nobbins – an ancient sign that the paying punters appreciated the efforts of the two fighters. It was like a throwback night in many ways, a night when the glamour of a world title belt was eclipsed by two scrappers in a six-round brawl. Stone lost a British title fight in

1994 and died two days later after collapsing in his girlfriend's arms. There is a statue of little Brad outside the Peacock gym in London's Canning Town.

In March, Glasgow's Pat Clinton won the WBO flyweight title when he beat Isidro Pérez on a slender split in his hometown. Clinton had lost a European title fight in Denmark, won the belt in Sardinia, and held the British title at flyweight. He was a double ABA champion, he'd boxed at the 1984 Olympics, and he was a fearless little fighter. His father, Billy, had been a Scottish champion. 'I remember my father telling me there's only two kinds of fighters – the ones who've got butterflies and the psychopaths; the psychopaths don't last too long,' said Clinton. At the Kelvin Hall that night a trio of great Scottish fighters stood in respect: Ken Buchanan, Walter McGowan and Jim Watt formed an honour guard for Clinton.

Clinton met Hitchin's Danny Porter in his first defence. Clinton had stopped Porter in a British title fight in 1989 and there was some criticism of the match when it was announced. Porter failed in British, European, Commonwealth and world title fights and in any other decade would not have got near a world title fight. However, in Glasgow in September he put in the performance of his life, went the full twelve rounds and pushed Clinton. 'I won that, I did enough,' Porter said late that night in the bar at the Albany Hotel.

There was a lot of screaming and moaning when Steve Cruz, the kid that had beaten Barry McGuigan in Las Vegas, was sanctioned to fight Paul Hodkinson for the WBC featherweight title in Belfast in April. Cruz had drink problems, had won just twice in three years, and had not fought in thirteen months since a stoppage loss. However, it was a good story: he was the boy that ruined the fighting Irish hero, the man that slayed McGuigan the Legend. Hoko ruined him in three easy rounds. It was sad to watch the Texas kid lose.

In May the proliferation of sanctioning bodies finally delivered something that old-timers could simply not comprehend: two British world champions at the same weight. In 1992 there were still a lot of men at ringside, working in the business, that had been involved in the forties and fifties. They had known a time when there were just eight world champions – boxers so distant and exotic that a glimpse or a chance handshake was cherished. Fight people like Danny Vary, Archie Kasler, Davey Jones, Les Roberts, Nat Basso, Danny Holland and dozens of others had their tales of shaking Rocky Marciano's hand, watching Sugar Ray Robinson train, driving Sonny Liston all over London. In May 1992 Britain had two world champions at featherweight. 'The game's gone,' Vary would often say.

Colin McMillan boxed a brilliant fight to beat Maurizio Stecca for the Italian's WBO featherweight title in the middle of May. There was a case for a shut-out, it really was that good. Warren made an offer to Hoko of £160,000 for a partial unification, and that offer would increase in the next few months. However, Eastwood, Hoko's promoter, dismissed the gesture. 'Colin can have the fight with Hoko and I will put it in the contract that his WBO title is not at stake,' said Eastwood. 'We're not interested in the WBO and don't want to get involved with them.'

It was a natural fight, and it would have been big.

In early September, McMillan travelled to Toulouse to watch Hoko defend his WBC featherweight title against Fabrice Benichou. The fight ended in the tenth, with Hoko narrowly in front on all three scorecards, when Benichou's lip was split so severely that there was no chance of him fighting on. Two weeks later it was McMillan's turn to defend his title at Olympia against Colombia's Rubén Palacios, a loser of eleven fights including a stoppage to Jim McDonnell in London in 1986. Palacios was rugged and there was a real concern about his selection. 'I rejected him as a challenger, he's not my choice,' insisted Warren, McMillan's promoter, before the fight. At the time McMillan had a non-licensed adviser called Jonathan Rendall, a journalist, and the pair had picked Palacios. The fight was ugly from the first bell and McMillan was rocked, cut, and the victim of constant illegal activity. In round eight, McMillan missed with a left hook; Palacios ducked under the punch and then brought his body up and into McMillan's shoulder. The left shoulder was instantly and visibly dislocated; McMillan switched to southpaw in desperation and pain. The referee missed it, but Howard Rainey in McMillan's corner saw it and threw the towel in. The fight was over after 1:52 of the eighth round, with McMillan in front by a tiny margin on all three score-cards. There was some confusion in the ring, an attempt to get the fight declared a technical draw, but it was given to Palacios as a technical knockout victory.

McMillan would be out over a year and he never recovered. Palacios never fought again and three days before what was meant to be his first defence, which was due to take place in Tyne and Wear against John Davison, he failed a routine HIV test. He was stripped of his title and died ten years later in 2003 at the age of 40. (McMillan, incidentally, was made to take an HIV test by the British Boxing Board of Control and passed.)

The Hodkinson fight was off the agenda for ever.

Johnny Nelson travelled to Hugo's Nightclub in Bealton, Virginia in May to fight James Warring for the IBF cruiserweight title. The memory of the De León draw, a stinker of a fight, had not faded. Nelson had won six times since that night, and left for America convinced he would win the title. It was another passive disaster for him. At the end of the fifth round, after fifteen minutes of a great hitless – but lively – mazurka, Ingle in Nelson's corner was frustrated and fuming: 'I'm sick of watching you – get out there and fight!' Nelson never listened. The career of the Entertainer, as Ingle had once dubbed him, was quite remarkable. After the loss to Warring on points, Nelson lost six of his next ten. He should have been gone, finished, retired in 1995, but he changed, he found confidence and power, and he went from December 1995 through to November 2005 unbeaten. He won twenty-one fights in a row and fourteen were for the WBO cruiserweight title. It's an end that would have been impossible to predict during any round in the De León or Warring fiascos.

There was a terrible night in July at the G-Mex for Warren. He had agreed deals with former Mickey Duff fighters Pat Barrett and Derek Angol and secured world title fights for the pair. Barrett had been due to fight Manning Galloway for the WBO welterweight title back in February, but the fight collapsed and Barrett only found out when

I attended a press conference at the Cumberland Hotel to promote the title fight. I'd been tipped off that Galloway was not boxing and I asked Duff why the fight was off. Duff exploded, screaming at me and demanding, 'What do you want? A fucking Pulitzer Prize?' Warren did a deal to get Galloway, who was a terrific operator, back and he simply knew too much for Barrett and won on points. Angol forgot the basics, lost his head after dominating for four rounds, and ran out of steam against Tyrone Booze. It was stopped in round seven, Angol's first loss in twenty-seven fights. It was Booze's first fight in nearly eighteen months. He was beatable, and it was a dreadful night for all involved.

Duff had been arguing all year with the people guiding the career of Lennox Lewis. He claimed that Frank Maloney had done a Cecil B. De Mille in reverse: 'He's taken a somebody and made him a nobody.' Duff had eased Frank Bruno back with two good wins in 1992: Bruno stopped the Cuban José Ribalta in two in April and then Pierre Coetzer in eight in October. I missed the second fight because Duff had banned me by then. Planned fights with Francesco Damiani and Ray Mercer never happened. 'Frank Bruno is not afraid of Lennox Lewis,' said Duff in April. 'If his people want to sit and talk, then I will sit and talk.'

Lewis knocked out Derek 'Sweet D' Williams at the Royal Albert Hall a few days later. There was betting outrage from the bookies when they initially offered 33-1 on the third. The odds were reduced to 7-4, Lewis finished it in the third, and the bookies paid out nearly £700,000. 'I will do the same to Bruno, and he knows it,' said Lewis. 'Don't listen to Mickey Bluff, I speak reality.'

In the early hours of the first day of November in front of a capacity crowd at Earls Court, the British boxing world changed. Lewis was matched with Donovan 'Razor' Ruddock. Razor had fought two brutal fights with Mike Tyson in 1991 and British heavyweights never beat fighters like Ruddock. It was a final eliminator for the WBC heavyweight title. Ruddock had former world champion Floyd Patterson in his team and he'd looked fantastic at the St Pancras gym in Kentish Town. The first bell sounded at 12.59 a.m. on 1 November.

Ruddock was dropped heavily and saved by the bell in the first. There was late-night chaos in the arena. In round two Ruddock was over twice, and the fight was finished after forty-six seconds. 'Ruddock was nervous before the fight,' said Lewis. 'When he got up, I looked at his feet. He was finished.' Lewis was cold when he fought.

'Since I started to work with Lennox he has started to look like Ali more and more each time,' said Pepe Correa, the volatile and never-understated trainer. 'He may just be the second coming of Muhammad Ali.' Correa was gone two years later. In June 2016, when Ali died, Lennox Claudius Lewis, to give him his full name, was one of the chosen to carry the Greatest's coffin. Now you see what I mean when I say British boxing changed for ever that night.

Barry Hearn had come up $300,000 short in that purse bid for Benn's WBC super-middleweight title fight against Mauro Galvano. The Italians badly wanted the fight on their soil, on their terms. It was a risk for Benn, and on the night, at a venue just outside Rome, it was extremely dangerous. Benn cut Galvano in round two with a legitimate punch and the fight was stopped during the break between rounds three and four. Galvano's people tried to get a technical draw, and that was how it was first announced. Benn and Galvano were raised on the shoulders of their people in the ring, Benn angry and Galvano relieved. Hearn, however, was still arguing for justice five minutes after the fight finished. 'It was a fair punch,' he screamed. The ringside officials called over the referee, Joe Cortez, and told him Benn was the winner. 'Justice was served, the kid deserved it,' said Cortez. Benn's first act as new champion was to push his way to the edge of the ring and clasp Eubank by the hand. They spoke, agreed to fight, and nodded. Meanwhile it was getting ugly, and armed Carabinieri joined Benn's fleeing party as the missiles started to fly. The smiling boxer was shuffled from the ring by an infamous group of Essex boys, two of whom would be shot to death one night in a Range Rover outside a village in Essex called Rettendon. Both Patrick Tate and Tony Tucker gave their man cover as he left the ring that night in Italy.

Two months later, in December, Benn stopped Welshman Nicky

Piper at Alexandra Palace in his first defence. It ended in round eleven, when Piper was just starting to tire. 'I was glad when it was called off,' said Jimmy Tibbs, who was in Benn's corner. 'I was thinking of Michael [Watson] and it was getting a bit uncomfortable. Nicky was brave.' Tibbs had been in Watson's corner the year before.

'I will not fight Nigel Benn now because of his mentality,' said Eubank. 'I don't want either of us to suffer what happened to Michael Watson.' He would change his mind ten months later.

At the end of 1992 Naseem Hamed was undefeated in six fights, still only 18 and dividing everybody he came into contact with. Reg Gutteridge called him 'the latest escapologist from Ingle's gym'. In the Wincobank gym, Hamed was stunning to watch. 'I've had him since he was seven and he's going to be a world champion before he's twenty-one,' said Ingle. 'I've spent over ten years of my life with him. I know what he can do and right now people are only seeing the tricks, the showman – wait until they see the fighter.' Brendan was wrong: Hamed was 21 when he won the world title.

In late December the WBC declared Lennox Lewis the heavyweight champion of the world. It was a mad year, a beautiful year.

The Contenders

In June, Carl Thompson went to Cleethorpes to beat Steve Lewsam for the vacant British cruiserweight title. The show at a holiday camp was promoted by Joe Frater, a Grimsby car dealer. Sweet Joe wore a velvet jacket and danced in the ring.

Naseem Hamed won his fourth fight when he stopped Miguel Matthews in the third at the Grosvenor House in Park Lane. Roy Francis, the ref, was not impressed with Hamed's taunting tactics and pulled him: 'Do that again, son, and I will personally throw you over that fucking rope.'

Barry Jones, 17, won three times and lost in the final at the European junior championship in April. The Eastern Bloc dominated. At the Olympics in Barcelona Robin Reid won a bronze at light-middle.

In November, David Haye won in a round at the Royal Garden Hotel on a testimonial night for former England ABA captain Johnny Banham. Haye was 12 years old.

From the Notepad

In July, the IBF pulled off a classic when it ranked Sheffield's Slugger O'Toole at six and Nottingham's Fidel Castro Smith at nine in their world rankings – you guessed it, one and the same man. Brendan Ingle liked to give his fighters creative names and that is why he changed Fidel to Slugger.

'I fought with the body of a man but the heart of a boy against De León – this is different, I'm a man now,' Nelson said before his fight with Warring. It was not different.

Two days after Lewis beat Ruddock, and on the same page in my notepad, Audley Harrison boxed at the Irish Centre, Camden Town, in the north-west London novices. I scribbled: '6.5. 15.8. Switch hitter. Like his style.'

'Fighting is the main thing, I don't know anything else,' said little Bradley Stone. 'It's the one thing I know really, boxing. I'm trying really hard, I'm going to make it.' Stone did try, and he fought for the British title. He is the kid star in Ron Peck's *Fighters*.

1993

'I've been here twenty years and he's been here twenty minutes and he's
getting all the publicity . . . I just told him to shut up and fuck off.'
Phil Martin on ejecting Chris Eubank from the Champs Camp gym
in Moss Side

'There is no blood on this floor. Out there Pat gets involved, his friends are
evil, and that is what burns a kid out, not this, not in here.'
Brian Hughes with a brutal assessment of a boxer's distractions

THE INCREASINGLY BIZARRE Chris Eubank started the year on a peace
mission in Moss Side and finished it fighting in front of 42,000 people
just a few miles away at the Theatre of Dreams. A draw in both
conflicts is about right.

In Moss Side there was a lot of anger at the perceived hijacking of
a sensitive issue by the fighter. At the start of January, Benji Stanley,
just 14, had been blasted with a shotgun and killed at Alvino's Pattie
and Dumplin' Shop. Eubank held a meeting on the subject in a sports
hall, and it was ugly at times. 'He's only here to sell tickets for his
fights,' one man said to the gathered group. 'Well, he's here and
nobody in Moss Side buys tickets to his fights,' countered another.
Eubank had earlier been evicted from the gym Phil Martin had built
from the ruins of a shop that was gutted by fire and hate during the
riots in 1981. 'I've been here twenty years and he's been here twenty
minutes and he's getting all the publicity,' said Martin. 'I was listening to him go on and I just told him to shut up and fuck off. I'd heard

enough.' Martin had three British champions at the time in Maurice Core, Frank Grant and Carl Thompson.

Eubank stayed six days on his mission before leaving to get ready for his first defence of the year and his sixth defence of the WBO super-middleweight title against Lindell Holmes at Earls Court in February. Eubank won on points. It was his fourth consecutive twelve-rounder.

Nigel Benn fought a few weeks later, in March, and was lucky to be saved by the bell at the end of the twelfth in his rematch with Mauro Galvano. Benn was caught, wobbled, and fell into the ring post as the bell sounded to end their WBC super-middleweight fight. Jimmy Tibbs was so concerned that he was up the steps. The verdict, once Benn had recovered from the genuine scare, was wide in the Londoner's favour. 'He caught me, I was hurt, and that's the end of the story,' Benn said. 'I got cocky, nearly paid the price, and then thirty seconds later all three judges went for me. That's why I'm the champion of the world.' The talk intensified about a return with Eubank. The problem was money: they both wanted too much.

In May, Eubank was in Glasgow and he looked weary; his timing was bad and he needed a finish that is often forgotten. It was his twelfth consecutive WBO title fight. 'Slow down? No chance, my bank manager will not allow it,' said Eubank. The challenger was Barney Eastwood's European super-middleweight champion Ray Close and it was expected to be an easy night for Eubank. In round eleven, when Eubank was trailing, he connected with a sickening right uppercut and Close went down. It looked like the fight was over and that Eubank had salvaged a lost cause once again, but Close somehow beat the count and survived the thirty-second onslaught to hear the bell. 'The ref should have stopped it when Close went down,' said Eubank. They were both exhausted in the last. It was a split draw, Eubank kept his title, and Close had a genuine reason to moan. He would get his rematch, but he had lost his moment. The scores were 115-115, 116-113 for Close and 116-112 for Eubank. No knockdown, no title, and Eubank needed a rest.

Benn was back in the ring in June having been promised a fight by south London's Lou Gent at Olympia. 'I will be in your face, not running and fighting you for every second the fight lasts,' said Gent. Benn smiled, reached out a hand to shake Gent's hand and said, 'Thanks, Lou.' Gent was not lying. Benn was caught and hurt in the third, but Gent, a battler from a different time, was down for a total of twenty-three seconds in three knockdowns in the same round. He somehow made it to the fourth and was rescued after two more knockdowns. Benn had his WBC belt, and now the rematch with Eubank was serious.

However, Benn had some trouble away from the ring when it looked like he and Tibbs had split. In early August Tibbs met with a couple of boxing writers at the Thomas A'Becket, the ancient gym in the Old Kent Road, and he was not happy. 'I'm not a greedy man,' he told us. 'I want what we agreed. This geezer told me that Nigel never wanted to talk to me. I'm disgusted and disappointed.' There was an agreement for £70,000 for the rematch with Eubank, and Tibbs said that Peter DeFreitas, a man with PETE tattooed across his knuckles, had made an offer of £40,000. It was resolved, the final figure private; dignity was restored.

'It's not just the training and the actual fight,' said Tibbs. 'It's holding concentration in the corner, holding his head when he drifts and telling him to concentrate. Against Eubank a lot of the fight is in the mind.' This is what a real trainer of boxers knows and what the pretenders claim to know.

The night in October at Old Trafford when Eubank and Benn met for the second and last time was truly beautiful. The first fight on the bill was Barry Jones of Ely in Cardiff. 'It was a long, long walk to the ring, but even at that early time there was a special feel in the air,' said the Welshman, who would win the WBO super-featherweight title in 1997. That week in Manchester had been hilarious at times with Don King in town to talk and lurid, conflicting stories from both camps – both belts were at stake. Men with names like Rolex Ray, Frank the Shirt, the Snowman, and Armed and Dangerous jetted in from Tenerife and mainland Spain. It was a happening.

The money issue had been settled when Eubank agreed a deal. 'We both knew that a million each was too much, so I agreed to take the smaller cut,' said Eubank. The official, guaranteed split was Benn £1 million and Eubank £850,000.

They fought each other to the very end that torrid night, their hatred never subsiding. It was tight, hard and intense in every round. In the sixth round Benn was deducted a point for persistent low punches, and that cost him revenge. It's that simple. The three judges only agreed on four of the twelve rounds and returned three contrasting scores, a verdict that broke Benn's heart: 114-114, a score of 114-113 for Benn, and the final score of 115-113 for Eubank from old docker Harry Gibbs, the referee in the infamous fight between Joe Bugner and Henry Cooper in 1971. Benn was distraught: without the loss of a point he would have won a split and slept easy for the rest of his life. The pair would never fight again but, a quarter of a century later, the rivalry has not subsided. It was a privilege to be there.

The loss of the big domestic featherweight showdown with Colin McMillan was still annoying Paul Hodkinson when he was getting ready for his February defence against Ricardo 'Colonel' Cepeda. 'I defended the best title, McMillan lost the worst title,' Hoko said. The WBC featherweight champion had to deal with Cepeda and his gobby translator, a New Yorker called Ralfie who looked and sounded like an extra from an episode of *Kojak*. 'Hodkinson likes to fight too much,' said Cepeda, who was Puerto Rican and spoke Spanish, through Ralfie. 'I will cut him early and in the ninth round he will be a bloody mess.' However, once Ralfie had translated with relish, there was a bemused look from Cepeda, who lived in the Bronx. Hoko retained in the fourth at Earls Court.

April was a cruel month for Hoko. He had to watch Steve Robinson win Colin McMillan's old WBO featherweight title and then he lost his WBC version. The £450,000 fight with McMillan was gone for ever.

The Robinson story was a fairy story, an unbelievable tale. It had all started the Tuesday before Rubén Palacios, the man that beat McMillan, was due to defend his title against John Davison in Tyne and Wear, when he failed that routine HIV test. He took the test two more times in the next twenty-four hours, and failed them all. 'It is sad,' said Ed Levine, the WBO's president. 'Rubén left Colombia to earn good money and he is returning with a death sentence.' Levine stripped him, and forty-eight hours before the first bell Robinson was found and sanctioned. Just a week before the fight Robinson had left his job making £53 a week at a warehouse in Cardiff. His record was thirteen wins, nine losses and a draw. He had only been in one twelve-round fight and he was fresh from a loss on points in France.

Robinson was paid twenty grand for the fight and he beat Davison in front of 3,000 sad fans. Davison was broken at the end of twelve rounds. It was a tight and deserving unanimous verdict. 'Steve Robinson proves that boxing is full of dreams,' said Dai Gardiner, who was in the corner when Johnny Owen had his final fight in 1980. 'The title means more than the money,' said Robinson, the first Welsh world champion since Howard Winstone in 1968. Davison never complained about the switch of opponent or about the two changes of dates before he finally got his chance. He was stoic, gallant in defeat. He fought one more time, a loss by stoppage to Duke McKenzie for the British featherweight title, before retiring.

Hoko was stopped a week or so later, caught and dropped in round seven by Mexico's Gregorio Vargas at the National Boxing Stadium in Dublin. Vargas would lose world title fights over twelve rounds to Floyd Mayweather Jr and John John Molina in the years to come. In Dublin he was too good, though he was trailing on all three scorecards before the end. Hoko, like McMillan, joined an orderly queue of boxers to relieve Robinson of his lucky belt. Well, that was the thinking.

In July, former British champion Sean Murphy was first in line to take Robinson's belt and he was knocked out with a right cross in the ninth, his heart as broken as his jaw. At ringside, McMillan was dismissive. He was next, an October date back in Cardiff at the Ice Rink, and he thought it would be a romp. 'I just hope the loser doesn't look silly,' McMillan said. 'I hope it is McMillan next because I'm sick of hearing how easily he will beat me,' said Robinson.

McMillan had been in Miami in January with Angelo Dundee as part of his rehab from the shoulder surgery. He injured the shoulder again and had a bolt inserted and a bone graft in February. He opted not to have a warm-up before Robinson – it was a mismatch in his eyes. It was a mistake. In front of 3,500, Robinson won a unanimous decision. McMillan went for an X-ray on a damaged right hand (internal bleeding, no fracture) and was left regretting tactics and not agreeing to a warm-up fight. Robinson made £250,000, but it was the win that mattered.

In July, Glenn McCrory went to Moscow for the first professional world title to take place in the city and lost on points to Al Cole for the IBF cruiserweight title. Big Glenn was dropped twice in the sixth but knew enough to hold and survive. The fight was not about the money for McCrory – he was making £25,000 – it was about proving he could still go the distance and belonged in a world title fight. McCrory never fought again, and that was the plan.

Andy Holligan was sent on a difficult mission in December, to meet Julio César Chávez in a bullring in Puebla, eighty miles from Mexico City. At 7,200 feet above sea level, it was cold. 'The kid was tough,' said Arthur Mercante, the referee, who was also the third man when Muhammad Ali met Joe Frazier in the Fight of the Century in 1971. Chávez was the WBC light-welterweight champion and unbeaten in eighty-nine fights. Colin Moorcroft and Frank Warren pulled Holligan out at the end of the fifth. 'I think this fight should end,' Mercante whispered seconds before it did.

In Scotland in May, Pat Clinton lost his WBO flyweight title to tiny Jake Matlala. The Scot was stopped in round eight, had one more losing fight, and then quit. On the same bill Paul Weir, having just his sixth fight, won the WBO minimumweight title when he inflicted a faceful of cuts on Fernando Martínez. The fight was over in round seven, and Weir was champion at a weight the Board did not even recognize. Weir was paid twenty grand for his first defence in October when he beat South Africa's Lindi Memani on points behind closed doors at Tommy Gilmour's St Andrew's Sporting Club. The boxing world had altered; just 700 watched a world title fight, and Weir was taken beyond eight rounds for the first time. All the old rules had gone.

Chris Pyatt, a veteran at 29, beat Sumbu Kalambay for the vacant WBO middleweight title in May and knocked out late replacement Hugo Corti in the sixth back at the Granby Halls in Leicester in a quick defence. There was bold talk of a fight with Roberto Durán; Pyatt wanted the winner of Eubank–Benn II.

Duke McKenzie lost his WBO super-bantamweight title to Daniel Jiménez on a tight majority verdict at the Lewisham Theatre: one judge went for a draw, two went narrowly for Jiménez.

Late replacement Lorenzo Smith was beaten over twelve rounds for the vacant WBO welterweight title by Eamonn Loughran at the King's Hall in Belfast. Barry McGuigan was there to shadow-box for twenty seconds to the delight of the 3,000 inside his sacred venue. 'It's a decent crowd but there are none of the diehards,' said McGuigan. They would come out twenty years later for Carl Frampton.

Lennox Lewis had a dozen wars at the negotiating table in 1993. Don King wanted him stripped in February, Riddick Bowe insulted him all year, and the deal to fight Frank Bruno was brutally shaped after months of dealing. A deal to fight Bowe in January collapsed when Frank Maloney suggested a unique purse split. 'Give the boxers six million each and the winner the other twenty million,' Maloney had told Rock Newman, the man in charge of Bowe. It never happened; Newman never got back to Maloney.

'I don't boast about the deals I've turned down, I boast about the deals I've made,' said Mickey Duff in April. 'I want the Bruno fight with Lewis and I want to talk about the actual money.'

In May, Lewis met Tony Tucker in Las Vegas, was paid $9 million by King, but refused to sign with the promoter for more fights. There was a relentless campaign of mischief by King's people to discredit Lewis and Maloney. 'Maloney is the Mighty Midget and he will ruin Lennox's career,' said King. Tucker was dropped in the third and ninth and Lewis won on points. It was good, but it failed to convert the American public.

The Bruno talks continued, a long flowing line of insult, impasse and slow progress. 'What Maloney knows about boxing you could put on the back of a postage stamp,' said George Francis, Bruno's trainer in August. It was finally agreed for October in Cardiff Arms Park, which was not Duff's choice, and by the first week in September 11,000 seats had sold. Maloney and Panos Eliades, the promoter, needed to sell 15,000 to break even. They made money in the end. Bruno had issued legal proceedings against Lewis over a comment and that was hanging high over the fight like a toxic cloud. There was no need for chairs or tables to be thrown or threats of death at any of the press conferences: when the pair were in the same room it was malevolent.

The doors opened and the fights started on the first day of October, but the principal prizefighters started to make their way to the ring on the second day of October. At 12.32 a.m. the covers came off the canvas. Mickey Vann, the referee, went in at 12.36 to inspect the ring. Bruno started to walk at 12.49 with plastic bags taped to his feet, and at 12.54 Lewis walked with his friend Anthony Gee holding the WBC belt high in the cold night air. It had been raining, drizzling, but it had stopped. The first bell was at 1.05. The richest fight ever to take place in Britain was underway.

It was stopped in the seventh when a savage final few punches from Lewis left Bruno in a bad way. Bruno's left eye was closing and his hands were rigid at his side, his body tilting like a giant shipwreck, at the mercy of anything that Lewis could find. It had been a battle of too much pride, too little skill and too much desire. It was a perfect mix. Bruno was winning on one scorecard and the fight was a draw on the other two. In the ring, Bruno's wife Laura was comforted by Lewis's mother Violet. An hour later and Laura was attacking Lewis for not being British like 'my Frank'. Lewis was truly exhausted, Bruno thoughtful. 'I will go home with my wife and children and see where I go from here,' he said. 'I'm a better fighter than I have ever been given credit for. I was four or five rounds in front, on my way to victory. That is the truth.'

The boxing obits for Bruno were written and broadcast, many of them savage in their dismissal. Lewis wanted him to walk away, the men in the Bruno business held their tongue. 'If I was looking after

Frank, I'd tell him to retire – today,' said Maloney, who delighted the tabloid pack when he said that Lewis was sleeping in the dressing room just twenty minutes before the fight. It's a funny business, the heavyweight business: one year later, after none of the big fights materialized, Lewis was knocked out indoors at Wembley and lost his world title; two years later, Bruno won the heavyweight world title by beating the man that beat Lewis.

It was another truly exceptional year.

The Contenders

British boxers were involved in a series of losing fights in exotic locations throughout 1993. Michael Ayers, an ABA champion with All Stars in 1986, went to Rome in April and lost on points to Giovanni Parisi for the WBO lightweight title. 'I need a knockout and I will get it,' promised Ayers. Parisi was too slick and won on points.

In the same month, Crawford Ashley boiled his body down to super-middle and was stopped in six by Michael Nunn for the WBA version of the title. Ashley moved back to light-heavyweight permanently after the loss.

Lloyd Honeyghan was back in Atlantic City and was stopped by Vinny Pazienza in round nine of a brutal fight. It was an unofficial light-middleweight world title eliminator. Honeyghan had just three fights left.

From the Notepad

'This is an odd fight,' said Dan Duva, part of the American arm of the promotion for Lewis–Bruno. 'How often do you get to hit a man who is suing you?' Dan was a lawyer and a very good one. He was certainly a very vocal one.

In March it was the end for Errol Christie – one final loss in Manchester, to Trevor Ambrose. It was pitiful to witness. 'There's no physical deterioration but his punch resistance is gone; that's it for Errol Christie,' said Phil Martin, who had been training him. 'I wish he had been with me from the start because he could have been a world champion.'

'This is my biggest payday,' said Andy Till, who was known as Stone Face. 'I'm looking forward to the day when I can give up the milk round.' Till retained his British light-middleweight title nine days later when he stopped Wally Swift Jr in the fourth round at the Royal Albert Hall. He was paid thirty grand for his work that night.

'If I fight this boy it will end in one round and it will be bad for him,' warned Riddick Bowe. He was ringside in Dagenham watching Herbie Hide stop Michael Murray to win the vacant British heavyweight title. Bowe dozed off at one point. The pair would fight.

1994

*'I hear Naz described as awkward and that is crazy. He is gifted.
The problem is that people don't know what a bolo punch is and
they don't recognize the skill involved when Naz slips a counter.'*
Brendan Ingle

*'When Lennox walked out I knew there was a problem, I could smell it.
He was only worried about his new braids and he kept looking at
himself. He wasn't there, he wasn't focused. I'd seen the Atomic Bull
and he was ready; he was throwing the right hand in his dressing
room – the right hand that finished Lewis.'*
Steve Head, legendary ringside security expert, on the night
Oliver McCall knocked out Lewis

IT TAKES LESS than a second in the boxing ring to finish a fight and for
a heavyweight that single second can be shattering. The repercussions
last a lot longer, as Lennox Lewis found out when he met Oliver
McCall.

Lewis was in the mix for a big fight in 1994. There was talk of
Riddick Bowe, talk of Evander Holyfield, but in May he was in
Atlantic City to stop the unremarkable Phil Jackson in round eight to
keep his WBC heavyweight title. Lennox never lost a round and the
early part of the summer was spent in hope of securing a massive
payday. Nothing happened. Then in August Don King placed a
million dollars on Oliver McCall to beat Lewis in their fight at
Wembley in September. Hey, it's a nice story, even if it's not true.

Lewis against McCall was a savage 211 seconds that will never be forgotten.

McCall had been on a tour of training facilities, a moving feast that was designed to keep him away from the crack pipe. He had trained with Julio César Chávez at altitude in Mexico, sparred behind closed and locked doors in Las Vegas, and finished in the English countryside at a health spa surrounded by women in towelling robes. 'McCall is an imbecile,' Lewis said at the Peacock gym a few days before the fight. McCall had been a sparring partner and one of his old bosses, Mike Tyson, called him from prison to wish him luck. 'I've been in more training camps than fights,' said McCall.

The 6,000 fans on the wrong side of midnight were stunned by the ferocity of the finish. Lewis was throwing a right when McCall's punch landed first. It was the start of the second round and Lewis was down, and hurt bad. He somehow got up at six and stumbled into the ref. The fight was rightly stopped after just thirty-one seconds. Frank Maloney and Pepe Correa screamed and pointed fingers in the aftermath, claiming their fighter could have continued. 'The referee was right – only thirty-one seconds had passed,' said McCall. 'Do you really think that he could have survived the round? It was right, and that skinny punk [Correa] was dissing me in the ring before the fight. He never said a word at the end.' At ringside, Panos Eliades, the liquidator turned promoter, was open-mouthed and confused. 'Why was he so open to the right?' he asked.

In the fall-out there was an inevitable cull, and Correa was sent back to America. A shortlist of replacements was drafted: George Benton, Jackie McKoy, Tommy Brooks and the Torch, my old friend Richie Giachetti. 'When Lennox got in the ring I didn't see the warrior thing I see in all great fighters,' said Manny Steward, who was in McCall's corner. The job of saving Lennox Lewis would eventually go to the man that masterminded his temporary downfall: Steward was offered the role.

In January, Herbie Hide and Michael Bentt exchanged a few insults. It quickly escalated and they had to be dragged screaming and kicking from a puddle on a hotel patio. Their suits were ripped, buttons long gone, and their fight at the home of Millwall – Senegal Fields as it was known – in March was on the boxing map. Hide was often unintentionally funny and just before the scuffle he questioned Bentt's thin attempt at proving his Britishness. Bentt had been born in London but lived and was based in America. Hide said to him, 'You are supposed to be a Millwall fan, but you think George Best played for Millwall.'

They met under a grim sky for Bentt's WBO heavyweight title and it was full of menace and hate. Hide was unbeaten in twenty-five fights, and he added Bentt to the stoppage column in round seven. Bentt never fought again and was rushed to the Royal London Hospital, Whitechapel, where eminent neurosurgeon John Sutcliffe studied the damage and declared that Bentt had a 'concussive brain injury', but was 'not bleeding inside the skull'. There was boldness in the celebratory talk back at the ground, about Hide fighting the division's big dogs. Barry Hearn laughed it off. 'Everybody knows how I operate and what I have achieved with Chris Eubank,' he admitted.

Hide would be out of action for one year. He met Riddick Bowe in Las Vegas when he did return.

There was despair for Nicky Piper in January when he was less than two minutes from victory against Leeonzer Barber for the WBO light-heavyweight title. Barber's face was disfigured by a terrible swelling on his right eye, and knowing he had a round to salvage the fight, he landed cleanly to send Piper down in the ninth. Piper got up, was dropped again, and then somehow got up again. The referee stopped it and Piper was left stunned on his feet, staring in amazement at Barber's grotesque deformities.

There was also a bad mismatch that January when Floyd Havard retired at the end of six rounds against John John Molina for the IBF's super-featherweight title. Havard was dropped in the third, had a broken nose and was losing every round. The retirement was the only sensible thing about the fight. At that point Havard had won and lost the British title, which he would win again. 'Molina was in a different class,' admitted Maloney, the promoter. 'But, I feel Havard could do well at WBO level.' That was catty from Maloney, but it was often heard at the time.

At the end of February, Nigel Benn took unbeaten Henry Wharton's best punches and retained his WBC super-middleweight title on points at Earls Court. It was a gruelling fight. 'I'd like to see Henry in with Eubank,' said Benn. 'His body shots will get through – you can't knock out Eubank with a head shot because his head is like granite.' Benn was caught with a left hook, dropped and pushed over for a disputed count at the end of the fifth round. Michael Watson was ringside in a wheelchair. 'Nigel is a good friend,' he said. Benn had to box, think, and take fewer risks than normal. He was 30, this was his forty-first fight, and the hard bouts and life in general had taken a toll on the Dark Destroyer. He had seven fights left; three he lost, three were easy, and one nobody will ever forget. Benn did take a break, let his body heal, and fought just one more time in 1994, in September, when he easily outpointed Juan Carlos Giménez in Birmingham.

Paul Weir relinquished his WBO minimumweight title, gained 3lb, and in February lost his first challenge for the WBO light-flyweight title to Josué Camacho. Tommy Gilmour, Weir's promoter, lodged an official complaint with the WBO. 'Paul deserved that, it's wrong,' said Gilmour, who was, like Duff, always screaming for his boxers. The title was vacant when Weir outpointed Paul Oulden in Glasgow in November. It was Weir's second world title and just his ninth fight.

Chris Pyatt had the easiest night of his life in Brentwood in February when he stopped Mark Cameron at the very end of the first round to keep his WBO middleweight title. In May, Steve Collins, once of Dublin and Boston, met Pyatt in Sheffield. Collins was trailing before finding the punches to stop Pyatt in the fifth round. Collins had some massive nights left.

At the Pond's Forge that night in Sheffield the real attraction was Naseem Hamed in the fight that is overlooked when critics try to discredit him. He won every second of every round against European bantamweight champion Vincenzo Belcastro, dropping the Italian for the first time in his career in round one and again in the eleventh. Belcastro was *The Ring* magazine's European fighter of the year, had lost two split decisions in world title fights, and later in 1994 lost another split decision in a world title fight. Hamed was just 20 and it was his eleventh fight. 'Sugar Ray Leonard showboats and he's a genius, the little fella does it and he's a flash bastard,' said Brendan Ingle. 'That was quality. That was brilliant.' Ingle was right. 'Don't call us, we'll call you,' Reg Gutteridge said. However, even Reg became a fan.

The fairy-tale continued for Steve Robinson with three defences of his WBO featherweight title, including two when he started as underdog. The first was in March in Cardiff against former world champion Paul Hodkinson, who had just signed a five-fight deal worth £1.2 million with ITV. It ended in round twelve with Hoko down and out, his face bruised, eyes nearly swollen shut, and the towel landing as the ref waved it off. It was Robinson's finest win. 'I will not get drawn into the same dogfight,' promised ringside guest and future opponent Duke McKenzie. Easier said than done.

In June, back at the National Ice Rink in Cardiff, Robinson went the full twelve and beat Freddy Cruz, a noted tough guy. It was a difficult fight for Robinson. In October, Cruz was back to fight Hamed in Sheffield and it was cruel to watch. A day before the fight I was with Hamed and Ingle when Cruz stood looking on in amazement. 'I came to fight a man, you are a boy,' Cruz said, and he meant it. Hamed was vicious and Cruz was brutally beaten and stopped in the sixth for the first time in fifty-seven bouts. Naz was ruthless. Cruz tried to duck out of the ring, his sore face hidden under a hood. 'Still think I'm a boy?' Hamed asked. Cruz said he was the best man he ever met.

At the start of October Robinson had met and stopped McKenzie at the usual venue. Poor Duke could not quite believe it; a crowd of 4,000 had come expecting it. On the night McKenzie looked like the kid, Robinson the veteran, and when the short left landed in the pit of McKenzie's stomach in round nine there was no chance of him beating the count. It was Robinson's fifth defence.

Eubank defended his WBO super-middleweight title in February in Berlin against unbeaten Graciano Rocchigiani in front of 9,000 at the Deutschlandhalle. It was a quality night from Eubank, who remained after the fight at ringside for over an hour to scrawl autographs and win hearts and minds. Rocchigiani had a conviction for pimping, had been wild, but planned to marry his girlfriend in the dressing room if he won. 'I like television, sex and pizza, but that has all changed now,' he told me before the fight. Presumably it was his fiancée's bridesmaids who threw the beer cups into the ring at the end before the extended love-in took place.

In May it was Ray Close in a hard rematch that was lightened by the appearance of a greened-up leprechaun in the Belfast ring before the introductions. The tiny actor threw sparkling slithers of silver all over the canvas and there was a desperate clean-up campaign. Don King was even kicking the stuff away; the tiny pieces were a hazard and could have got in a cut. Eubank won.

In July and August he was in back-to-back defences in fifty days. He narrowly outpointed Mauricio Amaral at Earls Court. In my notepad I wrote 'Amaral is a raw novice'. Eubank rejected any criticism of his win. 'Bad? On the contrary, I think I am very good,' he said. It was Belfast's Sam Storey next, and he was stopped in the seventh. Storey was a better fighter than that. The Storey fight was part of a deal with Sky and was watched by 320,000 – down about 10 million on Eubank's ITV audiences. In October, Eubank travelled to South Africa and won on points against previously unbeaten Dan Schommer. Dangerous Dan, who was from Minnesota, never fought again, and the truth is he never beat a decent fighter, but on the night he could have got the verdict. This was a bad fight and a lot of Eubank's good work was being forgotten fast.

His sixth defence of the year, in December, was in Manchester against Henry Wharton. The fight was set up beautifully when Wharton's manager Duff launched a most savage verbal attack on Eubank at a press conference. I was stunned, Eubank was speechless. Duff had devoted a life to the sport and he was not happy with some of Eubank's dismissive comments. 'I can assure you, you are the lowest of the low, you are scum,' said Duff. There was silence, just the flicking of camera buttons. 'He has made fucking millions and he doesn't deserve it. He's low-life scum. He exploits the game like a hooker; that is behaving like scum.' Barry Hearn, chairing the conference, turned to Duff: 'Mickey, stop. One more "scum" from you and you'll be escorted out.' After the conference Duff continued in every interview. He was genuinely upset. The following January he was fined five grand by the Board.

Eubank entered on a giant crane with fireworks illuminating his passage high above the 9,000 fans at the G-Mex. His performance was quite astounding and the win on points was described as stunning by many at ringside. It was his last world title victory. He would fight nine more times, win four, and lose five world title fights.

Two days after Wharton–Eubank, Frank Bruno agreed a deal with Frank Warren. It is just possible that Duff had heard about Bruno's plans when he lost his mind with Eubank. They were bold, bold plans involving Wembley Stadium, Oliver McCall and a world heavyweight title.

The Contenders

In June there was another appearance in Britain by Nelson Mandela's favourite boxer, Jake Matlala. This time he defended his WBO flyweight title when he stopped Francis Ampofo, who retired after nine rounds. 'I pulled him out when it was clear it was pointless letting him be a hero,' said Hearn. Ampofo would have eight more years of title fights and little Jake would be back in Britain four more times.

Eamonn Loughran retained his WBO welterweight title when he outpointed Alessandro Durán in Belfast. Eleven months later he did it again when he stopped Manning Galloway on cuts. Loughran should have, at some point, met the best British welterweights. Instead he continued beating WBO challengers until April 1996; during the three years he was champion Kevin Lueshing, Chris Saunders and Del Bryan held the British title. In April, Gary Jacobs stopped Durán in a defence of his European title. Jacobs was the best in Britain and it is a great shame he never met Loughran.

From the Notepad

Some memories never fade and Richie Wenton simply could not continue his fight against Neil Swain in October. Just six months earlier Wenton had stopped Bradley Stone for the British super-bantamweight title at York Hall. Stone walked from the ring, collapsed in his girlfriend's arms at home an hour or so later, and died after two days in a coma. It was Wenton's first fight since that night. 'Every second of every minute of every round, Bradley was on my mind,' he said. In the fifth he turned away and walked into the arms of Brian Hughes, his trainer. 'It's OK, son,' said Hughes. Wenton did fight again. 'I hear people tell me "It's cool, you didn't mean it",' Wenton said in 2002. 'I never meant it, but my fists killed him. That's the truth.'

Shaun Cummins went to San Remo in November to fight Agostino Cardamone for the European middleweight title. Cardamone got the decision, but he'd been dropped for a long, long count in round eight. I was ringside, and it was a disgrace. 'It was about thirty seconds in the end,' said Cummins. 'There was nothing I could do.' Cummins would die a grisly death in 2012 when a friend chopped him up, storing parts of his body in a freezer. The killer used one of the boxer's credit cards to buy a new freezer for the surplus body parts. He also bought a chainsaw.

1995

'Jimmy Murray did not die with a needle in his arm, he did not die up a backstreet, and my advice to young boxers is just keep boxing, stay off drugs.'
Kenneth Murray, father

'Naseem is no prince to me. He's a frog. I don't need him. I'm known in the United States. They've never heard of him. The day that fight happens, I'll beat him.'
Wayne McCullough starts to sell his fight with Hamed

FRANK BRUNO HAD refused to fall behind, refused to quit, and he finally won the world title he had been chasing after nearly fifteen years in the ring. He had fallen short in three world title attempts, left bloodied, floored and flawed in fights that could end a career. The national treasure, part heroic loser and part pantomime dame, just never knew when to quit.

Everybody in the Bruno business knew that, at 33 and in his forty-fourth fight, this was the very last chance. The man in the opposite corner outdoors at Wembley was Oliver McCall, the same man that had knocked out Lennox Lewis a year earlier. The fight had been pushed back to early September from 22 July and there were rumours that McCall had lost his way, had returned to the crack houses of Miami. He looked fine when he arrived, but he said some deeply stupid things about injuring Bruno.

However, this was a new Bruno, hardened by years of critics mocking his skills, his wins, and celebrating his losses. 'In Britain

248

sometimes they don't like a man to win,' he said before the McCall fight.

A crowd of 30,000 saluted Bruno on his way to the ring. They kept singing as the rounds unfolded. At ringside, Naseem Hamed and Nigel Benn, who retained his WBC title with ease on the undercard, stood from first to last measuring their hopes against Bruno's desire. George Francis was in charge of taking Bruno over the hill, the ferocious wall that he could hit, and beyond into what was an experiment in endurance. Bruno was relaxed, McCall often distant, and in round eight Bruno even switched to southpaw for forty seconds to take a breather. 'Frank did everything right, everything that we talked about – he took the right [hand] away,' said Francis. 'It was a controlled performance, the performance of a champion. I'm speechless.' At ringside, the murmurs of doubt were in decline as Big Frank delivered a boxing lesson.

McCall had a big last round. Bruno had nothing left in his stiff body, but he survived. The ring was invaded and Bruno was declared the new WBC heavyweight champion. Don King was not impressed with his fighter. There was no mourning for the fallen and he ignored McCall and started to sell Bruno–Tyson for 1996. 'It's King Bruno now and Mike is ready,' said King. Bruno was shattered and there was sensible talk of a six-month break to let his body heal. 'My head feels like ET,' said Bruno. The following day at a hotel near Bruno's home there was an informal gathering. Richard Pelham and Lawrence Lustig, two veteran boxing snappers, wanted a picture of Bruno sitting on a fallen tree. The three of us had to lift Bruno's legs for the pose – he was too exhausted to lift his own legs.

There was the expected rejection of the win by everybody in the Lennox Lewis business. Panos Eliades did offer Bruno two million quid to fight Lennox. There should have been a bit more respect; Bruno had been kicked too often. Bruno had his eye on far more for a second fight with Tyson.

Hamed had been chasing Steve Robinson for nearly two years when they met in the drizzle of a Cardiff night, under a canopy of hate. Hamed had ruined good boxers during the year as he moved closer to fighting Robinson. Armando Castro went in four, and Castro had eleven weeks earlier gone the full twelve in a world title fight with London-based Ghanaian Alfred Kotey. Sergio Liendo went in two, and was taken to hospital for a routine check. Liendo had never been stopped in fifty fights. 'Don't try this at home,' Hamed had warned viewers as he left his dressing room. It was a terrible ending. Enrique Angeles was stopped in two rounds in Shepton Mallet in May, and then 7,000 packed the Royal Albert Hall in July for fight number nineteen against former world champion Juan Polo Pérez. It was a party that night and Pérez was also wiped out in two rounds.

Robinson had defended his title at home in Cardiff against Domingo Damigella and then stopped Pedro Ferradas in round nine. He wanted more money for the Hamed fight, but there was a signed and sealed contract. Robinson's lawyers wanted quantum merit – the ability to alter an agreed amount – for the fight. It's what we call being an 'after-timer' in the boxing business.

The Cinderella Man from Ely had been a wonderful fairy-tale. He had won eight world title fights despite starting as the betting under-dog most times. Frank Warren had promoted six of them. The dispute lingered.

'Hamed will fight for the WBO featherweight title on September 30 in Cardiff and I just hope Robinson is in the opposite corner,' said Warren in early September. The WBO instructed Robinson that he had to fight Hamed or face stripping. So they met at the Cardiff Rugby Club at the end of September in front of 16,000, a crowd that would have been happier at a public lynching. Hamed was cut by a pound coin as he walked to the ring. He never stopped smiling. 'I can win world titles at three or four weights,' he said before the first bell. Robinson looked isolated in his corner, a few miles from his home yet totally alone.

It was over in round eight. Robinson was foolishly brave, dropped in the fifth and the eighth rounds. He'd always want a rematch. Hamed was world champion at 21 and unbeaten in twenty fights. He looked untouchable at that moment, the topic of a million supermarket conversations.

The unforgettable night at the London Arena in February when Benn fought Gerald McClellan for the WBC super-middleweight title ended in despair. The pair had thirty-three first-round knock-outs between them, McClellan twenty of the total, and his odds on a quick win were slashed from 14-1 to 4-1. Benn had split with Jimmy Tibbs over money and hired Kevin Sanders, a good operator from Peterborough, to be in the corner on the night. There was a further distraction with a tax bill. 'Nigel doesn't tell me about his finances, I'm just his manager,' said Peter DeFreitas. No fighter needs worries like that before a fight like this.

McClellan arrived in London with his exotically named personal bodyguard Hyacinthus Turnipseed. There was humour in the name only. McClellan also arrived with a reputation for dogfighting and brutality. The conferences were horrible, packed with evil. 'I'm prepared to die,' the American said on several occasions. He nearly did. I started my report in the *Daily Telegraph* with this deathless declaration: 'Gerald McClellan's final moments as a prizefighter were dreadful to witness.' It ended in round ten, with McClellan on his knee, blinking and slowly sinking into a dark vacuum that very nearly claimed him.

In round one, as he had predicted, he dropped and sent Benn tumbling through the ropes. Benn struggled, in what looked like slow motion, to grab a rope and pull himself back into the ring inside the ten-second count. He just managed it. The American boxer's cut-price corner, a study in amateurism, screamed that it was fourteen seconds, and they were probably right. A few extra seconds is all that is needed, and in the mayhem they were lost.

I was six feet from McClellan's corner and at the end of round three he told his trainer, Stan Johnson, 'Something's not right.' I witnessed the exchange and, in the middle of the night, Johnson confirmed the words.

Even that early in the fight, both were starting to show signs of the beating they were taking. Benn was dropped again in round eight. In round nine McClellan went down on his knee and complained of a head clash. He suddenly looked ill, a drained version of the athlete from thirty minutes earlier. He was down again in the tenth, up blinking and disorientated at the count of eight. There was a collective pandemonium in the London Arena, a feeling as intense as anything I have ever sensed at ringside. McClellan went down again for the full count, and it was over after 1:46 of the tenth. Many at ringside and in various broadcasting teams from around the world thought that he had quit. Even the great Reg Gutteridge, talking to 17.5 million viewers on ITV, got it wrong, and that was something he regretted for the rest of his life. People, strangers, embraced in joy and relief all over the Arena.

McClellan collapsed in his corner at 10.03 p.m. He was taken from the ring, and at 10.15 he opened his eyes. 'Relax, Gerald, take it easy, baby,' Johnson told him. The operation was over by one a.m. He had been in the gentle care of old-hand John Sutcliffe, a veteran of too many injuries. McClellan had had a large blood clot scraped from the surface of his brain. 'It came out with a bit of a vengeance,' Sutcliffe remarked. King and Warren remained at the hospital all night. Benn had also gone to the emergency room and was cleared to leave. He sat with McClellan before departing, surrounded, supported by and in the care of his concerned loved ones who lifted Nigel in and out of ice baths all night.

The surgery was a success, but McClellan had problems when he arrived back in America. He is alive but is blind and deaf. Benn's next defence was just a few months later, back at the London Arena, where he stopped Vincenzo Nardiello in eight rounds. 'It was not easy getting back in the same ring,' Benn admitted.

In October, after a British title fight at Glasgow's Hospitality Inn, there was an infamous death. On the 13th Jimmy Murray lost in the twelfth round with just thirty-four seconds left. His death was made official on the 15th. Drew Docherty retained his bantamweight title. It was a truly bloody, savage scrap. I had red spots on my notepad and I wrote: 'Canvas slick with blood here at the inhospitable inn.' The venue was packed: 300 people had bought standing-room-only tickets for £20; the 400 dinner guests had paid £50.

As Murray slipped down, not six feet from my seat, for the full count a riot started. Men were quickly covered in blood from smashed bottles. Some smeared their chests and faces in blood and re-created the fiction of the *Braveheart* film. The police did restore order and eventually sixteen idiots were arrested. The emergency ambulance staff had a struggle to and from the ring. Peter Littledyke, of the private ambulance service in attendance, confirmed the problem his staff faced as they ran a gauntlet of hate: 'They were knocked and battered on the way to the ring. To be honest, you would like to do a little more.' Murray's body was passed out of the ring in front of his mother, Margaret, who touched his leg. I was hopeful that awful night that I would never hear a mother wailing in despair again. I was hoping for too much.

'Jimmy Murray did not die with a needle in his arm, he did not die up a backstreet, and my advice to young boxers is just keep boxing, stay off drugs,' said Jimmy's father, Kenneth.

There is a statue of Jimmy Murray, professional boxer, near where he lived in Newmains. It's a harsh place for anybody, also known as Buckfast Valley in honour of the cheap booze that offered temporary obliteration. Murray wanted a different life.

Gary Jacobs, the former British welterweight champion, helped carry Murray from the ring in Glasgow that night. In August he had been in Atlantic City fighting for the WBC welter belt against Pernell Whitaker, who had held titles at three weights. Jacobs had waited patiently for his chance, waited like Mickey Duff fighters always did. It was a hard fight, much tighter than the unanimous scores suggest. Jacobs was dropped twice in the last, but he posed Sweet Pea plenty of problems. Two years later Whitaker finally lost the title to Oscar De La Hoya. 'I never had it easy, I never wanted it easy,' said Jacobs. 'I wanted to beat the best welterweight to win the welterweight title. I was old school.' He is right.

It took Dennis Andries ten minutes to walk from the ring to the dressing room in Glasgow in January after winning the British cruiserweight title. In the week of the fight Andries added five years to his age. 'I'm forty-eight now, not forty-three,' he said. Andries had lost over fifteen rounds for the British light-heavyweight title to Bunny Johnson in 1980. In 1995, the Hackney Rock, as Andries was often known, beat Denzil Browne in the eleventh round. It was his sixtieth fight.

Wayne McCullough had a chin of granite. He won a gold medal at the 1990 Commonwealth Games, took part in the 1988 Olympics, and reached the final at the Barcelona Olympics. He went to America, a wide-eyed kid from the streets of Belfast, to train with Eddie Futch when he turned professional. He won the WBC bantamweight championship in Japan in July, beating the local champion, Yasuei Yakushiji, on a split. In December, Wayne defended in Belfast at the King's Hall when he stopped Johnny Bredahl, who was unbeaten in twenty-six, in round six. McCullough made one final defence the following year, in Dublin, beating José Luís Bueno, and then lost the title away from the ring, beaten by the scales. He then moved up in weight, but over the next decade would fail in six attempts to win another world title. He remains a smiling fixture in Las Vegas whenever a big fight rolls into town. But his win in Japan was a proper win in a real world title fight.

After a year out of the ring there was a return to action for WBO heavyweight champion Herbie Hide in Las Vegas against Riddick Bowe. The fight in March did not end well for the Norwich boy. Hide was dropped nine times, seven for counts. He was 27lb lighter than Big Daddy Bowe. He was also being paid £2.3 million. It was finally stopped in the sixth round. 'Was I hurt?' said Hide. 'Ask Riddick Bowe if he was hurt. This is heavyweight boxing and everybody gets hurt.' In 2013 Bowe did a show with me in London and confirmed that the hardest he was ever hit was that night. Hide was still fighting fifteen years later, entering the Prizefighter competition at York Hall – a mad event where a boxer has to win three three-round fights in one night to take the cash prize. Hide won a fight, then pulled out with a cut. 'You know, against Bowe I should have boxed,' Hide told me in 2010. 'He was easy to hit and I was too fast, but he hit me on the back of the neck and that was it, I lost all feeling in my arms.'

It was the end of Chris Eubank's reign in March when he met Steve Collins at a venue called Millstreet not far from Cork. Eubank was unbeaten in forty-three fights and had been in nineteen consecutive world title fights since the contest with Nigel Benn in November 1990. Eubank touched down in round eight and Collins was dropped in the tenth. Eubank wasted a chance to end the fight by prancing. 'You'll regret not finishing him off for the rest of your life,' said Ronnie Davies in the corner at the end of the tenth. Collins took the WBO super-middleweight title with a tight decision.

They met again in Cork outdoors in September. 'I didn't think there was a man alive who could beat me twice,' said Eubank, who arrived at the stadium in an ambulance to avoid the crowds. 'He was expecting one thing and I did something else – he never adapted,' said Collins. The fight was a physical mess, too emotional in many ways. Collins had claimed he'd used a hypnotist to shut out pain; Eubank insisted hypnosis was a form of legal cheating. 'It's not hypnosis, it's called representational systems,' explained Tony Quinn, the mind coach who worked with Collins. 'It's all bollocks,' said Collins. 'I just got inside Eubank's head. There was nothing more sinister than that.' At the end of twelve rounds Collins won a split decision to leave Eubank considering retirement or a move to light-heavyweight.

Collins sneaked in a quick defence in Dublin, where he was born, in November when he beat Cornelius Carr, who had won the British title a year earlier. The Irishman looked tired.

The year ended with Mike Tyson circling Bruno. 'He's been in prison three years, out of the ring for four – I'm a better fighter now than I was the first time. This is my chance,' said Bruno. And he would get his chance in 1996.

The Contenders

Eamonn Loughran defended his WBO welterweight title against a guy called Tony Gannarelli, an American having his fourteenth fight. Loughran made two other defences in the year. He would have been in good fights with Jacobs in a parallel world, one where the WBO was absent. It is a pity.

The story of Paul 'Silky' Jones is odd. In November he won the WBO light-middleweight title when he beat Verno Phillips on points in front of a small crowd in Sheffield. He was stripped and never got another chance.

There would be another chance for Carl Thompson, one of Phil Martin's original British champions, after a dislocated right shoulder put an end to his vacant WBO cruiserweight title fight with Ralf Rocchigiani at the G-Mex in Manchester in the summer. Thompson had been on the canvas three times but was winning on all three scorecards when it was called off in the eleventh round. In 1997 Thompson would get sweet revenge in Germany and win the title.

January had started with Billy Schwer losing an IBF lightweight title fight to Rafael Ruelas in Las Vegas when his fragile eyebrows cut up badly and he was stopped at the end of the seventh round. In February, Drew Docherty, who would beat Jimmy Murray later in the year, was stopped by Alfred Kotey in four rounds for the WBO bantamweight title. Crawford Ashley from Leeds lost on points to Virgil Hill for the WBA light-heavyweight title in an outpost called Primm in Nevada in March. The same month, Paul Weir retained his WBO light-flyweight title on points, but was stopped in November by Jake Matlala and lost the belt. Robbie Regan's hard life continued in June when he retired at the end of nine rounds against Albert Jiménez for the WBO flyweight title, but then stopped Ferid Ben Jeddou for the IBF interim flyweight title two weeks before Christmas.

From the Notepad

In February, Bruno had knocked out Rodolfo Marin in sixty-five seconds and was ready for another fight when the finish was questioned. 'You don't think I hit? Well, go and feel his head, feel the lumps, and then tell me I didn't hit him.' It was the new Bruno.

'What's the problem with the Naz fella?' asked Brendan Ingle after the Robinson fight. 'They are critical because they don't know what is happening. He's not got a smashed-up face, a busted nose. He's a winner and he's from here.'

'Getting floored means nothing,' said James Oyebola. 'When you are knocked down it proves you have nerves [of steel] when you get up. I want it so badly that I get up.' An hour later Big Bad James stopped Keith McMurray in round seven. Eight months later he lost a British heavyweight title fight to Scott Welch.

1996

FRANK BRUNO HAD nothing left to offer but his large heart when he met Mike Tyson in a fight that was savage.

In February I was in Tenerife at Bruno's training camp and the ex-pantomime dame was angry. 'I'm getting darker, I want to fight now,' he said. His showdown with Mike Tyson was in March at the MGM in Las Vegas. Bruno was getting £4 million but wanted more. The fight was the first pay-per-view on Sky television.

The mood in Las Vegas that week was as ugly as I have ever experienced. There were so many warring factions. Tyson's men were horrible to Bruno's people, especially Laura, his wife. Laura was on the warpath, hunting down Don King and Frank Warren and making extra demands. It was all a bit demented. Tyson, nobody quite noticed, was serene and beautifully prepared. 'I'm going to shut King's mouth up and drop Tyson in his lap,' Bruno told the press. He sounded mean, and the 5,000 travelling British fans filled the MGM with the sounds of devotion.

Bruno entered the ring repeatedly crossing himself as he made his way through the ringside area. He looked petrified as he walked to the slaughter and the transformation was quite bizarre; all the fight had left him long before the walk to the ring. I would give the reason, but I would be sued. Tyson had run in without a care a few minutes earlier. He looked recovered from prison and a regime of harsh truths. Mills Lane, the third man of choice in the decade, pulled them together, and it started.

It began badly for Big Frank and he was tagged after ten seconds. 'He was much better than I thought he would be, much faster,' admitted Bruno. He survived until fifty seconds into round three when Tyson smashed his way through a high defence and sent Bruno down and out. Bruno, Lane and Tyson all finished on their knees that night in Las Vegas: Tyson praying, Bruno in ruin, and Lane watching from six inches away. It was a grim, temporary tableau that will remain forever in the minds of all those that witnessed it.

Aussie Joe Bugner took up two seats in Quaglino's restaurant, just off Piccadilly, in early January. He was in London to promote his fight with Hove's Scott Welch. The fight would take place in Germany in March. Bugner, fresh from winning the Australian heavyweight title, lost in the sixth. But in Quaglino's he had been unstoppable, telling me the secrets to staying young: 'Red wine, hard work, vitamin B and good sex. Sometimes the sex is the hard work.' His wife, Marlene, punched him on the arm. She punched him that way a lot, to be fair.

The British Boxing Board of Control had refused Bugner a licence to fight in Britain. 'The Board has given permission for Scott to fight Joe in another country,' said Frank Warren. 'It makes a mockery of their decision.' Bugner was not shocked. 'The Board has had it in for me since I started. I'm just a Hungarian to them. I beat Henry Cooper, I would have beaten Frank Bruno. I'm a legend. That's what Scott is fighting, a bloody legend.' After losing to Welch, the Legend had six more fights, won the lot, and beat James 'Bonecrusher' Smith for the

WBF heavyweight title in 1998, which was thirty-one years after his debut at the Hilton Hotel in Park Lane.

Two nights before Nigel Benn lost his WBC super-middleweight title, he walked along the Tyne in Newcastle. He was in reflective mood – troubled, I wrote at the time. 'I just want to retire, I've had enough, I'm tired,' he said. In the ring in front of 22,000 people who welcomed him like a returning hero he lost a split decision to South Africa's Thulani Malinga. Benn had two stitches in his mouth and both eyes were bruised, swollen and sore. He had narrowly beaten Malinga four years earlier. Benn left the ring, stopping just to kiss Michael Watson on the head, and closed the door on his dressing room. It looked like it was over, and perhaps it should have been.

A few days later Steve Collins retained his WBO version of the title when he stopped Burton's Neville Brown in Millstreet, the strange town near Cork devoted to drinking. Collins had the two wins over Chris Eubank, and that was something Benn considered significant. The pair were matched for July in Manchester in a fight billed as 'Ultimate Warrior?' It was a question the fight never really answered. In round four of a classic at the Nynex, as the Manchester Arena was then known, Benn twisted his right ankle and ended up on his knees in pain. He did get up, hobbling through a tricky survival routine until he had to turn away. The fight was over. Collins was in front on all three cards and both believed they would win by stoppage – Benn's retirement was on hold again. Collins had told Freddie Roach, his cornerman, that Benn could not hurt him. 'I will knock him out, relax,' said Collins. Benn, having retired for twenty minutes, declared his intention to continue. 'We were just getting warmed up, you know I like a fight – let's do it again, I'd like a rematch,' Benn said.

On the same bill, Malinga lost Benn's old WBC belt to Vincenzo Nardiello on points.

Benn–Collins II was made for November back in the same ring. It was captivating to watch both men fight like it was the end, and for one of them it was. At the end of six fantastic rounds Kevin Sanders, in Benn's corner, stopped the fight. Collins was in front and in control. The 21,000 fans were not impressed and booed as Benn and then Collins tried to take the microphone and talk. 'For ten years I gave blood, guts and tears but my body can only take so much,' said Benn. 'It's over.' Collins insisted Benn was the best British fighter in history, but was stunned by the sudden ending. 'I feel the public have been cheated tonight,' he said. 'You have to fight to the end.' Collins is a warrior, but Benn did fight to his end.

There was a wonderful cameo at the post-fight conference by Eubank, splendid in monocle and brandishing his latest cane. Collins spotted him as he was talking and asked, 'Can somebody get rid of that clown?'

Late that night I met with Sanders, who was emotionally drained. He explained his thinking. In 1994 he had been in the corner in Las Vegas when Robert Wangila, an Olympic gold medal winner from 1988, lost. 'Robert was down in the eighth, and in the ninth he was hit with seven punches. I will never forget those punches. He died a few days later. If I had been more experienced perhaps I wouldn't have sent Robert out for the ninth – I was not going to let Nigel go out for the seventh.'

At ringside that night in Manchester was Robin Reid, who had won a bronze medal at the Barcelona Olympics, and he studied Collins. 'I need a few more fights,' he sensibly said. The month before, Reid had travelled to Milan and fought in a hateful pit to stop Nardiello and win the WBC super-middleweight title. 'I got in the ring in Milan and I was not sure what the biggest danger was: fighting the world champion or the thought of beating Nardiello and having to get back through the crowd.' Reid was brilliant and cool, winning in the seventh.

Hamed fought four times in 1996 and each time he was forensically and unfairly evaluated by his critics. 'I'm the world champion, I'm twenty-one, I'm proud – what more can I do?' Hamed asked at a press conference in January. A few weeks later he made his first defence, as part of the Bruno–Tyson Sky bill, in Scotland, and it was over in thirty-five seconds, including the count. Said Lawal never had a chance and, to be brutal, never deserved his chance.

In June, Hamed sat in an ornate chariot and was carried to the ring in Newcastle by eight topless black men. He stepped from the moving throne and walked the last few feet across a carpet of rose petals. It made me laugh, but some of my colleagues were livid. In the ring was the number one challenger, an unbeaten kid called Daniel Alicea from Puerto Rico. In round one Alicea dropped Hamed – the first time he had ever been down. In round two Hamed knocked him out. 'I got caught, I got up, and I will tell you something – I'm glad I was taking his punches and not mine,' said Hamed.

Hamed was in Dublin at the end of August to fight Mexico's Manuel Medina. A few days before the fight I had been in a steam room with Hamed and a couple of others – his attempt to shift the cold that was sitting on his chest. Medina had held the world title twice, had fought as a boy from the age of fourteen in Mexico, and would win the world title again. At the Point Depot, where a few months earlier Wayne McCullough had retained his title in a controversial war, Medina was dropped three times and left in a terrible state when he retired at the end of the eleventh round. It had been hard for Hamed, but he was in front on all three scorecards. At the end of the eleventh the pair embraced, and seconds later it was over. Hamed could barely walk from the ring, but the capacity crowd cheered him: Irish punters know their boxing.

As Hamed reclined backstage, resting his head in the lap of British light-middleweight Ryan Rhodes, there was a mad inquest. McCullough got in first. 'I will knock Hamed out,' he said. He was reminded that his defence in March had only been watched by 5,000 and that he had been in hospital recovering for days after. In front of fifteen journalists, Frank Warren offered McCullough a million dollars for a fight with Hamed. It looked like we had a deal. However, a day or so later it was changed to a million pounds and a request that Hamed lose 4lb and fight at super-bantamweight. 'The Naz fella is the attraction, that is crazy,' said Brendan Ingle, Hamed's trainer.

Warren then made an offer to Marco Antonio Barrera. At about the same time there was an offer from Barrera's manager Ricardo Maldonado. It was for $1.7 million, the venue was Los Angeles, and once again there was an impossible request for Hamed to drop 4lb.

Ricardo's dollar gambit was safe: there was no way Naz could make the weight. The two men would eventually meet nearly five years later. The fight was five years too late for Naz.

There had also been an offer at the start of the year from Azumah Nelson for a Hamed fight. 'I like Hamed's style, but I will knock him out,' said Nelson, who was 37 when he made the claim; he was also the WBC super-featherweight champion.

In November, alongside Benn–Collins II, there was a final defence of the year for Hamed when he took two rounds to stop the Argentinian Remigio Molina, who was unbeaten in twenty-seven. Hamed was ready for 1997 and what would be the year of his life.

Barry Hearn had a terrible night at the Everton Park Sports Centre in April when his WBO welterweight champion Eamonn Loughran was dropped three times and stopped in fifty-one seconds by José Luís López. It was Loughran's sixth defence and it was also his last fight. 'I was cold, the dressing rooms were freezing,' said Loughran. Paul Weir had lost his WBO light-flyweight title to Jake Matlala on a cut; the rematch was brutal and Weir was over twice in the tenth before it was stopped in that round. There was an equally ugly row at ringside when ITV refused to screen the Weir fight, which Hearn had given them for free, because of an advert on Matlala's shorts. 'You should be ashamed of yourselves,' Hearn shouted at Reg Gutteridge and Jim Watt in the ITV commentary positions. The first Weir–Matlala fight had gone out at midnight on ITV and had been watched by 3 million people.

There was a classic fight at the Everton Park in February when local idol Shea Neary met American Terry Southerland at light-welterweight. In round two Neary was cut over the left eye; his eyelid was gaping open, blood everywhere in an instant. The ref pulled him over. 'He said to me, "I'm stopping the fight at the end of the round." I said to him, "I won't be here at the end of the round."' The blood was pumping out, covering everything, and the wound required seven stitches. Neary needed just one punch to knock out Southerland. There was bedlam at the venue when the American went down and out. Neary won a version of the world title in his next fight and remains a proper fighting hero in Liverpool.

Mickey Duff insisted that Henry Akinwande had the style to beat Tyson. Akinwande had left Duff after winning twenty-four of his twenty-five fights and was signed to King. Big Henry, born in Dulwich, raised in Nigeria, trained by Mick Costello at the Lynn club in south London and a veteran of the Seoul Olympics, was 6ft 7in tall. He won and retained the WBO heavyweight title in 1996, but never felt British. In 1997 he was certainly not British when he met Lennox Lewis in a shambles of a fight in Lake Tahoe.

Frank Bruno was gone – that is the story of the year.

The Contenders

Ensley Bingham was beaten on points by Ronald 'Winky' Wright for the WBO light-middleweight title. Wright ran from Bingo's left hook without apology.

In January, Daniel Jiménez, who had beaten Duke McKenzie in 1993 for the WBO super-bantamweight belt, was back in Britain to outpoint Drew Docherty for the WBO bantamweight title. Robbie Regan, in what would be his final fight, beat Jiménez to take the title on a night of raw emotion in Cardiff in April. Regan was fighting demons even then.

There was no luck for Richie Woodhall when he finally got his WBC middleweight title fight against Keith Holmes in Delaware in October. Woodhall had been number one contender for two years, and out of the ring for nine months waiting. He had an operation on his elbow before the fight; the alternative was to fight one-handed. 'I knew if I pulled out I would have to wait another year or two,' said Woodhall. He was trailing on points when he was stopped in the last round with just twenty-eight seconds left. He won a world title in 1998.

From the Notepad

That March in Las Vegas, the nastiness continued long into the night. Crocodile, one of Tyson's chief cheerleaders, attempted to make peace with Laura Bruno. It was not a good idea. 'Hey baby, your man was so brave, he can be proud he went down like a true champion,' Crocodile offered during a meeting in the tunnels at the back of the MGM. 'You can fuck right off,' Laura replied. A few minutes later she was leading two writers from the *Sun* into her husband's changing room for an exclusive. He never did meet with the rest of us that long night. He never fought again, but he was never out of the news.

'There is a window when Tyson and Lewis could fight without going to purse bids,' Panos Eliades told me in September. 'I can get around all the obstacles, no worry.' Tyson and Lewis met six years later.

1997

'Win or lose I'm taking Winky on a pub crawl round Salford.
I've never been off the beer this long in my adult life.'
Steve Foster before his world title fight with 'Winky' Wright

'Roberto was a dirty fighter and he was clever with it, but I knew
there was no chance of the referee throwing him out; I gave him
back a bit and just got on with it. It was a bloody good scrap.'
Dave Radford, a Yorkshire plasterer, on his fight with Durán in South Africa

LENNOX LEWIS WAITED in early January for confirmation that Oliver McCall would not be in prison or in rehab and would be in Las Vegas at the Hilton for their vacant WBC heavyweight title fight. 'It was a stressful time, we had no real idea what was happening,' admitted Frank Maloney, the boxer's manager and the man, back then, in the Union flag suit. As Kellie, twenty years later, she has never tried a Union flag dress.

McCall had got involved with a twelve-foot Christmas tree, a bottle of tequila and eight policemen in December and the Lewis rematch was in jeopardy. A stint in rehab, a conversion to Christianity and a travelling full-time drug counsellor combined to get him into Las Vegas four days before the first bell. Two nights before the fight a tiny contingent gathered at McCall's knee. He looked well considering he had been through a year of boozing, mayhem, crack cocaine and regular stays in rehab. 'This is my last fight, the last time I will bring up all of the hate and violence and the bad things in my life and turn them into aggression in the ring,' he said. 'It's not godly to do this for a living.' He sounded like he was ready, prepared for a fight. I should add that he took it all back the next day, but the look in his bright eyes was convincing when he said it.

'If Lennox loses he will be just another bum,' warned Manny Steward, the man in charge of Lewis's resurrection after the shocking loss to McCall in 1994.

The fight was a pitiful spectacle, a public humiliation that hurt the sport. McCall competed for two rounds inside the Hilton in front of 4,800 fans and then in the third started to walk away, pull faces and utter a few phrases. And then the tears came. At the bell to end round three Lewis stood and looked at him, and in McCall's corner George Benton and Greg Page had a look of horror on their faces. McCall never sat down, he just wandered, muttered and stood teetering unsteadily. Mills Lane, the referee, stood impassive, not quick to judge or chat. The fourth was a farce of a round. The crowd booed as McCall retreated in anguish, not throwing a punch, and Lewis followed. McCall was getting paid $3,075,500 and at ringside one or two concerned officials were looking on in alarm. His drug counsellor, Ruth Ferguson, should have been in the ring with him. Benton, a shooting victim from the streets of Philadelphia, and Page, a fallen champion with his own drug demons, recognized McCall's crack withdrawal, but the corner pair were not qualified to help their man. In the fifth Lewis went to finish – in the fourth he had been cautious – and after a couple of rights crunched home without reply Lane stepped in, at fifty-five seconds. McCall cried, engaged in some type of conversation, and was ushered quickly from the ring. The crowd chanted 'bullshit, bullshit' and aimed various missiles at the ring. Lewis was the champion again.

At the end of the fight everybody was a genius: everybody knew that McCall was a danger to his own health and everybody knew it would end the way it did. That often happens the moment a fight is over. However, it was clear from the third round on that McCall was having a breakdown. The following morning an urgent phone call came through: 'Oliver wants to tell his story – Hilton at eleven a.m.'

I went, and I'm glad I did: it was gold. 'Oliver had a plan,' Oliver said. 'They stopped me putting my plan into play. It was all going so well and then the ref ruined it for me.' At his side sat Don King, who the night before had vanished like a huge white lion sharing a stage with a man in a gold cape, with his concrete grin that never wavered. 'I believe I deserve a rematch, my plan will work,' added McCall. Even King was reluctant to endorse that fantasy. The Nevada State Athletic Commission fined McCall $250,000 and banned him for a year. McCall did fight again. He actually fought thirty-six more times before finally retiring in 2014.

Long before McCall's apology, Lewis was in talks for massive fights. The money dream was back on.

The next man for him was Henry Akinwande, who had given up his WBO heavyweight title to get his WBC shot. In January in Nashville, Akinwande had beaten Hove's Scott Welch on points in his last WBO defence. It was a difficult fight to watch. One judge gave Welch a round and that was a bad piece of scoring. The brutal truth is that Welch never started and Akinwande, who was only marginally more active and aggressive, was then dismissive. 'I was promised Rambo and got a bimbo,' he said. Welch deserved better, he was a lot better, and the fans certainly deserved much better.

Lewis–Akinwande was set for the tranquil casino haven on the shores of the ice-blue Lake Tahoe in July. A couple of things were said before the fight that I found alarming. One was from Maloney, who was having the time of his life as the manager of the heavyweight champion of the world. He told his fiancée, Tracey, that they would get married in a chapel at Caesars in Tahoe if Lewis won. 'If he loses, the wedding is off,' he insisted. The other was far more serious and came from Akinwande's mouth during a little sit-down a few days before the fight. 'When a fighter gets hurt, that's when you can see if a fighter has guts or not – I don't want to find out,' said Akinwande. Ouch, that's not good.

The fight took place in front of just 1,800 people in the Circus Maximus Theater in a tiny eighteen-foot ring. The small ring was meant to suit Lewis, to minimize the spaces for Akinwande to escape to. In the end it never left Lewis enough room and Akinwande never tried to escape, he just held and held until he was disqualified in the fifth round for not fighting. It was a disgrace. In the third, Lewis was dropped to his knee by a right – something he still denies and something that Lane, the ubiquitous third man for big nights, missed. Lane later apologized. The knockdown did nothing to inspire Akinwande. Twice Lane took a time-out and led Akinwande back to his corner in the hope that Don Turner, his trainer, could get him to fight. Nobody complained about the referee's highly irregular action. He just called it off. 'I'd seen enough, the guy never wanted to fight,' said Lane. At first Akinwande had his million-dollar purse suspended, but it was returned in full and he was not sanctioned.

'In my opinion Henry is lucky to get away with it,' said the British Boxing Board of Control's John Morris, who was the WBC supervisor for the fight. 'There should have been a penalty.' It was Akinwande's first loss in thirty-four fights. The London-born fighter would be scrapping for small purses for another eleven years, ending his ring career in six- and eight-rounders in Romania, Nigeria and Turkey.

And, Tracey became Mrs Maloney. It was a lovely ceremony.

Lewis did finally get to look mean in his last fight of the year when he met Andrew Golota in Atlantic City. The champion needed ninety-five seconds to separate the hope from the hype and leave the Pole needing a night in hospital under observation. The crowd of 14,000 were his fans and Lewis was under a fair bit of pressure before the first bell. A statement from the Atlantic City Medical Center in the middle of the night described the towering émigré as 'awake, alert and orientated' – three things he had certainly not been during most of the fight with Lewis. The win meant that the year ended with Lewis as the best heavyweight champion in the world.

Little Naseem Hamed fought five times in 1997, beating world champions and unbeaten fighters, and ended the year in an unforgettable brawl in New York.

In February at the London Arena, as part of a show with three world title fights, Hamed added the IBF to his WBO featherweight title when he knocked out Tom Johnson in round eight. The final right uppercut, thrown from the orthodox stance, connected flush and the poor American, who had arrived in London abusing Hamed, fell to the canvas like a large human puddle. 'Naseem is everything he says he is,' said Johnson when he was awake. The win meant that Hamed was the first British fighter to hold two belts at the same weight since Lloyd Honeyghan a decade earlier.

On the same bill in London Micky Cantwell lost a split to Jake Matlala for the WBO light-fly title. It was a grim battle, tight and hard. 'I thought I might have nicked it,' said Cantwell. In the south Londoner's corner, Jimmy Tibbs agreed. Matlala was a handful at 4ft 10in in his socks. Cantwell would get three more attempts to win a world title fight. Robin Reid found a knockout punch in round seven to leave South Africa's Giovanni Pretorius out for the count in their WBC super-middleweight title fight. His year would get much more difficult.

In May, Hamed was in a bad mood. 'He can come to the ring in a chariot, but he will leave on a stretcher,' said Billy Hardy. It was a very odd thing for Hardy to say. He had done all of his fighting in the ring up until that silly sentence. Hamed took it personally, and it was all over after just ninety-three seconds in Manchester. Hardy was on his knees, his nose broken, no chance of fighting any longer. 'I never wanted the fight, I was forced to take it because he was the number one,' said Hamed. There had been the threat of legal action by Hardy's management – Tommy Gilmour and Barry Hearn – to make sure the fight happened. Too many people in the boxing business on both sides of the ropes remained convinced that Hamed was some type of fake. Some sensible boxing men truly believed that he was rubbish.

Once again a couple of other world title fights took place in Hamed's slipstream that night in Manchester. Ronald 'Winky' Wright was too slick for Steve Foster and retained his WBO light-middleweight title in the sixth round. Foster had beaten former world champion Chris Pyatt to win the Commonwealth title in his previous fight. He had come a long way from the man that fought drunk, took any fight and was generally a bit of rogue. 'Win or lose I'm taking

Winky on a pub crawl round Salford,' said Foster. 'I've never been off the beer this long in my adult life.' There was an awkward moment at the end of the other championship fight when Reid kept his title with a masterclass against Henry Wharton. Mickey Duff had backed his man Wharton with fifty grand in a side-bet with Reid's promoter Frank Warren, but that was not the problem. Duff had said that he would retire from management, promoting and matchmaking if Wharton lost. It was not a bet, just a promise, and he went back on it. Reid looked classy, cool and relaxed. At the end of round ten Duff came over and confronted the ringside press. 'How you got it?' he demanded. He was not happy with any of the replies he received. One judge did return a drawn verdict, but that was way off.

In July and October Hamed was vicious and quite brilliant. At Wembley Arena in the summer 9,000 watched him destroy Juan Cabrera of Argentina in two rounds. In Cabrera's corner was Amilcar Brusa, who had worked with the great Carlos Monzón. 'I have never seen a fighter react like that – he has so much power and speed,' Brusa told a few of us after the fight; Cabrera quietly wept in the background. In October the carnival was in Sheffield. It was Hamed's first fight in his hometown for three years. When he'd last fought in the city he was living above his father's corner shop. A bunk-bed kid. Now he had made his mother and father retire and he was a million-aire. Hamed stopped José Badillo in the seventh and left the Puerto Rican, who had lost just once in twenty-one fights, in a dreadful state. The fight ended when Badillo's cornermen intervened: their fighter had a fractured cheek, a broken nose and a dislocated jaw. At ringside, New Yorker Kevin Kelley, a real fighter, was trying to be unimpressed, which was hard. 'C'mon, Kev, you don't mean that,' Hamed said. Their fight for December inside Madison Square Garden was on. 'It was like the old Naz tonight,' said Brendan Ingle. 'I told him to dummy, to shift, to use fractions and to get Badillo's mind. It was beautiful to watch.' It had been sweet, that is for sure, but there were some problems in their relationship. Money was starting to create friction, and that type of dispute in boxing is never healed.

That wonderful night in Sheffield had a dark side, though nobody knew as Hamed left the ring. In one of the undercard British title fights, Mark Winters had beaten Liverpool's Carl Wright on points at light-welterweight. A year earlier Wright had lost on points in a European title fight. The fight in Sheffield was a hard one but not brutal, and when it was over Wright sat down to watch the rest of the fights with his trainer Colin Moorcroft. Wright spoke to his fiancée, Nicola Tierney, after the fight. 'He sounded perfect, just a bit upset. He told me, "I've had enough."' As they were driving home, Wright complained of a headache; then he was sick and then he slept. Moorcroft went to a club called Appleby's, knowing Nicola would be there. He went in to find her – Carl was in the car. When Nicola and Colin got back to Carl he was having a spasm. They drove straight to hospital where he was given a scan. And then the situation worsened. Carl was transferred to Walton Neurological Unit after being given emergency resuscitation. He had the blood clot removed and made a stunning recovery. Two months later I went to see him and Nicola. 'He's the same Carl, just on a bit of a go-slow,' she said.

That Sheffield bill also featured the first world title win by Joe Calzaghe. Eleven years later he would retire undefeated after forty-six fights, including twenty-four world title fights. Calzaghe beat Chris Eubank over twelve relentless rounds. Eubank was down in the opening round, Calzaghe was staggered in the final seconds, and somewhere in the middle the pair punched each other to a bloody, bruised and exhausted standstill. Calzaghe got the decision, won the vacant WBO super-middleweight title, and was helped back to the dressing room by his father, Enzo. 'Gentlemen,' Eubank said, 'the show goes on; I entertain, I crave it. I took a gamble after a two-year absence. Joe Calzaghe is an exceptional fighter.' Eubank had replaced Steve Collins who'd retired, walked away insisting that Calzaghe had no experience. Collins had been waiting five years for a showdown with Roy Jones Jr. 'It's the only fight that motivates me,' he admitted.

Hamed went to New York in December and danced one crazy afternoon with Michael Jackson at the Blue Velvet gym. Hamed moonwalking and Jacko squealing – it was the oddest pre-title fight session I ever attended. It was weird cabaret, and Jackson, who had hosted Hamed at Neverland in October, was so relaxed he removed his gloves.

Little Naz knocked out Kevin Kelley in round four of a fight that was mad, thrilling and dumb. Hamed was dropped in round one, touched a glove down twice in round two and even touched a glove down in the fourth. Kelley was sent heavily over in the second and then again for the count in the fourth. Wow, it was ridiculous. One New York paper dubbed him Kid Counterfeit. Kelley, by the way, had been a world champion, held a version of the title at the time, and had lost just once in fifty fights. 'We all know what went wrong,' said Warren. 'I just hope that people recognize what went right: an unknown from Sheffield came to New York, set new featherweight records at the box office, attracted twelve thousand people, got up from knockdowns and knocked out the local hero. That's a bloody good British success story.' But Hamed and Ingle were estranged – that's the sad backstory to the glory in New York. It would not get any better, it never does.

The Contenders

Kevin Lueshing dropped and was then stopped by Felix Trinidad for the IBF welterweight title in January, and the same month Wayne McCullough lost a split, taking too many shots, against Daniel Zaragoza for the WBC super-bantamweight title in Boston.

Herbie Hide knocked out veteran Tony Tucker to win the vacant WBO heavyweight title in Norwich in June.

In September in Widnes, Reid was taken to hospital with exhaustion after beating Hacine Cherifi on a split to retain his WBC super-middleweight title. Three world title fights in seven months had left him exhausted, and in December he lost his belt on points to Thulani Malinga.

On 4 October in Calabria, Nigel Wenton was stopped by Giovanni Parisi for the WBO light-welterweight title, and on the same night in

Hannover Carl Thompson beat Ralf Rocchigiani for the cruiser-weight version on a split.

On the British leg of the Hamed–Kelley bill Barry Jones won the WBO super-featherweight title, Adrian Dodson was stopped by 'Winky' Wright for the WBO light-middleweight title, and Cantwell dropped down to WBO minimumweight and lost. Ryan Rhodes, dubbed 'Spice Boy' by Hamed, won the Lonsdale belt in a record time of ninety days when he stopped Del Bryan in March. In December he moved to middleweight and lost a tight decision to Otis Grant for the vacant WBO title in Sheffield. Spice Boy was only just 21.

From the Notepad

Lueshing left Nashville to visit his father in a Jamaican prison; he had not seen him for eleven years. His father had beat him with belts when he was growing up in London.

Mark Kaylor and Terry Lawless settled their financial dispute: Kaylor agreed a cash settlement and Lawless paid all costs.

In February, Hamed hired a tiny private plane to fly with me and former heavyweight contender Clifton Mitchell to watch Johnny Nelson win the European title in France. It was the start of Nelson's remarkable years.

Maloney, a veteran trainer called Bobby Paget, promoter Tony Breen and European light-heavyweight champion Crawford Ashley emptied the first-class bar on the Eurostar coming back from a hard defence by Ashley in Paris in May. I had to pour the quartet off in London.

In October, Billy Schwer collected 40 per cent of a £93,000 purse bid when he stopped Oscar Cano in Zaragoza to win the European lightweight title. Schwer's manager Duff admitted his purse bid was less than Schwer's end of the winning bid. It was good business for Billy, a seventies-style win.

In December, Herol 'Bomber' Graham won every second of every round against the crazy Vinny Pazienza in a bad fight at Wembley.

Paz, as he is legally known, had dabbled in porn, gambled, won a legitimate world title and then defied medical science by fighting on after breaking two vertebrae in a car crash. He'd been told he would never fight again He did, but not against Graham, who even at 38 looked like a ferocious ballroom dancer.

1998

*'I'm good for boxing in Britain because under Warren, boxing is in
danger of becoming a monopoly, but the WBU provides us
with a way to compete with him.'*
John Hyland, Olympian and promoter

*'Lewis has been lucky to fight guys that never came to fight. They either
break down or simply refuse to fight – well, now he's got a fight.'*
Shannon Briggs before he fell down in a world title fight with Lennox Lewis

NASEEM HAMED TURNED nasty, Joe Calzaghe was hit with injury,
Lennox Lewis lost his head, and Chris Eubank left the business after
two more memorable fights.

After the raw heroics in the win over Eubank there was a January
homecoming in Cardiff for Calzaghe's first defence of the WBO
super-middleweight title. One opponent fell through and then a
Croat called Branko Sobot was found. Poor Sobot was blasted in 1:35
of the third.

Robbie Regan, who had won the WBO bantamweight title in his
last appearance, was meant to be back in the ring on the bill. Instead
he had lost his licence after failing a British Boxing Board of Control
medical. 'I'm so sorry,' sobbed Regan. 'You fans have been fantastic
to me.' There would be more medical bad news for Welsh boxing
when Barry Jones, the WBO super-featherweight champion, was a
frustrated witness to three date changes for his defence against Julien
Lorcy in Paris. It was first planned for February, then 4 April, and

finally 16 May. Jones was getting a career-high sixty grand, but he failed a brain scan and lost his licence in April. 'It's terrible news, but it's my health,' said Jones. 'I was going to dedicate the fight to Robbie.' Jones was just 23, and was unbeaten in eighteen fights.

Calzaghe had problems in the gym before his April defence when he hurt his left wrist. All fighters, however, have to fight with an injury of some type. Richie Woodhall had lost his world title fight to Keith Holmes in 1996 just twelve days after keyhole surgery on his right elbow. Calzaghe forced Juan Giménez to quit at the end of the ninth round; the Paraguayan had been the distance in world title fights with Nigel Benn and Eubank. Calzaghe had an operation on the wrist, then hurt his left elbow and was out of the ring for ten months.

Incidentally, Benn was forced on more than one occasion during the year to deny rumours that he was planning a comeback. 'I'm never fighting again, trust me,' he said.

Eubank feared the end of his boxing life. His comments, nearly a decade earlier, had meant nothing. 'It's a mug's game,' he had said. The mad assault by Mickey Duff, when he called Eubank 'scum', was missing several points. I knew that he loved the sport he tried so eloquently to hate; he failed to convince me from the start.

In 1998, Eubank had two fights with Carl Thompson for the WBO cruiserweight title and both were quite breath-taking, the first of them a contender for Fight of the Decade. Nobody present or watching on television will ever be able to forget the fights.

The first took place in Manchester in April, and once again weight was a big issue before the fight. Eubank had never tried to deny the hardships he'd suffered shrinking his body to the 12st super-middleweight limit. He'd filled his suite with ripe cut fruit and sucked on the pieces. He'd had to remove his socks and his pants and suck in breath to slide just inside the hands of the tipping scales every time he fought at the super-middleweight limit. Before the fight with the Cat, as Thompson was known, Eubank had enjoyed the reduced regime, training in the cold of Bodmin Moor. 'I walk around at 13st 4lb – I might just come in at 12st 10lb and dance,' Eubank claimed.

Thompson was not listening. 'He's wasting his time with me if he is trying any mind games,' he said. Eubank weighed 13st 4½lb for the fight, Thompson a few pounds heavier, and neither came to dance.

The referee was Roy Francis, the third man in 1991 when Eubank met Michael Watson. The fight was a relentless battle with both boxers hurt, bruised and wobbled. In round four Thompson was down. There is a cliché about fighting to a standstill, but that night in front of over 20,000 people both men did fight to a standstill. They had nowhere to go and no energy to get there by the last round. At ringside, one or two people wanted Eubank pulled out during the final few rounds. It was desperately close, and at the end they stood either side of Francis, waiting and hoping that their physical sacrifice had not been in vain. The tight decision went to Thompson; two judges could only separate the men by a single point. Eubank, his left eye shut tight, dropped his head into his hands in utter despair and would spend two nights recovering from the fight in the Manchester Royal Infirmary. Thompson hobbled exhausted back to his dressing room.

In the emotional melee at the end I managed to grab Francis. He was drained. 'It was a hard last four rounds,' he admitted. 'It was a dilemma, but I had to give Chris every chance. It makes me feel like weeping. He's a guy I like so much. There's not many braver than him.' His comments were as brutally honest as the fight. Many felt the same way. Frank Warren was not talking about a rematch, he was talking about rest for both. 'That's a contender for Fight of the Decade,' he insisted. 'Right now, they need to do nothing for a long time.'

The rematch was there, and I knew Eubank would want it. 'I love this sport – the art, the single-mindedness and loneliness of it all,' he said. 'I love the victory when you are close to defeat.' That was Eubank's mind, not the throw-away quotes that got him headlines in 1990 and 1991.

The rematch was made for July in Sheffield – just ninety-one days after the first fight.

Eubank was still only 31. He had won nineteen consecutive world title fights and been for nearly a decade British boxing's biggest star. He had taken and passed two brain scans since the first fight. The second Thompson fight was his last. Thompson had won and defended the European title in overseas fights, taken the WBO title in Germany, and now, in his second defence, was once again the foreign fighter. 'It's been easy getting Carl ready,' said trainer Billy Graham. 'Eubank has done it all for me. Carl is motivated like I've never seen before.' It was the Eubank show once again. 'Nothing has changed since the first fight,' confirmed Thompson. 'I never expected there to be any change; I just train and fight. I leave the publicity and hype to fighters like Eubank.'

It was another hard fight and once again Eubank's left eye closed; it was shut tight by the end of the ninth and the doctor told the referee to stop it before the bell went for the start of round ten. Eubank was in front on two of the three scorecards and he complained, telling the doctor he could see. It was a lie. Eubank refused to shake Thompson's hand at the end.

There was a moment, a tiny incident that I have never forgotten, in Eubank's dressing room after the fight. I was sat next to him as he, between speaking, took his boots off. Every time he leaned forward a spot or two of blood dripped from his nose or his chin or lips. The spots landed on the floor between his feet, and each time he would wipe the blood away. He would lean back, talk, then lean forward, and there would be more blood. After about three wipes, he paused, clearly confused. He liked to keep things neat and tidy, and the tiny blood pools were ruining that. 'Finished? Ask me in September,' he said. He never fought again.

Hamed was truly ruthless in April when he made his tenth defence of his WBO featherweight. The man in the opposite corner was Wilfredo Vázquez, who had retained his WBA featherweight title three times in 1997 and had walked away from a defence to agree terms for Hamed. Vázquez, like so many before him, thought it would be an easy night; he was also getting $300,000, compared to the $82,000 he had been promised for the WBA fight. Hamed was brutal before the fight, fully dismissive of the Puerto Rican's credentials and of anybody critical of his lunatic fight with Kelley in New York.

Hamed dropped Vázquez five times and stopped him in round seven. He was, arguably, one of the top three fighters in the world right then. However, away from the ring his relationship with Brendan Ingle, his mentor and trainer for over fifteen years, was in ugly turmoil. Ingle said, 'They will pay ten per cent of four hundred, even ten per cent of two thousand, but once it gets to forty thousand or four million they start listening to everybody telling them the same story: "Why are you paying that much? You do the fighting." Well, I will tell you why: I've just spent fifteen years, seven days each week and about eight hours each day. That's why.'

In October, Hamed fought Belfast's Wayne McCullough in Atlantic City and it was a fight marred by too much hatred, nastiness and pride. McCullough, aka the Pocket Rocket, had been chasing Hamed for a long time. He was convinced that he would win and had been saying that for three or four years. 'I've studied him up close and I'm amazed that he has got this far,' said McCullough.

There were some travel issues before the fight and Hamed was late arriving in Atlantic City. He was not happy and there was an unnecessary edge to him. At the conference he was harsh on Ingle and it was uncomfortable. 'I've kept him, and that shows that being together seventeen years means more to me than it does to him,' said Hamed. 'I made him a million and right now I don't need a trainer.'

The undercard was stacked with British fighters. Ricky Hatton won for the ninth time, Robert McCracken for the thirty-second time, and Richie Wenton lost his WBO super-bantamweight title fight to Marco Antonio Barrera. It had been four years since Bradley Stone's death and Wenton would fight for another three years. Barrera's win moved him no closer to Hamed.

'I got to give it to Wayne,' said Hamed after his fight. 'I thought I'd KO him in the third round. I won easy, he has a hard head. Look at his face and then look at mine. He took a good beating. Next, I will KO Barrera.' Hamed had won a wide decision, never listened to a word his corner said and upset a lot of people. It was not a particularly dignified event to cover. I had it 7-2 after nine and then stopped scoring, and many in the crowd of 8,138 adopted a similar strategy: they'd come for the knockout, Hamed had promised it, and the Atlantic City crowd is a harsh crowd.

Lennox Lewis had been in Atlantic City in March to defend his WBC heavyweight title against Shannon Briggs as part of a March Badness bill. It was an emotional night. 'Lewis has been lucky to fight guys that never came to fight,' said Briggs. 'They either break down or simply refuse to fight – well, now he's got a fight.' It was a brawl, Lewis wanted a fight, and it nearly cost him his title. Briggs stunned and hurt him several times but was dropped three times and saved by the referee in the fifth. In late 2016 he was still fighting and still believing that he would get a world heavyweight title. His catch-phrase, 'Let's go, Champ', was heard at a dozen shows in Britain in 2016.

'Lennox got involved,' said Manny Steward. 'It happens, they get carried away with the emotions. He needs a big fight. I told him to challenge Holyfield.'

On the same bill it was the end for Herol Graham. It was his fifty-fourth fight – his first had been in 1978 – and he had won the British light-middleweight title in 1981. He had twice lost in world title fights and had been the middleweight division's invisible man for a decade. 'Without Herol there would not be a Naz,' said Glynn Rhodes, a product of Ingle's Wincobank gym and Graham's trainer in Atlantic City, the day before the fight. 'Herol's been ignored by all the great fighters and all the best British fighters. This is his chance.'

The 38-year-old was fighting the IBF super-middleweight champion Charles Brewer and, as Herol pointed out, nobody wanted to fight Brewer because 'he could bang and he was not popular'. The year before Brewer had agreed a fee to step aside and not fight Calzaghe. (They would meet eventually.) In round five Brewer was sent tumbling twice and he looked in distress. In the tenth, Graham was stopped. 'I was fine, I could have continued,' he argued. The three judges had the fight split, one for each boxer and a drawn score-card. In the dressing room, Frank Maloney, his latest promoter, cried with him. 'Herol came so close, this sport is cruel,' he said. Graham deserved so much more. He was 38-0 in fights when he dropped a wafer-thin decision to Sumbu Kalambay in 1987; he should have been given his chance long before that night.

Lewis never did fight Evander Holyfield in 1998. In September he beat Croatia's Željko Mavrović on points at the Mohegan Sun casino in Connecticut. The big Croat, with his Mohican hairstyle, was unbeaten in twenty-seven fights, seriously motivated by Darkie Smith, a trainer from Kentish Town, and he pushed Lewis for twelve rounds. At the post-fight conference it was difficult for Steward to conceal his disappointment. 'Lennox was fatigued from around the third,' he said. 'It was a strange fight.' Maloney glared over at him. Years later, when Lewis was long gone, he would always refer to Steward as a 'mercenary'. (That's not the full quote, by the way.)

There is no easy way to report the two WBO heavyweight title wins by the resurrected Herbie Hide, who was still only 26. In April, Hide stopped Damon Reed in fifty-two seconds – 'It's not a match I'm proud of,' said Warren – and in September he needed four minutes and four seconds to ruin Willi Fischer. They were bad fights.

In November, against a backdrop of south London splendour, Jane Couch became the first woman to compete under a British Boxing Board of Control licence. The Board had spent a fortune fighting Couch, and their entire strategy can be summed up in one demeaning sentence: she is a girl. That's it, I kid you not. Anyway, at Caesars in Streatham, formerly the Cat's Whiskers, Couch stopped Simone Lukic in round two. That, my friend, was history, and a dreadful mismatch. Couch was an old-fashioned battler and would quit after thirty-nine fights and several beatings; she was a girl, which is proven beyond doubt, but she was also a fighter. The predicted onslaught of some type of female freak show and takeover of British boxing never happened – still waiting.

The Contenders

In March, Richie Woodhall was too fresh for Thulani Malinga (who had become 42 overnight) and won the WBC super-middleweight title in front of 3,400 in his hometown of Telford. Paul Lloyd was stopped in the second by Tim Austin in a fight for the IBF bantamweight title. Austin had stopped or knocked out fifteen of his previous victims. Terry Dunstan lost for the first time when he was stopped in eleven by Imamu Mayfield for the IBF cruiserweight title.

Over 6,000 people filled a tent in Liverpool's Stanley Park to watch Shea Neary drop and stop Andy Holligan for the WBU light-welterweight belt. It was a memorable night, a terrific encounter, and a throwback to the seventies when the fight, not the fighter, was the attraction. 'We promised a war and we delivered,' said Neary.

In May, Spencer Oliver was rushed to hospital for emergency surgery to remove a blood clot when he was knocked out by Sergey Devakov in round ten of a European super-bantamweight title defence at the Royal Albert Hall. Oliver survived because of the rules and regulations in place because others had died or come close to death. He was having a Chinese meal a week after the fight. He remains a little miracle boy.

In September, Woodhall narrowly retained his title when he met late, late sub Glenn Catley. 'My instant reaction is that Glenn beat me,' admitted Woodhall. It was tight, not a travesty. Meanwhile, Mark Prince was stopped in round eight by Dariusz Michalczewski in front of 12,000 in Germany. It was the thirteenth defence of the WBO light-heavyweight title by the German-based Pole. (Prince would have a much harder fight later in his life, when his teenage son was stabbed to death.) On the undercard Hatton improved to nine and zero, and Wladimir Klitschko survived a knockdown in the opening round to win and make it 22-0.

From the Notepad

In January, John Fashanu appeared with Herbie Hide, as his adviser.

I never saw him again. Hide, meanwhile, was spending four grand on special guard dogs. 'They circle, but will only attack when I give them the command.'

There was a disturbing ring cameo by Jimmy McDonnell in February when he showed up for a danger fight on the Hungarian border with Slovakia. Jimmy Mac, who was training Hide at the time, had not fought since a knockout loss in 1990, and he lost on points. It was the last fight of his career. In 2016 McDonnell was training world champion James DeGale.

In March it was the end for Duke McKenzie when he was stopped in the first round on a show promoted by his brother, Clinton. 'I'm sorry, I've wasted your time,' said Duke to the fans. 'There is nothing left.' It was his forty-sixth fight. He won world titles at three different weights and has never received the respect he deserves.

John Hyland, who had lost a British title fight and fought at the 1984 Olympics, promoted the Neary–Holligan fight and was in bullish mood back at the old Moat House at the end of the night. 'I'm good for boxing in Britain because under Warren, boxing is in danger of becoming a monopoly, but the WBU provides us with a way to compete with him,' said Hyland. An hour later, at about 1.30 a.m., a policeman on a white horse, trying to keep order, was gently shoved by the crowd outside through a revolving door and into the hotel lobby. Neary was an attraction.

1999

*'I won my European title in Italy, defended it in France, and won my world
title in Germany. I have heard people boasting in many languages – it never
impresses me. Why should I listen to Nelson?'*
Carl Thompson on Johnny Nelson's latest insults

'Ryan went out on a suicide mission and got caught.'
Brendan Ingle after Ryan Rhodes lost a world title fight to Jason Matthews

THE WAIT WAS finally over for Lennox Lewis, the wait for recognition
continued to elude Naseem Hamed, Audley Harrison missed a
chance at glory, and from absolutely nowhere Johnny Nelson became
a world champion. It was a year of extremes, of arguments in court,
of cuts, mismatches and too much heartbreak.

Lewis and Evander Holyfield finally broke free from the negotiating table to fight at Madison Square Garden. The WBC, IBF and
WBA belts were the prize. Herbie Hide still held the WBO belt, but
nobody was talking about the kid from Norwich in New York. And
that is because the two finest heavyweights in the world, men that
should have met two years earlier, were signed and sealed to meet
each other.

The fight in March in front of 21,284 people was not particularly
memorable, a maul at times. Lewis was 6ft 5in and weighed 17st 8lb
compared to Holyfield's 6ft 2½in and 15st 5lb. Lewis had a couple of
big rounds, but Holyfield kept plugging away. It was not, as I said, a
great fight. At the end of twelve rounds Holyfield was marked, sore,

and had not done enough. Lewis had won, but he could have done a lot more, and in his corner there had been several stiff talks from Manny Steward. It was down to the three judges to confirm what we had just seen. A few people had it close, and that was, in many ways, understandable. There were others that thought Lennox had won ten of the twelve rounds. The decision was ready, and at that point nobody thought there was a problem. Then it turned very ugly.

The veteran South African judge Stanley Christodoulou scored it 116-113 for Lewis, Eugenia Williams scored it 116-113 for Holyfield, and Londoner Larry O'Connell, a twenty-three-year veteran of the judging table, scored it a draw at 115-115. There was outrage, chaos in the ring. 'I lost two rounds, no more than that,' screamed Lewis. 'Evander looked slow and old.' Ringside observers were, however, split, and several British newspaper sages agreed with O'Connell. The problem was that O'Connell never really agreed with O'Connell. 'I handed in my slip after each round,' said O'Connell, who had been a brilliant amateur boxer in the sixties for the Fitzroy Lodge in south London. 'I feel sorry for Lennox. I scored it as I saw it but my overall impression was that Lennox had won.' There was talk of a fix, the FBI made phone calls, newspapers published editorials that made no sense, corruption charges were threatened, and the three sanctioning bodies – having done nothing in over two years to get the pair in the bloody ring – suddenly unified to demand a rematch.

It was considered a high-profile bad decision, which is a decent enough description, but it was not the robbery some fools believe. The judges came under a lot of scrutiny – well, two of them did. Williams had only previously judged ninety fights, and that is, I'm afraid to say, nowhere near enough. She had actually only judged twenty-seven world title fights. 'She should never judge another fight,' said Bob Arum. 'I had it 10-2. It wasn't close.' Well, if that was the case, why not berate Christodoulou, who only gave it to Lennox by three rounds? Big Stanley left New York like some type of crusader against the might of boxing's corrupt heart. O'Connell scored a hard fight close. There was much bold talk of investigations, backhanders, odd payments into accounts, pictures with Don King as proof of illegality, and just about every other conspiracy theory available. The language was diabolical. The truth is that Lewis should have won, but it was not a disgrace and it was not criminal. Harry Gibbs, the referee that went against Henry Cooper in the 1971 fight with Joe Bugner, called O'Connell at home. 'I told him you have to call it how you see it and that is that,' said Gibbs, who died that November.

There was something of a fairy-tale, one with a painful ending, on the undercard to go with the mayhem of the main event. Howard Clarke, who was known as Clakka, from Warley fought Fernando Vargas, who was unbeaten in fifteen fights, all of them ending quick. Vargas was the IBF light-middleweight champion, an Olympian and a rising attraction. (He would go on and lose eventually to the fridge.) Clarke was in the ring as the challenger because he had pulled off a shock to beat ranked American Jason Papillion on points. It was the British shock of 1998. Clarke had won twenty-six of his thirty-eight fights and his participation was controversial, but Pat Cowdell, the great seventies amateur and eighties pro, was angry at any suggestion that Howard was in any way undeserving of his opportunity. 'If he was a cockney you wouldn't have written anything,' Cowdell said to Claude Abrams, editor of the *Boxing News*, during one lively exchange. Clarke was over four times and stopped in the fourth round. He was paid $30,000, which was not enough. 'One minute I'm nobody, the next everyone wants to interview me. It's like *Rocky*,' said Clarke, who followed the New York loss with sixteen consecutive defeats. He finally quit in 2007 with these truly amazing stats: 109 fights, 2 draws, 27 wins, 1 no contest and 79 losses. In late 2016 he had been suffering for a few years, the ghosts of sacrifices in the ring haunting what was left of his life.

In November Lewis and Holyfield did it all again at the Thomas and Mack Center in Las Vegas. 'I never did a proper job last time and I just hope we both try to knock each other out,' said Holyfield two days before the fight. It was what I wanted to hear. It was a much better fight, the seventh round was excellent, and it was a lot closer in many ways. At the end there was no confusion about the verdict, though: Lewis won on all three scorecards – I thought Holyfield was worth a draw – by four, six and two rounds. 'He did a lot better, it was harder than in New York,' admitted Lewis.

As a clear and alarming sign of the times, the IBO belt, which was vacant, was added to the WBC, WBA and IBF versions and left the ring with Lewis. It was a year when the IBO, the WBU and even the WBF staged too many fights in Britain, further confusing public perception; the WBO had weakened the strain, and the new sanctioning bodies, with their gaudy baubles, would often make a so-called world title fight a farce. Too many fighters I would consider third or even fourth best at their weight in Britain were turning their backs on the British title to fight for one of the new belts bearing the increasingly degraded label 'world champion'. Lewis now had four of them, and during the next few years Roy Jones, the American idol, would hold as many as six different world title belts. It was a nauseating alphabet soup, toxic but essential for boxers to get a living.

The first British boxer to win an IBO belt had been Northern Ireland's John Lowey in Chicago in 1995, and then Londoner Kevin Lueshing won the welterweight version in New York in 1996. In March 1998 the first IBO title fight took place in Britain when Patrick Mullings won the super-bantamweight version in Hull. By 2000 or 2001 some British boxers had made three and four defences. It was prolific, and the British promoters, especially Barry Hearn, loved it. In April 1999, after Hamed had stopped Paul Ingle, it was left to Kronk icon Tommy Hearns to close the show and bless the IBO with his presence. Hearns won an IBO title that long night in Manchester in a fight that was sad to watch: it took place against a backdrop of shuffling feet and people chatting as they left the venue. When the lights came on the cleaners were already picking up rubbish. The Hitman, as Hearns was known, had not even left the ring.

Hamed was no longer with Brendan Ingle. The rumours and the bad blood had all been true. 'I sacked myself,' said Ingle, 'let's get that clear. I could have continued with Naz and made more money. I'm not a mercenary. [Manny] Steward is a mercenary. He's a great trainer, but these days he's more of a mercenary.' But Hamed's twelfth defence, his twenty-ninth quick finish in thirty-two fights, that April against Ingle (no relation) was ruthless nonetheless. Ingle was over in the first, the sixth and in the eleventh rounds. He beat the last count but was saved from more hurt. Over 19,000 turned up at the MEN for the Hearn and Prince Promotions show. On the night Oscar Suárez started as the main trainer in the corner, but Manny staged a gentle coup once it became clear that Naz was not listening. The corner scuffling was short on dignity but made sense.

There was one more fight for Hamed in 1999: in October he beat César Soto on points in Steward's Detroit. It went the full twelve rounds and seemed to drag on for ever. (Wayne McCullough lost a WBC super-bantamweight title fight to Erik Morales in the main support.) Soto was the WBC champion, and that meant Hamed had won the WBO, the IBF, the WBA and the WBC belts at featherweight in four years and one month. A statistician might quibble, but Naz beat four legitimate champions holding the four legitimate belts.

In the camp for the Soto fight there were horrid rumours of friction, terrible sparring sessions and attempts by everybody to just get a bit closer to the little idol. Hamed lost 24lb, which means he started in camp as a light-middle, and there was a bizarre impasse on the day of the weigh-in when the Hamed camp, not Steward, attempted to introduce their own scales as the official championship scales. 'These Hameds are crazy,' said Bob Arum. 'Who's ever heard of bringing your own scales?' Soto, by the way, was still a good fighter at that point and Hamed won clearly. Sadly, his fighting life and personal life would get messier.

There was some joy for the Ingle gym in Wincobank, which has occupied a desolate spot on a steep hill on the outskirts of Sheffield since the seventies. Ingle and Johnny Nelson had been chasing Carl Thompson, goading him at every opportunity, and in March Nelson got his opportunity when he met Thompson for the WBO cruiser-weight title in Derby. 'If Carl tries to box he will get humiliated, if he tries to fight he's getting annihilated,' promised Nelson. 'You have to be far more than physically fit to beat me, you have to be mentally strong, and Nelson is not,' replied Thompson.

The fight was tense, and it ended in controversy: Thompson was over in the fourth and rescued in the fifth. 'I'm so angry,' he said. 'The plan was to come on strong later in the fight.' Nelson was sharp on the night. 'It's diabolical, my man's eyes are clear,' said Billy Graham, who had his young prospect Ricky Hatton carry Carl's belt to the ring. It was a sweet accomplishment for Nelson after his previous dismal failures. Nelson had been a pro since 1986, had lost five of his first eleven, and had been ostracized when he froze in two world title fights. 'This shows that Brendan's system works,' said Nelson. 'I'm a product of the St Thomas's gym, I started with no natural talent or ability. It's about experience and knowledge. This was payback.' Nelson and Hamed had been close.

Nelson won four more WBO fights in 1999, which included a shut-out in Las Vegas over Sione Asipeli, who was dropped heavily in the tenth, and a brawl with Bruce Scott. But he always had his critics.

'Johnny Nelson will be fighting and winning and not getting hit at fifty, just like Archie Moore,' promised Ingle. He was nearly right: Nelson went twenty-one fights unbeaten to the end of his career in 2005, when he was 38. He's threatened several comebacks, the latest in 2015.

In June, the combined knowledge of Ingle and Ernie Fossey in the corner could not help Herbie Hide when he, having started as favourite, was stopped in the second by Vitali Klitschko and lost his WBO heavyweight title. 'Ernie and I couldn't perform miracles,' said Ingle. Before the fight Norman Wisdom and Frank Bruno performed a raffle in the ring. It was a short pantomime, make no mistake. Vitali started to hurt Herbie early. 'Herbie was sloppy and boxed the wrong fight,' said Warren. 'He went head-hunting against a bigger puncher. That is stupid. I got him home advantage and he never had a plan.' In Kiev over 300,000 watched the fight on big screens in the main square.

At the world amateur championship in Houston in August there were cameos from Audley Harrison and David Haye. They could and should have gone further, reached the medal stages. The Cuban team was recalled to Havana by Fidel Castro and heavyweight Kevin Evans won the first medal ever by a British boxer; he lost to Felix Savon in the semi-final. In the final, Savon was gloved, had his headguard on and was ready to fight when Castro personally called Dr Alcides Sagarra, the national coach, and ordered the team to leave. Sagarra stood to attention as he listened – I know because I was six feet away. Haye and Harrison had pulled off a double act as singer and bodyguard to gain access to tables at the best clubs in Houston. After Harrison's loss to Turkey's Sinan Şamil Sam he asked Haye, 'Where we going later, the same place or somewhere else?' Harrison, in his defence, insisted that Houston was a fact-finding mission: 'I went to assess the opposition, to understand what I would have to do in Sydney [in 2000].' It worked. Haye and Harrison dropped decisions to the eventual winners.

The Contenders

Julius Francis was only a year away from Mike Tyson's fists, and the infamous boots he wore on that night, when in January he stopped Pele Reid (who'd started his career as just Pele) in round three at York Hall to retain his British heavyweight title. Big Julius was rampant in 1999 and made two more defences to win the Lonsdale belt outright; his win over Danny Williams, unbeaten in fifteen at the time, was a shock.

Joe Calzaghe beat Robin Reid in a tight brawl in Newcastle to keep his WBO super-middleweight belt, and on the same bill Richie Woodhall stopped Vincenzo Nardiello for the WBC title at the same weight. Calzaghe made one more defence before injuries kept him out of the ring for seven months; Woodhall lost the title in Telford to Markus Beyer in October.

Paul Lloyd, Kevin Lueshing and Billy Schwer all lost world title fights and all started as big underdogs. Lloyd was stopped in one round by Marco Antonio Barrera, Lueshing lost in three to Harry Simon, and Schwer, who had refused a lucrative step-aside offer, went the full twelve with Steve Johnston. No shame in any of those losses.

Bruce Scott, just sixty-two days after losing to Nelson, went to Germany at two weeks' notice and lost to unbeaten Juan Carlos Gómez in six rounds.

Paul Ingle went from losing to Hamed in April to winning the IBF version of the title when he beat Manuel Medina in November.

'I fought the wrong fight,' said Ryan Rhodes after he was stopped in two by Jason Matthews for the vacant WBO middle in July. Matthews had stepped in at five days' notice.

Howard Eastman, the British champion at middleweight, was never in contention; he defended his belt just once in 1999.

In a rare double knockdown, Terry Dunstan and Carl Thompson had their *Rocky* moment in Peterborough in December in the twelfth round of their vacant British cruiserweight title fight. Thompson, who fell to the canvas from exhaustion, beat his count and won with twenty seconds left. It was a tiny ring and a terrific fight. In commentary I said, and I wasn't kidding, 'There is a minute left and in a fight like this anything could happen.' It did.

From the Notepad

Michelle Sutcliffe, a mother of two teenagers, fought in Leeds. 'Jane Couch opened the door for all of us, even us mothers,' she told me.

Shea Neary hired Junior Witter for a day of brutal sparring before each fight. 'He stopped me in the amateurs – he gets my head right,' said Neary, who retained his WBU light-welterweight title in Dublin. It was Neary's tenth consecutive sell-out.

After a split with Don King there was a settlement of £7.2 million; Frank Warren got his fighters' contracts back and the TV got rights. He then secured a deal with ShowTime. Warren was optimistic about the future: 'I still have my heart, head and balls. It was a small price to pay to get my business back.'

Barry Jones sold 160 tickets in one pub in Ely for his fight on the Joe Calzaghe undercard in June. 'I would have sold more, but it was a quiet afternoon.'

Barry Hearn talked about a tournament involving sixteen heavyweights over one night on pay-per-view with forty grand for the winner. It would later be known as Prizefighter.

2000

*'I have been boxing for twenty-one years. I can't remember a part of my life
when I was not in a gym or boxing. It has been my whole life.'*
Billy Schwer

*'They all want to fight me. I bring the sparkle, the glamour and the money.
They want the money.'*
Naseem Hamed

AUDLEY HARRISON PUT an end to a thirty-two-year wait when he won
the most improbable of gold medals at the Sydney Olympics. He had
no right to win, no secret history to suggest a win, and no doubts that
he would win the gold at Darling Harbour; he knew that with the
gold he would be able to sit down to dictate terms for his occupation
of British boxing. The brave new world, according to Big Aud,
was a glorious paradox and it was a lunatic, joyful ride to the very
end.

Harrison was the first British boxer to qualify and was joined after
the last qualification event by his friend from the Repton club
Courtney Fry. In the end just under fifty British boxers, including
David Haye and Carl Froch, tried and failed to reach Sydney. Harrison
and Fry were the ninth and tenth Repton boxers to make an Olympic
squad under the guidance of Tony Burns. Fry lost straight away,
his mind on the death of a friend back in Britain and his new
child.

'I have to go to the negotiating table with a medal, I know that,'

Harrison had said in July at the Bethnal Green gym. The problem was that he had lost four of his last fifteen fights, had been beaten by two of the three top five at the Olympics, had flopped a year earlier in Houston, had a bad left hand – and he fell out with Terry Edwards, the GB coach, before the opening bell.

In the first round he was drawn against Russia's world amateur champion Alexei Lezin, who had beaten Harrison 6-1 in 1999. Harrison was trailing 8-6 when he stopped Lezin with one punch (a sudden stoppage by a nervous referee, and the Russians lodged an official complaint). It was a 'wow' moment. On the other side of the draw a German called Gengiz Koc, who had beaten Harrison twice, was left unconscious on the canvas for ten minutes by Cuba's Alexis Rubalcalba, who was slightly smaller than a family house. Rubalcalba was inside Harrison's head, I knew that from Houston in 1999.

Harrison scored nineteen points, his highest ever total, to beat Oleksiy Mazikin of the Ukraine to reach the semi-final and the land of medals. In that semi he beat Italy's Paolo Vidoz by thirty-two points and it was clear that the judges loved Harrison. He was in the final, but his hand was bad. In the opposite corner was a soldier from Kazakhstan called Mukhtarkan Dildabekov, the man who had slayed the colossal Cuban fighter. Just under a million people in Britain switched on their television sets on 1 October at about 4.50 a.m. to watch Harrison's emotional slice of history. He bashed poor Dildabekov and romped to super-heavyweight gold with a score of 30-16. The swagger was on, the gravy train was leaving the station, and Big Aud was at the table, telling everybody how to run their business. It was comedy gold and Olympic gold. 'I said I would and I did,' Harrison said. In December he had the first operation of the rest of his life when a surgeon fixed a knuckle on his left hand. He was 29 or 30, and the fun was about to start.

The professional year had started with Mike Tyson landing in London for a siege of the Grosvenor on Park Lane. He trained, he visited the mosque in Regent's Park, he shopped and he was generous with his time. A filmmaker called Dave Varley, from Leeds, made one of the finest boxing films about the visit having somehow found himself embedded with Tyson and his men. At the end of January Tyson walked out in front of a sell-out at the MEN (21,000 tickets went in forty-eight hours) to fight the British heavyweight champion and nice guy from south London Julius Francis. Big Julius knew his role and had trained with the army in Aldershot. 'I'm not fighting Mike Tyson the celebrity, I'm fighting Mike Tyson the boxer,' he insisted. The seclusion worked and Francis made it to round two, going down a total of five times. 'Too many people told me that Tyson was shot – they were wrong, and I was an idiot to listen to them,' said Francis in March on the night he lost his British title to Mike Holden. Francis was paid £320,000 for the Tyson fight and he received an extra forty grand for selling the soles of his boots as advertising space to a newspaper. 'I have no idea where those boots are now, I bet they are worth a fortune,' Francis said in 2014.

In the other heavyweight world, the real one, there was drama, patience and dominance from Lennox Lewis in three contrasting world title defences. Lewis was already starting to walk and talk like a boxing statesman, a man above any cheap shots, chat or stupidity. Thankfully he would revert, lose his mind a few times and get involved in some of the sport's highest-profile brawls in the coming years. But in 2000 he was coasting, splendid in his dominance. In April at Madison Square Garden he was vicious in destroying the previously unbeaten Michael Grant, who showed guts, in two rounds. Grant had hopped across from American football, knocked out dozens of willing men on his cynical path to the ring, and had then dared to challenge Lewis. 'He got what he deserved,' the champion said. In July, Lewis returned to London after six years and beat South Africa's Frans Botha, stalking the White Buffalo until a sickening right lifted Botha up and dropped him through the ropes. Botha beat the count and tried to walk forward, but Larry O'Connell waved it off at 2:39 of the second – the same O'Connell that had been savaged by everybody in the Lewis camp the previous year when he scored the first Evander Holyfield fight a draw. 'They gave me a bit of stick, nothing serious,' Larry told me after the fight. Michael Buffer had introduced the fighters – it was that type of night. Botha took his licks and then Buffer announced the result as cool as a midnight cocktail.

In his last fight of the year, in November, Lewis travelled to the Mandalay Bay in Las Vegas and ruined the plans of promoter Dan Goossen and David Tua. Before the fight Goossen, a lovely fella, took me to his suite somewhere in the clouds on about floor 121 to show me the Tua Man doll – well, more an Action Man with a moody haircut and a classic Samoan physique. 'I'm ready to roll with these now,' Dan said. 'All we need is David to win.' Hold those dolls, Dan. In all fairness a very different Lewis arrived for the fight and the respect before the bell continued for twelve rounds. 'I call on the warriors from my past to help me in battle,' said Tua, who had stopped, dropped or knocked out his previous eight. He could bang, but he was too short, and his ancestors back in Samoa, where David Tua Day had been declared by the president, were not listening. It was close to a defensive, risk-free masterclass from Lewis. Tua quit in 2013 after fifty-nine fights with just five defeats on points – nobody was silly enough to try and stop him. Dan died in 2014. Lewis only had four fights left, and each one was an event.

Naseem Hamed had an idea for his fourteenth defence of the WBO featherweight title at Olympia in March against South African Vuyani Bungu, who had been a brilliant super-bantamweight world champion for six years. Hamed's plan, after Steward had taken over when Hamed was drifting in the Paul Ingle fight the previous April, was to alternate his cornermen, giving Manny Steward and Oscar Suárez a round each. Amazingly both followed the plan – the first time I have ever seen such a thing – but after the fight there was a serious doubt that Steward would ever work with Hamed again.

Hamed arrived on a flying carpet, cross-legged and happy, and won in the fourth, which was impressive, but Bungu had been out for a year and was really still a super-bantamweight. Hamed had lost something; his defence was now a reaction to his caution and not part of his once glittering strategy. Hamed had just three fights left.

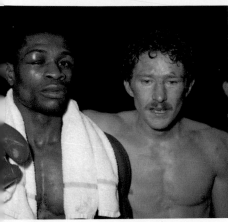

Left: Terry Marsh in 1986, a year before he too became world champion. His exit from boxing is still a mystery.

Below: It was a disastrous night for Herol 'Bomber' Graham (left) when he finally, five years too late, fought for the world title. Mike McCallum sneaked a split decision.

Bottom: A bad hair day and then a bad night in the ring for Nigel Benn under the big top at Finsbury Park. The great Michael Watson won in round six.

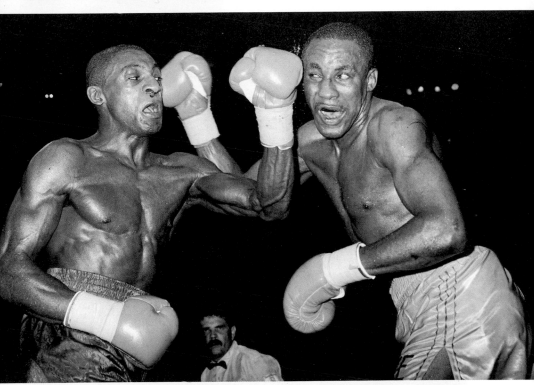

Above: Dave 'Boy' McAuley parries a long jab from Duke McKenzie in their IBF flyweight title fight. McAuley won on points.

Left: McAuley is lifted high by his cornermen, including Barney Eastwood at the front, after beating McKenzie. It was McAuley's third attempt at winning a world title.

Below: Lennox Lewis and Frank Maloney at a typically low-key press conference to promote the Olympic champion's third pro fight. The pair have changed quite a bit since.

Right: Michael Watson is poised and controlled in his first fight with Chris Eubank for the WBO middleweight title. The decision was front-page news.

Below: Three months later Watson is in a fearsome mood in the rematch with Eubank. The sickening result changed the sport.

Right: This picture is a guilty pleasure for me as Nigel Benn screams in victory. On the other side of the ring, Gerald McClellan collapsed and later required surgery.

Above: Joe Calzaghe in the shed he called home, a boxing gym that time forgot. Calzaghe was the no-thrills throwback champion, as was perfectly demonstrated in this win (*left*) against Eubank in 1997.

Below: Audley Harrison wins Britain's first gold medal in thirty-two years at the Sydney Olympics. His professional career was rather more complicated.

Above: Naseem Hamed arrives on his magic carpet to stop Vuyani Bungu in four savage rounds. The leopard-skin flying contraption was terrific; the fight a formality.

Below left: A lethal Lennox Lewis walks away from Mike Tyson in Memphis. It was a stunning end to a mad few days.

Below right: At the Athens Olympics in 2004, Amir Khan was just seventeen when he won the silver medal. He turned professional the following year and there hasn't been a dull moment since.

Above: Scott Harrison hoists his world title belt over the heads of Frank Warren and Frank Maloney. Harrison was an excellent but flawed fighter and the two Franks worked hard to keep him on track.

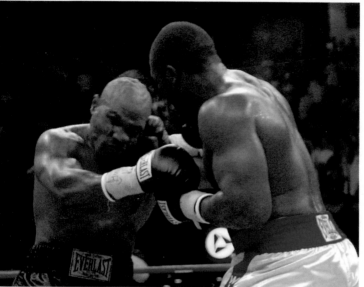

Left: Danny Williams on his way to his true moment of glory in a remarkable career. He stopped Tyson in four rounds.

Below: It's all over for José Luís Castillo and Ricky Hatton howls in delight in Las Vegas. He was exceptional that night and I interviewed him seconds later in the ring.

Above: Carl Froch went on one of British boxing's most amazing fight sequences. The Nottingham man divides opinion, but I've always had a soft spot for him.

Right: David Haye conceded about eleven inches and one hundred pounds to Nikolai Valuev, but outsmarted the Beast from the East.

Below: George Groves and James DeGale were kids in the same gym and they never liked each other. Groves won their pro fight and nothing changed.

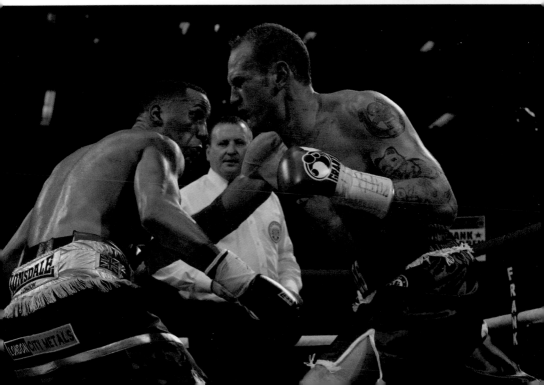

NICOLA ADAM

...IBLE OLYMPIC GOLD MEDALLIST

Above: Nicola Adams is Britain's most successful amateur boxer and an outspoken pioneer for the women's game.

Above: Tyson Fury steps out in a fur coat just a month or so after beating Wladimir Klitschko in November 2015. He had stopped smiling by the end of the year.

Left: New York belonged to Carl Frampton and his manager Barry McGuigan after the Belfast boxer upset the odds and beat Léo Santa Cruz.

Below: Anthony Joshua was still a novice when he won the world heavyweight title.

Time was running out, the decline was not going away, but sadly the delusion was intense. The level of hate between the Hameds and the working coalition of Brendan Ingle, former trainer, and Frank Warren, former promoter, remained high. 'I have three fighters to beat him now: Johnny Tapia, Marco Antonio Barrera and Acelino Freitas,' said Warren. He was right.

On Hamed's undercard, Liverpool's Shea Neary was stopped in round eight by Micky Ward and lost his WBU light-welterweight title. It was Neary's first loss in twenty-three fights, and Ward was two years away from his unforgettable trilogy with Arturo Gatti. The Ward–Neary fight was excellent; up close the punches sounded like two lumps of iron smashing into each other. It is not often that every punch is felt at ringside – perhaps it was the echo in the high-ceilinged building. It could have just been the gut refusal of either to quit until Ward went repeatedly for body shots to the liver (which should be illegal), turning each punch a fraction and landing in a slightly different place, and then finished Neary with left hooks. Two of the three judges had Neary in front at the end. Neary praised Ward to me when I saw him at two a.m. 'That was not normal, Ste, there was nothing I could do,' he said. It was a privilege to be ringside for that fight.

The Hamed sideshow stopped at Foxwoods Resort in Connecticut for what would be his last WBO defence. Hamed that August was barely recognizable, the kid that had stopped Steve Robinson in the drizzle in 1995 long gone. At Foxwoods, on a night of relentless thrills and spills, Hamed finally dropped Augie Sanchez, a kid from Las Vegas, in the fourth. The referee never counted, the boxer never moved. A few hours later, thankfully, he was discharged from hospital. Hamed had fallen into a fight and had been dropped in the second, hurt, and marked. He needed the sudden finish to stay unbeaten and, at the end, his American paymasters at HBO were happy. Seth Abraham, the boss, praised Hamed: 'He doesn't need to be protected and right now the only guy who walks into the ring an even bet against him is Floyd Mayweather.' At the time Mayweather was 4lb heavier and the WBC super-featherweight champion; just eight months later Mayweather told me how much he wanted to fight Hamed. Varley filmed the interview.

There was also talk at Foxwoods about a rematch with Paul Ingle – the American broadcasters would do anything to avoid screening Hamed against his mandatory, the Hungarian István Kovács. Ingle, incidentally, had stopped Junior Jones in the eleventh to retain his IBF featherweight title at Madison Square Garden when Lewis ruined Grant. It was a hard fight. Ingle had been dropped in the ninth and then turned the fight round. The Americans loved him. But he never agreed terms for a second fight with Hamed, and in October Hamed refused to take a 35 per cent cut in his HBO fee for a mandatory defence against Kovács. Hamed's people asked the WBO to create an interim title for the Hungarian, they refused, the belt was lost out of the ring, and Kovács won the vacant title in January 2001. Hamed's title days were over.

Ingle, instead, signed to fight South African Mbulelo Botile, who was moving up from bantamweight. Ingle passed his annual MRI before the December fight in Sheffield, part of a big bill headlined by Joe Calzaghe. Sadly, Ingle became the story. It came to an end, a horrible, bloody and silent end, in round twelve. Ingle was trailing by three, four and five rounds going into the last; in round eleven he had been dropped heavily. He glared at Botile and roared at the end of the eleventh and went back to his corner. 'He was talking, he was respond-ing, and he knew he needed a knockout to win,' said Steve Pollard, Ingle's trainer and friend. Ingle was talking, looking at Pollard, but he was also finished. He stumbled out for the twelfth with his nose broken, his swollen face smeared with blood and bruises, but spirit guided him to the middle of the ring and back into a fight he could never win. Pollard did the right thing: he's a fighting man and it's a tough business.

Just twenty seconds into the round Ingle was over for the full count. At first he seemed fine, exhausted and upset. He was sitting on the canvas and talking to Pollard and Frank Maloney, his manager. He was taken from the ring, but there was no sinking feeling, no sense of dread as he was packed off in an ambulance. The

Calzaghe–Woodhall fight started. 'We all thought Paul was just exhausted,' said Warren. 'I spoke to Frank and he agreed. Hindsight is a useless commodity. It would not have happened if we had known.'

Ingle was on the operating table forty-five minutes after leaving the ring. The safety measures set in place after the Watson–Eubank fight saved his life. The following Wednesday he was scratching his nose, eyes open, on his way back. Pollard and Maloney had to fight off the critics and accusations that they'd come close to killing their boxer by sending him out for that final round. They did the only thing they knew and deserved more support. Ingle had been in a lot of wars; he had won and lost four brutal title fights in either the tenth or eleventh rounds before Botile.

Calzaghe, incidentally, had no idea his friend was injured. 'I warmed up, went and fought, and only found out when I got back to the changing room – it ruined my night,' he said. Calzaghe had stopped Richie Woodhall in the tenth. Woodhall never fought again. It was Calzaghe's third win of the year. The first had been on Tyson's undercard in Manchester when he had beaten David Starie on points, and in August he'd stopped Omar Sheika in five torrid rounds at Wembley. Sheika had captivated the gullible with his speed and confidence at workouts. 'I have been studying Calzaghe for years, I have a plan, a strategy,' insisted Sheika. 'They all say that,' answered Calzaghe. The quality of his Sheika win is often neglected.

In back-to-back weekends in October the Conference Centre at Wembley was a scene of carnage. Colin Dunne and Billy Schwer met for the WBU lightweight title. It was a stunning fight. The crowd stood exhausted to the end, often slumping like battered boxers to their seats for the minute break. Schwer, on a lost cause, won the last, but it was not enough and he dropped a split. 'I have been boxing for twenty-one years,' he said. 'I can't remember a part of my life when I was not in a gym or boxing. It has been my whole life.' He had a couple left in him and would win and lose an IBO title. 'It was boxing, not Colin Dunne, that won tonight,' said John Hyland, the 1984

Olympian and promoter. The Dynamo still had a bit of fighting to do.

The following Saturday Danny Williams entered boxing folklore with a display of incredible bravery. Williams won the vacant British heavyweight title when he dropped and stopped Mark Potter in round six. The story of the fight was mad: Williams was over in the first, Potter in the second, and in the third Williams pulled out of a clinch and dislocated his right shoulder. It was hanging lame, visible from the cheap seats. At the bell to end round three, Jimmy McDonnell in the corner let Danny Tovey pop the shoulder back in. 'Be sensible for a round or two,' Tovey screamed at Williams. At ringside, Warren wanted the fight stopped. In rounds four and five Williams retreated, mostly just using the left, though he could use the right. In the sixth it popped out again. I swear I heard it at ringside and then clearly heard a yelp from Williams. The referee, John Coyle, took a look after fifteen seconds. Williams continued to move and his right arm was tight to his side: he was a one-armed fighter. 'I was ready with the towel,' said McDonnell. 'But in my head I could hear Danny saying, "Don't stop it, I only need one punch, one punch."' At ringside people were running back and forth, and then bingo. One left uppercut, screwed in blind, and Potter was over. He beat the count at nine and was dropped again. He never beat that count. Williams was flat on his back next to him, his right arm across his heaving body. The fight was over. At three a.m. Williams left the hospital with his right arm strapped across his body, his Lonsdale belt in a bag and his reputation made for ever.

The Contenders

On the undercard of the Williams–Potter fight, Ricky Hatton won the British light-welterweight title with one of his hardest fights, beating Jon Thaxton on points. Hatton needed twenty-eight stitches to close his wounds.

It was a mistake dropping Acelino Freitas, and Barry Jones knew that straight away. Freitas was the WBO super-featherweight champion, unbeaten in twenty-three, with twenty-three mercy stoppages or knockouts. He climbed up, dropped Jones a few times, and stopped the Ely idol in eight. It was not quite that simple – Jones had started to relax and enjoy it in rounds four, five and six – but Freitas closed it, and Jones never fought again.

In February, two unbeaten heavy punchers clashed for the vacant British light-middle title in Dagenham. Wayne Alexander knocked out Paul Samuels in the third. 'I have never been so exhausted,' said Alexander. 'It could have been me at the end.' Every punch was wicked and 2,000 people were treated to a rare, rare fight.

Johnny Nelson managed two WBO cruiserweight defences, Glenn Catley won and lost the WBC super-middleweight title on the road, and Robert McCracken was beaten in a WBC middleweight fight. McCracken had waited too long. Michael Brodie lost for the first time in thirty fights when he dropped a tight verdict for the WBC super-bantamweight title against Willie Jorrin. At minimumweight, Micky Cantwell lost a world title fight for the third time.

Esham Pickering was caught cold and done in seventy-two seconds for the WBO bantamweight title. Neil Sinclair dropped and was dropped by Daniel Santos in a WBO welterweight fight before losing in the second. Pickering and Sinclair were part of that brutal night in Sheffield when Ingle was rushed to surgery.

From the Notepad

In Glasgow in June, Mike Tyson wore a kilt and danced on a car. He then tangled with a Texan, clashed with a referee, and left in disgrace. There had been some trouble in London before he flew to Glasgow. He was later fined for the melee in the ring when he beat Lou Savarese. Junior Witter, one of Brendan Ingle's boxers, took a world title fight on short notice and lost to Zab Judah on the under-card. 'I knew it would make me a better fighter,' said Witter. It did.

An old friend called Cedric Kushner, who looked and moved like a walrus, was in London with Vuyani Bungu. 'Only in boxing can you be undefeated for eight years, defend your title thirteen times, lose to a great fighter like Prince Naseem and get asked if you're going to retire,' he remarked later that night.

In April, Richie Wenton was training at the Peacock gym in Canning Town, where the statue of Bradley Stone had been raised. 'I placed some flowers at Brad's feet the first day I trained,' said Wenton. In May he lost a British title fight.

2001

'Rahman was about to quit himself. His eye was bleeding. He looked at the ref and almost started walking back to his corner.'
Manny Steward on an alternative ending to the night Lennox Lewis
was knocked out

'I knew that if that second shot had gone in I would have won. I never got the chance, and when the right landed my hand went numb, and that was it for that hand for the rest of the fight.'
David Haye on his world championship final in Belfast

APRIL CERTAINLY WAS the cruellest month for Lennox Lewis when he went from a movie set to boxing purgatory in a few lazy weeks, and Naseem Hamed's mad roadshow crashed badly in Las Vegas in a year of misery and comic extremes in the British boxing business. An undercover operative at Disney World had a cameo, Herbie Hide had machine guns in his home, and Ricky Hatton had five WBU title fights.

When Hasim Rahman found out he had been picked to fight Lennox Lewis in South Africa for the heavyweight title he was at a training camp in the Catskill Mountains and sleeping in a bed Lewis had slept in. Rahman was a changed man from the kid that had been shot five times on the streets of Baltimore, arrested twelve times and found guilty of dealing drugs. In the ring he was unpredictable, powerful and vulnerable.

Lewis was late arriving at altitude in South Africa, nearly three weeks after Rahman. He had been filming scenes for a movie with Wladimir Klitschko in Las Vegas. He was only a few pounds heavier than normal, but he looked out of condition. 'I went running with him and after a mile he was struggling for breath,' said Frank Maloney, who had been with Lewis since 1989. 'I knew then he was in trouble and I told a few journalists, "He ain't got a chance."' It felt like a defence of the coming failure was being slowly built.

'Lennox is an enigma to all of us,' said Manny Steward, the trainer. 'We all wait to see what he does when he gets in the ring.' The odd gloom increased.

The fight in Carnival City was over in the fifth. The pair were sucking in rare mouthfuls of air, probing, missing and moving slow. Rahman pushed Lewis back with four jabs that missed, took a gasp of air and threw a right cross. It was the perfect punch, and Lennox went down on his back heavily. He was getting up at ten but it was too slow. Rahman was the champion, swamped by his people; ten seconds later Lewis was up and his eyes were clear – the same instant recovery as in the Oliver McCall fight. In my opinion, in both fights Lewis jumped up too quickly before his head had cleared.

'Rahman was about to quit himself,' insisted Steward. 'His eye was bleeding. He looked at the ref and almost started walking back to his corner.' Rahman was certainly not happy in the fifth. 'I got knocked down by a lottery punch and I was getting to my feet when the referee stopped it,' said Lewis, which was true, but a fighter has ten seconds only.

The Rock, as Rahman was known, and his people were not impressed. 'Let's not forget Lewis was running five miles at altitude and I kept hearing about how good he was in sparring,' said Rahman the morning after the fight. 'Suddenly I knock him out and the story changed: he has not prepared properly, he was going to pull out. Damn, it's a miracle he could get in the ring.'

There was a vicious fall-out inside the Lewis camp. Maloney would be a victim. Lewis had to call him to ask him to keep his mouth closed. The suits at HBO, the paymasters, had not agreed a deal with Rahman; they offered him $16 million for a rematch and watched in despair as the new champion did a deal with Don King. 'It's a shame what happened to that nice boy, Lennox. I feel for his lovely mother,' said King, who handed Rahman a cash advance of £200,000 on the £20 million deal.

A rematch was finally agreed for the Mandalay Bay, Las Vegas, in November.

'I will go on record and say that I will retire if I lose to this man,' said Lewis when we gathered in town for the fight. 'Beating me is the only credential Rahman has.' It was, in all fairness, the only credential Rahman needed.

The pair had scuffled live on American television when Rahman made a gay slur and Lennox invited Rahman to bring his sister the next time. The studio fight was ugly. 'I was glad to see that happen,' said Steward. 'I like a bit of tension in my fighters.'

Rahman was somehow getting paid less than Lewis. He looked uneasy all week and was still wandering the casino floor late into the night, every night. 'I don't feel like the champion,' Rahman said. His behaviour disturbed me; Lewis was calm, hard and focused. 'Having the crown doesn't make him a king,' said Lewis. In the crowds that gathered, eager like all Vegas crowds for blood, Don King walked tall, waving American flags, declaring the fight was as big as 'Ali and Frazier'. It was certainly big for Lewis, and he was the only calm soul in his gang. King had been on a plane on his way to Las Vegas that had hit terrible turbulence and he'd injured his neck. He'd gone for an MRI and the problem was pellets in the neck from a 1959 shotgun blast.

'Lewis has more talent than Ali,' said Steward. 'But all of his accomplishments will pretty much be forgotten if he loses to Rahman again. His legacy hinges on what he does in this fight.' Steward spoke in his usual thoughtful way and left us in silence. Yes, it was a big fight.

Lewis won rounds one, two and three. He boxed with his brain. Rahman was using the Lewis defence from South Africa: hands down, chin up. In the fourth, Lewis connected and Rahman was down, flat on his back, his head stuck between the prongs of King's crown logo on the canvas. It was an image to savour. Rahman scrambled up at nine, stumbled, and fell face first into the corner. It was revenge and redemption in one single right hand.

A few weeks before the fight it had been the end for Maloney; after twelve years and forty-one fights he was not with Lewis in Vegas. He found out he'd been sacked while roller-blading in Venice Beach, California. Maloney was offered a deal to remain and he called it a 'slave contract'. It was also revealed that a detective agency had been hired by members of Team Lewis to investigate Maloney. There was bold talk of racketeering, looting and defrauding. Nothing was ever proved and they were a disgraceful set of accusations. Pride clearly influenced his decision to walk. 'He's on two per cent – that's 240,000 for this fight,' said Warren. 'He's fucking crazy, he thinks he can get more for the book.' The book, *From Peckham to Las Vegas: No Baloney*, came out in 2003. It made some lawyers rich.

Back in April, Naseem Hamed landed in Las Vegas after a comedy camp in California. A film was made, with Hamed's assistance, of the preparation for his fight with Marco Antonio Barrera. In the film a confused, annoyed and disturbed Steward is asked about a sparring session he has just seen. He looks grim; Hamed looked terrible.

Barrera had avoided Hamed, and that is not open for debate. When Hamed was at his best the demands and ducks by Barrera were ludicrous. Now, the time was right for the brilliant Mexican. On the night, in front of 12,847 at the MGM, Hamed was poor, never really in the fight. I'm not sure I can think of a single British boxer whose career has been defined by just one single fight. It is always the Barrera loss – never Barrera avoiding him, never any of the wins, never the crowds, never the unforgettable nights, the ones in small venues long before he was a world champion. No, it all comes down to the Barrera fight, the shorts with 'Islam' on the back and a thousand pictures of him missing wildly or getting caught flush with hands down. Barrera boxed, picked his punches and stuck with a plan. Hamed had no plan, just his fists: in thirty-five fights that had been enough. Barrera had not wasted the years he kept Hamed waiting; Hamed, sadly, had. He talked of a rematch, but nobody was really listening.

Steward walked away wearily, insisting that he would need total control next time. Hamed limped away in shock, not making excuses and not offering any answers. He had started as a betting favourite and on the night maybe won three rounds.

There was briefly a chance of a dreadful April hat-trick of British defeats: Hamed went, then Lewis, and finally Joe Calzaghe was fighting Mario Veit, who was unbeaten in thirty. Calzaghe dropped him twice and stopped him in just 1:52 of the first to retain his WBO super-middleweight title in Cardiff. 'Joe is not like the other two, Joe lives and breathes boxing,' said Enzo Calzaghe. Later in the year Calzaghe had an easy win on the undercard when Mike Tyson fought in Copenhagen.

Audley Harrison finally named an opponent and May for his debut. The opponent was called Mike Middleton and one of his jobs was to work under cover at Disney World. He was brave and tough and he talked even braver and tougher. 'I'm all about heart and I never stop fighting,' he boasted. However, a sheet with his boxing record was given to the press and there was a sixty-day medical suspension on the bottom of it. That was the first of the errors by the men Audley had hand-picked to manage and promote him. The second was not to cross out a tiny piece in the standard British Boxing Board of Control contract. The failure to do so cost Audley about $40,000 because it entitled Middleton to a slice of the television revenue. The third mistake was not to know that Middleton was planning an unlicensed fight in Essex with an underground promoter. The fourth mistake was not to keep a close watch on Middleton, and that meant he could vanish. He did so, emerging smiling and joking at Frank Warren's office four days before the fight. Warren and Harrison had failed to agree a deal after the Olympics. 'I'm not a control freak,' said Harrison, which was questionable at the time. 'But, a lot of people have been shafted in boxing.' Harrison was only going to be part of the business on his terms and he was upsetting boxing people from the start.

Middleton's new agent was Andy Ayling, who had worked for Warren since the early nineties. 'This is diabolical,' he said. 'They have tried to deprive my boxer of the money he is due.' Nobody had tried to deprive him, the mistake was clerical, and it enhanced his fee. The BBC's Head of Sport, Peter Salmon, who had put in place Audley's deal with the broadcaster, had to call Colin McMillan, the former world champion, who was Audley's manager, to tell him the fight with Middleton had to happen. It was a ridiculous situation and McMillan and promoter Jess Harding had other boxers ready to replace Middleton. Two fighters were warming up at Wembley in the hour before the first bell, stripped, bandaged and ready: Gary Williams and Paul Fiske were both optimistic. However, a quick meeting took place at one end of Middleton's dressing room less than forty-five minutes before the first bell. Ayling was there, the Board's Robert Smith was the arbitrator, and Harrison's powerful legal double act, Jonathan Crystal and Robert Davis, were battling to keep the fight in bed. I was a silent witness to the deal. Big Mike was all set, the fight was on, and Williams and Fiske could get dressed. Middleton improved his pay from $5,000 to over $45,000. There was a rematch fee of $8,000 agreed. He is the highest-paid six-round fighter in British boxing history.

'I'm not a great fighter,' said Middleton. 'I will never be a contender, but I'm doing a service for all boxers.'

Somewhere in the background, lurking with a smile on his face, was Johnny Bos, the great fight fixer who had helped Mickey Duff make Frank Bruno twenty years earlier. It was Wembley, it was Bos, and it was over quick, just like the old days. The crowd of 8,000 loved it, and on the BBC over 6 million watched. Big Aud was big business. Middleton never quit, he went down swinging like he promised, and the fight finished at 2:45 of the first. It was a good watch until the end. Harrison did conduct himself with some dignity when the tone of the post-fight conference turned apocalyptic: the gold-medal hero had been a professional boxer for just 165 seconds and the end of his career was being discussed. 'This is just the start of the journey, stick with me,' said Harrison. It sounded more like a plea, and that is a shame.

In Belfast in June, Carl Froch won England's first medal at the world amateur championship, and ten minutes later David Haye won the second; Froch lost in the middleweight semi-final for bronze and

Haye went through at heavyweight to the final. He forced the Cuban Odlanier Solis to take an eight count in the first round of the final after Haye looked like he had delivered a knockout punch. Haye won silver when he was stopped on his feet in the third. 'I hit him with a right uppercut and I saw him go,' said Haye. 'He drops and then he wakes up.' Solis won three world championships and an Olympic gold in 2004. The success of Froch and Haye, both of whom had tried and failed to reach the Sydney Olympics, was a pivotal event in many ways for GB amateurs and over the next dozen or so years British boxers won medals of all colours at every major global event. The wilderness years of the seventies and eighties were gone.

The British boxing lunatic of the year was Howard Eastman, a man with parrots and demons. He had a televised scuffle with Robert McCracken in Hull at ringside. 'Whose bright idea was it to get these two together?' screamed Sky commentator Ian Darke. Eastman stopped McCracken to retain his British and Commonwealth middleweight titles and win the European belt in April. There was chaos in Eastman's corner and Darkie Smith had to take over. McCracken was dropped in the tenth, stopped, and never complained. He would later train Eastman.

The win secured Eastman a trip to Las Vegas and a fight with William Joppy for the vacant WBA middleweight title. Eastman blew the fight, it's that simple. He never worked enough. Joppy finished with the left side of his face a swollen mess and he was dropped heavily in the last. One judge gave Eastman the last 10-7, the other two went 10-8. It was not enough, and the scores were 113-113 and two for Joppy 115-112 and 114-112. The real story of the fight was Eastman's furious fall-out with New Yorker Al Bonanni in the corner. Bonanni kept pushing Eastman to do more work and to stop showboating. 'I told the kid he was fucking up, he had the fight won if he got busy, and he told me I was sacked, and I told him I resigned!' Bonanni said. Eastman wanted to report Bonanni to the local commission for abusive language. But Bonanni was right: in Las Vegas against Joppy, Eastman missed a chance. He would get another world title fight in 2005, and was still boxing in Jamaica in 2014.

The Contenders

Ricky Hatton won five WBU light-welterweight fights and all finished inside five rounds. Johnny Nelson added the WBU heavyweight title, which was arranged at just twenty-four hours' notice, to his WBO cruiserweight belt, which he also defended twice. Wayne Alexander was another to agree a fight at short notice – just over twenty-four hours – when he met WBO light-middle champion Harry Simon, and lost in the fifth. 'I couldn't say no,' said Alexander.

There was an ugly end in round three for Bristol's Adrian Stone when he met Shane Mosley for the WBC welterweight title at Caesars Palace in Las Vegas. Stone was out before he hit the canvas. Shane stood over him, concerned. Stone recovered, but took eighteen months out from the ring.

Glenn Catley went on the road to Quebec and lost in round seven to Eric Lucas for the vacant WBC super-middle title. The proliferation of titles meant that Peter Culshaw defended his WBU flyweight title and never fought Damaen Kelly, who defended his WBU version. The British champion at fly was Jason Booth and he never defended his title in 2001. More titles and less clarity.

Michael Gomez lost, won and then defended his British super-featherweight title. Gomez had been born in a ditch when his dad crashed the car carrying his pregnant mother. Life had not got any easier. 'He has bad friends and they are like cling film,' said Brian Hughes, who worked with the boxer. Robin Reid, another Hughes fighter, defended his WBF super-middleweight title four times in 2001. Reid holds a bizarre British record: he fought for seven different versions of the world title. He held three.

In a genuine crossroads fight Scott Harrison stopped Steve Robinson in November for the British featherweight title. Robinson had been part of a boxing fairy-tale, had held the WBO featherweight title, and made seven defences; Harrison would win the same belt the following year. Harrison's endgame would be grisly.

From the Notepad

A Belgian dentist called Phillipe Fondu told a small lie to a big Russian in November. 'Hey, Steve, I said that York Hall is the Madison Square Garden of London,' Fondu recalled. 'He was very excited.' The Russian, a kid called Alexander Vasiliev, lost to Johnny Nelson. The vacant WBU heavyweight title was the prize. Fondu was a crucial element from about 1990 in the British boxing business, importing losers week after week. He'd once had a career in big game hunting.

Floyd Mayweather Sr shared his thoughts on a beaten Naseem Hamed. 'The greatest circus in the world just got condemned: Prince Naz needs a whole new makeover. I'm not the guy to change it. You know why? You ain't got nothing to work with.'

In the weeks of confusion before Audley Harrison named his opponent I grabbed Johnny Bos to try and talk specifics. 'If I go and give you the names and you run the names in your paper, what would he need me for?' Bos told me. 'He would be getting it all for free, and I'm not big on giving it all away for free.'

In June at Wembley, Eric Esch aka Butterbean weighed 23st 13lb when he flattened Doncaster's Shane Woollas in round one. 'He might be fat, but he can't half whack,' Woollas said. The show flopped.

2002

'Mickey Duff did every possible thing he could to keep me from being a success and I did every possible thing that I could to make him lose sleep. We would sit around thinking of ways to wind him up. As soon as we got him ranting and raving we were happy.'
Frank Warren

'I might stammer, some people might say I'm stupid, but I'm not going to be one of those boxers who will end up skint.'
Herbie Hide

THEY STOOD AND looked at each other over the heads of security guards, swapping malevolent stares in the Memphis ring just seconds before the start of the fight that took six years to make. Mike Tyson and Lennox Lewis began their unfinished business without shaking hands.

They had thrown punches, bitten each other and traded the lowest insults during months of selling. A date at the MGM had fallen through and Las Vegas lost out on one final carnival celebration of Tyson's life. Lewis needed a tetanus jab for the bite on his thigh after an aborted conference in New York in January. 'I don't hate him, I just want to beat him,' said Lewis. At the same conference Lewis connected with a right.

In the days before the first bell, as the city filled with craziness, the boxers were at locations in Tunica, a sad gambling retreat sixty minutes from Memphis, and the contrast was brutally clear: Lewis was calm, Tyson as agitated as a junkie late on Saturday night. 'I'm ready to crush his skull and shut up his cheerleader [Manny Steward],' he said in Tunica that week when three busloads of press had driven to him. In Maui, a few weeks earlier, he had gathered in a splendid flowered garden to open his heart. 'I have episodes and sometimes I have episodes at work,' said Tyson. 'No one cares about my health as a person – people only care if I'm healthy enough to fight.' Steward was worried about Lewis getting disqualified. 'If he hits me after the bell, which is one of his favourite fouls, I will hit him back,' Lewis vowed. 'I'm not afraid to go back at him.'

Tyson had lost 60lb to get his body ready. Lewis was 15lb heavier, five or six inches taller, and he had a thirteen-inch reach advantage. Tyson had none of the skills he'd had ten or more years earlier. Lewis was a slight betting favourite, but only slight.

In the ring Lewis was flawless, savage and pitiful. Tyson was fighting a lost cause. 'Get this man out of there before you get caught with some crazy shit – this man is finished,' said Steward at the end of the fourth round. A round later he was even stronger: 'You got a dead man in front of you – let shit go and let's finish this motherfucker.' Lewis kept moving, jabbing and looking for openings. This was never going to be a stupid fight.

At the end of round seven there was despair in Tyson's corner. He was cut over and next to both eyes, and in the round Lewis had been brilliant. 'You got to turn it ugly, man,' implored Tommy Shields. Tyson looked up in shame: 'I can't get off, I'm done.' Lewis was ready for the eighth. Tyson sucked in a breath and stepped forward to the slaughter. It was arguably his bravest act as a boxer.

Tyson went forward, two jabs and a right forcing Lewis to the ropes. Then the jab started again. Lewis connected with a right uppercut, then a left, and Tyson's legs folded. His heels hit his arse but he did not go down. The ref stepped in and gave Tyson an eight count. There was bedlam. 'You OK, Mike?' Eddie Cotton asked. Tyson nodded but stood still, and over came Lewis. Right uppercut, right cross. Bang, bang. Tyson never turned away and he never threw a punch. One single right ended it, and Tyson twisted like poured syrup to the canvas. He was looking up at the lights, ignoring the noise, blood from each cut slowly flowing down his cheek and dripping to the canvas. He moved at seven, nearly got up before the count was over. I was standing there watching this. The official time was 2:25 of round eight.

'I apologized to Lennox for all the things that were said,' said Tyson, his face still wet with blood and tears. 'I love Lennox, I respect him; he was a master boxer tonight. I would love another chance, I would appreciate that.' There was no chance, no appetite for a repeat of the beating.

A few weeks before he travelled to Portland, Oregon to fight Roy Jones Jr for six different world title belts, Clinton Woods took the *Sun*'s Pat Sheehan carp fishing. Woods caught a two-pounder. 'Pat, tell 'em it was at least three pounds,' said Woods. That was typical of him. 'If he has a bad night and I have a very good night, I can win,' Woods said when he arrived. At his side Dennis Hobson, the Sheffield scrap dealer, his friend and promoter, nodded. 'It's a hard night, make no mistake,' he said. Hobson had managed to get Woods $900,000. Jones claimed that he wanted to fight Woods in Sheffield and insisted that the BBC, who would screen it, put him on *Top of the Pops* with one of his songs. The BBC agreed and then Jones changed his mind and Woods packed his bags for the long trip. Jones was the best fighter in the world right then.

'I will never be in a blood, sweat and guts type fight,' said Jones. 'I'm Roy Jones Jr, not Rocky Balboa.' Six months later he gained 20lb and won the heavyweight world title in Las Vegas when he easily beat John Ruiz. He was a master.

In Portland that September night Woods had no fear. It was finally over after eighty-nine seconds of round six. Woods was out on his feet when Hobson threw in the towel. 'The first thing I did after the fight was thank Dennis,' said Keith Woods, Clinton's dad. 'I know how brave he is. He was never going to quit.' The ref had come over at the end of the fifth and was in danger of getting assaulted for asking if Woods was prepared to continue.

Woods had held the British, Commonwealth and European

light-heavyweight titles to earn the Jones fight. He had done it the old way, the way the men did in the seventies. He would win a world title three years later.

It was a big year for Ricky Hatton, and it started in February when 12,000 people paid to watch him beat Mikhail Krivolapov at the MEN in Manchester. The figure was a shock: Hatton with his WBU light-welterweight title and a career fought exclusively on Sky had become a major attraction. It ended in the ninth.

In June over 18,000 were in the same arena and Hatton started as a slight betting underdog against Belfast's Eamonn Magee. Magee was the Commonwealth champion and the survivor of a near fatal assault or two and a punishment shooting – he was shot in the leg by the IRA in 1992. He was a proper handful. 'Hatton is easy to hit, he never moves his head, he can't back up, he marks up – this could be one of my easiest fights,' said Magee. The show was given the title Anarchy in the UK. Johnny Rotten considered an offer to introduce the fighters. In round one Hatton was over for the first time in his career. He survived the round, and the rest of the fight was hard. At the end Hatton took a close decision. 'I have no idea what Magee is made of,' Hatton told me late that night. 'I hit him with everything. He never moved.' Magee quit in 2007. He lost six times in total and was never stopped. He beat good fighters, but his loss to Hatton was special. In 2015 Magee's son, also called Eamonn, was stabbed and killed. He was just 22.

In Hatton's third fight of the year the ring was invaded by the father and trainer of his opponent. Hatton was always a rough/dirty fighter. In round one, and at the start of two, against Kentish Town's Stephen Smith there had been a few elbows, shoulders and butts going in. At the end of the first a right dropped Smith and he was cut by the right eye. The pressure continued in the second and Smith's eyebrow was split by a wayward elbow. A body shot landed and he was down again. He was hurt, and that was when Darkie Smith left the corner, climbed through the ropes and got involved. Darkie showed Mickey Vann, the ref, what had happened. Stephen tried to steer Darkie out of the ring. Vann kept his distance as Darkie trundled, seething, back to the corner. 'Ricky was butting and using his elbows and I couldn't let that happen – I would not have let that happen to any of my fighters, not just my son,' said Darkie. The fight was over after twenty-eight seconds of round two: Vann disqualified Smith for the invasion of his dad. 'Darkie jumped in there to save his son getting hurt, that's all it was,' said Ray Hatton, Ricky's dad.

In Newcastle at the end of the year Hatton knocked out Joe Hutchinson in the fourth. All year Hatton had been stalked by Junior Witter, who was the British champion. 'He is afraid to fight me and at each of his fights I get surrounded by security,' said Witter. Hatton was just starting to get angry with his would-be rival: 'He is annoy-ing me now and I hope a fight at Maine Road can be arranged for next year.' It never was – they never fought.

There was a harsh start to the year for Joe Calzaghe in April when 5,000 watched his WBO super-middle defence against Charles Brewer, who had to lose 2lb at the weigh-in. The first round was so good that nobody heard the bell. Brewer, the man that had rallied to stop Herol Graham in 1998, had been dismissive of the Welshman: 'I look at Calzaghe and I see a boy – he can't move, he can't punch, and I will show that he can't take a punch.' Calzaghe won clearly on points. In the summer, 6,000 came out to the castle in Cardiff to watch twelve rounds as Calzaghe beat Miguel Jiménez. It was not a great fight: Calzaghe damaged his left hand again and Jiménez just wanted to survive. There was a streaker at one point.

In November a deal was reached to fight Bernard Hopkins, possibly at the Millennium Stadium in Cardiff the following April. That never happened. In December in Newcastle, alongside Hatton, Calzaghe stopped Tocker Pudwill – which is one of boxing's finest names – in two rounds in front of 11,500. Calzaghe and Hatton would dominate British boxing for another six years.

After three fights in his first year there were five in 2002 for Audley Harrison. His win over Dominic Negus in July was lively. Negus touched down in round four and Harrison took an illegal shot. Negus jumped up, ran over and butted Harrison. Two blatant fouls, but no chance of a double disqualification; Harrison won on points after six. 'I admit to getting a bit over the top, but he took a liberty with that punch,' said Negus.

Harrison had his first professional fight in America in November on the Arturo Gatti and Micky Ward undercard in Atlantic City. Two days before the fight he kept me waiting for sixty minutes for an interview. He was there the whole time on the beach, twenty metres away, on one of his phones. I guess I deserved it: I had been truthful about some of his performances. Harrison stopped Shawn Robinson in the first. He had thirty-one words in the local paper. 'Robinson was not a bum when [Danny] Williams stopped him, now I stop him and he's a bum. It is not fair,' said Big Aud. That's his opinion.

In Glasgow another Harrison, Scott the featherweight, won a throwback fight when he beat Julio Pablo Chacón for the WBO featherweight title in October. Chacón had stopped István Kovács, the man Naseem Hamed vacated the title to avoid, to win the belt and made two defences before Harrison beat him. At ringside people hugged at the final bell. Jim Watt and Ken Buchanan were there to salute their heir in front of 5,000. At the hotel, Chacón's people were angry with the scores and accosted Dave Parris, one of the judges. Dave is a big lump and that complaint was dealt with very easily.

Hamed was back in London for a fight in May, and it was bewildering. He easily beat Spain's Manuel Calvo on points, but from the seventh the punters at the ExCel (12,000 tickets were sold) left in their thousands. It was Hamed's first fight since the Marco Antonio Barrera loss and much was expected, promised and not delivered by the fallen maestro. 'I understand the booing, they don't under-stand the art of boxing,' said Hamed at the end. Manny Steward was gone, and Oscar Suárez, who was a nice fella, worked solo.

Hamed had lost 40lb for the IBO featherweight title fight and still failed at the weigh-in. He was talking of a Barrera rematch, three fights with HBO, and dominance once again. Very few of us were listening as he rambled on. I had been smuggled in after a successful request from Team Hamed for me not to be part of Sky's broadcast team for the fight. I did a preview show with Ian Darke for Sky on the

Friday night, Team Hamed complained, and I had to be sneaked in twenty-four hours later. Hamed never fought again. It was one of the saddest nights I have had at ringside.

At the Commonwealth Games in Manchester in July and August there was a fabulous vanishing act by David Haye. He won a fight, then disappeared to London without permission or letting anybody know to have a bicep examined. There was a tear; he was out of contention and unrepentant. 'I was not going to risk my future just for the Commonwealth Games,' insisted Haye. In the finals, David Dolan, Darren Barker and Jamie Arthur won gold medals. The real story was Haye. 'It's odd because the England team will think that it doesn't matter if my arm is hanging off, you still fight, you still want gold,' said Ian Irwin, the squad coach. Over three decades covering the amateurs I saw Irwin stretched to breaking point so many times. He was a decent man.

At the end of the year Haye made his debut behind closed doors at York Hall and forced Tony Booth, who lost for the seventy-third time, to quit with an injured rib after two rounds. It was a Eugene Maloney show (brother of Frank), and the doors were still locked at the old hall because Haye had to fight an hour before they opened and dash to the BBC's Sports Personality of the Year award. He was not yet a contender, but he was a face. He was the one in the white suit sitting next to David Beckham.

The Contenders

At one truly crazy point in May there were twenty-one British world champions, including Lennox Lewis, holding versions of the title sanctioned by men governing the WBC, WBA, IBF, IBO, WBO, WBU, WBF and IBA. That is eight sanctioning bodies at work in Britain and at the same time only nine British title fights took place.

It was, in many ways, a bad year for the domestic scene. Johnny Nelson had a difficult night in Copenhagen, getting up from a knockdown to stop Ezra Sellers in round eight. In November he retained his WBO cruiserweight title for the tenth time with a split draw against Guillermo Jones in Derby. The Entertainer was slowing down and would fight just once each year in 2003, 2004 and 2005.

Takaloo was six when he arrived from Iran. He stacked and rented deckchairs in Margate. In 2002 he defended his WBU light-middleweight title against Gary Logan and lost on points to Daniel Santos for the WBO version in August. 'I still dream of being like Rocky,' Takaloo said.

Colin Dunne lost his WBU lightweight title to David Burke, who had been at the Atlanta Olympics. Dunne, who trained as a jockey until a late growth spurt, fought for and lost a British title fight in 1996 and then won and defended the WBU belt eight times before Burke. At the time Bobby Vanzie was the British lightweight champion but he never defended the title in 2002. Vanzie would walk away from the sport in 2004 to devote his life to the Church.

From the Notepad

When Audley Harrison fought in Atlantic City there was an emotional introduction for Gatti and Ward. Michael Buffer hit his finest form: 'This is for the undisputed never surrender blood and guts championship of the world.' Nice.

In October there was a murmur that Hamed would return against Manuel Medina in 2003 with Maurice Core, former British light-heavyweight champion, in his corner. Never happened.

At the Tyson–Lewis fight a section of the car park at the Pyramid was converted into a harem and touting empire. Tickets were going cheap in the last hours before the fight. There were many colourful deals available in that sideshow retreat. I toured the site with Crocodile, part of Tyson's retinue. After the fight one fan was shot dead and another shot in the face. I left at four a.m. after my TalkSport duties and the city was horrible.

2003

'If you let fighters fight who they want to fight, the public would have a great night out. However, at the end of the day they would have a short career. You have to learn your craft, get your experience on the undercards and improve: Audley Harrison is not the future of boxing.'
Frank Warren

'The ref was a joke, the scoring was a joke, and I had no chance. It's 2003 and I thought I would get a fair shake.'
Robin Reid on his world title fight in Germany against Sven Ottke

CONCERNED VOICES HAD been raised in private, and in public, and they added intrigue when Vitali Klitschko agreed to fight Lennox Lewis for the heavyweight title in Los Angeles on a June night. Vitali stepped in just two weeks before the fight when Canada's Kirk Johnson injured his chest. Lewis had not fought since the slaughter of Mike Tyson the previous summer and the bold talk of a rematch. Purses in excess of $30 million and showdowns with Vitali all looked like empty boxing chat until Johnson pinged a muscle. Lewis considered the Canadian a bigger threat. I certainly never did.

It was to be the London-born boxer's last fight. The bloody slugfest – it was the night Lewis had a brawl – and the ugliness of Vitali's slashed face in defeat made it an unforgettable fight. Lewis was trailing on all three scorecards when the doctor pulled the Ukrainian out at the end of the sixth round. At the Staples Center in LA they had stood and fought and delighted 15,939 people (8,490 paid) in every round until the end; the crowd booed and jeered the merciful conclusion. Klitschko required plastic surgery to close the holes and punctures on the left side of his face. 'They were caused by punches, not butts,' insisted Lewis. 'He is claiming they were butts. I was ready to take him out.' A total of nearly seventy stitches sealed Vitali's face and made him human again.

'I will know when it is time to quit, and that time is not now,' insisted Lewis. 'I will give him a rematch and bust up the other side of his face.' The line got a few laughs, but was a bit disrespectful. 'He has never fought as badly as that,' insisted Manny Steward. Lewis was also the heaviest he had weighed in forty-four fights, and at 37 he had nothing left to prove. He would have got to Vitali and, anyway, winning on cuts your fists have inflicted is a legitimate way to win. There was no trickery, no foul play at work. Lewis opened up Klitschko's face and the doctor was right. We started to miss big Lennox the next morning.

In the same month there was a sensational short fight in Cardiff when Joe Calzaghe met Byron Mitchell. It was over in the second – the type of round that wins Round of the Decade titles. Mitchell had lost his WBA super-middleweight title on a split decision to Germany's Sven Ottke in March. It had been a cruel decision; he was younger than Joe and had never been stopped. In round two Calzaghe was dropped for the first time in thirty-six professional and more than 120 amateur contests. He was gone – I was ten feet away, standing up and watching his eyes. Mitchell smiled at his corner. Calzaghe's eyes went from glazed to icy-cold clear in a second as he stood, and he was angry. Then it was Mitchell's turn to go over, stumbling and hurt. The American beat the count but had no reply to Calzaghe's next attack. It was over officially at 2:36 of that second round.

'I will know when to quit,' said Calzaghe. 'I will not go out like Lennox risking my reputation in fights like that.' Lewis–Klitschko had taken place the previous Saturday.

After the win there were the usual frustrating claims and counter-claims about big fights. It is a feature of British boxing that good fighters always want big fights and they are not easy to arrange; the proliferation of belts had made the situation worse, the task even trickier. 'I have been promised some of the best fighters in the world over the last five years and have had to just sit and watch as they have refused to fight me,' said Calzaghe. The fighters had also been able to win other world titles, get a good living and not worry about Calzaghe. The perfect example was Ottke, the IBF champion. He was world champion from 1998 until 2004, lived just a few hundred miles away in Berlin, and beat six Calzaghe victims in his twenty-two world title fights. Sven, who spoke perfect English, was a nice guy and he retired undefeated after thirty-four fights in 2004.

Late that night in Cardiff, Frank Warren was talking and eating fish. 'The deal with [Bernard] Hopkins was done last year, it was done; Hopkins then demanded that his £1.8 million purse be doubled. Just like that.'

Calzaghe was out until the following February, the big fights he wanted still nearly three years away.

After easing back under the radar in 2002 following his long-overdue medical clearance, Wayne McCullough moved to featherweight, travelled to Glasgow in March, and fought Scott Harrison for the WBO bauble. McCullough had failed a routine brain scan in October 2000 when a cyst on his brain, which had shown on scans in 1993 and 1995, was suddenly deemed a risk. He kept passing scans, the British Boxing Board of Control kept refusing him. In 2002 things changed, he fought in Belfast, and then secured the Harrison fight.

It was a rough night for Wayne and the fight could have been stopped at any point beyond round eight. At the end of the eighth, Peter Harrison, in his son's corner, looked across the ring at Kenny Croom, in McCullough's corner, and motioned for him to stop it. He never did. At ringside there were calls for McCullough to be rescued, saved from his own proven bravery, but he survived until the end. He went off to hospital to recover. The decision was a shut-out and the celebrations muted.

At the post-fight conference Harrison was asked about McCullough's condition and replied, 'My job's to just keep fighting:

the corner, the referee, his manager – it's their job to stop it at the right time.' It was a fine statement. McCullough's manager, who was sat at ringside ignoring all cries to end the fight, was his wife, Cheryl.

In July, Harrison got it all wrong and lost the title on a split to the Mexican Manuel Medina. There had been rumours before the fight about Harrison's lifestyle and the boxer had defended his friends: 'It's important to keep your roots, keep your mates. They're no' gaun to try and rip you off.' It was a good fight, and Medina, having his seventy-sixth contest, just did enough. It was his nineteenth world title fight and the fifth time he had won a title. 'I have no idea what went wrong, no excuses and no idea,' said Harrison. The boxer was distraught, leaving the venue with a tiny silent group. There were others, people that knew his late-night habits, with some idea.

The rematch was set for November, back at the Braehead in Glasgow, and Harrison gained 50lb – well, he ran up the foothills of Ben Nevis with a 50lb pack on his back. The boxing scholar had started to lose his way and he was paying penance, pushing his body savagely.

The Braehead was uncomfortable for Medina's return. I had predicted a late stoppage, based on a meeting with Harrison. He was possessed by the July loss, grieving for the defeat, and he started furiously. Medina was over in the first, dropped twice in round ten – bloodied, his nose broken into a grotesque swollen lump – and he was sent down again for the final time after just thirty-one seconds of round eleven. At the end the Scot was up by six points and twice by a score of eight points. Harrison that night was simply irresistible. It's always nice to get a perfect prediction.

After twelve rounds the officials at ringside did their best to turn a great fight into a farce at the MEN in October. In the ring Michael Brodie and In-Jin Chi had fought each other to a standstill, altering each other's features in the process, and they both stood exhausted waiting for the verdict on their vacant WBC featherweight title fight. They had to wait fifteen minutes before a majority win for Chi was announced. It looked like the right decision. It was tight, but Brodie had been dropped in the second and had had a point deducted in the opener for illegal use of his head. The deduction, so early in a fight, seemed terribly harsh. The Korean and his people celebrated and went back to the changing room; the crowd of less than 5,000 traipsed out into the Manchester night. Brodie, with both eyes closed, walked forlornly to his own dressing room.

At ringside, however, a closer look at the scores revealed an error, and fifteen minutes after declaring Chi the winner the result was changed to a draw. The final scores were 113-113 twice and one of 114-112 for Chi. The real travesty is that without the point off in the first round Brodie would have won the title.

At the post-fight fall-out the WBC's boss, the infamous José Sulaimán, forgot he was not in his Mexican stronghold and came close to getting a slap from Steve Lillis, the finest boxing tabloid journalist of his generation. It was both comical and very serious for the pompous Sulaimán. Lillis had asked Sulaimán, who admitted responsibility for the miscalculation, if he was going to suspend himself. It did not go down well with the WBC's El Presidente and to this day Lillis is still unable to travel to Mexico.

Chi was back the following year for the rematch.

In the same month Michael Gomez and a hundred sombrero-wearing fanatics travelled from Manchester to Edinburgh for a lost cause. Gomez was, in his own words, 'a sacrificial lamb' sent to lose against Alex Arthur, the Prince of Edinburgh and the unbeaten British super-featherweight champion. This fight and the tales of the travelling crew of Gomez diehards has become the stuff of legend, the type of night that hundreds have subsequently claimed to have been at. The venue was hostile, as expected. 'They called me Gypsy scum and English bastard,' said Gomez. 'I was born in a ditch, I never had anything – how did anybody think a few words could hurt me?'

There was always a flipside to the anarchic Gomez – the ability to box to rule, to follow instructions and to think. Gomez had left Brian Hughes and was working with Billy Graham; Ricky Hatton was part of the corner. Arthur had been all smiles at the weigh-in but he'd needed three trips to the scales. The fight was over with just two seconds left in the fifth round after Arthur had been dropped three times. He twice jumped up fast, his heart too simple to understand that he was going to lose for the first time and he needed the extra seconds. The Scot had no chance of beating the third count. He was fearless, Gomez was ruthless, and the delight was infectious at the fight with the flying sombreros.

It was, however, the type of fight that leaves both men changed.

The eventful career of Audley Harrison continued with six fights, a hearing, many insults, and his departure for America. At the start he'd talked too much, weighed too much and fought too little. He was a different beast in 2003. In June he announced a change: 'I'm off to America to accelerate the learning curve.' He had three quick wins, one in a Miami nightclub where the tickets were twenty bucks, once he moved his base to the US.

In February there had been an outburst from Harrison after he won in London and his genuine rival, Danny Williams, lost a European title fight in Berlin. Williams was stopped by Sinan Şamil Sam, the Turkish boxer who beat Harrison at the 1999 world amateur championship. 'Danny has been like a cockroach on my back and I'm glad I've washed him off,' Harrison said after watching Williams lose. 'I was his PR machine. He doesn't deserve a fight with me now. He fought like a frightened cat.' It would be two long years before they met. Williams defended both his British and Commonwealth titles later in the year.

Harrison's most notorious fight was at York Hall in May when he stopped Blackpool playboy Matt Ellis in the second. It was a decent win, and Big Aud reminded everybody that twelve months earlier Frank Warren, who had been the Olympic champion's nemesis since Sydney, had offered him half a million to fight Ellis. The deal was withdrawn when Ellis was knocked out by a travelling Kazakh.

At the end of the Ellis fight, Herbie Hide approached the ring. Harrison started talking to him, Hide was talking back, people were jostling, and then it went seriously wrong. Hide had to be ejected, the chairs at ringside were all over the place, and people were trampled. I was part of the BBC broadcast team and we did our post-fight analysis in the middle of a wrecked York Hall. A woman called Flatona Bak wrote a letter of complaint to the *Boxing News*, and the British Boxing Board of Control called an emergency meeting for June. Nobody was hurt, it was all handbags, and twenty minutes after the so-called riot Hide walked back in! I think he'd lost a button off his shirt. At the hearing Harrison and his promoter, Jess Harding, were fined £1,000 and Hide £500. 'It doesn't make sense for a heavy-weight to stay in Britain and moan about their situation,' Harrison said after leaving the hearing in Hammersmith. 'I don't care about the people that want me to fail.' I was not one of the people waving him off.

Ricky Hatton and Junior Witter were matched at Maine Road, the late home of Hatton's beloved Manchester City, for the summer. It never happened. Witter won a version of the European light-welterweight title and Hatton defended his WBU version three times. In March, Hatton went straight to a plastic surgeon to close a cut above his right eye after beating Vince Phillips on points at the MEN. Hatton never lost a round, and every round was hard. 'It was the most vicious fight that I have ever been involved with,' he said. The cut took twenty-two stitches and kiboshed the Witter fight. 'I desperately want that fight,' said Hatton. 'Witter is like a boil on my arse and I want to get rid of him.'

The Contenders

David Starie and Robin Reid both lost decisions to Sven Ottke for the IBF super-middleweight title in Germany. Reid was harshly treated by the referee and at the end of the fight somebody poured a bucket of ice over the ref's head. Also in Germany, in November, there was an escape for Johnny Nelson in his fifty-seventh fight when he narrowly beat Alexander Petkovic to retain his WBO cruiserweight title.

Belfast's Damaen Kelly went to Colombia and lost in a flyweight world title fight to unbeaten Irene Pacheco.

Clinton Woods and Jamaica's Glen Johnson could not be

separated at the end of twelve rounds when they met for the vacant IBF light-heavyweight title in Sheffield. 'I never get justice, never,' Johnson cried at the end. The pair had two more fights, both memorable, and every round, all thirty-six of them, was close. 'I still dream about fighting him,' Woods told me in 2013.

From the Notepad

When Hatton beat Phillips there was a truly unique ticket deal available: Frank Warren offered entry in exchange for a gun, and over a thousand weapons were turned in during the amnesty.

In May, at the first Female National Amateur Boxing Championship, held in Hendon, Nicola Adams won. There was no joy for Tamasin Mallia at bantamweight. She lost for the fourth time. 'Now I have to do the horrible bit,' she told me after the fight. 'I have to call my five-year-old, Tommy, and tell him that I've lost again.'

In Hackney it took me two days but I tracked down Kirkland Laing for a ten-minute BBC film. He was not in a good way, drinking heavily and still doing crack. 'I was a good fighter, I could have been a great fighter,' he told me. He shuffled off, full beard, dog at his side, a cross between a boozed-up Santa Claus and Fagin. Three weeks later he was in intensive care after a suspicious fall from the roof at the flats. I had a call at five a.m. to tell me he had been pushed.

'This stuff is incredible,' said Manny Steward when he was at the Fitzroy Lodge gym in south London. He was talking about some of the contraptions Freddie Hill had removed from his Lavender Hill gym and put on the walls at the Lodge. Steward took pictures. Hill died in April, a great lost coaching guru.

At the London ABA finals Frank Bruno sat down next to me. 'No questions, Mr Bunce,' he said. He then told me that he was coming out of retirement to fight Audley Harrison. 'He's like a ripe orange that is ready to be plucked,' Bruno remarked. Big, sad Frank was sectioned six months later.

2004

*'I consider myself one of the greatest and I know I did it with dignity
and I know I have come out at the right time.'*
Lennox Lewis

*'It was getting closer and closer and Hopkins was getting greedier
and greedier. He never wanted it, he bottled it.'*
Joe Calzaghe on yet another collapsed fight with Bernard Hopkins

THE YEAR BELONGED to an unknown teenager from Bolton and his great Olympic odyssey.

Amir Khan was a late selection for the European championship in February in Pula, Croatia. He was just 17. Many in boxing thought he was too young and he lost to a Georgian in the opening series of fights. Twenty-two other English, Scottish, Welsh and Irish boxers lost in the same round and cried over their ruined Olympic dreams. All medal winners were guaranteed a place in Athens.

Khan was then sent in March to Plovdiv, Bulgaria, where he qualified for the Olympics and won the best boxer of the tournament award. No other British fighter qualified for Athens. Some had five and six fights and fell short.

In June, Khan went to Jeju in South Korea for the under-19 world championship. 'The officials were not happy, but Amir knew he had to go,' said Shah, the boxer's dad, who travelled to America, Greece, Croatia, Bulgaria, Italy, Germany and South Korea with his son in the twelve months before the 2004 Olympics. In Jeju, Khan boxed five times in seven days to win gold, and again he was recognized as the best boxer of the tournament. He was the only winner not from Cuba or the old Eastern Bloc. He beat the Cuban world youth champion, the Kazakh and the Uzbek on his way to gold. The Olympics were less than fifty days away when Khan returned. It was, in any year, a stunning achievement.

However, after an easy win it looked all over in the second round in Athens when Khan met Bulgaria's Dimitar Stilianov. I had asked about a return flight; it was a lost cause, and after the pain of Atlanta, when I sat for too many days not working, I was ready to leave. Stilianov had twice been European champion, including a few months earlier in Pula, and had won a silver medal at the world championship. No British boxer had won a European title since Frankie Taylor in 1961. Khan gave Stilianov a boxing lesson, then he stopped the Asian champion, and in the semi-final he chased the Kazakh. It was crazy. Khan was 17 and in the Olympic final against Mario Kindelán, Fidel Castro's favourite fighter and the reigning world and Olympic champion. Kindelán had won the world amateur title three times, and had beaten Khan at a pre-Olympic event in Athens, the score 33-13. 'I had never ever seen a tape of him, but I left the ring knowing that I could beat him,' said Khan.

The Bolton carnival arrived that final Sunday: the full Khan family, the full Khan friends, and just about every British athlete not competing somewhere. 'I worked all my life for this,' said Mick Jelley, the coach at Bury where Khan boxed. Jelley and Shah had been companions on the road and Shah, at the time, helped out with the juniors at the club. Jelley is still training fighters, and at the Rio Olympics a kid called Muhammad Ali from Bury represented Great Britain. Little Ali started to box because of Amir. 'It makes me so proud,' said Jelley in May 2016.

There were a lot of tears on that final day. Khan pushed and chased the greatest Cuban of his generation, arguably the greatest Cuban amateur ever, until the final bell. It was silver, not gold, but it was not the end. 'Right now, I'm just Amir Khan from Bolton. I have the silver medal from the Olympics, but my story is not finished,' Khan told me three weeks after the Olympics.

In December, just ninety-six days after the final in Athens, Khan fought live on the BBC at the Olympia in Liverpool against an American called Michael Evans. Khan dropped Evans and won easily. It was his nineteenth fight of the year and he was still only 17.

There'd been a claim in October that the ABA would find £70,000 to keep him amateur, and at the same time Frank Warren said that he was not chasing him. There was a plan by Warren to get Khan and some other amateurs on a Joe Calzaghe undercard in February 2005. It never happened, and Khan decided in late December that he would enter the 2005 ABA championship.

At heavyweight, a long way from the Bambi innocence of Khan, there was a spectacular series of fights involving Danny Williams. He lost his British title in January to Michael Sprott, had two quick wins, and was then selected for slaughter by Mike Tyson in late July. It was an odd selection, and an odd homage to Ali from Tyson: the fight took place in Muhammad Ali's hometown of Louisville, and it was all a bit confused. One thing was for certain: Williams was there to lose.

'Tyson is not great any more,' said Williams in the days before the fight. 'I know the first three rounds will be hectic, I know that – after that I can win.' In the gym, over five weeks of training in America, Jimmy McDonnell had worked on his fighter's mental side. McDonnell had eliminated doubt, and in Louisville they were a strange, calm pair. Tyson was working with Freddie Roach and he had brought his pranksters and foul-mouthed jesters as players to his glorious side-show attraction. There was fear in Kentucky for Williams.

In round one Williams took a terrible beating. He could have been stopped if he had shown any weakness to the referee. He survived, and dug his feet in the canvas so deep that it came close to swallowing his boots. He was slugging it out with Mike Tyson in front of 17,000 people in the fight of his life. Tyson was like the old Tyson in the first and the second, and after three Danny was down; but by then Tyson's survival minutes were finished. Williams now had him where he wanted him. What is often missed when the fight is reviewed is the dirty tactics used by Williams. In round three he lost a point for a wayward elbow and another for a low blow. It was all part of an endgame nobody predicted outside of the tiny Williams travelling gang.

It was all over for Tyson in round four. He sat on the canvas after sixteen punches had bounced off his bald head looking out at nothing, his eyes the deadest I have ever seen in a living person. He would have one more fight and dozens more falls before finding something like peace. A Tyson deal with Bob Arum worth $80 million was withdrawn that night. Tyson left the ring in a wheelchair and went off to have his damaged left knee examined. 'Mike got hit with too many punches and he needs to make some decisions,' said Roach.

'I proved I'm a warrior,' said Williams. 'I was not going to lose and I could feel his power going. My plan was to box, but when he hit me in the first, I said, "Yeah, let's go to war." I knew I was here as the knockout job, I was here to be sacrificed.'

There was a massive effort by too many of the press on both sides of the Atlantic to condemn the win once it had happened and that was wrong, unfair on Danny and Jimmy Mac. Tyson had looked sharp all week, he was terrific early in the fight, and there was the Arum deal hanging over the night. It has to be said that Bob Arum does not often make mistakes when he plans a future for a fighter. Danny's win was legit.

'He never spoke to me before, during or after the fight,' said Williams. 'He ignored me and never acknowledged me at the end, and that is a bit strange.'

There was a wonderful surprise for Williams in the ring when Zoe, the mother of his two children, appeared. She was there in secret, Williams had no idea, and he proposed to her after the fight. She accepted.

The win made Williams popular, and before he left Louisville there were offers. Evander Holyfield was mentioned, a rematch with Tyson was an option, but Williams talked of new WBC champion Vitali Klitschko on the night, in the dark hours after glory. 'I want

Vitali, it's that simple,' was his deathless comment. In December, at the Mandalay Bay in Las Vegas, they met.

'Danny can knock out anybody,' insisted Frank Warren. 'He begged me for Vitali and he's got Vitali.' Williams was making $1.3 million. 'The Tyson fight changed my life, but it never changed me – this is the only fight that matters,' said Williams.

The Klitschko fight was horrible to watch. Williams was dropped four times, beaten in every round and stopped in the eighth in front of 9,000 people. He went to hospital for six hours for a scan, to get his eye stitched and his shoulder examined; he was free to leave at dawn. 'I'm not going to quit,' he said. 'Bruno never quit when he lost world title fights and I will never quit.' There were few easy answers to what went wrong in Las Vegas and not one excuse was offered. 'I will not put Danny in a fight like that again,' said Warren. 'He needs to consider his health, not just his money.' Danny Williams would still be fighting and losing a decade later.

'I've been matched in some dumb fights in my life but this is the dumbest,' said Arthur Williams, a former world champion, before he was stopped in the third round by David Haye in May. Haye's next fight, his eleventh, was against Carl Thompson at Wembley in September. Thompson was having his thirty-ninth bout, and was 40; the IBO cruiserweight title was one of the prizes. It was a painful night for Haye and he was stopped on his feet and in the referee's arms in round five. The inquests were held at ringside that night. 'He's ruined now,' said Lloyd Honeyghan. 'He looked real heavy as he got tired,' added Kevin Lueshing. Adam Booth, the man in Haye's corner, kept it positive: 'If he hadn't taken the fight, David wouldn't have learned the lesson. It was still a public humiliation and it should have been a mismatch.' He did learn a lesson or two and had a quick win in December.

Thompson had beaten South Africa's Sebastian Rothman in yet another gruelling classic in February. Thompson was over once, Rothman twice. There had been a problem that night with Thompson's gloves: Richie Davies, the referee, noticed before the first bell that the attachment holding the thumb to the main glove had been cut.

Thompson was suspended for six months by the British Boxing Board of Control and Maurice Core, his friend and trainer, was initially refused a new licence. On the night of the Haye fight, Core was in the corner. Thompson had just one more fight, a win, and retired in 2005.

In February, Lennox Claudius Lewis made his retirement from boxing official. The WBC were hounding him, desperate for him to continue fighting and give Vitali a rematch. Lewis did his own thing. He was 38, had fought in seventeen world title fights, and won the title for the first time in 1993. He'd fought and beaten eighteen world champions during his career. 'I'm going out like Rocky Marciano and Gene Tunney,' said Lewis, his mother Violet grinning in the front row. 'They both retired as world champion and like them I will never come back. I consider myself one of the greatest and I know I did it with dignity and I know I have come out at the right time.' There was a standing ovation when he finished talking. He did, for a few years, have to deny rumours of a return. 'It was never close; when I said I was done I was done,' he told me at the Muhammad Ali exhibition in London in early 2016.

Ricky Hatton, Joe Calzaghe and Scott Harrison had a total of nine world title fights during the year. Calzaghe was dropped by the Egyptian Magician, Kabary Salem, in October at a bad time in his life. He was going through a divorce and was still frustrated as he waited for a big fight. Calzaghe had stopped an Armenian in February. The real problem was in June when a fight with Glen Johnson, the IBF light-heavyweight champion, collapsed in the final few days. Calzaghe had a bad back, but he had also been arrested and released after an incident with his wife. It was an ugly time. Johnson, instead, took a fight with and knocked out Roy Jones in a defence.

Hatton won four times, three of them in front of crowds of over 17,000 at the MEN. He had to meet a replacement when Brazil's Kelson Pinto pulled out a few days before a fight, and by October he was not happy. Pinto was unbeaten in twenty-one at the time, nineteen of them quick; in September he lost to Miguel Cotto for the WBO light-welterweight title. 'That was my fight,' Hatton said. 'I want it written in capital letters that I will fight anyone, and it's not about the money. I'm sick of excuses – they are bad for me because they make me look like the one that never wanted the fight.' Hatton was a very angry man.

Harrison walked through three fighters at the Braehead, including his mandatory and a man that had never been stopped. He won in the fifth, the third and the first rounds. In July he was cleared of assault. It was the start of the chaos for Scott.

The other Harrison, Big Aud, remained unbeaten, won three times, and in March picked up the WBF heavyweight title when he stopped the Dutch Richel Hersisia in four rounds at Wembley. He made the front cover of *Ring* magazine the same month, one of three men identified as holding the future of heavyweight boxing in their hands; the other two were Dominick Guinn and Joe Mesi. 'My future in the UK is not looking good,' said Harrison before he met Tomasz Bonin in June. 'I have no idea when I will fight here again – I have not been appreciated.' He was back the following year, in the ring with Danny Williams.

The Contenders

There was no justice for Michael Brodie when In-Jin Chi returned to Manchester: Brodie was stopped in round seven of his WBC featherweight fight.

In September, Johnny Nelson moved closer to inevitable retirement when he retained his WBO cruiserweight title and stopped Rüdiger May in seven rounds. The same month, Carl Froch won the vacant British super-middleweight title in one round against Derby's Damon Hague. Froch had won the Commonwealth title in March. That night in Nottingham both Froch and Hague went to the ring before the fight to ask for calm from the Derby County and Nottingham Forest fans in the audience. There was no trouble. He was still four years away from the world title.

The IBO dominated with twenty-one fights, four featuring British boxers in both corners. There was a return for Argentina's Sergio

Martínez, who stopped Richard Williams to retain his IBO light-middleweight title. Martínez stopped Williams and Adrian Stone in Britain in 2004, and by 2011, when he was the middleweight world champion, he was one of the biggest stars in boxing.

The Brian Magee and Robin Reid IBO super-middleweight fight at the King's Hall in Belfast in June was a bit wild. Magee was over twice, lost a point for hitting and holding, and lost his title on points. Reid was roared home from ringside by his friend the Snowman, who had been in Milan, Newcastle and Nuremberg for all of his world title fights.

From the Notepad

When Clinton Woods lost a tight decision to Glen Johnson in February for the IBF light-heavyweight title, Neil Port was part of his corner. Porty, who was 40, was a big lump, 16st and 6ft 2in, but in October he decided he wanted to be known as Penny. Nobody in the Sheffield boxing business was bothered when he showed up in a boozer wearing a dress. 'He's Porty, he's me mate,' said Woods. Seven days before Christmas, Porty was stabbed and killed. The doctors fought for five hours to save him – he was tough. In 2005, Porty's eldest son was sentenced to six years for the manslaughter of his father.

In June, Audley Harrison wrote a letter to Vic Wakeling, the head of Sky Sports, offering to co-promote a British title fight against British heavyweight champion Matt Skelton. It never happened.

In April, a man called Maurice 'Termite' Watkins arrived at the Fitzroy Lodge gym in south London with eight potential Iraqi Olympians. Five other boxers and two officials had been stopped and held at the Kuwaiti border by Special Forces. Watkins had fought for the world title one night in Las Vegas on a Muhammad Ali undercard before working in pest control and getting the gig in Baghdad to kill giant rats: they were feeding on the dead. Watkins had got a boxing programme going in 2003. He managed to get one fighter to Athens. 'Termite seems like a nice enough fella,' said Mick Carney, the boss at the Lodge. 'He's not all the ticket, but I admire his guts.'

In Bolton, six weeks after the Olympics, I went with Amir Khan to the Kebabish Chippie. Every dish had 'Amir' or 'Khan' in the name. We still queued for our food. Amir was like that.

2005

'Boxing is a sport where a lot of guys get publicity that can't fight and a lot of guys who can't get publicity can fight.'
Howard Eastman, the fighting philosopher of Battersea

'The closest that he's ever been to fifteen stone was when he was on a pebble beach.'
Dean Powell on yet another hefty heavyweight import

ONE OF THE finest nights in British boxing history took place in Manchester in June when Ricky Hatton met Kostya Tszyu for the IBF light-welterweight title. The doors were locked before midnight at the MEN, the bars finally closed, and for about an hour 22,000 stood and sang in hope and anticipation.

Hatton was unbeaten in thirty-eight fights and had never been anywhere near a fighter like Tszyu. The Russian-born Australian, known as the Thunder from Down Under, was on a run of nine world title wins, seven of them quick, and getting him to Manchester for a two a.m. fight had cost Frank Warren a lot of money. Tszyu had beaten the very best at his weight, including Sharmba Mitchell in three and Zab Judah in two; Floyd Mayweather was not interested after watching Tszyu ruin men he knew.

Hatton and Billy Graham entered the ring with a version of 'Blue Moon' filling the sweltering arena with noise. They were the underdogs, a couple of friends with too many memories, and the Tszyu fight was finally the real test. 'I asked for it, I got it, and I had to prove

I could win it,' said Hatton. The fight was relentless, brutal, and so technical at times that Hatton had to fight for every inch. He also responded to Tszyu's dirty tactics with a series of borderline shots, including a damaging full-contact hit below the belt in round nine; Australian reports insisted that their defeated hero was forced to pass blood after the fight. Slowly Tszyu started to lose the fight, and by about round eight he had begun to surrender a few inches. At the end of round eleven he looked a forlorn figure as he stumbled back, bruised, cut and aching in every part, to his corner. Hatton sat down at the same time, looked up at Graham, and the pair knew that the final three minutes would be the hardest of his life. 'I never had a lot left, I was knackered, but I knew I had three minutes,' said Hatton. Tszyu had less. 'He's gone, he's finished,' Graham insisted. At that point Hatton was leading by one round, three rounds and five rounds. All he had to do was stay on his feet.

In Tszyu's corner the veteran Johnny Lewis, the Australian Angelo Dundee, looked at his boxer and then glanced across at Hatton. 'I didn't want to put Kostya in a position I would have regretted and I told him that the fight was over. He looked down, and that was it.' Two days later, when Tszyu and Lewis arrived in Sydney for a press conference, Lewis was embraced by Tszyu's wife. 'She thanked me, and that was the only confirmation I needed – I did the right thing.'

After the fight there was a split with Warren, who had paid Hatton over £6 million during his career. It was not a pretty split, but they never are in the boxing business.

Hatton worked with Sheffield's Dennis Hobson for his fight in November when he added the WBA light-welterweight title to the IBF belt. He stopped Carlos Maussa in round nine with a brutal finish from a single left hook in front of 12,000 in Sheffield. Maussa had knocked out Vivian Harris to win the title in June, and Harris had been one of Hatton's biggest critics. Harris had also asked for too much money to fight Hatton.

By two a.m. Hatton was finished with the plastic surgeon: a total of fourteen stitches had been used to close cuts over his left and right eye. The bad cut over the left had happened in the first thirty seconds of round one. During the fight Mick Williamson, aka the Rub, had worked like a lunatic, his magic swabs, all soaked in adrenalin, a blur in each hand as he fought to close the wounds and keep Hatton in the fight. Hatton had been too excitable, too wound up, and that made him fight reckless. Stuart Pearce, the Manchester City manager, had carried Hatton's belt to the ring. 'I could feel the tears before the first bell,' he admitted. The Maussa win is always overlooked.

Naseem Hamed was ringside with Hatton's friend, Marco Antonio Barrera. 'I will be back, next summer, and I would like Marco again,' said Hamed, who was 31 that night; the IBF and WBC champions at featherweight were both 32. 'I'm looking at offers at the moment,' he added. It never happened.

It was the end for Scott Harrison. Incidents away from the ring increased, and in the ring he was fortunate to escape with a draw in January's defence against Victor Polo, who is possibly one of the unluckiest boxers in history. The Colombian had lost three split-decision world title fights before the draw with Harrison.

Hanging over the Scot's head was an assault charge against a policeman after a struggle in a taxi, and he was banned from every pub and club in East Kilbride. After the Polo fight he talked of envy and betrayal. 'There is always somebody that says something,' Harrison said. 'All I want is a quiet drink and somebody has to say something. I do have a short fuse, and that causes problems.' There would be more arrests and more sad skirmishes over the next twelve months as his life collapsed. In May 2006 he was arrested at the Lomond Park Hotel 'on suspicion of possession of drugs'. The charges were later dropped. He had been out of the ring six months at that point and would not fight again until 2012. A lot of fights were made, then scrapped, and Harrison was involved in some horrible incidents. He needed help in late 2004, not bollocking and condemning in 2006. In harsh terms, he was an addict.

In June he met Michael Brodie in Manchester in a show the night before Hatton–Tszyu. 'He's already talking about retirement and that is never a good sign,' said Harrison. It ended for Brodie after forty-six seconds of round four. Brodie took four years out, returned in 2009, and lost his last fight to Anthony Crolla. There had been some bad blood with Brodie for a few years – Brodie had twice pulled out of fights with Harrison after Warren had won purse bids – so it was a satisfying win for Harrison. The Mancunian had held the British title back in 1997 after a great fight with Neil Swain, lost a disputed world title fight in 2000, and met In-Jin Chi twice. Brodie had some problems away from the ring too, and Harrison was too much on the night.

The last fight of Harrison's WBO reign was against Australian Nedal Hussein at the Braehead in November. It was the Scot's eleventh consecutive WBO title fight. Harrison had gone back to the foothills of Ben Nevis to prepare; his body looked good but his face had the tight lines of a man suffering under an addiction or two. He won comfortably over twelve rounds, but the real fight was on the safe side of the ropes, and he was losing that one. The people close to him knew that he was in turmoil. 'He was a troubled young man,' said Frank Maloney. He certainly was. He was also a terrific fighter.

In 1997, Clinton Woods won the vacant Commonwealth super-middleweight title; two years later he won the British light-heavyweight title; and in 2002, 2003 and 2004 he failed in world title fights. He was British boxing's invisible warrior. In March 2005 he met a convicted killer called Rico Hoye from Detroit. Hoye had the swagger and was unbeaten in eighteen fights, with fourteen ending early. The Magna Centre in Rotherham was heaving, and Woods bashed Hoye from corner to corner and stopped him late in the fifth. Hoye was also the betting favourite.

Woods beat Julio César González over twelve in his first defence in September. Woods went the full twelve rounds thirteen times in his career, and seven were world title fights. That is a proper professional.

It was a fight made in 2000 and spoken about for five years until they finally met in December at the ExCel. Audley Harrison was back from making his fortune in America, and Danny Williams was still recovering from meeting Mike Tyson and Vitali Klitschko in a twenty-week period in 2004. The vacant Commonwealth heavy-weight title was the side prize to a fight that attracted a big house of 14,000. 'If I can't beat Danny Williams then I'm not the fighter I claim to be,' said Harrison. 'I've had enough of this now,' warned Williams at the final press conference. 'If anything else is said it might just kick off.' Backstage they hated each other.

Harrison, unbeaten in nineteen, started as the favourite. Williams had walked out on a British title fight with Matt Skelton in July, never fully explaining his midnight flit. There was brave talk of a new Audley, the Audley we had only glimpsed so far, and once again there was a fear that Danny the weary hulk would be too slow, would lack edge, and would lose without breaking a sweat. It was, in short, an intriguing fight. Sadly it was poor on the night, and Williams won a split decision. 'Nobody deserved to win,' said Claude Abrams, editor of *Boxing News*, from the seat next to me. He had a point.

Harrison was typically unrepentant about his negative per-formance. 'I heard the jeers, that's expected, it's the anti-hero thing,' he claimed. 'I'm not going to lie, I lost some confidence. If my mind's not focused, I can come across as scared to be hit.' The clutching, hitless waltz did have one knockdown in round ten when Harrison was dropped. He had been dumped by a wild clubbing right, and in that moment the articulate Olympic champion and self-proclaimed future of boxing had looked desperate; not badly hurt, just lost. The jeering crowd stopped, but not for long. Thankfully, 2006 was a much better year for British heavyweights.

'I've got an Olympic medal, I've won three versions of the world title and I've been on the top shelf,' said Robin Reid in August. 'I can beat Lacy.' A week later, talk of a Joe Calzaghe fight with the American intensified when Reid lost to Jeff Lacy in Florida for the IBF and IBO super-middleweight titles. A deal, a verbal deal, was reached for a fight with Lacy in Cardiff in November. It never happened. Reid had been stopped (he retired at the end of round seven), dropped four times, and left the ring convinced that Lacy was dirty and that he would beat Calzaghe. Reid was deducted two points, one for a bad butt and the other for holding to survive. The Lacy win convinced just about everybody that he would easily beat Calzaghe.

In 2005, Calzaghe defended his WBO super-middleweight title twice, going over old ground and stopping Mario Veit in Germany, when he claimed to have put a ten-grand bet on a stoppage win, and in September outpointing Evans Ashira in another shut-out in Cardiff. A fight with Brian Magee collapsed in March, the Lacy fight was pushed back, and there was talk of a move to light-heavyweight for a fight against Clinton Woods. 'He loses all his big fights, he needs me more than I need him,' said Calzaghe. 'Joe Calzaghe has never had a bloody big fight, a hard fight, and he's talking bollocks,' replied Woods.

The last days of Johnny Nelson's career took place in Rome in November. In the ring before the fight against Vincenzo Cantatore there was a bizarre attempt by Nelson to get inside the Italian's head. He performed a quite stunning box splits – that's the one where your legs are out sideways. It was nuts. Nelson won on points, it was a split, and he never fought again. It was his thirteenth defence and the fifty-ninth fight of a career that had started in 1986 in obscurity in Hull with a £300 purse. Nelson lost that one – he lost his first three fights. It had certainly been a hard road to glory for him.

On the undercard in Rome was Enzo Maccarinelli, and the plan was for the pair to meet. A date was arranged, but Nelson had a freak accident while running when his patella tendon snapped. He had an operation on the knee, the Maccarinelli fight was put back, and then Nelson was injured again. The Rome fight was the end for the Entertainer.

It was the start of Amir Khan's professional career in July after several confusing months as an amateur. In February, Khan had entered the ABA championship, fighting in Preston at light-welterweight for the East Lancs, Cheshire, Cumbria and Isle of Man title. It was a boisterous crowd of 3,000 in the Guildhall. In the semi-final Khan was dropped in round four by Craig Watson. He was hurt, but survived to win 21-9, and then beat Liam Dorian in the final. He stopped his next opponent at the Olympia in Liverpool, which was a change in venue to allow 1,100 extra Khan fans in, and then he withdrew. The next round was in Norfolk, at Gorleston near Great

Yarmouth, and Khan's club, Bury, had originally been offered ten tickets. The venue capacity was 820 and a revised offer of forty-five tickets was made. 'What happens if five hundred people show up and I have just ten tickets?' asked Asif Vali, who was Khan's personal manager and a family friend. 'If there is any trouble it will all be blamed on Amir, and that is not fair.' Khan withdrew from the championship.

There was a far more cunning and productive plan. 'I will go back down to sixty kilos to fight Mario Kindelán,' insisted Khan in March. 'I'm getting stronger and he's just getting older.' The fight was made for Bolton in May – Kindelán's last, Khan's goodbye, and the start of ITV's new love affair with the boxing business. Khan won on points and turned professional live on television. 'I plan to leave boxing at twenty-five after winning world titles, because I don't want to keep taking punishment,' Khan said that night.

The first of Khan's four professional fights in 2005 took place back in Bolton when London's David Bailey received two counts of nine and was stopped in 109 seconds in front of 6,000 devoted fans.

The Contenders

It was hard to keep Wayne McCullough down and he lost twice to Oscar Larios for the WBC super-bantamweight title in America. He retired in the Las Vegas rematch in July.

Howard Eastman got another world title fight when he met Bernard Hopkins in LA in February for the WBC, WBA, IBF and WBO middleweight titles. Hopkins was 40, it was his twentieth defence, and he won by nine, six and four rounds on the night. Eastman had Robert McCracken in his corner and was paid £535,000. The fight was shown in the UK on Setanta. Eastman blamed the referee, blamed Hopkins for not fighting, and forgot to blame himself for not doing a thing in rounds one, two and three.

In October in Liverpool, Khalid Yafai and Anthony Ogogo won the world cadet championship. There were thirteen champions and only three were not from Cuba or the old Eastern Bloc. Yafai won a world title in 2016 and Ogogo an Olympic bronze medal in 2012.

David Haye won the European cruiserweight title in just forty-five seconds, and Carl Froch defended his British and Commonwealth super-middleweight title once.

From the Notepad

There were a lot of angry people when Simon Block, general secretary of the British Boxing Board of Control, said, 'Sky has taken a national sport in 1995 and turned it into a minority sport ten years later.'

In July, a butcher called Mark Krence from Chesterfield was having a bowl of cereal when Dean Powell, the matchmaker, called. Fourteen hours later Krence was in Bolton fighting for the British heavyweight title, a replacement for Danny Williams, against Matt Skelton. Williams had vanished late the night before. 'Danny is a coward,' said Skelton, who retained his title against Krence. Four months earlier Williams had gone to Bedford, Skelton's town, in an open-top bus to challenge the champion. 'He's scared to fight me,' said Williams. They would fight twice in 2006.

2006

THE LONG WAIT for vindication finally came to an end for Joe Calzaghe in March when he touched gloves with Jeff Lacy at two a.m. for a fight that would change his life.

Calzaghe had been WBO super-middleweight champion since 1997, he had made seventeen defences, and he had fought a relentless struggle for respect. He had sat helpless, often injured and always innocent, as fights with Roy Jones, Bernard Hopkins and Glen Johnson evaporated. He was avoided, but doubters insisted he was fortunate.

Lacy arrived in Manchester with an arrogant entourage of American fighting sages, his unbeaten record of twenty-one, and the backing of just about every boxing journalist in the world. The young American was the IBF champion, he was the one featuring in fantasy fights with the ailing greats of the sport. 'Jeff Lacy is the saviour of boxing all over the world,' insisted Gary Shaw, the American's promoter. Shaw's declaration was met by a chorus of hallelujahs from the travelling party. Frank Warren, on the table next to Shaw, looked over: 'Not here, no need for a saviour here, thanks – we are doing OK.'

It was the most perfect fight I have ever witnessed, a fight where every move, every drama, every punch seemed to be choreographed to perfection, and over thirty-six minutes every tiny detail unfolded as predicted. Two nights before the fight I was with Enzo Calzaghe and Joe – they were up late to try and get ready for the two a.m. bell – and the fight was explained to me. 'This is going to be the easiest night of Joe's life,' said Enzo. 'It's impossible for people to prepare to fight Joe; once they get in the ring they realize that there is nothing they can do.'

Lacy lost every round and was dropped, helpless and ruined, in round twelve, but somehow survived to the last bell. Calzaghe stood over him for a second and screamed. It was an unforgettable fight. The Americans stood in the blood-stained ring at the end, shocked at the destruction of their fighting superman. 'It could have been stopped at any point in the last three rounds,' said Calzaghe. 'I knew from about round three that he had no idea what to do – he survived on his heart.'

It was a long night, and at 5.15 a.m. I got a taxi back to the hotel.

A few days later there was a meeting at an Italian restaurant. A few of us gathered to reminisce with Joe, Enzo and Frank. There was talk of Hopkins once again, and Mikkel Kessler, the unbeaten WBA champion from Denmark. Kessler added the WBC belt in October. Suddenly, he was high on the agenda.

'I'm scared of losing, I never want to lose, and that is what motivates me,' said Calzaghe. 'My dad, Enzo, has always been my biggest influence. We argue and fight, but he's my dad and he never gets the credit he deserves.' Enzo had once been the opening act for the Barron Knights, a travelling troubadour and gentleman.

In October, a fight with Sakio Bika at the MEN was ugly, rough and bloody for Calzaghe. 'I will be the same physically for this fight as I was for the Lacy fight,' he insisted. 'But, I don't really know how I will be mentally.' He won by wide margins, but was cut over the left eyebrow and his aching hands hurt. 'Bika caught me with some terrific head-butts,' said Calzaghe. 'He is one of the strongest men I have met and certainly the dirtiest.' Calzaghe had four fights left after Bika.

The Scott Harrison decline and fall continued in 2006 and was dreadful. He was arrested in April when police used tear gas to flush him and two others out of a bar. The following month he was arrested again; this time drugs were mentioned. A fight with his number one contender, scheduled for March, fell through. A fight in September against Juan Manuel Márquez was talked about, a defence at the Braehead in November was planned.

Harrison had been imprisoned in Spain, having fled there to avoid the confrontations in Glasgow. There had been an assault charge: a Spanish man had lost a tooth and needed five stitches in his mouth. A policeman, also involved in the fracas, claimed that his eye had been damaged. It was a misunderstanding with a taxi after training, according to Scott. Peter Harrison went to see his son in the Spanish prison. It was Costa Hell, as the papers said. 'I need to know if he is still my wee boy,' Harrison said. 'I believe he can still defend his title in December and, as a former boxer, I know one thing: any fighter's toughest contest is outside the ropes.' Father and son sat opposite each other, peering through filthy plastic and speaking on sticky phones. 'I felt like his inner strength was burning through the plastic. It was the most emotional moment of my life.'

The WBO waited patiently. Warren tried to make fights happen and Harrison was in turmoil. A fight in December was agreed with east London's Nicky Cook, the venue the ExCel, and it was a good fight. Cook was unbeaten in twenty-six and the European, British and Commonwealth champion. Harrison was released, and there was a conference of assurance in November. 'Prison has given me more discipline,' he said. 'In there it was like the UN and a lot of the others gave me their fruit and yoghurt to help with my diet. Prison has made me stronger.' One convict made him a skipping rope, another made him some weights with concrete. 'Scott has been banged up in prison, wondering if he will get out,' said Warren. 'He's here now, fucking up for it, and that takes some guts.'

He looked good, but in a telephone conference call with Cook there were raw moments. 'You sound a bit ragged, mate,' said Cook. 'Shut the fuck up,' Harrison screamed back at one point. 'Does he need help?' said Cook one afternoon at his gym. 'I don't know or care how Scott Harrison is. I'm not a shrink, I'm a fighter.'

The fight collapsed. Harrison was advised to withdraw by a doctor, who had been monitoring his weight loss. Dr Niall MacFarlane was blunt: 'Kidney failure was a real danger. He trained in prison but, really, the food he was given was not giving him adequate nutrition. The kidneys weren't working properly and that could have gone to acute kidney failure.' It was over. A dejected Cook beat a journeyman instead.

The following day, Harrison said, 'The blame game has gone on too long, it's time for some uncomfortable truths.' There was talk of a return to the ring in early 2007, and that never happened. Harrison's return came in 2012, Cook got his title chance the following summer, and I'm not sure a single lesson was learned. Harrison was sick, a drunk, an addict; he was suffering from depression and he faced criminal charges in two countries. He needed professional help, not a return to the ring. The choice to try and fight was his, and it was the wrong choice.

It rained in Boston like the apocalypse was due when Ricky Hatton moved to welterweight to fight Luis Collazo for the WBA title. The May fight was Hatton's only outing in 2006 and it was difficult, close at the end. 'The mad thing is that people expect me to just walk through him and that is not going to happen,' said Hatton before the fight. In round one, after about twelve seconds, Collazo was over, caught with a left hook. It was an awkward knockdown and the American, who had been at welterweight for ten years, was tough enough and knew enough to push Hatton until the final bell. The judges went for Hatton twice by three rounds and once by just one. Hatton had surrendered his IBF and WBA light-welterweight titles because of forced mandatory defences. He also gave back the WBA welterweight belt when it was obvious he was not going to fight his German mandatory. After the fight he talked about meeting José

Luís Castillo and Floyd Mayweather. He seemed to know his destiny, even if he was not sure about his weight. 'Ricky is the best light-welter in the world,' said Billy Graham. 'Why did TV insist he move up to 147lb? I argued against it, but no one listened. Too often the trainer is seen as the poor relation. I will make my voice heard before Ricky fights again.' Billy did, and Ricky returned to light-welter the following January.

The long-running verbal battle between Hatton and Junior Witter took a very serious twist in September when the Sheffield fighter won the WBC light-welterweight title, beating DeMarcus Corley at the Alexandra Palace in north London. It was a glorious win for Witter, part of the maverick camp run by Brendan Ingle on a hill outside Sheffield. 'I've had my downs in the last five or six years,' said Witter. 'It's been difficult. I don't feel like I've had a single break. Now, I'm the man.' Witter had lost just once in thirty-six fights: his world title fight defeat to Judah in 2000 had been followed by eighteen wins, fifteen of them quick. It had looked like he would follow Ingle's great middleweight Herol 'Bomber' Graham straight into the record books without a world title.

Sadly, Corley's coach, Roger Mayweather, was banned from working in the corner, but he still found some time to share his opinion of Witter before the fight. 'I ain't seen shit to lose a second of sleep over. He can't punch, he's got no balance, and his chin is up in the air. This fight is over.' Great stuff. Witter won easily, romping home by scores of six rounds twice and three once. Late at night in the silent area behind the vast building I spoke to Ingle. He was as happy as I have ever known him. He liked to beat the Americans and their gobby trainers. 'Remember, Steve,' he said, 'I take a kid at six or seven – I work from nothing – that is what I do. The truth is that so-called great trainers in America do the easy work. They get fighters that people like me have been making for years.'

The top three British heavyweights finally met each other in a series of good fights after a few years of circling and insults. In February, Danny Williams beat Matt Skelton for the Commonwealth title. Skelton had started to box at 35 after a career in K-1 fighting in

Japan. Williams beat him on a split, but in their rematch in July Skelton, who was 39, won on points. Both fights were gruelling. In June and October, Scott Gammer, just to confuse the issue, won the British title at heavyweight when he beat Mark Krence and made a defence against Millwall's Micky Steeds. It made no sense, but it kept the title busy. Williams would meet Gammer in 2007.

In December it was rematch and revenge for Audley Harrison. He was matched with Skelton, but the big Bedford man withdrew, and at eight days' notice Williams stepped in. Williams had been in training for eight weeks: 'I knew somebody would pull out.' He was 20lb lighter for this fight than he had been for the Skelton rematch in the summer.

'I had to fight a different fight, I had to show that the first fight was not really me,' said Harrison – and the first fight had been terrible. Harrison caught Williams with a left uppercut in the first round, split his nose. The gash would need seven stitches. In the second, Richie Davies, the ref, called for the doctor to inspect the nose. 'Just one or two more rounds,' one of the two examining doctors said. At the end of the second Williams sustained another cut, this time under his left eye. This would also need seven stitches. The third was a real battle. Williams was hurt, then he hurt Harrison, and was then dropped. Poor Danny got up, tried to fight back but was dropped again. This time when Williams was back on his feet it was waved off, at 2:32 of the third. Harrison had won his gold medal in October 2000, and six years later, this was his finest win.

'Audley won, no excuses,' offered Williams. 'Maybe it is time for me to quit.' Well, Danny kept fighting: the Harrison fight was his forty-second, and in November 2016 he met a 53-year-old German for his seventy-fifth. 'I have to fight, I have to pay for my kids to get the education I never got,' Williams told me in 2015. He is one of British boxing's great treasures.

The Contenders

Amir Khan had the first of his six wins in 2006 in January. 'I think I can be world champion before I'm twenty-one,' he said. He was 20 (and three weeks) at the end of the year.

Young Muttley beat Michael Jennings for the British welterweight title. He was given that name because his dad was known as Muttley.

A young kid called James 'Chunky' DeGale from Dale Youth beat Russia's Dmitri Chudinov at York Hall in an amateur international. Jamie Cox, Frankie Gavin and Tony Bellew also won as England beat Russia 6-2.

David Haye made three defences of his European cruiserweight title, and in the last, in November at York Hall, he stopped Italy's Giacobbe Fragomeni in nine rounds. Fragomeni had beaten Haye 11-1 in an Olympic qualifier in 2000, a decision that remains one of the very worst I have ever seen.

Enzo Maccarinelli defended his WBU cruiserweight title for the seventh time, won Johnny Nelson's old WBO cruiserweight title and made a defence. He never fought Nelson, but he would get Haye.

Clinton Woods retained his IBF light-heavyweight title twice, beating Jason DeLisle in six and finally getting the verdict over Glen Johnson. Woods and Johnson fought thirty-six torrid rounds, not one session was easy.

Carl Froch stopped Brian Magee at York Hall and then Tony Dodson in Nottingham. Both fights were for the British and Commonwealth super-middleweight title. The Dodson scrap ended in the third and was ugly; Froch had knocked heavily into Dodson during the introductions. It was a nasty side of Froch that too many people forgot about.

In Hartlepool, Michael Hunter was a boxing industry. He was unbeaten in twenty-seven and had held the British, Commonwealth and European titles before he lost to Steve Molitor for the vacant IBF super-bantamweight title in November.

From the Notepad

It was a bad year for cruiserweights I had known. In May, former British champion Tee Jay collapsed in a lift and died. He was 44. His coffin was the biggest I have ever seen and even his father, the legendary Akay Isola, chuckled when he saw it. At the service, which was at the Grand Mosque in Regent's Park, Ron Shillingford, author of the boxing bonkbuster *No Glove, No Love*, told me that he had recently been in prison talking to prisoners. He had seen Tee Jay's old sparring partner and the first man to win the British cruiserweight title, Sammy Reeson. 'Sammy sends his regards,' Ron told me.

In September, former Premier League player Curtis Woodhouse had his first professional fight at the Grosvenor House in Park Lane. Dean Powell was his manager and his debut was live on ITV4. 'The man you are fighting is fucking useless,' Powell assured Woodhouse, the sinking feeling in his gut making him feel sick. Curtis won on points, was nervous, and I said he was naive. He was. I was convinced he had no chance of ever winning a British title. Eight years later he proved me wrong, and it was a delight.

In 2016, Jeff Lacy returned to Britain for a fight outside the British Boxing Board of Control's jurisdiction. He lost on points to Portsmouth's Tony Oakey in Bristol.

There was a horrible death in December when Gary Barker, just 19, was in a car crash. Barker, who boxed for the Repton like his brother and father, was a national junior champion and had won the Commonwealth junior title. He would have a final cameo in the British boxing business one night in Atlantic City seven years after his death.

2007

'I was dead surprised. The phone went and he said, "Hey, Ricky, it's Tom." I said, "Tom who?" He said, "Tom Jones." I said, "Bollocks." But it was, it was Tom Jones.'
Ricky Hatton

'I have waited and I have done it the old way, and to be honest there are not enough fighters prepared to go down the traditional roads of British, Commonwealth and European. That is the only way to become a real fighter.'
Alex Arthur

IT WAS LAS VEGAS in January. The fake lakes froze, volcanoes fell silent in the frost, snow was on the boulevard, and in every single casino, flop and bar the talk was about Ricky Hatton.

He was back at light-welter, back fighting for his old IBF title, and the unbeaten Juan Urango, the champion, was in the opposite corner in a converted ballroom inside the Paris. Hatton had been in Las Vegas for two weeks; he had converted a city and caught a cold. His chest was bad – he should probably have pulled out. 'I was not great,' he admitted. 'But every single day I walked up and down and saw hundred-foot screens showing me bashing up Collazo. That's Vegas, and that's the Vegas dream for fighters.' He used words like 'popcorn' to describe how excited he was when he first saw his face on a huge screen; he explained what it meant, and the local television crews were assigned to monitor the invasion. As many as 6,000 fans made the journey. It was less than four weeks after Christmas. Hatton won clearly, nearly a shut-out, and he slipped £1.2 million into his pocket. He had a date to return in June, and an opponent.

Floyd Mayweather was invisible that January. In May, at the MGM, he won a disputed split decision over Oscar De La Hoya in a fight that generated $250 million. 'Ricky Hatton had his chance last year,' said Leonard Ellerbe, who was Mayweather's man on earth. 'He said no twice, asked for ridiculous money, and now the door is closed on a Hatton fight.' However, it seemed Las Vegas wanted it. 'This city needs fights between fighters who fight and don't dance,' said Bob Arum, the boxing Lord of the casino city.

José Luís Castillo never danced. He had met Mayweather twice, lost a bad decision once and was outpointed in the other fight. The Mexican had been in some savage brawls, had met the best. He smiled all week as he and Hatton shook hands and nodded for the press in June.

'Before the Castillo fight it was mental in the changing room,' said Hatton. 'Oasis was on, it was like a mad house in there; I was hitting the walls. My old friends were there, they'd had a few scoops. That's how I like my changing rooms.' Wayne Rooney was also in there, and at one point Castillo's kids came in – they had on their Castillo head-bands – to meet the footballer. The fight was at the Thomas and Mack, just a mile from the brightest of the lights, and 13,044 were inside. When Hatton left to walk to the ring, Rooney was carrying one of his belts. As they were held by the TV director for a minute or two in one of the venue's tunnels, Ricky looked at Rooney, who had the belt above his head and was shaking. 'Fucking hell, Wayne. Who's fighting? Me or you?'

It was pure adrenalin from that point. Hatton was sharp, Castillo was sharper. In round four time stopped for the poor Mexican when Hatton slotted in the finest punch of his career under his opponent's right elbow. Down went Castillo with a yelp I heard at ringside. 'I thought Castillo would get up. Nobody else would, but that tough little bastard would,' said Hatton. Castillo wanted to get up, but it was impossible. The fight was over at 2:16 of the fourth and Las

Vegas, the centre of the boxing universe, belonged to Hatton and about 8,000 British fans.

What happened next is crucial. 'There was more action in the four rounds tonight than the whole of Mayweather's career,' Hatton told the HBO interviewer. It was played out live inside the venue to roars from the crowd. I was doing the interview for Setanta and was in the ring, six feet from Hatton, when he said it. I knew why he said it. A few miles away in a private house, hefty with bling attachments and obedient friends, Mayweather was watching. He called his lawyer. Hatton left the ring, had a shower, and was singing, shouting and drinking. He took just one call in the dressing room, his towel close to slipping off. It was De La Hoya, the fight's promoter. De La Hoya had just spoken to somebody. 'Ricky, let's go get Floyd.' The fight was announced six weeks later.

'They should put a swivel on his head because he gets hit too much,' said Floyd Mayweather Sr. The son called his opponent Hatton the Hobbit. The best insults came from Roger, the uncle. 'This guy brings the same thing Sylvester Stallone brings to the table,' he said. 'He brings his name, his face, and it is going to get busted up. This is nothing but a *Rocky* movie.'

In September, Hatton and Mayweather went on a five-city tour that lasted just five days. 'I just want to go home and have a bath, I have had enough of him,' said Hatton in Manchester, which was the final destination.

The fight was set for December at the MGM. The Spice Girls were moved from there to Mandalay Bay. A move from Las Vegas to the Staples Center in Los Angeles was considered too much of a risk for the travelling British fans. Hatton was in town, and on edge. Billy Graham closed the gym to the public. 'He's more nervous than I have ever seen him,' said Graham. 'It's nothing to do with getting hurt, it's to do with just what is at stake.' Hatton truly believed that Mayweather could not hurt him, and that was a basic flaw, a mistake that made him lose his way once the bell sounded.

That week in Las Vegas was part of the most amazing experience I have had in over fifty visits to the oasis. Bars at the MGM came close to closing because they nearly ran out of booze. The singing, the fans, the noise, the love for Hatton was a seven-day union. It made no difference what time of day or night it was, the noise never dropped in the MGM. It was a privilege to be part of it. Over 25,000 British fans had come to town.

At the weigh-in on the Friday I caught my first glimpse of the disaster. Hatton slashed his fingers across his throat to signify the end for Mayweather. I had never, in fifteen years of watching Hatton, seen him do anything like that. Graham was concerned, the Mayweathers relaxed. 'How can you say you are a trainer of champions when your fighter has a smashed-up face? Billy Graham don't bring shit to this fight,' Roger Mayweather said. It had been about six months of abuse from the Mayweathers.

Tom Jones sang Hatton into the ring, into a cauldron of tears and sudden fears that was overwhelming. Mayweather never flinched. Hatton was screwed too tight, and that was bad; Mayweather moved, tucked, hit, held, and made life difficult. Hatton chased, never moved his head, and, slowly, most of the claims from the Mayweather clan started to look like the awful truth. In round ten Hatton was dropped by a punch that had no apology. He got up but he was down again. It was waved off as Graham threw the towel in.

After the fight Mayweather was generous, respectful, and displayed impeccable manners. He knew he had broken Hatton in the ring. Hatton never made an excuse. Graham was stunned. He looked ill after a fight that had gone so spectacularly wrong.

The next day Hatton, his face cut and horribly bruised, was back next to the same ring to finish third in the BBC's Sports Personality of the Year. Had he beaten Mayweather, he would have won. Instead the winner was Joe Calzaghe, and nobody disputed that decision.

Nearly 90,000 people had watched Calzaghe live in 2007 in two contrasting fights at the Millennium Stadium. In April a man called Peter Manfredo Jr, who had been in an American reality TV show called *The Contender*, arrived in Cardiff with little chance of upsetting Calzaghe. Manfredo was a good talker and over 35,000 attended his boxing wake. 'All the pressure is on Joe,' he said. 'It's his hometown and I'm expected to lose. I've got no pressure.' The end of the Manfredo fight was predictable and he was stopped in the third. Manfredo complained, his management complained, Calzaghe complained, and most people in the Calzaghe business complained. It remains the only so-called premature stoppage I have ever seen where everybody involved moaned. 'I made him look third rate, he was third rate,' Calzaghe commented.

In November it did get very serious for Calzaghe when a fight with Denmark's unbeaten Mikkel Kessler took place in front of 50,500 at the stadium. It had been difficult to arrange, but in July Frank Warren had announced the fight, a deal with Setanta and a new deal with ITV. 'People have been writing me off,' said Warren in a 6.15 p.m. conference call. 'I'm still here and boxing is not dead.' Kessler was the WBC champion, unbeaten in thirty-nine fights and in a sequence of five fine world title wins. The Danish fighter, whose mother was British, was seven years younger. Calzaghe was in his twenty-second consecutive WBO title fight, his twenty-first defence since beating Chris Eubank in 1997. 'I'm not ready to retire, I could go on until I'm fifty,' Calzaghe said. 'The fear of losing motivates me. I know that the 2007 Joe Calzaghe beats any Joe Calzaghe from five or ten years ago.' His last loss had been in 1990 in Prague at the European junior championship. 'It took me weeks to get over it,' he said.

Often when two unbeaten fighters meet, especially at this level, the fight falls short. In the Cardiff ring under a canopy of song, a classic unfolded. I had it 4-3 to Kessler after seven, and then Calzaghe applied some adjustments – the type of science a fighter never gets credit for. Something that Enzo Calzaghe had said echoed in my head: 'His opponents can write things on blackboards, plan, talk, and then Joe changes during the fight.' Joe changed, and from round eight he left Kessler in his slipstream. The Dane actually looked puzzled at one point, struggling to understand why he was missing. Calzaghe admitted he was hurt in the last, and that is how champions end title fights. 'If you fight guys like Mikkel you get hit and you get hurt,' said Calzaghe. He won by six rounds and four rounds twice. Kessler bowed his head in defeat, praised Calzaghe, and returned to

Denmark; he won a world title the following year, beat Carl Froch in 2010, and retired after losing a rematch with Froch in 2013. 'The night in Cardiff was the most amazing of my fighting life,' Kessler said, and a lot of people agreed with him. 'It is the best night I've had in boxing,' said Warren. The crowd filed away at 2.30 a.m.

Calzaghe promised to burn his plastic sweat suit and move to light-heavyweight. A fight with Bernard Hopkins was mentioned again, and the day before Hatton met Mayweather there was a verbal flashpoint between the two in the press room at the MGM. It was not chance, Hopkins was too calculating for that. The fighters were surrounded, both taking questions, both relaxed, and then Hopkins went to leave, paused, and pushed back into the melee, coming face-to-face with Calzaghe. 'I will never let a white boy beat me, never,' he said, and then he was gone. The fight was made. Less than forty-eight hours later Calzaghe, with a battered Hatton at his side, was handed the Sports Personality of the Year trophy by Lennox Lewis. Enzo, the devoted dad, was in tears when he was handed Coach of the Year. He deserved it.

David Haye started his year by gaining 17lb and knocking out a heavyweight, and then, in November, he won two cruiserweight world titles near Paris when he survived a knockdown to stop Jean-Marc Mormeck. Poor Tomasz Bonin lasted just 105 seconds at Wembley in April, and then Haye fled with Adam Booth, his friend and trainer, to Northern Cyprus for three months of isolation in a gym the pair built near Girne. (The secret gym, incidentally, is cleverly constructed inside an old building.) In the Mormeck fight, which took place in a bear-pit, Haye was over in the fourth and straight back up. 'We practised a roll; we knew there was a chance David would get dropped,' said Booth. The end came in the seventh. Mormeck was wrecked but he was also leading on two of the three scorecards. Setanta had picked the fight up less than twenty-four hours before the first bell. Enzo Maccarinelli was in the studio at Input, where over a thousand live boxing shows have been recorded, to accept Haye's challenge. 'You want to fight?' Haye asked. Big Enzo said yes, and it happened the following March.

Maccarinelli had defended his WBO cruiserweight title three

times in 2007, the best of them the dancing and thinking masterclass against Wayne Braithwaite in July. 'He hit me early and that made me think again about having a war. I'm not an idiot,' said Maccarinelli. On the Calzaghe–Manfredo undercard Maccarinelli stopped Bobby Gunn in the first round. Gunn is a fun guy and before the loss his manager, Joe McEwen, told me, 'Bobby is on a quest to become the toughest, most devastating and vicious fighter since Jack Dempsey.' In 2016 the quest was still on, and Gunn had become the bare-knuckle champion of the world.

The Contenders

In July, Amir Khan had to get up from a disturbing knockdown to stop Willie Limond and win the Commonwealth lightweight title. Khan then made two quick defences, but the memory of the knockdown lingered; doubts were there. In February, Graham Earl had been involved in a brutal five-round brawl when he lost to Australia's Michael Katsidis for the interim WBO lightweight title. The fight had looked over about five times, with both boxers out on their feet, before the end. Earl was stopped in just seventy-two seconds by Khan in December.

Gavin Rees jumped up two weights to pull off the shock of the year in July when he fiddled his way to a wide points win over Souleymane M'baye for the WBA light-welterweight title. Junior Witter made two defences of his WBC light-welterweight title, including an impressive stoppage of Vivian Harris in September. Hatton had the IBO version at the time, and that made three British world champions at light-welterweight.

Alex Arthur had given up on a Scottish super-fight with Scott Harrison and won the interim WBO super-feather title in July. He beat Stephen Foster Jr, whose father was the Viking, in a December defence in Edinburgh.

Nicky Cook had to wait until July for his WBO featherweight title fight and was stopped in the eleventh, when he was trailing on two scorecards, by Steve Luevano.

In September, Clinton Woods, in his only fight of the year, repeated a points win over Julio César González to retain his IBF light-heavyweight title.

Wayne Elcock had won and lost the WBU middleweight title, and in September he pulled off a shock to outpoint Howard Eastman for the British middleweight title. The Eastman win secured Elcock an IBF title fight in Switzerland against Arthur Abraham. Elcock was stopped in five.

Carl Froch stopped Robin Reid in a British super-middleweight defence. In 2010 Froch beat Abraham in arguably his finest win. Froch was three years too late to fight Calzaghe.

In Leeds, Carl Johanneson slipped under the radar in two quality defences of his British super-featherweight title: he beat Ricky Burns on points in February and stopped Michael Gomez in October. He was stopped himself in a European title fight in the middle.

In Chicago at the world amateur championship in October and November, Frankie Gavin, from the Hall Green club in Birmingham, boxed six times in ten days to win the first gold medal by a British or Irish boxer at the event. There were bronze medals for Bradley Saunders and Joe Murray. All three automatically qualified for the Beijing Olympics.

Audley Harrison was out cold in February in the same Wembley ring that had hosted his triumphant return from Sydney over six years earlier. The crowd jeered and laughed as he was attended to by medics after Michael Sprott sent him tumbling to dreamland. It was the low point of the year, a damning end to a once brilliant love affair with the British public.

From the Notepad

It was my job in Las Vegas at the Sports Personality of the Year awards to get the trophy back from Joe Calzaghe (I had been asked to deliver it from London) and keep it safe. I got it back and took the gleaming, hefty beauty on the most amazing of Las Vegas journeys. It went in and on bars, restaurants, pools, limos, roller-coasters, more bars, roulette tables, poker tables, and finally came to rest at dawn in a buffet surrounded by bleary-eyed folk eating prawns the size of kittens for the real breakfast of champions.

Billy Graham pulled a glorious all-night drinking session in a bar at Caesars Palace in June after Hatton beat Castillo. He was there with his hat at two a.m. and still there, with his hat, at nine a.m. 'Boxing saved me,' Graham said. 'I was homeless, I had nothing. Now, to make this type of money I would have had to rob a bank.'

'I got hit, I got dropped, I got stupid and I came back,' said Khan after beating Limond. He was bright-eyed in the dressing room, but there was a gathering of long faces that night. Khan would utter the same words again and again. His lasting attraction is that he always comes back.

In April, Antony Fowler, from the Golden Gloves club in Liverpool, beat George Carmen from Dale Youth at under-63kg in the quarters of the junior ABA championship. In 2016 Fowler, still an amateur, went to Rio; Carmen had retired from the pro game with bad eyes in 2014 after seventeen fights. There is nothing simple, easy to predict or standard about the path a young boxer follows.

There was a moment of comedy when the full HBO camera team, a humourless squad of about ten earnest people, arrived at Joe Calzaghe's dirty, freezing and possibly condemned gym to start filming promos. 'They thought I had set them up,' said Enzo. The gym was an abandoned rugby club. Joe never warmed up, stretched, warmed down or had a shower (there was no shower!) at any point in his career. 'He gets up in the morning, he walks to the shop, he walks here – why does he need to warm up? He's bloody warmed up!' said Enzo, the 2007 Coach of the Year.

2008

'Does he think I will run at him and fight like a nutter? He's even more arrogant than I thought.'
Joe Calzaghe on Bernard Hopkins

'I'm not going to say that I'm the greatest British fighter of all time but nobody had my support. That is my greatest achievement in boxing.'
Ricky Hatton

THE HILLS SURROUNDING the Calzaghe gym in Wales are often wet with rain or mist, and under a trickling shower, in the grey gloom, Joe Calzaghe talked through his fight with Bernard Hopkins. 'He's old, he's desperate, and do you really think I would agree to this fight and go to America if I thought I was going to lose?' said Calzaghe that afternoon under the dripping trees.

Hopkins had the fight he wanted, a fight inevitably pushed through after his comment in Las Vegas at the end of 2007. 'My mouth only ever works with my brain,' he told me in Philadelphia in March. 'Do you think I said that and never thought about what would happen? Do you think a man that beat the streets, beat the legal system, beat the boxing system would say something like that without thinking?' The following day I visited a school with Hopkins, a school in a white neighbourhood of the city. The head teacher came out, spoke to us, and talked about the fifty flat-screen computers Hopkins was buying. Hopkins asked for that bit not to be part of the thirty-minute film for the BBC.

They met in April in Las Vegas at light-heavyweight, and there was a scare less than sixty seconds after the first bell at the Thomas & Mack when Calzaghe was on the floor. 'I knew there was something wrong – what was I doing on the canvas?' Hopkins had his chance, and he let it slide. The American tried just about every trick, many of them dirty, to win. At the end of twelve rounds one judge went for Hopkins by a round and the other two went heavily for Calzaghe. In the aftermath, Calzaghe spoke of retiring, fighting Antonio Tarver, and even Oscar De La Hoya. There are always crazy ideas at the end of big fights in Las Vegas.

Hopkins, by the way, went on to win, lose and win again the light-heavyweight world title and had his final fight in late 2016. He was 51 and he was still moaning about the Calzaghe verdict.

The last fight for Calzaghe was in front of 14,152 at Madison Square Garden in November, and he beat Roy Jones Jr on points. It was easy, but Calzaghe was dropped again in the opening round. It was a ruthless display by the Welshman, not so easy to watch if you liked Jones Jr. The offers mounted for Calzaghe from a dozen fighters, all piling up long before Jones had been iced down, patched up and presented at the post-fight conference. 'Those pitty-pats were a lot harder than I thought,' Jones admitted. Sadly, the American continued to fight for far too long. Calzaghe was quick to let people know what he thought about his future: 'I don't want to fight until I can't fight any more. There is only so far you can go before getting beat.' He walked away at 36, unbeaten in forty-six fights. He never truly considered a return, though he was angry for a year or two at the relentless insults from Carl Froch. 'I'm done, I've done my fighting, it's too late,' Calzaghe said.

One prepared in a tin shack set against the wind on a hill in Swansea and the other trained at five different Miami gyms and shared a fifty-third-floor apartment. In March, after eighteen long months, David Haye and Enzo Maccarinelli met at the O2 in front of 20,000 people. Haye had the WBA and WBC belts, Maccarinelli the WBO, but they were fashion accessories. It was a rare British world title fight: they were number one and number two in the world; Chris

Eubank and Nigel Benn had not been one and two when they fought in the nineties.

'If Haye catches me clean I will go, I know that. I'm not stupid,' said Maccarinelli. Haye had said the same thing, but he had missed the final conference and had instead met with the press in the foyer at the O2. It was 2.30 a.m. when the bell sounded. Haye had walked to the ring, Maccarinelli had run. There was something wrong, it was obvious. Months later he admitted he had been ill. There was nothing in the first, it was 2-1 in Haye's favour according to the three judges, and then Haye landed flush in the second. Maccarinelli was down, stumbling, lost against the ropes when it was called off. It was a tense, great short fight. 'I'm disgusted with myself,' said Maccarinelli. It was a hard loss to accept – it's hard for a fighter to recover after losing to a man he has been told has no power, no chin, no heart and can't make the weight. 'I made everybody believe I was dead at the weight and it worked,' insisted Haye. 'Enzo fought the ideal fight to get knocked out.'

Just to confirm that making the cruiserweight limit was not a problem, Haye moved to heavyweight for ever. 'It's time for a bit of glamour in the heavyweight division,' he said. 'I think there is an opening in the heavyweight division, and even if there was not an opening, I would still be going in.' On the same night that Haye beat Maccarinelli there was a dreadful WBC heavyweight title fight between Nigeria's Samuel Peter and Kazakhstan's Oleg Maskaev in Mexico. Haye was right, the heavyweight division needed him. 'He's not big enough,' warned Frank Maloney.

Eight months and 17lb later Haye was fighting Monte Barrett, a decent American. Barrett was not the first choice. 'It seems heavyweights in America lack the motivation and just eat all day and come up with excuses to not fight me,' said Haye. 'They are jealous.' Barrett was dropped five times, and it ended in the fifth. Haye was clipped, off balance, went over and was hit by a late left hook in that fifth round. Richie Davies, the ref, took a point off Barrett, and seconds later Haye knocked him out. Haye was a heavyweight and his next fight, so he said, was Vitali Klitschko, a ringside guest.

'I know they will not let me fight Wlad, I know I will get the statue,' added Haye in December. 'Lennox couldn't hurt him, but I will end his reign.'

After twenty-three wins Carl Froch met unbeaten Canadian Jean Pascal for the vacant WBC super-middleweight title in front of 10,000 in Nottingham. It was the type of legitimate fight, a fifty-fifty, that made Froch's years as champion so refreshing. He wanted the adulation that Calzaghe had never bothered chasing and he truly believed he could get it by fighting the very best. Froch took a clear decision and it was not just another award of a bauble to the first available winner. Froch had made it the proper way, won a real title. He had been a bit careless, but at this level, when two unbeaten boxers fight to the very bitter end it is too much to expect defensive wizardry. Pascal and Froch fought like desperate men in an old-fashioned fight. On the same bill Tyson Fury made his debut, stopping a Hungarian in the first round.

In May there was an emotional homecoming for Ricky Hatton at the City of Manchester Stadium in front of 58,000. Hatton beat Juan Lazcano in a shut-out over twelve rounds for the IBO light-welterweight title, but that is not the story of the fight. Hatton was not right; his timing was bad, he flinched, and he looked uncomfortable at times, nervous, jaded. To be brutally honest, he looked finished. The denial was deep that night. 'I made some mistakes against Mayweather, but not as many as some people are claiming,' said Hatton in his defence, knowing the problem was the defeat in Las Vegas and not the Lazcano win. There was talk of a rematch with Floyd in front of 100,000 at Wembley, talk of other super-fights, and very little was said about the obvious flaws. I wrote that he was easier to hit than at any point in his career, and more alarming was his 'sudden reaction' when caught. He looked uncomfortable. The press coverage was brutal. Hatton took some of it personally. 'All these people are moaning, but who is there coming up to take my place?' he asked.

Billy Graham left after the Lazcano fight. The pair had been together twelve years through forty-five fights. 'I love Ricky and I always will,' he said. 'I will never have anything bad to say about him.' Sadly and predictably there was a nasty fall-out, and the pair never spoke for nearly a decade.

A fight back in Las Vegas was scheduled for November, and then the Hatton tale took a very odd twist. Hatton hired Floyd Mayweather Sr as his coach. 'Billy had lost a bit of enthusiasm,' said Hatton. 'He told me that he was physically fucked and had to have needles in his hands so that he could do the pads with me.' Hatton also finally admitted that he was poor against Lazcano: 'My brain was in bits in that fight.' He talked of falling back in love with the sport. It looked that way, and Daddy Mayweather just soaked up every second of praise. 'The old days are coming back,' promised Mayweather. 'I make good fighters better and I do it my way, I do it the old-school way. I'm the professor of boxing and I don't need people telling me. I tell people.' In August, Roger Mayweather had one last word on Graham's departure: 'The man got rich and don't know shit.' Graham was in Atlanta at his new home, living a different life and looking after his snakes. 'I needed a break from the business,' he told me in 2015, after seven years of silence.

Hatton looked happy to be back in the city that had adopted him the year before. He walked to the ring in his fat suit, playing his Ricky Fatton role. He had to beat Paulie Malignaggi, the truly wonderful New Yorker, to salvage his career. 'He's taken his eyes off me and that is both stupid and disrespectful,' said Malignaggi. Hatton had promised a thinking fighter and he looked sharp stopping Malignaggi in round eleven. Poor Paulie screamed the placed down. 'I'm fine, don't stop it!' he pleaded. Too late, Ricky had won nine of the ten rounds. The Oasis brothers were there, Liam and Noel, and when the fight finished Hatton went off on tour with the band.

There was a shocking end to the first part of Amir Khan's boxing career when, after three wins in 2008, he found himself opposite unbeaten Breidis Prescott one night in September at the MEN. Prescott had been in Miami but he was from Colombia, and not a scenic part of Colombia. A camera crew from Sky had gone to film him and taxi drivers had refused to take them to Prescott's side of town. He had knocked out seventeen of the nineteen men he had beaten. He was tall, looked more like a butterfly stroke specialist. An hour before the fight I spoke to Khan's promoter, Frank Warren. There was concern, and it was justified. Khan was dropped heavily, not a slip or a clip, after thirty seconds. He was gone, but he climbed up, went straight at Prescott and was sent down and out. It was a heavy knockout, yet he was still struggling to try and get up. It was over after fifty-four seconds. It was 11.16 p.m, and the inquest started a few seconds later. Khan's new coach, a man called Jorge Rubio, was sent back to Miami. 'Rubio might be a good coach, but he is a bad matchmaker,' said Warren.

Khan packed his bags, went to Los Angeles and walked into Freddie Roach's Wild Card gym. There was no publicity, no cameras. Khan sparred with Manny Pacquiao and it was savage from the first day. 'I had to find out if the kid could fight,' said Roach. At night the kid from Bolton cried. It was a long, long road back and he was still only 21. A fight was made with Oisín Fagan for the ExCel in December and Khan won in a scrappy two rounds. Dean Powell replaced Rubio in the corner because Roach was busy with Pacquiao in Las Vegas. 'He's not far from a world title,' said Roach. 'I'm just trying to teach him some patience.' Ten months after the Prescott loss there was a world title fight for Khan. It remains British boxing's most outstanding salvage job.

In the Olympic middleweight final James DeGale, from the Dale Youth club in west London, was blatantly bitten on the chest in the opening round by the crudest Cuban. DeGale boxed with intelligence for two rounds, had a lead of 10-4, and then sensibly tried to protect the lead in the last two rounds. It was an ugly spectacle but at the end of eight mauling, pushing, shoving and biting minutes DeGale won the gold, 16-14. In the semi-final he had beaten Ireland's Darren Sutherland 10-3. 'James uses the computer brilliantly, he got his tactics right,' said Sutherland, who had spent time with Brendan Ingle in Sheffield and would turn professional with Frank Maloney in London. Sutherland had previously beaten DeGale four times out of five. DeGale had beaten an Egyptian, an American and the Kazakh Olympic champion from 2004 to reach the semi-final. It is the finest gold medal ever won by a British boxer. David Price, who'd needed nine fights to qualify, and Tony Jeffries won bronze medals, but there was a confused end to the Olympics for world amateur champion Frankie Gavin when he failed the weight and never boxed. 'It was a great team, we had never put together a team like that,' said Terry Edwards, the coach. By the end of 2016 three of the eight had won professional world titles. After winning the gold, the bookies put a 20-1 price on DeGale winning either a WBC, WBA, IBF or WBO world title; Gavin was 3-1 and Billy Joe Saunders 10-1.

The Contenders

'I wouldn't hire these two as sparring partners,' said Maloney when Setanta hired him as a pundit for the Ruslan Chagaev and Matt Skelton WBA heavyweight title fight in January. Chagaev won, and it was not a classic.

Gavin Rees lost his WBA light-welterweight title to Andriy Kotelnik when he was stopped with just twenty-six seconds left.

After four defences and three years as champion, and with a new caravan at Cleethorpes, Clinton Woods lost his IBF light-heavyweight title on points to Antonio Tarver in Florida. 'I got £240 for my first fight,' said Woods. 'Boxing has taken me to some great places and changed my life.'

In May, Junior Witter lost his WBC light-welterweight title in a tight split decision to Tim Bradley. Witter was dropped in the sixth by Bradley. Witter had been paid £300 for his first fight.

In Atlantic City in June, Kelly Pavlik, unbeaten in thirty-three, stopped Gary Lockett in three rounds for the WBO middleweight title. Lockett never boxed again and started to train fighters.

Alex Arthur had his interim WBO super-featherweight title upgraded to full WBO status and then lost to Nicky Cook. At the same weight there was a bloody brawl for the British title when Kevin Mitchell stopped Carl Johanneson in the ninth.

Twelve years after winning his first British light-middleweight title, Ryan Rhodes did it again when he beat Gary Woolcombe at

York Hall in front of his oldest friend, Naseem Hamed. 'I'm here for the Spice Boy, only now I call him Old Spice,' said Hamed. And Kell Brook, crafted in the same Sheffield gym as Hamed and Rhodes, became Brendan Ingle's latest champion when he won the British welterweight title.

From the Notepad

Hopkins had a theory, and he was probably right: 'Fighters will die before they quit, but the father? A father will stop his son from getting executed.'

Witter was angry two days before he fought Bradley, pulling me to one side in Nottingham. 'What more do I have to do to get a fight with Hatton?' he said. 'It should be me in the ring and not Lazcano.' The loss finished any hope of the fight ever happening.

'I was driving my taxi the night Audley won the Olympic title,' said Martin Rogan, minutes after beating Harrison on points in December. The Irishman had won Barry Hearn's inaugural Prizefighter tournament at York Hall in April, taking the £25,000 prize after winning three times in one night. It was the first and still the best Prizefighter. 'I think boxing is under threat from MMA and companies like the UFC are giving fans exactly what they want,' warned Barry Hearn that night. 'Prizefighter is boxing's fight back.'

In Las Vegas, before Calzaghe–Hopkins, there was a quiet moment with Lennox Lewis. 'Vitali's wife is desperate for me to fight him again,' said Lewis. 'I have put a price of £70 million on the fight. It ain't happening, I'm a happy man.'

There has to be some sympathy for Hull's Luke Campbell. In November, buried between the Hatton, Calzaghe and Haye fights, he won the European amateur title, the first British winner in forty-seven years. 'This is the start, I'm looking at London in 2012,' Campbell said. His win at the London Olympics did not go under the radar.

2009

*'If Amir loses he will have to go home and get a real job, and
if he wins he will end Marco's career.'*
Freddie Roach

*'Part of the beast that is David Haye I created. I'm coming
back to destroy a part I left behind years ago.'*
Audley Harrison

IT WAS SIGNED and sealed for David Haye to fight Wladimir Klitschko
in June before a bad back, the collapse of Setanta and a secret meeting in Berlin changed everything. Haye swerved the Klitschko
brothers and agreed a deal to fight Nikolai Valuev, the Beast from the
East.

Over 60,000 tickets had been sold for the fight with Wladimir at
the Veltins Arena in Gelsenkirchen. Haye had been in and out of
Germany, annoying the Klitschko boys, wearing on one visit a T-shirt
with a grisly image of him holding up the two severed heads of the
brothers. 'They both hated me, they could tell I was not scared,' said
Haye. The deal for the fight was agreed at a series of meetings in
April, and Haye's signature was meant to secure silence. 'This is a
slave contract; when I win I have to keep fighting Klitschkos for life,'
said Haye. 'I have to accept it because I want the fight.' The bit about
fighting a Klitschko until they got revenge was a joke and it upset the
man that ran the Klitschko empire. 'David is not allowed to discuss
the terms, the contract,' insisted Bernd Bönte, the snow-haired

former television producer in charge of the Klitschko show. Every day there was a new rumour, a sickening feeling that the fight would collapse, and inevitably it did. Big Wlad was fuming: 'Haye needs to stop fighting with his mouth and find the bravery to meet me in the ring.' Haye asked for a six- to eight-week postponement, but it was known he was looking at other options. Haye claims he was close in July to agreeing a deal to fight Vitali. 'It's one signature away,' he said. Then Valuev became the focus of Haye and Adam Booth, his promoter, friend and coach. Secret meetings took place in Berlin, a three-day conference was held at the Grosvenor House in London, and the deal was done. Haye v. Valuev for the WBA heavyweight title in November was a stunning announcement, a great piece of secrecy.

The experts were divided. Brendan Ingle laughed: 'Haye will stand him on his head.' Barry McGuigan was concerned: 'Valuev will eventually overpower him.' Haye was 99lb lighter and about eleven inches shorter. Valuev had been dubbed the Beast from the East by Frank Maloney during his brief period in charge of the Russian in 1996, when he fought at Battersea Town Hall. A sad backstory emerged in the days before the first bell in Nuremberg. 'My childhood was trashed,' Valuev told a few of us in Germany. 'It was sport, only sport. People looked at my size and wondered what I could do for them. I had no childhood, and that is why I don't box with passion.' It got better. His favourite author was Agatha Christie, and he showed us a well-thumbed translated edition. His grandfather was eight feet tall and a paid assassin. Valuev added that he liked to hunt wild boar and bears on his own. A seven-foot-tall man weighing 21st with Agatha Christie for company and a rifle in his hands stalking bears. 'That is how I will celebrate beating Haye.' He was a glory to cover.

Haye won by not getting hit, by not getting sucked into a clinch, by moving. 'Don't you dare go looking for a knockout,' Booth told him several times at the end of rounds. Haye injured his right hand at some point after the third and did manage to nearly topple Valuev in the last round. 'I never said it would be pretty or easy beating the giant,' said Haye. It was the end for Valuev, who slipped away with his ballerina wife to read British fiction and hunt.

'He can't hurt me, he is too small to hurt me,' said Ricky Hatton two days before fighting Manny Pacquiao. Hatton ended a dreadful April training camp in early May by climbing through the ropes at the MGM in Las Vegas. It is estimated that 18,000 British fans travelled out for the fight and that took his total for five fights in Las Vegas to just over 90,000, according to US immigration figures. It was over before it had started, arguably finished in the weeks and days before the first bell. Hatton had over-trained, peaked too soon, and knew he would lose as he was walking to the ring. The camp had been a disgrace. Hatton went down for the full count, remained on the canvas for over two minutes. Pacman, as the Filipino is known, had dropped Hatton in the opening round with a southpaw right hook then flattened him in round two with just one second left before the bell. Hatton made £12 million, allegedly, taking his career earnings to £47 million.

The turmoil in the Hatton camp had been open and hostile, with Floyd Mayweather Sr showing up late for training and insisting on Hatton sparring close to the fight. There was escalating conflict between Mayweather Sr and Lee Beard, who was also part of the coaching team. Beard knew Hatton would get knocked out – he blamed it on Mayweather Sr. Mayweather Sr blamed it on Hatton for training twice each day, once with him and then once with Beard. 'It ain't my fault he's going at it twice every day,' he said. Mayweather Sr had wanted to eliminate any lingering doubts he had, and demanded Hatton spar fiercely far too close to the fight. Hatton claimed his pride kept him from refusing. He was marked during the week of the fight, subdued, and the rumours were savage: everybody in Las Vegas knew he was getting a hiding in sparring. One of the sparring partners, Erislandy Lara, had recently defected from Cuba and would go on to win a world title of his own. The sessions with Lara had simply been too hard, and Hatton's father, Ray, had argued for the fight to be postponed. Hatton, to be fair, never let the chaos before a fight become the substance of excuses; those that were in Las Vegas and close to the camp know just how divisive Mayweather's role became. The pair split late that night. Hatton said of Mayweather's departure, 'He zipped up his zoot suit and scurried away sharpish.' The exit was too late to prevent the toxic fall-out. That was the end of that, though not the end of Hatton.

The Super Six tournament for super-middleweights was launched in July with press conferences in Copenhagen, New York and Berlin. Nottingham's Carl Froch was named in the original line-up, alongside Andre Ward, Andre Dirrell, Mikkel Kessler, Arthur Abraham and Jermain Taylor. It was a draining tournament that finished in December 2011. The plan was for twelve fights between the six boxers over an eighteen-month period, and it remains a brilliant but flawed concept. Too many boxers came and went before the final fight.

Before the grand launch, in April, Froch went to Foxwoods, Connecticut to defend his WBC title against Jermain Taylor. It was an ugly few weeks for Froch and his promoter, Mick Hennessy. There was no TV deal in place and the fight was eventually screened on delay by ITV. 'Who the Froch is Froch?' said Taylor's promoter, Lou DiBella. 'They are acting like they are the champion,' countered Hennessy. It was a classic fight. Froch was dropped in round three and trailing on two of the three cards going into the twelfth and last round. Froch then dropped and stopped Taylor with just fourteen seconds left on the clock. DiBella had an answer to his question.

In October the Super Six started and unbeaten Andre Dirrell arrived in Nottingham with Gary Shaw at his side to try to unsettle Froch before the first bell. There always seemed to be a sense that Froch was easy to spook and opponents constantly tried. Froch had his insecurities, like all great fighters, but he was mentally tough once it was fight time. 'This fight is easy for my kid, Froch is too slow,' said Shaw. Robert McCracken, in Froch's corner, knew it was not going to be easy for either of the fighters. 'Dirrell will be a pain in the arse for a few rounds,' he said, and he was right. 'All this switch-hitting rubbish makes a fighter vulnerable,' said Froch. 'I keep hearing about his speed – well, if speed is the only problem I've got, I'm in for an easy night.' It was not an easy night. At the end of twelve rounds Froch won a split, and he deserved it. Late that night at the fight hotel, after he had been hollering and screaming at ringside, Shaw sat down and admitted his man had lost. 'He's still a kid, he will be back.' Ward had stopped the betting favourite Kessler on cuts, and Abraham had knocked out Taylor. The first round of the Super Six was over.

Amir Khan's waiting was also over, and his world title fight was skilfully delivered. Remember, you get what you negotiate, not necessarily what you deserve, in the boxing business. Less than ten months earlier Khan had been knocked out by Colombian Breidis Prescott in Manchester. Prescott looked like he had been put together by a granite sculptor and the finished monster had shoulders like wings of muscle. The massacre had lasted less than a minute, the damage was fearsome, and the recovery by Khan had been magnificent. Two fights later he was back in the Manchester ring to fight the Ukrainian Andriy Kotelnik for the WBA light-welterweight title.

In March, Khan had met Marco Antonio Barrera in front of 18,000 in Manchester. It was a great piece of matchmaking by Frank Warren. Barrera was a seventy-two-fight veteran and had been scrapping for pesos since he was 15. There was blood, a lot of blood, and Barrera had skimped on a cutsman. On the day I wrote: 'I suspect that cuts will be a factor and possibly the decisive and generous factor in helping Khan.' There was pressure, Barrera was not quite finished. ('If Amir loses he will have to go home and get a real job,' Freddie Roach had warned.) The Mexican was cut in the first and rescued in the fifth; he needed thirty-three stitches to close the wound above his left eye. 'He never hurt me, he was too fast,' Barrera said.

The Kotelnik fight was delayed for three weeks because the champion had toothache. Roach, who had Khan in Los Angeles at the Wild Card gym from April, doubted the excuse. 'Kotelnik is not ready – this is a good delay for us,' he insisted, and he was right on the night. In the fight, Khan boxed to Roach's directions, never deviating or taking the type of risk that led to the Prescott loss. At the end of twelve rounds it was a virtual shut-out with one judge scoring it 120-108 and the other two returning identical totals of 118-111. Khan was the champion of the world, and that was a relief for everybody in the Khan business. Kotelnik trudged away with his swollen features tucked into a blood-stained towel. He'd thought it was going to be an easy night. Roach was delighted; Khan was the twenty-fifth world champion that he had worked with. He said, 'Amir showed some old-school moves that people don't get to see any more. Fighters don't feint any more or go to the body like Amir did tonight.'

There was some bold and misguided talk about a fight between Khan and Hatton. Both Khan and his promoter, Warren, wanted Hatton to turn his sabbatical into permanent retirement, but that never stopped the speculation. In December he made a quick defence when he knocked out Dmitri Salita, the Orthodox Jew with the unorthodox number one ranking, in seventy-six seconds. 'Amir can be better than Naz,' said Warren. 'It's all about dedication and sacrifice.'

The Contenders

Michael Jennings had filled halls in Wigan, Widnes and Warrington, and in February he walked out at Madison Square Garden to fight Miguel Cotto for the vacant WBO welterweight title in front of a full house. 'He never gave me an inch, not one second to breathe,' said Jennings. It ended in the fifth round.

Two British veterans had fights for their old titles: in August, Clinton Woods went back to Florida and lost to Tavoris Cloud for the light-heavyweight title, and Junior Witter was stopped by Devon Alexander for the WBC light-welterweight. Nicky Cook lost his WBO super-feather to Román Martínez, who was unbeaten in twenty-two, and on the same bill at the MEN, Enzo Maccarinelli was stopped by London-born Ola Afolabi for the interim WBO cruiser.

Kell Brook made two easy defences of his British welterweight title and would win a world title in 2014. Bristol's Lee Haskins defended his bantamweight title twice and won a world title in 2015. Nathan Cleverly won four British and Commonwealth light-heavyweight fights by stoppage. And the British middleweights were very lively: Wayne Elcock was done in three by Matt Macklin, who vacated, and then Darren Barker won the vacant title. Barker–Macklin became a soap-opera fight and it never happened.

The future of British amateur boxing was secured when the GB Olympic boxing gym opened at the EIS in Sheffield. British amateurs finally had a gym, a programme and the funding to become a dominant force. At the London Olympics in 2012 they would come first in the medal table, beating the Cubans and the Russians. The slow process to excellence had started with Audley Harrison winning gold in 2000, the first British boxing gold for thirty-two years. In August it was announced that three of the thirteen women's weights would be included in the Olympics from 2012; the GB trio of Nicola Adams, Natasha Jonas and Savannah Marshall all had to lose or gain weight.

From the Notepad

'Terry's job was to get the best money and the worst opponent for his boxer and when I suggest an opponent, his immediate reaction is no', said Mickey Duff talking about Terry Lawless, boxing manager and Duff's partner, who died on Christmas Eve in Marbella, Spain.

'I had promoted 512 matches and the majority I knew the result before I sat down. The public buy a ticket to find out what I already know,' Barry Hearn explained before his brainchild, Prizefighter, moved to the ExCel in London's Docklands for Heavyweights III and the return of Audley Harrison. Big Aud won, by the way.

The sympathy vote of the year was easily won by Hatton's brother, Matthew. In November he fought Lovemore Ndou for the IBO welterweight title on a show promoted by his dad, Ray, and his brother, with his mother, Carol, in the front row. He won clearly, I thought, but it was scored a draw. 'I might take them off my Christmas card list,' said Matthew, who was a much better fighter than he was ever given credit for.

Freddie Roach was ruthless in Las Vegas before Hatton met

Pacquiao: 'I will be disappointed if the fight goes longer than three rounds.' He was not disappointed.

A tour by Mike Tyson was chaotic. The fallen idol cancelled shows, was late on stage, and at his rambling best. He did, however, buy a few pigeons from Horace Potts of Bloxwich.

Afolabi was born in south London and eventually found his way to Roach's Wild Card gym. 'I washed the snot and blood off the walls for a few bucks, that was how I survived,' he told me in 2014.

It is possible that Gary Jackymelon was the second best junior boxer, just behind Errol Christie, in British history. He fought for the Blackwell Miners Welfare Club and won four schoolboy, two junior ABA and two NABC titles. He was beaten four times in ninety-seven fights and was lost to the game by the age of 18. He dropped dead in September, and I made a pilgrimage to the club near Nottingham where it all started.

Setanta collapsed in the summer, and between September and December I took a one-man show on the road, ten shows in eight cities in three countries. I sold seven tickets in Sunderland, did slightly better elsewhere, and was joined on the road by Haye, Christie, Macklin, Matthew Hatton, Dirrell, Steve Foster, Dave Coldwell, Big Joe Egan, Stinky Turner, Carl Thompson, Jim McDonnell, Cleverly, Maccarinelli, Marty Rogan, Paddy Barnes, Wayne Alexander, John Ingle, Paddy Considine, Vince Smith, John McDonald and Johnny Harris, and dozens of other fighters. Kevin Mitchell from the *Observer* also came out.

2010

'He never thanked the fans after Pacman. He watches that fight again and
again. He has panic attacks and is being treated for serious depression.'
Ray Hatton on his son Ricky's troubles

'I'm here in his backyard, the underdog, and that's because I want
to be a real champion – I don't want to fight any handpicked
unknown fighters and then brag about my defences.'
Carl Froch on fighting Mikkel Kessler in Denmark

IN MANY WAYS the thoroughly modern heavyweight world champion
David Haye deserved a low canopy of cigar smoke to give his fight with
John Ruiz the added authenticity of a genuine throwback brawl.

Haye was in a Sky pay-per-view defence of his WBA title against
Ruiz at the MEN in April, and it was a riot from the opening bell
until the end in round nine. Haye dropped Ruiz in the first, fifth and
sixth rounds and was deducted a point in the wild opener when he
hit the American on the back of the head. Ruiz had not been stopped
in fifteen years and nine of his eleven world title fights had gone the
full twelve. Haye was a glorious if controversial remedy to a heavyweight division in decline, and 19,200 people left the steep-seated
Manchester fight sanctuary singing and smiling.

'Valuev was a freak show, Ruiz was a real fighter, and he had beaten
hard men,' said Haye. 'This is what I promised – real fights, knockdowns and a bit of drama. This is the answer to the boring Klitschko
shows.'

A few days later there was sweet revenge for Audley Harrison when he knocked out Michael Sprott to win the vacant European title. 'It was my last chance,' admitted Harrison. 'If I lost it was all over. Now it's interesting because traditionally the European heavyweight champion gets a world title fight.' And, to add to his unsubtle hint, he reminded Haye that as an amateur he had been knocked out by Coventry's Jim Twite. 'He should focus on his own career and not worry about mine,' replied Haye.

It was inevitable that the estranged friends would fight. 'I don't want this fight,' insisted Haye. He was probably telling the truth. But it was on, and the opening press conference at the hotel in south London where Haye spent a lot of nights was tremendous fun. 'Audley doesn't deserve this chance but the people believe he does and that is enough for me,' said Haye. 'It's called the Sweet Science,' said Harrison, and Haye interrupted: 'No, it's called a public execution.' The pair had once been inseparable, but a couple of incidents and time had ruined their friendship. There had been a sparring session in 2006 in Miami in front of Lennox Lewis when Haye, who was sharp, took a liberty with Harrison, who was not fit. Then, in about 2008, Harrison claimed Haye had not helped him by adding him to a promotion. 'I helped set all these fighters free,' insisted Harrison. 'I showed Hatton, Calzaghe, Khan and Haye how to do it on their own. I led the way.' Haye laughed off the claims. 'The truth is we fell out because he is bitter and twisted. I've done it and he hasn't: it's not complicated, he's jealous.'

Some 20,000 people packed the MEN in November. It was a rotten fight. In the third, Harrison toppled over after fewer than a dozen punches in total had been thrown. Haye made a fortune. 'It was not my fault,' he said. The negotiations for a fight with Wladimir Klitschko continued.

The venue for Carl Froch's second fight in the Super Six tournament was the home of Lego in a remote corner of Denmark, and he started as a slight betting underdog against Mikkel Kessler. However, just seven days before the fight a postponement was announced. Froch had gained 7lb at a barbecue, his elbow was injured and his eardrum was damaged; but the problem was not Froch's permanently broken body, it was the treacherous volcanic ash cloud. In the end Froch and Robert McCracken, his coach, took a white-knuckle ride on a tiny plane and landed a few days before the first bell. I saw the pair an hour after they arrived and they both looked ready to vomit.

The fight was always going to be exceptional and, like the Andre Dirrell fight, it was screened on Primetime. Froch had won the WBC title in front of 3 million viewers on ITV at eleven p.m. at night and had been in a televised wilderness since then. 'It's hard to be diplomatic,' said Mick Hennessy, Froch's maverick promoter. 'I've sat with television executives and I've heard that Carl Froch is too old, he turned pro too late, he lacks power – I've listened to the bullshit again and again.' It was hard for Hennessy to be diplomatic when he was arguing for his fighters.

It was close on the night. Froch was dragged deep into a brawl and Kessler fought the fight of his life to take the decision. Calzaghe never said much after his great British rival lost to Kessler, a man he had so wonderfully defeated. He never had to: some things in boxing are best left. 'I went over to Kessler's backyard, I went to Jermain Taylor's backyard, and I took on the unbeaten kid Dirrell,' said Froch. 'I was in the deep end and that's why I have no respect for Joe Calzaghe.' The Calzaghe–Froch enmity would continue for a long time.

'I got it wrong in Denmark,' insisted Froch. 'I stood in front of Kessler and tried to take him out with every punch. I was flat-footed, and the longer the fight went the more drained I felt.' Kessler had to take fourteen months out after the fight with a serious eye injury; Froch limped home to Nottingham to try and put his body back together. He had a gap in his luggage where the WBC belt had been.

The next fight in the Super Six was against Arthur Abraham, and it looked like Froch would have to go back on the road. A Monaco date in October was a compromise after Froch refused to fight Abraham in Germany. At that point in the Super Six Abraham had knocked out Jermain Taylor with just six seconds left in the last round and then been disqualified in the eleventh against Dirrell. The fight was set for Helsinki, and it took a lot of threats and deals.

On the night it was minus eighteen, a frightening cold. Five Live's Mick Costello nearly froze solid searching for a taxi. In the ring Froch was simply brilliant, winning every second of every round against Abraham. It was a flawless display, and at the end of several rounds McCracken and Froch stood and talked. 'I was telling him that he had to keep boxing and to forget any crazy ideas about knocking out Abraham,' said McCracken. As a bonus, Froch won back his old WBC super-middleweight belt. Pascal, Taylor, Dirrell, Kessler and Abraham was a sequence of fights to rival any in British boxing history. The last three had been tucked away on Primetime pay-per-view.

In May, Amir Khan defended his WBA light-welterweight title against Paulie Malignaggi at the Felt Forum, which is the basement venue at Madison Square Garden. Khan stopped the New Yorker in round eleven, which is exactly what Ricky Hatton had done two years earlier.

Oscar De La Hoya was Khan's new promoter and he agreed a December fight against Marcos Maidana at the Mandalay Bay in Las Vegas. The Argentinian had stopped twenty-seven of the twenty-nine men he had beaten and his only loss was a shameful robbery in a world title fight against Andriy Kotelnik in Germany. Roach took Khan to the Philippines to spar with Manny Pacquiao. Khan had salvaged his career by moving to the west Hollywood gym that Roach built and ran, but the Maidana fight was a real test. It was the type of fight that could sit comfortably in any epoch.

In round one Khan was caught, hurt, wobbled; then, with a second or two left in the opener, he slotted in a sickening left hook to the body and Maidana was down. In round five Maidana lost a point for using his elbow as a fist. The tenth was dreadful for Khan and he was out on his feet after just thirty seconds, his eyes rolling like lemons in a cheap one-armed bandit. He somehow survived the round and got the decision. Khan was 24 and no longer Kid Khan. 'I hurt him, he hurt me – what a fight.' What a fight it was, and the man that ran the gym at the end of many a boxer's rainbow was delighted.

'Amir can be the pound-for-pound king in five years,' said Roach.

Hatton was back in the news in the summer when he was splashed in the papers after a night of passion and cocaine. The pictures were damning. 'He said he had to drink to hold his head high,' said Ray, the boxer's father, who also revealed that his son had been repeatedly watching the Pacquiao fight. 'He has panic attacks and is being treated for serious depression.' Hatton was a long way from an easy fix.

At the Boleyn Ground in Upton Park in May, Stinky Turner, a schoolboy finalist from the seventies, and his band The Cockney Rejects performed a version of 'Bubbles' when Kevin Mitchell walked to the ring. Mitchell was unbeaten in thirty-one and had looked very calm when beating Breidis Prescott in late 2009, but there'd been no pressure that night. Mitchell was a West Ham fan and 20,000 of the faithful had come out to support him against Australia's Michael Katsidis. The WBO's interim lightweight title was the prize. Mitchell was far too emotional, playing to the stands and trying to match Katsidis. He was stopped, on his feet but hurt, in round three; he made it easy for the Australian. 'I'm not happy,' said Jimmy Tibbs, Mitchell's coach. 'Kevin didn't live the life for this fight.' Mitchell sat there and nodded. 'It's not been great,' he said. 'If Kevin doesn't want to do it, then I'm not going to finance it,' added Warren. It was not a great post-fight conference: it never is when a young unbeaten fighter gets so seriously turned over. Katsidis kept smiling, holding his tongue before laughing and saying, 'Hey, I never heard any of this before the fight, and if Kevin had won we wouldn't be hearing it now.' He had a point, but he was wrong – little Kev had not been living the life.

On the undercard, Danny Williams lost his British heavyweight title in what should have been his last fight. He was ruthlessly stopped, dropped twice, by Dereck Chisora, and eventually saved in the second round. Chisora was fighting for the thirteenth time, Williams for the fifty-first. 'Danny has been a great warrior and I hope he retires,' said Warren. 'If not, I hope the Board stop him fighting.' Danny Williams never stopped, the Board had no right to interfere, and he had another twenty-four fights.

Even in boxing, a refuge for many on the edges, Jason Booth is extreme. He had been on the booze, lost his way, and it looked at times like he had no future in the sport. In September he came so close to beating Steve Molitor for the IBF bantamweight title. It was a majority, one drawn score and two for Molitor, who had been world champion on and off for five years. Booth had turned pro in 1996, won his first British title in 1999, and last fought in 2016. In 2005 I was in Nottingham to film his brother, Nicky, and went to see Jason. He was in bed, drinking cans of cheap lager, watching TV and getting fat. It was 10.30 in the morning. 'I've lost my motivation,' he told me.

The Contenders

Ricky Burns was close to becoming the forgotten man of Scottish boxing when he met unbeaten Puerto Rican Román Martínez for the WBO super-featherweight title in September. Martínez had not lost in twenty-six fights. Burns was over in the first, but when the fight finished he was the champion. It was a shock, a fine performance. The Scot retained the title in December.

It ended in tears for Rendall Munroe in October when he tried something so few British boxers have pulled off and travelled to Japan for a world title fight. Munroe was a binman in Leicester, and if he won he was still going to be a binman. His fans wore Hi-Vis jackets to his fights. He lost on points to Toshiaki Nishioka, a very good champion, for the WBC super-bantamweight title. One month before Munroe fought, the Liverpool idol Alan Rudkin died. In 1965 Rudkin lost on points over fifteen rounds to the legendary Fighting Harada in Tokyo for the bantamweight world title. The binman was walking in the shadows of greats.

Nathan Cleverly won the interim version of the WBO light-heavyweight title in December. The same weekend Wladimir Klitschko pulled out of a heavyweight title fight with Dereck Chisora with just twenty-four hours to go before the first bell. 'He does not want to fight me, I can tell from his eyes, he's gonna pull out,' Chisora had insisted on the Thursday night. On Friday afternoon Klitschko pulled out, claiming he had torn an abdominal muscle. It was odd.

James DeGale won the British super-middleweight title in his ninth fight when he stopped Paul Smith just twenty-eight months after taking gold in Beijing. 'I couldn't see the punches,' Smith tried to explain. His face was a web of cuts and bruises and he just could not grasp what had happened. The pick of the undercard when Smith lost was a ridiculous British light-heavyweight fight. Tony Bellew somehow survived shocking knockdowns in the first and second to stop Ovill McKenzie in round eight.

From the Notepad

When Hatton had his cocaine problem in the papers, one of the men to stand at his side was Junior Witter. 'I don't see why he should be banned,' said Witter, who had spent many years waiting to fight Hatton. 'It was for recreational use, not performance-enhancing.'

Mike Tyson was back in the UK on tour and shared his thoughts on the current heavyweights. 'I've watched the Klitschkos and they are competent boxers, and Haye needs a bit more time,' Tyson said. 'I'm proof that the glory as world heavyweight champion does not last for ever.' They loved him in Peterborough and Doncaster.

The July date for the long-overdue British middleweight fight between Darren Barker and Matt Macklin fell through. Barker had been at altitude in Tenerife and Macklin at Roach's Wild Card gym, where he'd had his nose broken in a sparring session. 'They just queue up to spar, I had no idea what their names were,' said Macklin. 'That is how Freddie runs the gym. It's brutal.'

In May a boxer called Shaun Gray died. He was 35 and his best fighting days had been twenty years earlier when he boxed for West Ham under Micky May. He won seven junior titles, finished twenty-eight of his thirty-two wins by knockout or stoppage, and remains the most fearsome under-17 boxer I have ever seen. Grown men discussed his career at the funeral in Canning Town like they were talking about a world champion. His brother, Patsy, also a schoolboy champion with West Ham, had died seven years earlier. They had been addicts, but were both in recovery when they died.

2011

*'I don't want to look back on my career and see bum after bum.
I'm a boxer with pride.'*
Tyson Fury

*'I have spent the last twelve months sulking and you know how low
I have been. I have let myself down. That's over, and now
I'm happy and ready to get on with my life on my terms.'*
Ricky Hatton on his way to an early recovery

THE JULY WEEK in Hamburg for David Haye against Wladimir Klitschko started so well with endless promises, and then the weather changed. The rain fell in a torrential wall and a sore toe became the most famous exhibit from a forgettable night.

Haye delivered his WBA belt, Klitschko had the IBF, WBO and IBO versions, and the boxing world longed for and needed a real heavyweight scrap: so many of Klitschko's opponents had folded shamefully, fallen exhausted, broken, fat, and at the painful end of the champion's jab. Many of these overweight American challengers were a disgrace. Haye had preached an alternative fight, a fight where Klitschko was dragged kicking and screaming from his comfort zone; he'd also promised not to join the endless list that would not be missed.

'David has made the same mistake that everybody makes with Wladimir and dismissed his speed – it's a bad mistake,' said Emmanuel Steward, the man that had transformed Wlad from a big athlete into a proper heavyweight champion of the world. Haye was defence number ten and only one of the previous nine had heard the final bell.

At the weigh-in the British fans, some queuing since seven a.m., roared at the arrival of Wladimir, who had his brother and shadow Vitali in his immediate slipstream. 'Shit Ivan Drago, you're just a shit Ivan Drago, shit Ivan Drago,' they chanted. The boxers exchanged a genuinely chilly final stare after stepping on and off the scales. Klitschko was 17st 5lb, Haye 15st 3lb, and for the stare-down Klitschko stood on his tiptoes. Haye tried to laugh it off and I sensed something was not right. It looked like the first sign, a single piece of recognition that Big Wlad was serious. In every conversation with Haye since 2008 it had been obvious he thought that he could knock out Klitschko.

'I'm as big as you need to be,' said Haye. 'If size was everything then Valuev would be the greatest heavyweight in history.' Haye smiled for the fans, clenched a fist, got a cheer and vanished down a back stairwell.

Wladimir had been in reflective mood earlier in the week. 'David thinks that I have never had a hard time, never suffered and have just beaten men he calls bums. He is wrong. I will get respect for the forty-nine men that he called bums and I will add his name to the list. I was destroyed when I lost twice in twelve months. I was at the bottom and I had to fight my way back. I know what it is like to have nothing.' It was another sign.

On fight morning I spoke to Gary Logan, who was part of Haye's travelling team. Logan had lost three British title fights, had fought forty-two times and was an old boxing head on relatively young shoulders. 'He's got a bad toe,' he told me. 'It's not good.' It was 7.30 a.m. on the day of the fight and I dismissed the news. A toe, a bad toe? It was a sign I missed.

The rain threatened the fight at one point. It ruined the night and meant nobody could sit in any of the seats on the pitch at the Imtech-Arena, which created a nasty tension, with thousands standing ten or more deep just outside the ringside perimeter and just under the giant canopy. Haye got lost on his way to the ring; Wladimir was led along a direct route and never had to push and shove any fans. It was another sign. 'I plan on giving him a lesson about respect and that is why it will be long,' Wlad had promised. During the introductions it looked like the towering Ukrainian was licking his lips. Haye was his supper.

In the fight, and from the very start, Haye never mastered the jab that kept hitting him and he was caught with enough right hands to prove a lot of people wrong: there was nothing wrong with his chin. Haye dug his boots into the canvas, bit down on his shield and tried to counter. The months of pad work with Adam Booth, his partner in the great Klitschko hunt, wearing six-inch platforms had been in vain. It was the speed, as Manny had warned. 'After five or six rounds he was not responding to what I was telling him,' said Booth. 'That's wrong, not an excuse, just a fact.' It was hard, a depressing ritual of Klitschko sticking out a jab, holding, pushing Haye off, and looking for an opening for the right hand. 'I was not going to quit like so many have done,' said Haye. But he was hurt.

It was a wide win for Wlad, and then the fun – or the horror, depending on where you were sitting – started. Haye appeared at the post-fight conference in sandals. Wlad, Manny and Bernd Bönte, the Klitschkos' business partner and promoter, were in playful mood. Bönte and Wlad had been terrorized by Haye for a long time. 'We expected more, we are disappointed in Haye,' said Steward. 'You will have success at a certain level but at my level you will always be a loser,' added Klitschko. Haye was helpless under fire, and then he made a dreadful mistake: he mentioned the broken toe.

'A broken toe? Really? If you keep talking you will end up like a sore loser,' said Wlad. 'A fighter, David, must never say he has a broken toe.'

Haye insisted it was not an excuse. 'You beat me fair and square, you had a masterful game plan, but this didn't help,' he insisted.

Somebody shouted, 'Show us the toe!'

I shouted, 'No.'

It was too late, and with a helping hand from Booth, David Haye, who that morning had been the heavyweight champion of the world, stood up on a table in his black flip-flops and let the world see his red toe. 'It looks like a bee sting,' offered Wlad – arguably the most brutal putdown in the annals of boxing trash talk.

It was a horrible end, and in October, as promised, Haye retired. He wanted out before he started to 'slur', and he had achieved his three objectives: win world titles, secure a financial future and get out in his prime at 30. He was back in the ring nine months later.

Carl Froch wanted to take a cut in pay to get his fourth fight in the Super Six in Nottingham and not Atlantic City. It made sense: his last two had been on the road. In June he met and beat Glen Johnson, the Jamaican-born light-heavyweight and great rival of Clinton Woods, to retain his WBC title. Johnson was a late replacement in the Super Six, coming in when Mikkel Kessler withdrew. It was hard, Johnson is hard, and Froch won clearly, but one judge returned a drawn verdict and that is always a risk when you fight overseas. The fight was on Sky – the third broadcaster to screen Froch's world title fights. The win meant Froch was in the final against Andre Ward, the 2004 Olympic light-heavyweight champion. Ward had fought three times, twice in his hometown and once a few hundred miles away.

The pair met in the final of the Super Six tournament in December. There was no great compromise and Froch had to return to Atlantic City. He had fought in six world title fights in four countries against the very best. On the night Ward was too slick, too clever and slippery for Froch. 'Andre never gets the credit for what he does,' said Virgil Hunter, who had been with Ward since the boxer was a child. 'I still think on a good night I could beat him,' said Froch. It was not a good night, and that is what Ward does – he makes men fight his fight, he smothers work, and has brilliant timing. At the end of round nine and again after eleven, Robert McCracken asked Froch, 'Are you listening, Carl, are you listening?' Two of the three judges had it close at 115-113 for Ward but the British judge, John Keane, scored it 118-110. Froch has never tried to claim the fight was close. 'He's ugly but he's good at it,' said Froch.

There was a bad-tempered end to the first of Amir Khan's three fights in 2011. There had, in fairness, been a bad-tempered start to the negotiations for Khan to defend his WBA light-welterweight title against Dungiven's Paul McCloskey. 'The deals placed on the table were an insult to Paul,' said Barry Hearn. 'Amir can't fight himself and I'm afraid you have to pay opponents to step in the ring with you and pay them fairly.' It was made, and at the conference in Manchester before the fight there was the first appearance of Barry's son, Eddie, wearing his promoter's hat. 'I won't try and sell you tickets,' said Eddie. 'I won't need to. I will sell you Paul McCloskey, the undefeated European champion. This is about dreams, Paul's dream.' It was sell, sell, sell from the start.

Khan was winning a technical fight when there was an accidental clash of heads in round six. The referee called 'stop' and led McCloskey away for inspection by the British Boxing Board of Control doctor. The fight was stopped. The Northern Irish fighter was stunned, his corner furious. Eddie had to calm his dad during the ring melee. Eamonn Magee, who'd once dropped Ricky Hatton in the same Manchester ring, closed the cut above the left eyebrow in about three seconds. In the dressing room ten minutes later he showed me the cut in detail. 'It's nothing, tiny, barely bleeding,' Magee reasoned. It did require seven stitches, but that, in Magee's world, barely qualifies as a scratch.

The ref and doctor got it wrong that night. Khan had not lost a round, but McCloskey and his 9,000 travelling fans deserved a proper ending.

In July at the Mandalay Bay in Las Vegas, Khan met Zab Judah. It is the forgotten fight in Khan's career. Judah was the IBF champion and had held world titles at two weights. This was Khan's show, the kid from Bolton topping a Las Vegas bill against an American world champion. 'It will be man against boy,' warned Judah, who had just found religion. Khan stopped him in round five. 'I think Amir is in front of Manny [Pacquiao] right now,' said Freddie Roach. 'It took Manny eight years to get to the point where he became unbeatable. Amir has been with me three years and he's getting closer and closer.' Pacquiao was Roach's finest creation, so this was serious praise.

A few months later, a couple of weeks before Christmas, the Khan carnival came to a controversial end in Washington DC. Khan and his team acted like they believed they were bullet-proof before the Lamont Peterson fight. Nobody in boxing has that much protection. Peterson had lost just once in thirty-one fights, he was not dead at the weight, and he was just two years older than Khan. Over 9,000 tickets had been sold, some as cheaply as $25, for Peterson's homecoming. Peterson had once been homeless, sleeping on the DC streets to survive. The bookies had installed Khan as a prohibitive favourite.

In round one Khan dropped Peterson twice – only one was ruled a knockdown – but it was not over. It was a good, tight, even fight after that first round. Khan lost a point in round seven for pushing Peterson's head down. It was innocuous, but illegal. The ref, a guy called Joe Cooper, was inexperienced. Khan should have been told not to push Peterson's head down again by his corner. His corner needed to let the referee know that Peterson's head was dangerous, make the ref think twice about what he was doing. Men like Mickey Duff, Angelo Dundee and Dean Powell would have been driving Cooper crazy, pointing out the dangerous head and screaming. Instead there was silence, and then in round twelve there was disaster: Cooper took another point off Khan for the same lame infringement. The fight was lost. The scores confirmed the calamity of the deductions: two judges went for Peterson 113-112 and the third went Khan wide with 115-110. If Khan had not lost the points he would have kept both his titles. 'It's not my fault, I never took his points away,' said Peterson. A rematch the following March fell through when the American failed a drugs test.

After a comical press conference when Tyson Fury hired two dwarfs as security for Dereck 'Del Boy' Chisora, the pair met at Wembley for the British and Commonwealth heavyweight titles. They were each unbeaten in fourteen, and Fury was able to control the fight and win a clear decision in front of 1.6 million people on Channel Five. 'I respect Del, he came to fight,' said Fury. There was premature talk of a fight with Wladimir Klitschko.

Four months later, in November, Fury was dropped by Neven

Pajkić in the first round, dropped the Sarajevo-born Canadian twice in the third, and won a slugfest. It was before this fight that Fury talked about his 'depressive mode' and the pressure and expectation on him. 'The boxing keeps me sane,' he said. 'I still get challenges from Gypsies. They get a few beers in them, start jumping about thinking they are Tyson or Ali, throwing punches, swearing and jumping around with their fat bellies. I'd love to knock a few of them out.'

At the Dale Youth gym on the ground floor of Grenfell Tower, near Shepherd's Bush in west London, there were pictures of James DeGale and George Groves on the wall, separated by a few inches. The pair had been boys at the gym and Mick Delaney, the coach there for thirty years, insisted they were just two schoolboy boxers. 'We were never close: I never really liked him and he never really liked me,' said DeGale. In 2007 at Brent Town Hall Groves had beaten DeGale in the north-west London divisional championship. It was tight, the pair never shook hands. It was also big news, and I announced the result live on BBC London. DeGale was national amateur champion in 2005 and 2006 and Groves won the same weight in 2007 and 2008. In the months before the Beijing Olympics the pair were training at different times in the gym, being kept apart by the men at Dale Youth. 'It was not ideal,' said Delaney. It was not ideal for the GB selectors. A tournament was held in Sheffield to settle the problem: Groves lost twice and DeGale won twice, beating the men that beat his rival. DeGale got the Olympic slot, won the gold, and they both turned professional.

They met for the British and Commonwealth super-middleweight titles in front of 18,000 at the O2 in May. DeGale had fought ten times, Groves twelve, and once again it was close. One judge scored a draw, the other two went for Groves by just one round. The fight did nothing to heal the hate, and even in January 2017, after DeGale's draw against Badou Jack in New York, there was fresh talk about a third fight with Groves. It is a long, unique and spiteful rivalry.

The Contenders

British boxers were in world title fights in eight divisions and six countries, and it was often hard. Matthew Hatton lost a decision to Saúl 'Canelo' Álvarez for the WBC light-middleweight title in January. Ryan Rhodes went to Mexico in June to fight Álvarez and was stopped in the last round. Brian Magee lost an IBF super-middleweight fight to Lucien Bute in March, but won the interim WBA version in July against Jaime Barboza in Costa Rica. Felix Sturm was fortunate in two defences of his WBA middleweight title against British boxers: in June he got a split over Matt Macklin and in December he escaped with a draw against Martin Murray. The Macklin fight was bad. Another Murray, the Manchester lightweight John, was stopped in New York by Brandon Rios. Both Murray's eyes were closed in a nasty fight for the vacant WBA title. Ricky Burns made two defences of his WBO super-feather title and in November moved to light-weight and outpointed Michael Katsidis to win the WBO lightweight belt. It was a masterclass from Burns. Nathan Cleverly also made two defences of his WBO light-heavyweight title, and the second, against Tony Bellew in Liverpool in October, was lively. It was tight, and Bellew lost. There was no robbery in Liverpool that night.

From the Notepad

'I'm just a pro boxer with a young family, a mortgage, and I'm fighting to earn a living. I'm also Ricky's lickle brother,' said Matthew before the Álvarez loss.

In Las Vegas, Amir Khan bumped into his great rival Tim Bradley. 'You need to grow some balls,' Khan told him. 'He never said a word but some of his team started to get brave.' You can take a kid out of Bolton.

Kevin Mitchell was in a dark place in May. 'I have blown all my dough on cars and watches. I have spunked hundreds of grands.' He beat John Murray in July to ease his pain and got another world title fight in 2012.

In November, Audley Harrison was on the BBC's *Strictly* with his left knee in a brace, his ankles in bulky supports and his ambitions soaring. 'The time is right for me to fight again,' he warned. Ron Boddy insists that DeGale did shake hands with Groves after the fight. 'He told George to go and win the title.' The Boddyman is seldom wrong on tiny boxing details.

2012

'I remember David as a little boy and it will not be easy to take him out.'
Audley Harrison on his fight with David Price

*'I'm six foot nine, I'm eighteen stone, I've got a heart of a lion
and I can punch – I wouldn't want to fight me.'*
Tyson Fury

IT IS HARD to fully appreciate the pure mayhem of the day and night in Munich in February when Dereck Chisora pushed Vitali Klitschko, David Haye hit Chisora, and an armed squad of police came to my hotel door at four a.m.

It had been a bad week, with Chisora slapping Vitali at the weigh-in and then spitting water in Wladimir's face in the ring before the introductions. Don Charles, coach and long-suffering friend of Chisora, was concerned. 'The slap was not meant to happen,' he said. An hour before the fight there was a truly ugly stand-off in the dressing rooms when Wlad, who was there as an official observer, demanded that Del Boy take off his bandages and wrap his hands again. That did not go down too well and some quick diplomacy was needed. In the WBC heavyweight title fight itself, held in the beautiful Olympic boxing venue, a capacity crowd of 13,000 witnessed the hardest fight Vitali had been in since the 2003 loss to Lennox Lewis. Once the bell went, once the first punch had been thrown, a calm Chisora went looking for the upset. The final scores were harsh on him.

An hour later was when the story of the night started and the memories of the fight faded quickly. Vitali, Chisora, Charles, Frank Warren and Bernd Bönte were at the press conference when David Haye arrived. Haye had been with me on BoxNation, but was at the press conference after German TV asked him to attend. At that point he was close to ending his retirement and agreeing a fight with Vitali in Germany in June. Haye took up a standing position at the back of the room and started to heckle. It was innocent stuff, at first. Chisora asked him about his toe and that got a laugh. Haye was silent for a second, Adam Booth, his coach, at his side.

'Chisora showed heart,' said Bönte. 'You showed your toe.'

The mood was changing.

'If Haye is a fighter, he should fight me. I will give you two slaps,' said Chisora.

'Let's fight,' said Haye.

'I've got a great idea,' said Warren. 'Dereck fights Haye and the winner fights Vitali.'

That got a polite chuckle.

'Sounds like the perfect plan,' said Bönte.

Then Haye turned it back on Chisora: 'Vitali said he would knock me out, do you think you can?' It was an immediate challenge.

'Be quiet – can security get him out of here?' said Charles, who could sense Chisora would go and confront Haye; Charles also knew that Haye was not joking.

The security remained close to the top table.

'I'm coming down,' said Chisora.

He got up and went to meet Haye. Nobody stopped him, the gathered and assorted hacks let him through. The pair were face-to-face for a few seconds before Haye threw the first punch. He was still holding a soft-drinks bottle in his right hand when he landed just under Chisora's chin. They scuffled, pushed each other, and were pushed and pulled by people getting involved and caught in the fight's natural violent movement. Booth was hit on the head by a tripod and Haye was swinging the tripod. Charles had his jaw broken when Haye cracked him with a right. Real fights, fast, violent clashes, do not follow any of the choreographed rules of fake fights. This was savage, quick, confusing and bloody. Haye managed to get out. Chisora was left threatening violence, but he did apologize to a dazed Booth.

Haye jumped in a van and, just as it was pulling away, somebody looked behind and there, staggering in the middle of the road, was Booth with blood running down his face from the scalp wound. It had just started to snow again. The van's driver stalled in panic and Jim Rosenthal, fresh from six hours of presenting, took over at the wheel. The sirens were blaring as the van left and a dozen police cars were travelling at speed in the opposite direction. Haye and Booth were on the floor between the seats. At the hotel there was a quick turnaround. Haye remained in the van, parked in a playground of snow. I cleaned Booth's wound and off he went to the airport to catch the first plane.

A few hours later there was a knock on my door. I peeped through – somebody had ordered me a Village People tribute band. There was one guy in a full leather coat, another with a bike helmet and shades (at four a.m.!) and another in a tight T-shirt and baseball cap. I opened the door, toeing the blood-stained tissues through the bathroom door and out of sight just in time. 'Is Haye here?' the man in the coat demanded. The police left after a few minutes.

The following morning, long after Haye and Booth had landed in London, the German police grabbed Chisora and Charles at the airport. They were held for questioning and released.

Haye–Chisora was made official in early May and would take place in July. It was not called a rematch and it operated under the auspices of the Luxembourg Boxing Federation at the Boleyn Ground in east London: Chisora's licence had been suspended by the British Boxing Board of Control and Haye had relinquished his when he retired. There was a tough Board directive issued in May warning that any licence holders involved with the fight would have their licence terminated. Haye and Chisora met at conferences and at the weigh-in, which was held in front of 600 at the Odeon in Leicester Square, but were separated at all times by a steel fence. It was wonderful and necessary pantomime. 'He would be lighter than me if he was not so fat,' said Haye. Chisora replied, 'How's your toe?' Haye was 15st, Chisora 17st 9lb.

It was a great fight, and it ended in multiple embraces. Chisora was dropped heavily twice and stopped with just one second left in round five. Haye was just in front but Chisora looked stronger at the start of the fifth round. It was memorable for the 30,000 punters. Haye retired again.

Carl Froch is a truly remarkable man. In May he agreed for the short-end money to fight Lucian Bute for the IBF super-middleweight title. Bute was unbeaten in thirty, two years younger in life and years younger in boxing terms, and making his tenth defence. 'Carl is in the last-chance saloon and he knows it,' said Eddie Hearn, the sole boxing promoter operating on Sky. 'It's me again with an unbeaten champion, a good fighter. That is exactly what I like,' said Froch. There was a lovely story about Bute playing 'hostile crowd noise' in his gym in Canada to prepare for the Nottingham fans. It was never going to be enough; Froch walked out majestic, regal and serious to a raw greeting from 9,000 fans. It was his first fight in Nottingham since October 2009 and he knew it was 'all or nothing'.

Froch was ruthless, Bute looked shocked by his mistake in accepting the fight. In round four Bute was hurt near the bell and staggered back to his wide-eyed corner. They let him out for the fifth, but they all looked sick as he walked to his end. Froch sent him sprawling down the ropes and the referee was stopping it after sixty-five seconds as the corner surrendered. A split second before it was official, Hearn vaulted into the ring howling in relief and joy. It was a bit messy. Froch was back as world champion, an overnight success after ten years.

A rare thing happened in November: Froch took an easy fight. Yusuf Mack, a father of ten, arrived with Philadelphia boxing royalty, Buster Custis and Brother Nazim Richardson, in his corner. It was Froch's delayed homecoming, the softer touch that all fighters get for their first defence. Mack was down twice and stopped in the third. Mack's life had been hard; he was a father at eleven and revealed in 2014 that he was having affairs with transgender women. One daughter suggested he kill himself. 'I thought about it,' he admitted.

In July, after four years operating under the strict protocol of Freddie Roach's terms of survival, Amir Khan fought like a lunatic against unbeaten Danny Garcia. When Khan's rematch with Lamont Peterson had collapsed after the American tested positive for synthetic testosterone, Garcia, the WBC champion, had agreed terms. Khan was back as the main attraction at the Mandalay Bay and fought two sensible rounds before getting caught and dropped in the third. His legs deserted him, but he tried to fight his way back. 'Amir was wild,' confirmed Roach, unable to hide the disappointment. Khan's eyes cleared during the break, he went out for the fourth, was over twice and pleading for it to continue when it was stopped. It was a disturbing final round and at 25, after twenty-nine fights and a hard life since the Olympics at the tender age of 17, there were many that thought Khan was finished.

But there was a win in December, a stoppage in Los Angeles, and a different man was in Khan's corner. Khan had walked away from Roach and started to work with Virgil Hunter, the man behind Andre Ward. There had been too many gym wars with Roach, and Khan needed protection from his own bravery. 'Amir can listen and that is crucial,' said Hunter. Part of Hunter's regime was analysis, the ability to talk through the screaming ruins of his lost fights.

In the last rounds of Ricky Hatton's prizefighting life he was talking to himself as he started to take too many punches. The uneasy retirement finally ended when Hatton met former world champion Vyacheslav Senchenko at the MEN, his personal ring, in November. Hatton had not fought since the loss to Manny Pacquiao in May 2009. 'I want to know what is left and that's why I have picked Senchenko,' said Hatton. Every ticket, just over 19,000 of them, had sold before the Ukrainian's name was mentioned. This was a goodbye fight and the fans, the thousands that had gone on the road, wanted to be there. The tales from the gym were mixed, but after two years of suicide attempts, cocaine binges, rehab visits, brutal splits with his family and false starts, it was sensible just to ignore the gossips.

Senchenko survived the crowd and a few rounds of vintage Hatton, and then took the idol apart. Hatton went down and out, retching for breath and taking the full count in round nine. It was over, but he delayed the announcement for an hour, and even then there were American members of his promotional team talking about a Las Vegas fight, one final jolly boys' party for the faithful.

The eight GB members of the Beijing boxing squad had turned professional before the first bell at the London Olympics. It was a harsh reality for the men in charge of picking teams, a massive disadvantage against the Cubans, Russians, Kazakhs and Uzbeks. Still, Luke Campbell and Anthony Joshua won gold, Fred Evans a silver and Anthony Ogogo a bronze. The women competed at three weights: Nicola Adams won gold and Natasha Jonas missed out on a medal when she lost to Ireland's Katie Taylor; it was Taylor's hardest fight on her way to gold. The Belfast duo of Michael Conlan and Paddy Barnes also won a bronze. Joshua was world heavyweight champion before Rio in 2016, Campbell had lost, Ogogo was two months away from a disturbing loss, and Evans had vanished. Olympic medals are not instant pro currency. Nicola Adams turned professional in early 2017.

The Contenders

There was interim title madness with Scott Quigg in a technical draw against Rendall Munroe and then winning the rematch for the WBA super-bantamweight title, Martin Murray winning the interim WBA middleweight title, and Brian Magee the interim WBA super-middle version. In December, Magee was stopped by Mikkel Kessler for the full WBA title.

In January, Derry Mathews was stopped by Emiliano Marsili for the IBO lightweight title. Mathews stopped Anthony Crolla to win the British lightweight title three months later but lost the title to Gavin Rees when he was stopped in nine in July. His year was not finished: he lost in Prizefighter in October to Terry Flanagan. Dirty Derry, as he is known, is a modern throwback.

Nathan Cleverly made two defences of his WBO light-heavyweight title, one in Los Angeles.

Ricky Burns beat Paulus Moses in March and stopped his friend, Kevin Mitchell, in Glasgow in September. 'We were mates before the fight and we are mates now,' said Mitchell after losing in the fourth. 'I never underestimated him, he is just so much better than I thought.'

Darren Hamilton had slept rough on the Bristol streets, moved to London, found a gym, and in May beat Ashley Theophane to become British light-welterweight champion. Theophane would become part of Floyd Mayweather's Money Team, but had boxed for All Stars when he was an amateur. Hamilton and Theophane were hard, unglamorous operators.

From the Notepad

When Cleverly beat Tom Karpency in February, the plan was to get Karpency back for Enzo Maccarinelli to knock out. 'The fight Wales wants is me and Nathan,' said Enzo. Nice idea, never happened.

Audley Harrison ended his latest exile in May. 'If I can't beat Ali Adams then I don't deserve to be boxing,' he remarked. Aud had said the same thing several times. He won, and then fought David Price for the British heavyweight title in October. 'I remember David as a little boy and it will not be easy to take him out,' said Aud. The dilemma was avoided as he was knocked out cold in eighty-two seconds.

The win did not impress Tyson Fury, who lost on points to Price in 2007. 'I will not stand there like Audley,' he said. 'It will take a few rounds and then I will knock out Price.' Fury won three times in 2012, including an eliminator for the WBC title.

During the Olympics the job of vacuuming the ring canvas between sessions was left to 1984 bronze medal winner Bobby Wells. 'It's not a comeback,' Wells told me.

Burns was in typically honest mood before beating Mitchell. 'I feared for him during his bad days.' There had been serious turmoil in Mitchell's life since the Michael Katsidis loss in 2010.

In October, Manny Steward died suddenly, and Lennox Lewis was emotional. 'He got me through some of my toughest fights and I'm only sad that I couldn't do the same for him.'

Kieran Farrell had a fit in the ambulance after losing on points to Crolla in December. He recovered slowly, and there was no surgery. 'I couldn't put my socks on when I first came home,' he said. He also revealed that he had gained 18lb between the weigh-in and the fight. Once again losing weight was a factor in a boxing head injury.

2013

'I was under a bit of pressure before the fight with people driving me mad and I know now why I never sold tickets – I moved about two hundred for this fight and they all wanted to talk to me; I had to go out the back for a snout to get a bit of peace and quiet.'
Johnny Greaves on the problems of being popular an hour before winning his final fight to end his career (won four, lost ninety-six)

'It's a setback, and heavyweights have setbacks. In two or three fights this will all be ancient history.'
David Price on his first loss

IT WAS SUPPOSED to be so easy for Carl Froch in November when he met George Groves in Manchester in his second fight of the year. His routine defence came so close to being his final appearance.

In May, Froch had boxed quite brilliantly to get revenge over Denmark's Mikkel Kessler in front of 19,000 at the O2 on a Sky pay-per-view card. Froch kept his IBF super-middleweight title and added Kessler's WBA version in a fight where the cheap baubles, studded with fake diamonds and vulgarly fur-lined, looked like the tacky attachments they are. On the night, which started late for the HBO cameras, the fight was poised after six rounds, but by the end of round eight Froch was looking stronger. I was working on Five Live with Ricky Hatton and he said to me at the start of round nine: 'Froch is unbeatable tonight, unbeatable.' In round ten Froch's knees finally dipped and he was forced, ragged and exhausted, to hold and survive. In the last two rounds Froch came back. The boxers fell into each other's arms at the final bell. Their bruises and cuts were disguised by cosmetic dabs, but the damage from a fight like this, at this stage in a good fighter's career, can run a lot deeper. Froch got the decision, clear and beyond doubt. Kessler never fought again.

Froch talked about a risk-free fight in November and then a meeting with ringside guest Andre Ward at a stadium in May 2014. 'I would beat him easier the next time and the first fight was not close,' said Ward. It looked like a done deal, and Groves was selected as the November date, a British kid with pedigree and a win over James DeGale in his nineteen unbeaten fights. He was not quite a sacrifice, but he was certainly not meant to be a test.

'Groves is dangerous because he's unbeaten, young, and that means he will be foolish,' said Froch. 'He is annoying me. He is proud and I know it will be hard.' There was a ringside divide on the night between those that thought there would be a fight and those that thought Froch was going to walk through Groves. There was very little middle ground as the lights dimmed and the pair made their way through 19,000 to the ring. Groves had his new man, Paddy Fitzpatrick, with him in the corner. Adam Booth, his old coach, was next to me working for Five Live. He was nervous, but confident Groves would win.

Froch was dropped in round one when a big right connected cleanly. He went down in a heavy and damaged heap. He was gone, finished, but he found his balance, got up and fought until the bell in a round that no witness will ever forget. The fight's pace continued, Froch was hurt again, Groves put under pressure, and by about round six Groves was in front. Froch had recovered from the knockdown and was coming back into the fight in round nine when he caught, hurt and sent Groves stumbling into the ropes. He connected again. Groves came off the ropes and staggered in front of the referee, Howard Foster; Froch was chasing and hitting him when it was stopped. The time was 1:33 of the ninth, and for ten minutes the fans booed. It was over, Froch had won a timeless classic.

The debate had started long before the three men left the ring: was it stopped too early? I had seen Groves sag on the ropes, his body disturbingly limp for a second or two, and it was a second later that Foster stopped it. I had no problem with the stoppage.

'For a few rounds it looked like Carl Froch's career was over,' said Eddie Hearn. 'He took a hiding in there at times. I just had no idea at one point how he was going to turn it round.' Froch was still dazed in the aftermath, admitting with a smile that he couldn't remember the knockdown.

'I'm a victim of my false reputation for being chinny and of Carl's reputation for being a warrior,' said Groves. 'Froch's boxing celebrity status has stood in the way of me becoming world champion.'

Late that night Robert McCracken, Froch's coach and long-time friend, was still recovering when I met with him in the fight-hotel bar. There was a vile storm of controversy growing online and ugly, untrue conspiracies about Foster. However, at one a.m., nobody knew how big the story was going to be. 'We might not see Carl again,' warned McCracken. Twenty feet away a group of men were relaxing, drinking, chatting and laughing. They had all been at the fight, working; one of them was Howard Foster, blissfully unaware about what was coming. He would receive death threats in the next few weeks.

Darren Barker was broken and had no right to be in the ring in August, looking over at Daniel Geale before their IBF middleweight title fight. Barker's hips had been operated on, he had survived a street attack that left him unconscious, and he would never recover from his younger brother's death in a car crash. Gary was his inspiration. Barker had lost a world title fight in Atlantic City in 2011 when Sergio Martínez stopped him in round eleven for the WBC's diamond belt. He was back in Atlantic City for Geale, armed with desire that defied category. In round six the Australian connected with boxing's fiercest and most clinical finishing punch when a short hook connected under Barker's right elbow. Barker went down. All bets are off when that sort of punch lands. He was on all fours with his head and face buried in the canvas. That was when something helped him get up. 'I could sense his spirit telling me to get up,' Barker said. 'I knew it was Gary, I saw his face.' Nobody could quite believe he beat the count. At the end of twelve rounds Barker won a split decision.

Barker's body was close to ruined when he went to Germany for his first defence in December. He got paid for the risk of fighting Felix Sturm. His right hip hurt from the first seconds; his movement was limited and he was caught and dropped twice. He was on his feet when Tony Sims, his coach, threw the towel in. Barker never fought again and just might be the happiest retired boxer in British history.

Matt Macklin and Martin Murray both met Sturm in world title fights but they never met each other, and neither fought Barker. It was a unique triangle of talented British middleweights that missed each other. Barker–Macklin was on and off for nearly three years.

'Twice I have accepted a Macklin fight,' said Murray. 'I'm not in this sport to be a superstar, I'm in this sport to support my family. I don't need any excuses.' In April, Murray went with a travelling party that included Hatton to Argentina to fight Sergio Martínez. It was hostile; the fans were locked in a secure area for their protection. Martínez had not fought in his home country for ten years and had just been voted the most popular Argentinian sportsman, beating Lionel Messi. He was a great mystery. He had won three fights in Britain in 2003 and 2004, returned to Spain (where he was based), and finally in 2010 won the WBC middleweight title. He beat Barker and in 2012 stopped Macklin. The Murray fight was his sixth defence.

It was a night of developing natural disasters and the fight was brought forward ninety minutes when a violent storm approached the 50,000 fans. Murray was brilliant. Martínez was bullied and dropped in round eight. He was dropped again in round ten, but it was ruled a slip. He was given twenty seconds to get up. At the final bell all three judges went narrowly for Martínez with an identical score of 115-112. 'I didn't do enough,' said Murray. 'He's the champion and that's the way it works.' It was tight, Murray was honest.

Eight weeks later Macklin was paralysed by Gennady Golovkin in three rounds for the IBO and WBA middleweight titles. 'There was nothing I could do,' he said. 'He cracked my ribs and he enjoyed it.' Golovkin was just finding his feet in 2013. Martínez, his natural rival, had one fight left and in 2014 he cashed out with a payday in New York against Miguel Cotto. He lost and quit.

In the seventies the walls at the Felt Forum, the venue in the basement at Madison Square Garden, would sweat on Friday fight nights. In April it was Tyson Fury's turn in the ancient ring. He was in New York to fight Steve Cunningham, and the American was not impressed. 'I've been in camp with the Klitschko brothers and if they were six foot, they would both be good fighters,' said Cunningham. 'If Fury was six foot, he would be nothing.' Fury had dismissed Cunningham's street credentials. 'Why is it that all American fighters have to talk about gangs, guns and going to prison?' said Fury. 'Forget all that nonsense talk and answer me this: how much to get my Twitter name on the bottom of your boots? I can reach millions that way.' The Americans were not impressed, and veteran coach Nazim Richardson dismissed Fury: 'Fury is like the new Primo Carnera.' That's a big insult, a suggestion that he was manufactured, had no talent, and was only there because of his size.

In round two Fury stood in front of Cunningham and was caught and dropped heavily. It was foolish to stand with his hands down. Cunningham had been the cruiserweight world champion. He was smaller by about five inches but in his previous fight he had lost a heavyweight title eliminator by a split decision. He could fight, and he was motivated. Fury survived, and in round seven he put together a combination, which included an elbow, and Cunningham went down and out. Fury was trailing on two of the three scorecards at the time. 'I got caught, went down, then got up to win,' said Fury after serenading the crowd with a song from the ring. 'It's what real fighting men have to do.'

It had started for Audley Harrison in 2001 when he became an instant millionaire on his debut, and it finished in seventy seconds against Deontay Wilder in Sheffield in April 2013. Harrison was 41, had just won his second Prizefighter tournament, and was taking a risk fighting Wilder, unbeaten in twenty-seven with twenty-seven stoppages or knockouts. Wilder did hit Harrison when he was down. Harrison never fought again, but he kept threatening one more last fight.

On the same night in Sheffield Amir Khan survived a nasty fourth-round knockdown to beat Julio Díaz over twelve rounds. It was Khan's only appearance in 2013; he no longer looked like a kid and he no longer fought like a kid.

In August there was a shocking weekend in Cardiff for WBO light-heavyweight champion Nathan Cleverly. In April he had retained his title for the fourth time with a win over his mandatory, Robin Krasniqi. Over 6,000 fans packed the arena in the summer to see Cleverly fight Sergey Kovalev. The night before the fight, Kathy Duva, Kovalev's promoter at Main Events, told me she was shocked anybody thought Kovalev would lose. 'Are you guys all crazy?' she asked. A few minutes earlier Cleverly's father, Vince, had told me that beating Kovalev would not be a problem. Dean Powell, the matchmaker, knew it was not easy and was concerned on the day.

The Russian was unbeaten in twenty-two, had stopped nineteen, and eighteen of them had been in rounds one, two and three. He was ruthless but Cleverly was sharp, confident and not bothered by Kovalev's power in the first two rounds. In round two Kovalev was cut over the right eye. He was moaning and he spat out his gumshield. He was not happy, and that meant he was angry. The third round was bad. Cleverly was too brave, had no respect, was dropped twice and finished the round stunned and stumbling in the referee's arms. It could have been stopped then. It was not, and Cleverly came out for the fourth – came out for definite slaughter. After twenty-one seconds he was down again and it was off. It was Cleverly's first loss in twenty-seven fights.

Less than four weeks later Dean Powell was dead. I had known him since 1986 when I went to Dudley amateur boxing club to interview Ronnie Brown, the coach. Powell suffered from depression and had taken his own life.

The Contenders

In January it looked like Froch would have to fight Adonis Stevenson, his mandatory. Stevenson moved up, won the IBF light-heavyweight title, and stopped Tony Bellew in November.

Gavin Rees lost to Adrien Broner for the WBC lightweight title in Atlantic City.

Matthew Hatton went to South Africa and lost on points to Chris Van Heerden for the IBO welterweight title in March.

Dennis Hobson, the Sheffield promoter and elite ducker and diver, put on a bold fight outdoors in Doncaster in May when Jamie McDonnell won the vacant IBF bantamweight title. McDonnell left Hobson, was stripped, and in December Hobson put Stuart Hall in with Vusi Malinga for the same vacant title. Hall, a veteran of several lost years in Ibiza, won a brutal fight. 'It's been a tough year,' said Hall. 'I've been back on the tools [roofing] to make a few quid. I've been down to my last hundred a few times. It's Christmas now in every single way.'

Ricky Burns had an easy defence of his WBO lightweight title in May and was in a real fight in September when he met Raymundo Beltrán. Burns was dropped in round eight, had his jaw broken in round three, and narrowly retained on points. It was his ninth consecutive world title fight and he was exhausted. He denied making weight was a factor.

Scott Quigg had two fights in six weeks, one a draw, the other a win, and he was upgraded from interim to full WBA super-bantamweight champion. In Belfast, Carl Frampton had started to talk about Quigg and won twice. Both camps made and rejected offers, traded insults, and started to sell their 2016 fight.

Scott Harrison lost for the last time when Liam Walsh beat him over ten rounds for the WBO lightweight title at Wembley. Harrison was 35, his face too easily betrayed the timeline of his descent, but he was stoic in defeat, a great neglected and sad British tale. Liam's brother, Ryan, dropped a decision to Lee Selby in October for the British and Commonwealth featherweight title.

Kid Galahad, the latest product from Brendan Ingle's gym in Wincobank on the outskirts of Sheffield, won the vacant British super-bantamweight title when he stopped Jazza Dickens. 'The Kid is the latest, not the last,' warned Ingle. Herol Graham had been Ingle's first British champion, in 1981.

From the Notepad

It looked like David Price was two fights from a Klitschko bout when he sold out the Echo in Liverpool to fight Tony Thompson in February. 'In this country the demand to step up is greater than anywhere else,' said Price. It was his sixteenth fight and it was over in the second. Price's eardrum was damaged, his legs and unbeaten record gone. Thompson was 41 and still a good heavyweight but, with odds of 80-1 on a win in two rounds, it was a terrible shock. 'In two or three fights this will all be ancient history,' said Pricey.

There was another victim when Frank Maloney, Pricey's promoter, went to hospital with a suspected heart attack. Maloney never wanted the rematch and was not happy when Lennox Lewis appeared as Pricey's new adviser. They met in July, same venue and same winner. Thompson was dropped heavily in the second and then stopped an exhausted Price in round five. 'The adrenalin drained me; my body wasn't doing what my mind wanted,' said Price. 'He was gassed, he should have finished it when he put Thompson down,' said Lewis. It was too much for a tearful Maloney. 'I'm finished,' he said.

In October, Anthony Joshua made his pro debut at the O2, and on the same night in Moscow, Wladimir Klitschko was paid $17.5 million for beating Alexander Povetkin. They were a long, long way from ever meeting on that night.

In September, David Haye pulled out of a fight with Tyson Fury less than a week before the first bell. 'He's bottled it, I told you it would happen,' said Fury. Haye showed pictures of a cut over his left eye. It had needed six stitches and was opened by Croatia's Filip Hrgović. 'My sparring partners were better than Fury,' Haye countered. A new date was announced for 2014, but in November Haye had a five-hour operation on his shoulder. The subscapularis and bicep tendon attachments were ruptured. Fury lost the fight again. It was a terrible time for him.

In March, Michael Norgrove, a pro having his sixth fight, collapsed in round five at the Ring in Blackfriars. He fell gently into the arms of the referee, Jeff Hinds, and was lowered to the canvas. He died in early April, the first casualty in a British ring since October 1995. He was winning the fight that killed him.

2014

*'I lost the lottery-winning ticket twice. The money was there and
then it was gone. It was heart-breaking, and all people
seemed to talk about were my tweets.'*
Tyson Fury on his two cancelled fights with David Haye

*'You know Harry Levene used to say: "It doesn't matter if you are
rich or poor – as long as you've got money." That's right,
but you need to have fuck 'em money.'*
Mickey Duff with a deathless addition to an ancient boxing axiom

IN THE END the money did talk and Carl Froch met George Groves
again in front of 80,000 people at Wembley in a fight that would
either ruin or make his reputation.

The verbal and physical skirmishes, which had started at the end
of the first fight when Froch initially refused to shake hands, continued until every available seat was sold. Froch never wanted the
second fight. Groves had to fund a journey to the IBF in New Jersey
where he pleaded and lobbied for a rematch, presenting an eclectic
dossier to reinforce his claim. He had evidence from a psychologist
who had studied Howard Foster, the referee in the first fight. Groves
calculates that he spent £20,000 of his own money. It worked: the IBF
sanctioned a rematch.

'He tried to price himself out, ignore me, insult me, and I know he
was forced to take the fight,' insisted Groves. It was not that simple.
Froch had no idea if he was going to continue fighting and then the

sums started to add up, people started to murmur, there were doubts. 'Money talks,' said Eddie Hearn, the promoter of the fight. 'This fight was always going to happen.' It was made for Wembley Stadium in May.

'I was guilty of mentally not taking him seriously,' said Froch. 'My body was right, I took no shortcuts in the gym, but my mind was wrong. I did think about walking away, but I want to beat him again.' Top fighters want to quit and not leave behind a single question if they go on their terms. Joe Calzaghe and Lennox Lewis had timed their exits perfectly, and Froch wanted the same.

Groves entered the playing field in a double decker bus. Froch looked harder, meaner and angrier than ever. Robert McCracken had dismissed claims by Paddy Fitzpatrick, the maverick coach with Groves, that the camp was in crisis and that Froch was struggling. 'He's been to see a quack quack,' said Fitzpatrick. 'There is nothing Froch can do to deal with Groves.' There was, even in the vast open-sky venue, a powerful sense of intimacy at ringside. The fight had significant meaning and the many hateful encounters had created a mood.

It was slower than the first fight, more cautious, and smarter from Froch. Groves was relaxed, perhaps too relaxed, but at the end of round seven I had it 4-3 to Groves. One of the three judges agreed with me, but it was irrelevant. 'I hit him with the left, moved him, and then let the right go. Boom!' said Froch. Groves was caught flush and was out before he hit the canvas. His left leg tucked and stuck under his thigh. He woke, moved, the leg sprung free, and it was stopped at 2:43 of round eight. They did eventually shake hands, but the hatred remains. 'I made a split-second mistake, I opened my shoulders – it happens in boxing,' claimed Groves, and that is all it takes at the top level.

Froch never retired that night but he knew when he peered in the dressing-room mirror that it was over. There were few visible blemishes; the real wounds were all part of his long and documented suffering in the years devoted to becoming a wealthy prizefighter. His body was held together in too many places by gristle and hope.

The Titanic Quarter in Belfast was blustery at seven p.m. and freezing cold under the darkest of skies three hours later when in September over 16,000 roared Carl Frampton to the IBF super-bantamweight title.

Frampton had stopped Kiko Martínez in 2013, but since that night the Spaniard had won the title against an unbeaten fighter in America, defended against one former champion in Spain, and taken the money to fight another former world champion in Japan. Martínez stopped all three, was fearless, brave, and convinced he would win. 'He's a different fighter now, I know that,' said Frampton. The fabled fighting city had fallen in love with Frampton. It was lazy to call him the new Barry McGuigan, but no other Irish fighter had come close to the love and adoration McGuigan enjoyed during his short reign as champion. 'He's better than I ever was,' said McGuigan. It certainly felt like Frampton was close to the same affection, close to being a real idol in a divided city unified by its fighters.

Frampton dropped Martínez in round five and was excellent until the final bell. He won on points, and his face and body formed a sore skin-map of suffering – bruises, lumps, cuts and a left hand so bloated it looked like it belonged to a drowning victim. The following morning Frampton could barely walk to his car, both hands lame and his face swollen and purple. 'I just need some rest,' he muttered.

Kell Brook told me in late 2013 that he was ready to walk away from boxing after yet another world title fight collapsed. 'What more can I do? I've been waiting, I'm ready, and I will fight anybody,' he said. In August he travelled to Carson, a suburb of Los Angeles, to fight IBF welterweight champion Shawn Porter, who was unbeaten in twenty-five fights. This was the modern version of the lost causes from the fifties, sixties and seventies that British boxers accepted and went on. At the end of round ten, Dominic Ingle, in Brook's corner, told him, 'You can win this, there's nothing in it.' Brook had a good eleventh round and did enough in a hard fight that had its ugly physical moments. It's always a joy when a British boxer in America makes the Americans complain. Nigel Benn had famously infuriated the Las Vegas faithful in his foul-filled stoppage of Iran Barkley in

1990. 'I love sticking it up the Yanks,' Benn had boasted. Porter's people moaned about Brook's tactics and forgot to mention their boxer's punches to the back of the head. The British judge, Dave Parris, scored it a draw, the two American officials went wide for Brook. It was a good win.

Less than four weeks later Brook nearly died when he was the victim of a machete attack in Tenerife. He was left in a puddle of his own blood at dawn after a bewildering night of drinking with people he had only just met. He looked sickened in the photographs, snapped at the hospital, and even the obligatory thumbs-up from Hearn, who flew in on the day of the attack, looked limp. The assault remains an unsolved mystery.

If a fighter is dependent on the mercy of his cornermen for more than a round or two it can make watching from ringside disturbing. In November it was obvious that Dereck Chisora was struggling in his rematch with Tyson Fury. He had been thumbed in the eye in round two, was trailing, was cut, and was offering very little other than his courage. 'I was ready to stop it from about five,' admitted Don Charles in Chisora's corner. At the end of round ten it was stopped. 'No more, it's over,' Charles told Chisora. There was no complaint.

Fury had fought as a southpaw, using every inch and pound of his advantage to control a fight that had looked competitive until the roar of the capacity crowd of 18,000 at the ExCel drowned the first bell. Fury was patient, hard to hit and composed – he fought like Wladimir Klitschko had, putting brain before stupidity. 'That was the real Tyson Fury in there, that is the man I see every day,' said Peter Fury, the fighter's uncle and coach.

In June, Fury had been fined fifteen grand by the British Boxing Board of Control for a rant about Chisora, and in September he'd shown up for one press conference with white tape over his mouth. He never uttered a word. I hosted two very public head-to-heads with the pair before the fight; the one in Manchester was a bit mad, but the one in London was a love-in. 'C'mon, Big Del, give us a hug,' said Fury. The pair shook hands and talked sensibly about dignity and the honour and privilege of fighting for the British title. Heavyweights have always been a contradictory fighting species.

The Fury fight finished just after 1.30 a.m. at the end of a night of boxing that had started at four p.m. There were three other British title fights. Frankie Gavin met Bradley Skeete and retained his British welter title on points, and Liam Walsh did the same at super-feather against Gary Sykes. The fourth British title fight that night was special. 'I will knock out Average Joe Saunders, no doubt,' said Chris Eubank Jr. It was a fight that had required expert negotiating skills to put in place and keep in place. Both boxers said they wanted it, but that is seldom enough. Frank Warren danced a few magic steps to deliver the pair. Chris Eubank Sr was increasingly involved and pulled his son out of a conference, claiming he thought Saunders would lose his cool. 'He is not a good example as a champion,' said Eubank Sr. At an earlier conference his son had travelled on his own, showing up early and fulfilling every obligation graciously. 'Boxers should show up, get it done and dusted and everybody goes home,' said Warren. 'It's just trivial crap: I could understand if there is a dispute over money.'

On the day that Eubank Jr failed to show I diverted to Brighton, to the smelly subterranean gym that Eubank Sr had used and which was now the base for his son's preparation. Ronnie Davies, the coach of both, was also there. 'This kid is special, we have not seen anything like his best yet,' said Davies. At that time Eubank Jr was unbeaten in eighteen, his last ten having ended quickly; the victims were mostly reliable imports, men that try enough to get paid but not enough to win a round. Eubank lacked the title-fight rounds, had barely lost a round in his eighteen fights, and Billy Joe Saunders had been the full twelve five times. The bookies made Eubank a slight favourite, but the rounds were always going to be the difference in the fight.

It was a fight of two halves: Saunders won the first six, Eubank the last six, and the judges went for a narrow split decision. Sadly, the two boxers never gained any added respect for each other and all attempts at a rematch in 2015 and 2016 ended with bitter accusations and crude online assaults. Saunders left the ExCel ring as the British champion: it was his fourth defence of the title he had won when he beat Nick Blackwell in 2012.

In Glasgow at the Commonwealth Games in July and August, nine boxers from the home countries won gold medals. Nicola Adams won at flyweight, the first boxing gold medal for a woman at the Commonwealth Games. It was a bit of a British celebration to be honest, with many fighting friends from the GB squad. Josh Taylor, part of the GB team at the London Olympics, won gold at light-welterweight for Scotland. Paddy Barnes, best man at Frampton's wedding, and Michael Conlan won gold for Northern Ireland. Conlan won his final against Qais Ashfaq from Leeds with stitches and all sorts of stuff keeping a nasty gash above his right eye closed. The cut was from the semi-final and it would have ended a pro fight. Conlan was brilliant in the final.

The decision to drop head guards, which had been universally used since the 1984 Olympics, caused confusion (though not for the women, who were still required to wear them). Nobody really had any idea how to deal with cuts. Men fought with fantastic wounds. Amateur boxers since the early eighties had never had to worry about cuts because the rim of the head guard offered padded protection to brows. The absence of any protection from wayward heads, elbows and legitimate punches only made winning a major amateur (a word destined to be dropped) tournament even more of a crazy lottery. 'I like fighting without head guards,' said Barnes. 'But, fighting six times in ten days is impossible.'

The Contenders

Ricky Burns lost his WBO lightweight title to Terrence Crawford. Nobody quite realized how good Crawford was.

Stuart Hall beat Martin Ward on a cut in March, but lost his IBF bantamweight title to Paul Butler in June. Butler relinquished the title to move back to super-fly. In October, Hall lost to Randy Caballero on points for his old title, which was vacant. Hall had been in four world title fights in ten months and it is one of British boxing's most improbable tales.

Enzo Maccarinelli lost to Jürgen Brähmer for the WBA light-heavyweight title when his right eye was sucked under a grotesque swelling and he was pulled out at the end of round five in Rostock. He was trailing on points but still in the fight. The promised rematch never happened. 'The phone went dead, I never heard a word,' said Maccarinelli.

Scott Quigg made three defences of his WBA super-bantam title and Jamie McDonnell won the vacant WBA bantam title, and defended in November.

Paul Smith's loss to Arthur Abraham for the WBO super-middleweight title in September forced the WBO to hold an inquiry. Smith lost the fight, but it was competitive, and the final scores were extremely harsh: one judge only gave Smith one round. There would be a rematch.

Tony Bellew got revenge over Nathan Cleverly when they met at cruiserweight (an increase of 25lb) in November. Cleverly still looked like he was suffering from the Kovalev loss and he would drop back down to light-heavyweight; Bellew was finally at the weight he should have been fighting at years earlier.

The endgame for former Premier League footballer Curtis Woodhouse was close to fantasy. Woodhouse had won twenty-one and lost six fights when he met Darren Hamilton for the British light-welterweight title in Hull in February. Woodhouse won a split, lost the title to Willie Limond in June, and never fought again.

From the Notepad

In the summer Kellie Maloney appeared and little Frank, the fighter, apprentice jockey, trainee priest, publican, manager and promoter, was gone. 'It's just a huge relief to put an end to a bad few years,' she told me. Maloney had suffered a heart attack, her dad had died, she was separated from her beloved second wife, had tried suicide, and in 2009 she was the first through the door to discover her unbeaten boxer Darren Sutherland hanged in a south London bedsit. It had been torture. The new Maloney was just like the old Maloney, only in a skirt. Also, a bit of the nineties sparkle and mischief was back.

When Eubank Jr met Saunders there was a familiar feel for the two cornermen. Ronnie Davies, with Eubank, had been in the corner when Eubank Sr had beaten Michael Watson in 1991. In Watson's corner on that night at White Hart Lane was Jimmy Tibbs, and he was with Saunders at the ExCel. 'There are a lot of memories when I meet Jimmy,' said Ronnie, who was five and zero in meetings before the fight. They had each reached the junior ABA finals together in the early sixties. They were pure, throwback boxing men.

In August, the former British light-middleweight champion Jamie Moore was shot in Marbella. He was outside the house where he was staying at about 3.30 a.m. when a man in a mask approached with a gun. 'I thought it was a wind-up and then he started firing,' said Moore. Five bullets were fired, two hit home, and then the assassin paused and fled. Moore was on the floor in his own blood and helpless when the gunman quit. The police insisted it was mistaken identity. Moore returned to Manchester for his slow and painful rehab before he was back in the corner.

Anthony Crolla's January 2015 world title fight was postponed in December when somebody threw a concrete slab on his head. He stayed on his feet, broke his ankle, fractured his skull and ended up in hospital, stuck in a dreadful limbo not knowing if he would be allowed to fight again. He was cleared to fight the following March. Crolla only had the injuries because he had chased two burglars and had grabbed one when the other hit him with the slab. 'I never went down,' said Crolla.

2015

'Terry is like me. He came from the small halls, the social clubs, and he's a real working-class boxer. He never had the funding or the benefits. He's done it the hard way, he's done it my way.'
Ricky Hatton on Terry Flanagan

'I had no choice, brudda, I'm not scared and it's the world title.'
Ovill McKenzie, on travelling to Argentina for a fight at just eleven days' notice

IN A YEAR when a record twenty-two British boxers took part in thirty-two world title fights it was Tyson Fury's shocking win over Wladimir Klitschko in front of 50,000 that deserved all the praise. It was a win for history, not part of the endless recycling of championship belts.

Klitschko was in his twenty-eighth world heavyweight title fight, he had stopped or knocked out fifty-three of his sixty-four victims, and ring giants are not undone by insults, cheap tricks or promises. 'Fury is like Haye and like Chisora: they are all good talkers, but I know what he will do,' said Klitschko, who had developed boxing's finest deaf ear. In the days before the fight Klitschko suddenly changed and became darker and meaner. 'How does Wlad know what I'm going to do – I don't know what I'm going to do!' said Fury.

At the hotel bunker on the edge of Dusseldorf city centre, Fury had surrounded himself with big men: his father, Gypsy John, and his uncle, Peter, stood as sentinels on each excursion during the final days, and a selection of brothers and cousins added to the bulk. The weigh-in was behind closed doors – a security issue rather than a security problem. 'My brother Peter has done a magnificent job and now my son, who I still think of as a six-year-old, is ready,' said John. However, dozens of other heavyweights had arrived ready to fight Klitschko and then suffered terrible defeats.

On the day of the fight Asif Vali, who had worked with Amir Khan after the Olympics, led a tiny delegation to the arena and they discovered two inches of extra foam under the canvas. Wlad knew Fury would move and the extra padding would have drained him, ruined his plans. There was an ultimatum or two and the padding was dragged out. I bumped into John Fury in the lift at the hotel at about three p.m. and he gave me a piece of the padding. It was comical, thick and impossible for legs. 'Tyson is resting, we handled this,' said Gypsy John, who had once shared Billy Graham's Phoenix gym with a teenage Ricky Hatton.

An hour before the fight Vali struck again when he demanded that Wlad remove and put on his bandages and all the tape one more time. Vali was entitled to ask, he was the designated observer, and he was doing exactly what Wlad had tried when Vitali met Chisora. 'That can get inside a fighter's head,' Lennox Lewis told me at ringside. We both agreed it would not have happened if Manny Steward was still alive and in charge of Klitschko. Nobody told the Klitschko brothers what to do in Germany, but Vali had twice penetrated their arrogance and accepted levels of intimidation. In the ring, after Rod Stewart had murdered a song and left in a cream puff, Klitschko looked tense; Fury's twinkling eyes had gone blank and his smile was no longer friendly. 'He knew then, I can tell it in a man, that it was over for him,' said Fury.

It is too easy to forget how hard Klitschko tried in the opening round to knock out Fury. He dug the toes of his vast white boots deep into the canvas looking for the power to land his right and end the fight. Fury danced, he moved, he jabbed, he held, he smiled and he talked. 'I did stuff that no other boxer had ever done against him,' said Fury. 'He's a perfectionist and I made him uncomfortable.' Fury never panicked, and that is what separates the good heavyweights from the great ones.

Klitschko knew he was beaten long before his old friend Michael Buffer announced the result – with so little enthusiasm that I actually wondered at ringside if his microphone had been sabotaged. I thought it was closer than the three judges, and perhaps that is because on my travels I have seen so many fine performances reduced to farce by incompetent decisions. Fury was brilliant, Klitschko was totally beaten.

Fury left the ring with the WBA, IBF, WBO and IBO belts. The IBF bauble was gone the following morning when Mick Hennessy, who had been with Fury from the start, refused even to negotiate for a fight against an unknown Ukrainian. The IBF had made the man their mandatory – a dumb decision. At breakfast Fury wore sandals, his toes covered in plasters to treat the giant blisters on his dancing feet. His face had just a few marks. He looked a little sad in his family huddle – the new heavyweight champion of the world with nobody to fight. 'That might be it; that might be as good as it ever gets. I did think that at the time,' said Fury a few months later. Over breakfast in Dusseldorf it looked like that was exactly what he was thinking. In the lobby, Gypsy John was still holding court. 'I feel like I have lived a hundred lives. I'm a happy man,' he told me.

Klitschko vanished after the fight, a totally broken man. He had been knocked out earlier in his life, but he had never been given a boxing lesson. Trust me, the boxing lesson hurt him more.

A few weeks before the Fury fight, in a venue on the outskirts of Buenos Aires surrounded by too many men with guns, a tiny group from London's old East End walked to the ring. They were not a shy and retiring gang. Jimmy Cliff's 'You Can Get It If You Really Want' was playing as Ovill McKenzie weaved through the ropes. McKenzie was a warrior and had taken the fight at just eleven days' notice. 'I had no choice, brudda, I'm not scared and it's the world title,' he said. It had taken twenty hours to get there, but in McKenzie's career that is like a second or two. In 2000 the Jamaican boxing authorities ran out of money, he was not sent to the Olympics, and in 2002 he ended up at the Peacock gym in Canning Town. He lived in the shed on the roof, where boxers from a dozen countries kipped in bunk-beds three high. 'They were the roof warriors,' said Martin Bowers, who runs the gym with his brother Tony. McKenzie moved from the shack to Derby and lost six of his first eleven fights. 'I took bad advice and hard fights.' It never really got any easier: he won the Commonwealth light-heavy title in 2006, lost it the next year, won Prizefighter in 2009, lost back-to-back fights to Tony Bellew, won and lost against Enzo Maccarinelli, and finally won the British title in 2014. When he accepted the fight against IBF cruiserweight champion Victor Emiliano Ramírez he had won twenty-five and lost twelve.

Ramírez had the look of a cartoon bad guy, one of the silent henchmen from a spaghetti western, the kind of man that never lasts long, either shot or eviscerated early, but always leaves an impression. McKenzie conceded nearly 10lb, boxed like a dream, and won by three or more rounds. The judges were nearly fair: one went for Ramírez, one for Ovill and one for a draw. It meant the Argentinian kept his title. There was talk of a rematch, but a year later, when McKenzie had a fight with Marco Huck for the IBO title signed and sealed, there was a problem with a routine medical. Ovill had felt breathless after a hard training session, nothing serious. In November 2016 he was forced to retire with a heart condition, which put an end to his extraordinary career.

In the increasingly confusing governance of boxing just about anything is acceptable, and at lightweight, middleweight and super-middleweight there was chaos. At lightweight four British boxers fought seven times for three different belts; at middleweight it was three in four fights for three belts; at super-middle, the home for so long of British dominance, five British boxers were in six fights for the four main belts. It is hard to know where to start.

The WBA excelled with leniency and lunacy. Chris Eubank Jr won their vacant interim middleweight title in February and made a defence in October. However, fourteen days before his defence a kid from Venezuela also won the vacant WBA interim middleweight title. Martin Murray was stopped by Gennady Golovkin in a triple world middleweight fight in Monte Carlo in February. Murray went into round eleven, further than anybody had managed with Golovkin. In December, Andy Lee, who was born in London, lost his WBO middleweight title to Billy Joe Saunders. It was a tight decision but Saunders had dropped Lee in round three to deserve the title.

The lightweight situation, compounded by the injury status of Anthony Crolla, was even more bizarre. In April, Derry Mathews, who had beaten and drawn with Crolla, won the WBA's interim title. He never defended. The following month Kevin Mitchell was stopped by Jorge Linares in a bloody and memorable slugfest for the WBC version. Something very odd happened in July when Crolla and Terry Flanagan, both from Manchester, fought for versions of the world lightweight title in back-to-back weekends. The pair had even briefly gone to the same school, St Matthew's RC High School in Moston. Flanagan stopped dangerous Mexican José Zepeda in round two for the WBO title, and Crolla, by now the have-a-go hero, was unlucky to only get a draw against Darleys Pérez for the WBA version. Flanagan stopped Diego Magdaleno, which was impressive, in October. A few weeks later Crolla knocked out Pérez with the sweetest of left hooks to the ribs. Just before Christmas Mitchell was given another chance – it would be his last fight – and was stopped by Ismael Barroso for the interim WBA title.

At super-middleweight the WBA sanctioned Frank Buglioni to fight Fedor Chudinov for their title. Buglioni had been in a Fight of the Year contender in May when he drew with Lee Markham, and against Chudinov he displayed tremendous heart to lose on points. In May, James DeGale made history when he became the first British gold medallist to win a professional title; he was the third to try. DeGale beat Andre Dirrell for the vacant IBF title and made a defence against Lucian Bute in December. George Groves dropped a disputed decision to Badou Jack for the vacant WBC version in September. Groves was over in the first but did more than enough in the remainder of the fight. He vanished afterwards and was inconsolable. Arthur Abraham had beaten Wayne Elcock in a defence, lost to Carl Froch, and in February he outpointed Paul Smith again. In November,

Abraham's luck nearly deserted him and he scraped a split decision over Martin Murray for the WBO belt at the weight. It meant Murray had lost to some of the finest middleweights and super-middleweights in four world title fights over a three-year period. 'I fight the best, no cheap talk from me,' Murray said. He could have won three titles at that stage with kinder judges.

The year ended with a scrap like something from a small hall in the seventies when Anthony Joshua and Dillian Whyte showed just how important it is to win a British title. They had met as amateurs in Whyte's first and Joshua's fifth fight; Whyte had won, dropping Joshua. 'It matters, don't worry about that. He can say it means nothing, but it does,' insisted Whyte. Joshua was unbeaten in fourteen, Whyte in sixteen, and there was far too much pride in the ring that night at the O2. It was a sell-out, a capacity house for two novice heavyweights, and that is because the punters knew it mattered. It did. In round seven Whyte went down and was stopped. Joshua confirmed again that he could fight.

The Contenders

Carl Frampton kept his IBF super-bantam title in two contrasting fights. In February he was ruthless stopping Chris Avalos in Belfast, and then he went to Texas in July, which never made any sense other than financial, and was reckless against Alejandro González. Frampton was dropped twice in the first round, caught cold by a dangerous man, but he won clearly on points in the end. 'It was a blessing in disguise,' said Frampton, and he knew that his super-bantamweight days were nearly over. He wanted the Scott Quigg fight before moving on. On the same July night at the Manchester Arena, formerly known as the MEN, Quigg dropped Kiko Martínez twice in a short brawl, won in two, and put some pressure on Frampton. The negotiations continued, and the hate remained between the men dealing with the numbers behind closed doors: Barry McGuigan and his sons did not like Hearn, but everybody at the table knew a fight had to be done.

Kell Brook defended his IBF welterweight title twice and had an easy night both times.

Liam Smith, one of the four fighting Liverpool brothers, won the vacant WBO light-middleweight title in October and made a quick defence in December.

Lee Selby was brilliant when he stopped Evgeny Gradovich, the unbeaten champion, to win the IBF featherweight title in May at the O2. The official result was a technical decision when the fight was stopped in round eight with Gradovich cut; the official ending saved Gradovich a beating. Selby made one defence in America, winning easily and pocketing a vast sum from his new paymaster, Al Haymon. 'There is no way I could go anywhere near that figure,' said Hearn, who had put the Gradovich fight together.

Jamie McDonnell twice went to Texas, twice went the full twelve, and twice narrowly beat Tomoki Kameda to keep his WBA bantam title. At the same weight, Bristol's Lee Haskins, who'd beaten McDonnell over eight rounds in 2008, won the interim IBF belt when he dropped and stopped Ryosuke Iwasa in the sixth. It was one of the best wins by a British boxer all year. In November, Haskins was upgraded to full champion when Randy Caballero failed to make the weight for their fight in Las Vegas. Haskins refused a catchweight fight.

Paul Butler dropped back to super-fly and was knocked out by Zolani Tete, a South African of real quality, in March for the IBF belt at that weight. Butler got in three quick wins before the end of the year and each was necessary to recover his confidence. Tete was lethal.

In May at the O2, when he was the underdog, Nick Blackwell, a one-time unlicensed fighter, won the British middleweight title at the third attempt. Blackwell, boxing to strict orders from Gary Lockett in his corner, stopped John Ryder in round seven. Blackwell made two quick defences before the end of the year.

From the Notepad

Errol Christie, a real golden boy of boxing in the eighties, was waiting for prescription eye drops in a chemist when a special anti-terrorist unit bundled him to the ground. It was a mistake, but he took a knock to his ribs. 'I knew what to do, I let them put the cuffs on me,' said Christie, a veteran of years fighting on the streets of Coventry. The armed police apologized. He went to hospital to get the ribs checked, had an X-ray, and the ribs were all fine. But the doctor spotted something else. Poor Errol was diagnosed with lung cancer and chemo started. I saw him a week later and he was getting ready for another fight. 'I don't smoke, Steve,' he said. 'I think it was all those smoky working men's clubs and halls. They were always full of smoke.' He is right, they were. He was 52 when he was diagnosed in March.

DeGale had lost four times to Darren Sutherland before beating the Irishman at the Beijing Olympics. When DeGale won the world title, beating Dirrell in May, he had his great rival's initials on his shorts. Sutherland hanged himself in 2009. 'He was special to me,' said DeGale.

Whyte and Joshua had fallen out quite seriously but were forced to sit and talk by American heavyweight Kevin Johnson when all three were hired hands at a Klitschko training camp in 2014. Johnson read the riot act, told the pair to stop acting like idiots. 'Kevin told us straight and we agreed to hold it back, be cool: we knew we would fight, why fight for free?' Whyte told me in October.

Frampton's opponent in the Texas fight, González, was found with two other men in an abandoned truck in Guadalajara a year later. All three had been tortured, one was naked, and they had all been executed.

2016

*'There has been a lot of chaos in Tyson's life since he won the title
and people have found him guilty of many things before he has
been tried, before the evidence. I know the truth, he knows the truth.'*
Peter Fury

'Get your hands off me or I will knock you out, you lanky cunt.'
Carl Frampton to Eddie Hearn at a press conference

IT WAS WITHOUT doubt the year of the British heavyweight, the year when more British boxers fought for world titles and were in more world title fights than any other year.

Anthony Joshua won the IBF heavyweight title in April when a man called Charles Martin arrived in London to defend his belt and collect several million dollars. Martin was unbeaten, untested, the luckiest champion in the IBF's history, and the worst to hold their belt. He was their thirteenth champion and his reign, which ended after ninety-four days in just ninety-two seconds of round two, is the second shortest in boxing history. Martin had sauntered to the ring, nearly splitting his snug shorts as he flexed in the ring. He had come in wearing a tacky gold crown on his head which looked like a freebie from Burger King; he looked like that was where he had finished his conditioning. He was smiling at the end when he was counted out. Joshua had hurt him, sent him sprawling the moment he connected cleanly. Eddie Hearn, Joshua's promoter, had pulled off a great coup in getting Martin to London for sacrifice and he should get credit for that. Joshua simply did what he had to do.

'I'm not just a beach-body-looking boxer,' said Joshua after the win at the O2. 'I will walk through Tyson Fury.' It was an uncharacteristic comment from Joshua; perhaps the adrenalin helped. Anyway, he was the sixteenth British boxer to fight for the world heavyweight title in fifty years.

Fury had been ringside in New York in January when Martin forced an injury stoppage against Vyacheslav Glazkov to win the belt. It was the belt that had been stripped from Fury before Christmas. Fury was ticking over, waiting for news of a rematch with Wladimir Klitschko and looking at the WBC champion Deontay Wilder. There was no great sense of fear in March, no panic in the life and times of Fury.

In June, Joshua stopped Dominic Breazeale in round seven. Breazeale and Martin had both, at different times, been part of a grand scheme by a reality television executive to find the new heavyweight. The pair had been part of a lunatic carnival involving a total of over eight hundred eligible men. Breazeale and Martin were the best, which is alarming. Joshua looked tired against Breazeale, predictable, but just too good for the American. It was physical heavyweight boxing at its most basic, devoid of guile, art or cunning. 'Nobody can take his punches,' enthused Hearn. The truth is that nobody at that level had the skills to defuse his punches, move and build a strategy. However, that is less of a tidy axiom than Hearn's often repeated claim; just because a convenient axiom is repeated all the time it does not become any truer. 'He's the best heavyweight prospect for a long, long time,' Lennox Lewis told me one day at the Muhammad Ali exhibition at the O2. 'I just want to see him keep learning – he's not there yet.' In August at the Olympics in Rio, Joshua admitted he had been tired by the relentless schedule. 'I'm getting there, I'm getting there,' he said one afternoon in the media tent. I think that Martin and Breazeale, both unbeaten, were ideal opponents for Joshua's sixteenth and seventeenth fights; the problem was the IBF belt, which confused the issue and undermined the credibility of the two heavyweight title fights.

In Joshua's third fight of the year, in Manchester in December, the fall guy was Eric Molina, who looked bad and fell over far too easily in round three. There had been rumours of rifts, bad sparring sessions, and Molina was the least dangerous opponent on all the lists of prospective opponents that Hearn teased the media with. It was also the first fight where Joshua officially worked with Robert McCracken, the GB coach, who assumed his good and proper role as official coach. The pair had worked together for every fight since long before the Olympics, now it was official. Joshua entered the ring knowing that ringside guest Wladimir Klitschko would join him in victory to announce their fight. There was relief at the end.

'I'm realistic,' said Joshua. 'There will always be somebody to beat, another guy, a better guy. I beat these guys, and I will beat Klitschko; I might have to beat Haye and then, when he comes back, I will beat Fury. That is the way. I just have to keep winning.' Anthony Joshua has always been the most realistic person in the Anthony Joshua business.

Fury was gone by the time Joshua biffed roly-poly Molina that night in Manchester. He had pulled out of a planned October rematch with Klitschko. He was dangerously low, despondent and angry. A positive test for cocaine was revealed. By the time Joshua, cheered by 20,000, walked across the ring canvas for an easy night of massacre, all of Fury's belts had been claimed back. He was suffering, and a long process of recovery started. 'It's a hard sport to love all the time,' said Fury. 'I've had terrible setbacks.' There was genuine pity from boxers when Fury's descent became known.

David Haye had ended his exile in January with a mismatch live on the television channel Dave. He won in round one and over 3 million watched the sideshow. He was back at the O2 in May and this time he finished it in the second round. He was a lot bigger – about a stone heavier – a bit slower than before, but as dangerous as ever. Haye had Shane McGuigan in his corner, a shrewd switch, after ending his partnership with Adam Booth. Haye had talked in January and June about a fight with Joshua, Fury, and even of his wild idea for redemption in a rematch with Big Wlad. However, his next fight was created after a series of finely choreographed confrontations with Tony Bellew. It is a script that nobody could have written at the start of the year and nobody could avoid at the end of the year.

Bellew had won the WBC cruiserweight title in May at Goodison Park, where he had been man and boy on the terraces, when he survived a knockdown to stop Ilunga Makabu in round three. It was, as Bellew said, a fantasy come true. He defended the title against Haye's mate BJ Flores in October. It was a bad fight, Flores was down so many times, and the farce ended in the third. However, Flores was there for another purpose; he was just a Trojan horse on the night. Hearn had tweeted that it would 'go off', and it did. Haye was part of Sky's team at ringside, and when it was over Bellew took the microphone and started to give Haye some stick. At one point Bellew jumped down from the ring – there was a vast clear area at ringside just like there is at the wrestling – and continued. Luckily, Dave Coldwell, a foot shorter and about four stone lighter, was able to pull Bellew back into the ring. It was fabulous stuff. 'He's a cruiserweight just like me, he has the same dimensions,' said Bellew. 'I'm a bit fatter, he's a bit better looking. He only went to heavyweight because of the money. Right now, I'm his biggest purse, and he knows it.' At ringside Haye was acting like the worst pantomime villain in history and never once pretended he was going to storm the ring. Bellew is an expert at the 'hold-me-back' action, Haye a raw novice. 'I could probably beat Bellew with one punch,' Haye said.

The fight was agreed and announced in November, and a different Haye showed for the conference. There was a scuffle and a short shot was thrown in the thick of the melee. It was genuine and nasty, and the O2 sold out in minutes. 'He hates it when I remind him he is skint,' said Bellew. The words no longer held any humour. 'I will shut Hearn up, Bellew will be unconscious, and then I'm coming for Joshua,' said Haye. 'I will put you out of business. What has Hearn ever done?' Hearn reacted fast: 'I made this happen. I'm paying you and you are fighting for me. That's what I've done.' They all left the table prowling.

Carl Frampton and Scott Quigg finally got made and took place in

Manchester in February. It was an odd fight, strange from the start, and at the end of twelve rounds Frampton won a split, which was bad, and left with his IBF belt and Quigg's WBA version. It was not a Frampton masterclass, but it was a strange performance by Quigg. It happens. Quigg had his jaw broken in round four and never offered that as an excuse. He started slow and there was simply no urgency in the first half of the fight. Frampton had an easy night in the hardest fight of his life. Perhaps it was the pressure, perhaps Joe Gallagher in the corner was hearing the wrong thing from the people near him. Boxing is a sport packed with errors, mistakes are made, and on the night both Quigg and Gallagher, two proper boxing men constructed far from any bright lights and wealth, got it wrong.

Frampton went to featherweight (Quigg would follow him) and agreed to fight unbeaten Léo Santa Cruz in New York in July for the WBA's so-called 'Super' featherweight title, which is an extra belt that allows the men that run the sanctioning body to generate more cash. Frampton was the underdog, Santa Cruz was talking about moving up as many as three weights to win more world titles. 'I only got this fight because I was dropped in the González fight,' said Frampton. 'I know why I'm here.' The shift to featherweight had eased Frampton's weight issues and he was relaxed throughout the secret extended stay in the New York area. Frampton and Clan McGuigan had touched just about every bar, shop, barber and city hall in the whole metropolitan New York area that had any Irish connection. The city was his long before the first bell at the Barclays Center in Brooklyn. On the night he was totally inspired, brilliant. Many consider it the finest performance by any boxer all year. One judge returned a draw – one of the foulest scores in years – but the other two went heavily for Frampton. The pair agreed a rematch in Las Vegas.

In Rio at the Olympics, Nicola Adams was untouchable, winning gold again at flyweight. In May she had won the world amateur title. At super-heavyweight, Joe Joyce, from Sid Khan's Earlsfield club in south-west London, lost a disputed decision in the final against Tony Yoka for silver. There was an outstanding bronze for Joshua Buatsi in the light-heavyweight division. Buatsi, a member at the South Norwood and Victory club in London, won three times, beating two seeds before losing in the semi-final. Boxing needed three medals to retain the funding.

Amir Khan and Liam Smith both lost in big fights to Saúl 'Canelo' Álvarez. The news in February that Khan was moving from welter-weight to fight Álvarez in Las Vegas at middleweight was a shock. The fight was made at 155lb, five pounds inside the middleweight limit. Khan was in the fight, moving well, and then in round six he was dropped for the full count. There was a lot of righteous postur-ing about the shift in weight, but the final punch would have sent a small elephant to dreamland. In September, in front of over 50,000 people in the stadium where the Dallas Cowboys play, Smith took his WBO light-middleweight title to Texas and started as champion against the Mexican. In June, Smith had made an easy defence in Liverpool. Sadly, Álvarez was ruthless on the night, mixing punches from body to head with the help of his elbow, shoulder and his own head. Smith was down in rounds seven, eight and nine. It finished in nine after a body shot.

Gennady Golovkin filled the O2 in September to defend his three middleweight titles against the IBF welterweight champion Kell Brook. It was another fight that few believed would ever happen. Brook had had an easy defence in March, agreed to gain the weight, and the fight sold out. It was savage from the very start, one of those fights where the punches crack and the pain can be heard. In round five, Dominic Ingle, who has known Brook for over twenty years, threw the towel in. Brook complained at first, but soon realized his friend had saved his career. Brook had a fractured right eye socket. 'I needed two eyes to fight and I couldn't see,' said Brook. At the time of the stoppage one judge had Kell in front, the other two had it scored a draw. 'Wow, Kell Brook never knew how to lose. I'm glad that Dom stopped it,' said Abel Sánchez, Golovkin's coach. It was Golovkin's seventeenth defence and all had ended early. Once Brook's swollen face had returned to normal he was sent for an operation. 'Kell's surgeon went up through his gum, his front teeth, moved an eye to one side and then sorted out the fracture,' said Ingle. It was a horrible loss and a sensational fight.

The Contenders

At lightweight, Terry Flanagan defended his WBO title three times, and Anthony Crolla stopped Ismael Barroso in seven rounds and then lost his WBA title in a war against Jorge Linares. The Linares fight was the type of fight a boxer needs time to recover from. A rematch was planned.

At light-welter there was a tough night for Las Vegas-based Ashley Theophane when he was stopped by Adrien Broner in nine for the vacant WBA title. The same title, still vacant because Broner had failed to make the weight, was then won by Ricky Burns six weeks later in Glasgow. Burns became only the third British boxer to win world titles at three different weights and squeezed in a defence in October.

At bantam, Lee Haskins had a defence in May, and then in September repeated a win from 2012 to narrowly beat Stuart Hall to retain his IBF version. Jamie McDonnell kept his WBA with wins in April and in Monte Carlo in November. There was just one win for world champions Lee Selby at feather, James DeGale at super-middle and Billy Joe Saunders at middle. Bob Ajisafe went on a lonely mission to Moscow and lost on points for the IBO light-heavyweight title. There were defeats for George Jupp in Mexico at super-feather and little Charlie Edwards, in just his ninth fight, at flyweight. Stephen Smith, part of the Smith brotherhood, lost twice at super-feather, both on points and both to good champions.

Nathan Cleverly finally found some form and stopped Jürgen Brähmer to win the WBA light-heavyweight belt, and Khalid Yafai beat Luís Concepción for the vacant flyweight title. Yafai is the third member of the 2008 Olympic team to win a world title. His younger brother Gamal won the Commonwealth super-bantam title in March, and the baby in the family, Galal, fought at the Rio Olympics. All three came from Frank O'Sullivan's conveyor belt at the Birmingham City club.

There was a nasty British light-middleweight fight in Cardiff when Liam Williams stopped Gary Corcoran. The ref had to warn them to keep it clean after less than twenty seconds.

In December, Dillian Whyte's defence of his British heavyweight title was downgraded to a non-title fight after Dereck Chisora picked up and threw a table during a press conference. The fight was fantastic, Whyte won a split decision, and they will do it again, hopefully with the Lonsdale belt as the prize.

There was a fantastic piece of boxing skill from Bradley Skeete to win the British welterweight title from Sam Eggington. It was a reminder of what the noble art is all about, and that is something that is often forgotten when the tables are flying, the millions are being made and the insults are being thrown.

From the Notepad

Frank Bruno wanted to fight again and handed a dossier to Robert Smith, the boss at the British Boxing Board of Control. 'I have known Frank since our Young England days and I was disappointed when he gave me the documents.' Bruno was 54. 'I'm being mugged off by so-called promoters,' he said. 'I'm coming back.' The story vanished a day later.

Nick Blackwell started the year as the British middleweight champion and ended the year as one of the silliest, bravest and luckiest British boxers in history. He lost his title to Chris Eubank Jr in March. It was a gruelling fight. 'Why hasn't the ref stopped the fight?' Chris Eubank Sr asked his son at the end of round eight. At the end of round nine, this is what Gary Lockett in Blackwell's corner said: 'He's got nothing, now go out and work him over.' At the same time, less than twenty feet away, Eubank Sr said: 'I don't want this to go to points – I want you to take him out of there.' It was vicious, and it ended in round ten.

Blackwell collapsed after posing for a picture or two. He was rushed to hospital, his brain was scanned, and he was placed in a coma. He was not operated on – the bleed was not serious enough

– and after a lonely vigil at his bed by his family, he recovered.

Blackwell was fine. He was soon in the gym helping Lockett with other fighters. He was also given £70,000 by a British former world champion to help him. In September, Blackwell was in the corner with Lockett when Dale Evans beat Mike Towell. A day later Towell died after an emergency operation. Blackwell and Evans went to the funeral.

Blackwell talked about how much he missed fighting. In November he was back in hospital, and this time the surgeons cut into his skull to relieve the pressure from a bleed on the surface of the brain: Blackwell, without telling a soul that cared, had been to a gym and sparred. It is possibly the dumbest thing I've ever known a boxer do. Two Board licence holders were suspended for their role in the stupidity. Lockett was furious, Blackwell so lucky, and in late December he opened his eyes again.

I make no apologies for this brutal, beautiful and frustrating game.

ACKNOWLEDGEMENTS

My thanks to everybody who helped along the way – too many to mention by name, but you know who you are.

There are thousands of facts, dates, names, weights, fights and other details in this book. I am sure there are a few mistakes – apologies in advance.

PICTURE ACKNOWLEDGEMENTS

Every effort has been made to trace copyright holders. Any who have been overlooked are invited to get in touch with the publishers.

First section

Page 1
Chris and Kevin Finnegan: © Sport and General/S&G and Barratts/EMPICS Sport; José Urtain and Henry Cooper: © S&G/S&G and Barratts/EMPICS Sport; Joe Bugner and Henry Cooper: © PA/PA Archive/Press Association Images.

Page 2
Jim Watt and Ken Buchanan: © SMG/Press Association Images; Chris Finnegan and John Conteh: © PA/PA Archive/Press Association Images.

Page 3
Richard Dunn and Bunny Johnson: © S&G/S&G and Barratts/EMPICS Sport; John Conteh and Jorge Ahumada: © S&G/S&G and Barratts/EMPICS Sport; Alan Minter and Vito Antuofermo: © Popperfoto/Getty Images.

Page 4
John Stracey and Dave Boy Green: © PA/PA Archive/Press Association Images; Dave Boy Green: © PA/PA Archive/Press Association Images; Jim Watt: © PA/PA Archive/ Press Association Images.

Page 5
Maurice Hope and Rocky Mattioli: © PA/PA Archive/Press Association Images; Clinton McKenzie: © Sport and General/S&G and Barratts/EMPICS Sport; Cornelius Boza-Edwards and Carlos Hernandez: © PA/PA Archive/Press Association Images; Tony Sibson and Marvin Hagler: © S&G/S&G and Barratts/EMPICS Sport.

Page 6
Charlie Magri and Terry Lawless: © United News/Popperfoto/Getty Images; Frank Bruno and Terry Lawless: © PA/PA Archive/Press Association Images; Pat Cowdell: © Gerry Armes/Birmingham Mail/Popperfoto/Getty Images; Mark Kaylor and Errol Christie: © PA/PA Archive/Press Association Images.

Page 7
Mark Kaylor and Errol Christie: © Sport and General/S&G and Barratts/EMPICS Sport; Barry McGuigan: © PA/PA Archive/Press Association Images; Glenn McCrory and Tee Jay: © Bob Thomas/Getty Images; Dennis Andries: © Sport and General/ S&G and Barratts/EMPICS Sport.

Page 8
Tim Witherspoon and Frank Bruno: © PA/PA Archive/Press Association Images; Mark Kaylor and Herol Graham: © Sport and General/S&G and Barratts/EMPICS Sport; Lloyd Honeyghan: © *The Ring* Magazine/Getty Images.

Second section

Page 1
Tusikoleta Nkalankete and Terry Marsh: © Bob Thomas/Getty Images; Herol Graham and Mike McCallum: © David Jones/PA Archive/Press Association Images; Michael Watson and Nigel Benn: © Adam Butler/PA Archive/Press Association Images.

Page 2
Dave McAuley and Duke McKenzie: © PA Photos/PA Archive/Press Association Images; Dave McAuley: © S&G/S&G and Barratts/EMPICS Sport; Frank Maloney and Lennox Lewis: © PA/PA Archive/Press Association Images.

Page 3
Michael Watson and Chris Eubank: © MM/S&G and Barratts/EMPICS Sport; Chris Eubank and Michael Watson: © S&G/S&G and Barratts/EMPICS Sport; Nigel Benn: © Sean Dempsey/PA Archive/Press Association Images.

Page 4
Joe Calzaghe: © David Davies/PA Archive/Press Association Images; Chris Eubank and Joe Calzaghe: © Chris Smith/Popperfoto/Getty Images; Audley Harrison: © Tommy Hindley/Professional Sport/Popperfoto/Getty Images.

Page 5
Naseem Hamed: © Adam Davy/EMPICS Sport; Lennox Lewis: © Nick Potts/PA Archive/Press Association Images; Amir Khan: © Getty Images/Stringer.

Page 6
Frank Warren, Scott Harrison and Frank Maloney: © John Gichigi/Getty Images; Danny Williams and Mike Tyson: © Matthew Stockman/Getty Images; Ricky Hatton: © Mark Robinson.

Page 7
Carl Froch: © PA Wire/PA Archive/PA Images; Nikolai Valuev and David Haye: © Alex Grimm/Bongarts/Getty Images; James DeGale and George Groves: © Nick Potts/PA Archive/Press Association Images.

Page 8
Nicola Adams: © Mark Robinson/Getty Images; Tyson Fury: © Eamonn and James Clarke/Press Association Images; Carl Frampton: © Anthony Geathers/Getty Images; Eric Molina and Anthony Joshua: © Peter Byrne/PA Archive/Press Association Images.

Thanks also to the Repton Boxing Club for their hospitality for the front cover photography shoot.

INDEX

ABOUT THE AUTHOR

Steve Bunce has worked as a journalist and broadcaster since 1984, writing about boxing for the *Daily Telegraph* for a decade and since 1999 at the *Independent*, as well as having a column in *Boxing Monthly* and for ESPN.com. He has been at six Olympic Games, reported on more than fifty fights in Las Vegas and covered bouts in over twenty countries. He is a regular on BBC Radio Five Live, working on their monthly show since 2004, the weekly podcast and all major live fights. He has been part of the broadcast team at BoxNation since 2011 and also holds various ridiculous records on the BBC's award-winning *Fighting Talk*.